# THE IRIS FAMILY

# THE IRIS FAMILY

## NATURAL HISTORY
## & CLASSIFICATION

PETER GOLDBLATT
JOHN C. MANNING

TIMBER PRESS
*Portland* ✦ *London*

Frontispiece: *Neomarica coerulea*

Peter Goldblatt, B. A. Krukoff Curator of African Botany, Missouri
Botanical Garden, St. Louis; John C. Manning, Research Scientist,
South African National Biodiversity Institute, Kirstenbosch, Cape Town

All artwork by the authors unless otherwise indicated.

Published in 2008 by
Timber Press, Inc.

The Haseltine Building
133 S.W. Second Avenue, Suite 450
Portland, Oregon 97204-3527
www.timberpress.com

2 The Quadrant
135 Salusbury Road
London NW6 6RJ
www.timberpress.co.uk

Designed by Christi Payne
Printed in China

Library of Congress Cataloging-in-Publication Data

Goldblatt, Peter, 1943-

    The Iris family : natural history and classification / Peter Goldblatt, John C.
Manning.
        p. cm.
    Includes bibliographical references and index.
    ISBN-13: 978-0-88192-897-6
    1.  Iridaceae. 2.  Iridaceae--Classification.  I. Manning, John (John C.) II. Title.
    QK495.I75G625 2008
    584'.38--dc22

                                            2008002937

A catalog record for this book is also available from the British Library.

# CONTENTS

*Color plates follow page 112*

# PREFACE

The *Iris* family or Iridaceae are almost worldwide in distribution and one of the most important plant families in horticulture. Genera such as *Crocus* and *Iris* are significant components of the floras of parts of Eurasia, and *Iris* is also well represented in North America. *Gladiolus* and *Moraea* are large genera and major constituents of the flora of sub-Saharan Africa and southern Africa. There are now believed to be more than 2,000 species of Iridaceae worldwide, but there is a marked center of diversity of the family in sub-Saharan Africa and a concentration of species in the temperate south of the African continent. More than 1,000 species of Iridaceae occur in southern Africa alone, marking it as one of the largest families in that rich flora and one contributing nearly 5% of the total species there. *Sisyrinchium,* with more than 140 species, is the most speciose genus in the Americas, where many more genera occur, several important in tropical horticulture. Yet there is no single volume that deals exclusively with this group of plants. This book aims to fill this gap by presenting an overview of the Iridaceae by summarizing all that is currently know about the family.

Simple statistics about the Iridaceae have until now been difficult to obtain and are often mislead-ing. In the 1970s, before our work on the family began, reliable sources estimated that there were some 1,000 species in the family. Our own estimates, made periodically, have generated higher figures: 1,700 species in 1990, 1,850 species in 2000, and we now estimate that there are more than 2,000 species of Iridaceae, making it one of the larger families of the monocotyledons. The number of genera of Iridaceae remains problematic, but for other reasons. Some authorities entertain differing philosophies about plant classification and recognize more than 75 genera, for example, by splitting the genus *Iris* into several smaller genera or by finely dividing the bulbous species of South and Central America based on minutely different features. Here we admit just 66 genera and try to follow, as far as current knowledge permits, a natural and phylogenetic generic concept, only possible when species relationships are well understood. It follows that as we learn more about relationships, most often using the base sequences of DNA, the way we understand genera may continue to change. While we wish we could present a final account of the Iridaceae, the history of plant taxonomy tells us that change is likely. Taxonomy truly is an unending synthesis, and this volume is just one more step in that process. Nevertheless, we

9

hope our efforts will establish a new baseline for the knowledge of the *Iris* family.

Our work incorporates, for the first time, the results of molecular DNA studies of New World members of the Iridaceae, contributed in part by the Mexican botanist Aaron Rodríguez as well as by ourselves and colleagues. This work, using sequences of several plastid and nuclear genes, shows that several small genera, mostly poorly defined, are embedded within larger genera. A prime example is the American genus *Tigridia*, within which are nested small, seemingly distinctive genera. The resulting conclusions are unavoidable, that these nested genera must be included in *Tigridia* in order to maintain the principle of a natural or, more correctly, a monophyletic classification. This principle, simply stated, requires that all members of a lineage bear the same generic name. Alternative classifications based not on the relationships of members of a lineage but on particular sets of morphological characters, called a phenetic classification, can be but are not necessarily arbitrary, being based on those characters deemed important by particular experts. In other words, appearance alone does not always tell us how species are related. We can be misled by parallel adaptations for particular life forms, growth habits, or pollination systems.

As far as possible we have made this book accessible to all readers without oversimplifying the information. This means avoiding jargon, or even unnecessarily technical terms, when what they mean can as easily be expressed in conventional words. Readers will, therefore, not see the word *ensiform* but instead the plain English *sword-shaped,* nor *distichous* when *two-ranked* does the same job. A certain amount of technical terminology has to be used (there are no simpler terms available), and a glossary is provided to aid readers.

We have made a number of taxonomic changes in the volume. The new genus *Afrocrocus* is described here to include the western southern African *Syringodea unifolia,* a species very different from the remaining members of that genus. DNA sequences and some associated morphological features also provide evidence that several genera of the New World tribe Tigrideae cannot continue to retain generic rank. These are *Ainea, Colima, Fosteria, Rigidella,* and *Sessilanthera,* all now synonyms of *Tigridia,* and *Cardiostigma,* included in the past in *Calydorea,* is now also placed in synonymy in *Tigridia.* The Bolivian genus *Cardenanthus* is subsumed in *Mastigostyla, Kelissa* and *Onira* are included in the temperate South American *Cypella, Tamia* is included in *Calydorea,* and *Tucma* in *Ennealophus.* We have accordingly made new taxonomic combinations for the type species of these synonymized genera as follows: *Afrocrocus unifolius* (Goldblatt) Goldblatt & J. C. Manning; *Mastigostyla boliviensis* (R. C. Foster) Goldblatt; *Tigridia convoluta* (Ravenna) Goldblatt; *T. conzattii* (R. C. Foster) Goldblatt; *T. latifolia* (Molseed & Cruden) Goldblatt; *T. longispathum* (Baker) Goldblatt; and *T. oaxacana* (Molseed) Goldblatt.

## ACKNOWLEDGMENTS

Many people assisted with various aspects of the book, and we particularly want to thank those who allowed us to reproduce their photographs; these include Dan Blanchon, Maurice Boussard, Blaise Cooke, David Du Puy, Gérman Roitman, Minoru Tomiyama, Wolfgang Wranik, and George Yatskievych. Over the years Alberto Castillo, of the Ezieza Botanical Garden, Argentina, has provided examples of South American species for study and, with Roitman, has proffered advice on South American species about which we know all too little. We especially thank Mary Stiffler, librarian at the Missouri Botanical Garden, for her cheerful and untiring help finding literature for the study, much of it obscurely referenced. Timber Press generously offered helpful comments and advice throughout the preparation of this volume, which is much improved as a result.

This work would not have been possible without the support of Peter Raven, president of the Missouri Botanical Garden, who has always encouraged of our research in the *Iris* family and, not least, for inspiring this volume. Likewise, grant funding for many years from the U.S. National Science Foundation and the U.S. National Geographic Society made possible field expeditions to Africa and the Middle East. We are also indebted to the Stanley Smith Horticultural Trust for past subsidies for book publication; the present volume also received a publication subsidy from that organization.

# INTRODUCTION

One of the larger families of the monocots, the Iridaceae comprise plants with an extraordinary diversity of large, brightly colored flowers, exceeded in their gaudiness and complexity only by the orchid family. Consider just the genus *Iris* itself, and its modest-sized to large flowers in a variety of wonderful shapes and a seemingly endless range of colors, and then realize that the Iridaceae also include a host of other genera—*Crocosmia, Crocus, Freesia, Gladiolus, Tigridia*—just to name a few well-known examples, and we see just how diverse the flowers of this family really are. Different as these genera are from one another, they nevertheless belong in a single plant family. The Iridaceae are one of some 14–20 families that are today recognized as belonging to the order Asparagales of that large group of flowering plants, the Monocotyledonae (monocots for short), that have a single embryonic leaf and very often narrow leaves with parallel venation.

The family characters of the Iridaceae reside in a few critical features of the leaves and flowers. And as in the orchids, the Orchidaceae, another member of the Asparagales, the diversity of the flowers of the Iridaceae signals a floral biology of fascinating diversity, involving a multitude of different pollination strategies and intimate associations between pollinating insects or birds and particular flower types. Yet until now there has been no single source available dealing with the biology and modern classification of the Iridaceae. Thus, this volume aims to present a present an authoritative account of the family and its natural history. No modern systematic treatment of the Iridaceae exists either, and older accounts are thoroughly out of date because of the many changes to its classification resulting from new research, much of it in the field of molecular systematics, which uses DNA sequences to discover the genetic relationships of organisms. This volume therefore has a dual function. First, it presents an outline of the important morphological, anatomical, and chemical characteristics of the family, relating them to its biology, natural history, and evolution. Then, in the second part of the book, the classification is outlined, followed by a detailed treatment of the genera. Traditional binary keys are presented to facilitate identification. Each genus is described, and complete nomenclatural data are included so that all generic names, whether currently recognized or not, are accounted for.

All members of the Iridaceae can be recognized by their petaloid (soft-textured and colorful) perianth, or corolla, in which the three tepals of the inner whorl and the three of the outer whorl are alike in texture and general shape, and often in color. This type of perianth, a feature of all families of the Asparagales as well as the related order Liliales, distinguishes them from other monocots, such as grasses, reeds, and palms, in which the perianth is either very reduced or with the members of one or both whorls firm-textured or dry and often green or brown. What sets the Iridaceae apart from other asparagalean or lilialean plants is the male part of the flower, the androecium, which consists of only three stamens, where in most related families there are six. The flowers of the highly specialized Orchidaceae, in contrast, usually have only a single stamen. Like the orchids, the Iridaceae have flowers with an inferior ovary, with the single exception of the rare Tasmanian genus *Isophysis*.

Apart from their flowers, the Iridaceae can usually also be recognized by their characteristic leaves, sword-like and oriented edgewise to the stem with two identical surfaces. Such leaves are termed isobilateral and unifacial. In contrast, typical leaves have upper and lower surfaces of different appearance or anatomy, or both, usually held with the upper surface facing the stem; such leaves are termed dorsiventral and bifacial. The genera of Iridaceae have one other significant characteristic that sets them apart from all related families: scattered cells in most of their organs contain solitary spike-like crystals of calcium oxalate, called styloids, as well as small cuboidal crystals, also composed of calcium oxalate. This compound is found in most plants but is most often stored in very different, needle-like bundles, called raphides. Thus this aggregation of some 66 genera (no two experts agree on exactly how some of the genera should be delimited) and about 2,000 species that we recognize as being closely related and forming a single family, the Iridaceae, can be distinguished by independent sets of vegetative and reproductive features. Evidence from DNA matches this correlation exactly, and molecular sequences of several plastid DNA regions likewise show the Iridaceae constitute a single lineage.

The information detailed here largely follows botanical tradition in dealing first with the range of external form found in the Iridaceae. Then there is discussion of anatomical and microscopic features, including embryology, pollen, and chromosomes. Chemical characteristics are of little more than minor importance in plant classification and receive appropriately scant attention. An account of the classification of the Iridaceae follows, in which we outline the historical developments in interpreting relationships within the family and show how this has led to the most recent classification, which incorporates evidence from DNA sequences. An account of the natural history of the family focuses on the many intimate associations between flowers and their pollinators but also links specialized features of leaves, fruits, and seeds to their functions and adaptations. The economic importance of the Iridaceae is, in a sense, that part of the natural history of the family that concerns human–plant associations rather than plant–animal associations. The adaptive link is largely missing here, of course, as human uses of any Iridaceae are too recent to have influenced the evolution of the family beyond the development of horticultural strains or cultivars.

Despite its beauty, worldwide distribution, and importance in horticulture, there are no general books about the family that place its botany in a modern context and present its features in a coherent manner, or review its evolution and classification. This volume attempts to do all this by outlining in a series of chapters the important vegetative and reproductive features of the family and relating them to their roles in the lives of the plants. Particularly fascinating in this respect is the close correlation between the structure, color, and physiology of the flower and the various pollination strategies

**Table 1.** Classification of the Iridaceae. Subfamily names have the suffix -oideae, and tribal names, -eae. Treatment of Tigridieae is provisional pending further study. *Belamcanda, Hermodactylus,* and *Pardanthopsis* are included in *Iris,* following Tillie (2001) and Goldblatt and Mabberley (2004). Only important generic synonyms are indicated.

Iridaceae, 66 genera, c. 2,025 species
  subfamily Isophysidoideae, 1 genus
    *Isophysis,* Tasmania, 1 species
  subfamily Patersonioideae, 1 genus
    *Patersonia,* Australia, Borneo, Sumatra, New Guinea, 21 species
  subfamily Geosiridoideae, 1 genus
    *Geosiris,* Madagascar, 2 species
  subfamily Aristeoideae, 1 genus
    *Aristea,* sub-Saharan Africa, Madagascar, c. 55 species
  subfamily Nivenioideae, 3 genera, 15 species
    *Nivenia,* Cape region, South Africa, 11 species
    *Klattia,* Cape region, South Africa, 3 species
    *Witsenia,* Cape region, South Africa, 1 species
  subfamily Crocoideae, 29 genera, c. 1,025 species
    tribe Tritoniopsideae, 1 genus
      *Tritoniopsis* (including *Anapalina*), southwestern and southern Cape, South Africa, 24 species
    tribe Watsonieae, 8 genera, 111 species
      *Cyanixia* (= *Babiana socotrana*), Socotra, 1 species
      *Zygotritonia,* tropical Africa, 4 species
      *Savannosiphon,* southern tropical Africa, 1 species
      *Lapeirousia,* tropical and southern Africa, 42 species
      *Pillansia,* Cape region, South Africa, 1 species
      *Thereianthus,* Cape region, South Africa, 8 species
      *Micranthus,* Cape region, South Africa, 3 species
      *Watsonia,* southern Africa, 51 species
    tribe Gladioleae, 2 genera, c. 260 species
      *Gladiolus* (including *Anomalesia, Homoglossum, Oenostachys*), Africa, Madagascar, Eurasia, c. 262 species
      *Melasphaerula,* southern Africa, 1 species
    tribe Freesieae, 4 genera, 26 species
      *Crocosmia,* tropical and southern Africa, Madagascar, 8 species
      *Devia,* western Karoo, South Africa, 1 species
      *Freesia* (including *Anomatheca*), eastern tropical and southern Africa, 15 species
      *Xenoscapa,* southern Africa, 2 species
    tribe Croceae, 14 genera, c. 595 species
      *Radinosiphon,* southern tropical and southern Africa, c. 2 species
      *Romulea,* Africa, Mediterranean, Canary Islands, Arabian Peninsula, Socotra, c. 92 species
      *Afrocrocus,* southwestern South Africa, 1 species
      *Syringodea,* southern Africa, 7 species
      *Crocus,* Europe, Asia, North Africa, c. 85 species
      *Geissorhiza,* South Africa, mainly southwestern Cape, c. 86 species
      *Hesperantha* (including *Schizostylis*), sub-Saharan Africa, c. 82 species
      *Babiana* (including *Antholyza*), southern Africa, c. 90 species
      *Chasmanthe,* southwestern South Africa, 3 species
      *Sparaxis* (including *Synnotia*), Cape region, South Africa, 16 species

      *Duthieastrum,* southern Africa, 1 species
      *Tritonia,* south tropical and southern Africa, c. 30 species
      *Ixia,* southern Africa, c. 67 species
      *Dierama,* tropical and southern Africa, 44 species
  subfamily Iridoideae, 30 genera, c. 900 species
    tribe Diplarreneae, 1 genus
      *Diplarrena,* Australia, Tasmania, 2 species
    tribe Irideae, 5 genera, c. 508 species
      *Iris* (including *Belamcanda, Hermodactylus, Pardanthopsis*), Eurasia, North Africa, North America, c. 280 species
      *Dietes,* eastern and southern Africa, Lord Howe Island, 6 species
      *Bobartia,* southern Africa, mainly Cape region, 15 species
      *Ferraria,* southern and southern tropical Africa, c. 14 species
      *Moraea* (including *Barnardiella, Galaxia, Gynandriris, Hexaglottis, Homeria, Roggeveldia*), mainly sub-Saharan Africa, also Eurasia, c. 198 species
    tribe Sisyrinchieae, 6 genera, c. 175 species
      *Libertia,* South America and Australasia, c. 12 species
      *Orthrosanthus,* South and Central America, and Australia, 9 species
      *Olsynium* (including *Chamelum, Ona, Phaiophleps*), South America and western North America, c. 12 species
      *Sisyrinchium,* South and North America, c. 140 species
      *Solenomelus,* South America, 2 species
      *Tapeinia,* South America, 1 species
    tribe Trimezieae, 3 genera, 42 species
      *Trimezia,* South and Central America, c. 20 species
      *Pseudotrimezia,* eastern Brazil, c. 12 species
      *Neomarica,* South and Central America, c. 12 species
    tribe Tigridieae, 15 genera, c. 160 species
      *Alophia,* tropical South America, Central America, Mexico, southern North America, c. 5 species
      *Calydorea* (including *Catila, Itysa, Tamia*), South America, c. 16 species
      *Cipura,* South and Central America, c. 9 species
      *Cobana,* Central America, 1 species
      *Cypella* (including *Kelissa, Onira, Phalocallis*), mainly temperate South America, c. 30 species
      *Eleutherine,* South and Central America, West Indies, 2 species
      *Ennealophus* (including *Tucma*), South America, 5 species
      *Gelasine,* South America, c. 6 species
      *Herbertia,* southern South America, c. 7 species
      *Hesperoxiphion,* Andean South America, c. 4 species
      *Larentia,* northern South America, Mexico, c. 4 species
      *Mastigostyla* (including *Cardenanthus*), South America, mainly southern Andes, c. 20 species
      *Nemastylis,* Central America and southern North America, 4 species
      *Salpingostylis,* Florida, 1 species
      *Tigridia* (including *Ainea, Cardiostigma, Colima, Fosteria, Rigidella, Sessilanthera*), Mexico, Central America, Andes, c. 55 species

used by different members of the family to attract specific insects or birds to visit and pollinate them. The volume ends with a complete account of the genera now recognized as belonging to the family and reviews in turn their main attributes, geography, and ecology. A table of the current classification of the family (Table 1) will aid understanding of the chapters that follow and includes the geographic distribution of the subfamilies, tribes, and genera, and the number of species in each group.

# PLANT FORM

## ROOTS

Slender feeder roots are found in most Iridaceae. These roots, as in most monocotyledons, are adventitious, arising not from the primary root of the seedling but from some other part of the plant, typically the stem. Species with bulbs and corms also develop conspicuous, thick contractile roots at certain stages of their growth cycle. The contractile roots serve a vital function in pulling the corm or bulb of a seedling or young plant deeper into the ground to a suitable depth, presumably to limit predation and prevent damage by desiccation. Distinctive fleshy roots (or root tubers) are found in *Sisyrinchium* subgenus *Echthronema* and in *Iris* subgenera *Nepalensis* and *Scorpiris* (the so-called *Juno* irises), the latter of which also have a bulb. These fleshy roots serve as storage organs in the same way as corms and bulbs.

Remarkable spiny roots that loosely surround the corm are produced in *Moraea ramosissima*, probably as an adaptation to protect the nutritious, starch-filled corm from being harvested and eaten by small rodents, as well as the major consumers of corms, baboons and porcupines.

## ROOTSTOCK

In many monocots the organ from which the roots emerge is a specialized, largely or entirely subterranean portion of the stem, for convenience called the rootstock. It is treated separately from what would normally be called the stem, that is, the aerial stalk bearing leaves, branches, and flowers. Prostrate and creeping to suberect stems bearing roots on the underside and thus termed rhizomes are probably the ancestral condition in Iridaceae and are found widely across the family. The rhizome is sometimes very short and represented by an erect segment of stem tissue, the root crown, for example, in species of *Olsynium* and *Sisyrinchium*. Some species, especially annuals of the genus *Sisyrinchium*, essentially have no rootstock at all, merely a mass of fibrous roots at the base of the stem. The rhizome produces a cluster of leaves at the growing tip, or shoot apex, followed later the same year or in the next by a terminal flowering stem. Further growth of the rhizome continues from buds lateral to the terminal flowering stem. In the Neotropical genus *Trimezia* the rhizome is more or less erect, somewhat swollen, and often surrounded by distinctive and sometimes slightly fleshy leaf bases, and it has been considered intermediate between a rhizome and a corm (or even a bulb). In the Mediterranean *Iris tuberosa* (often treated in the past as a separate genus *Hermodactylus*), the rootstock is an unusual, slender, tuber-like rhizome, unique in the family.

The shrubby southern African genera *Klattia, Nivenia,* and *Witsenia* have a large woody underground stem, called a caudex, in which the woody tissue is generated by secondary growth at the base of the stem. A few species of the Australasian *Patersonia* have a similar woody rootstock, produced by secondary growth. The caudex has the important function of producing new shoots and stems after fire; it is resistant to destruction from all but the hottest bushfires.

True bulbs, comprising a few fleshy leaf bases attached to a short portion of stem tissue, occur in all genera of the New World tribe Tigridieae. Similar bulbs also occur in *Iris* subgenera *Xiphium* and *Hermodactyloides* (the latter also known as section *Reticulata*). The species of *Iris* subgenus *Scorpiris* (*Juno* irises) also have a bulb-like rootstock, to which are attached fleshy, tuberous roots. Filled with stored carbohydrate and protein, the fleshy leaf bases of the bulb are enclosed by dry, brown to gray or red layers, called tunics.

Corms, in contrast to bulbs, are entirely derived from stem tissue and in this origin are similar to rhizomes. They differ from the latter mainly in being compact upright organs that are replaced anew each year. The corm of the previous year is usually more or less, or even entirely consumed during each growth cycle. Sometimes, however, the wizened remains of the old corms persist below the current corm, sometimes for years. In nutrient-poor soils, organic matter is slow to decay, and we have counted as many as 35 corm skeletons in plants of

the southern African genus *Pillansia*. Corms store starch-like carbohydrate food material of complex chemistry, which is mobilized to provide nutrients to the plant when the corm sprouts, allowing it to grow very rapidly.

Two basic types of corm are found in the Iridaceae (Figure 1). In subfamily Crocoideae the corms, usually consisting of three to several internodes but sometimes as few as one, have a distinct central zone of vascular tissue (the stele), and they produce roots from the lower half. The corms are enclosed in tunics of dry tissue derived from the bases of the lower leaves, and they often have a very distinctive appearance, either of woody or fibrous tissue, specific to a genus or species. The other type of corm in the family is found in the genera *Ferraria* and *Moraea* (Iridoideae: Irideae). In these two genera the corms lack a central ring of vascular tissue and have accordingly been termed astelic. The new roots in these corms are produced from the base of the apical shoot, not from the corm tissue at all. In *Ferraria* the corm consists of more than one internode, and the old corms are not fully resorbed annually but persist for many years. The corm tunics are membranous and have usually completely disappeared by the time plants come into flower. Corms of *Moraea* are, by contrast, just a single internode long and are usually completely resorbed annually. They are enveloped by well-developed tunics that accumulate from year to year. The tunics are often distinctive for species groups and subgenera, and may be more or less woody, coarsely fibrous, or sometimes cork-like, providing important characters for classification and identification as they do in Crocoideae.

The basally rooting corms of subfamily Crocoideae originate in two distinct ways. In tribe Watsonieae and the taxonomically isolated genus

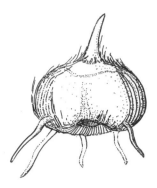
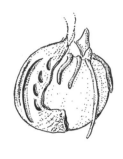

**Figure 1.** The two main types of corms of the Iridaceae, with tunics partially removed to show corm surface: (left) typical basally rooting corm of Crocoideae, (right) apically rooting corm of *Moraea* (Iridoideae).

*Tritoniopsis* the corm is derived entirely from a lateral bud in a leaf axil at the base of the flowering stem, and the corm is thus axillary in origin. In nonflowering plants, however, the new corm arises from the apical bud, which would otherwise give rise to the flowering stem rather than a lateral bud (De Vos 1977). In the remaining genera of Crocoideae the corm develops through enlargement of the basal internodes of the flowering stem, or axis, itself and are thus axial in origin. In this type of corm the apical bud of next season's growth cycle is axillary in origin and in mature corms can be seen to lie immediately adjacent to the base of the old, decayed flowering stem. In practical terms, the difference between the two corm strategies lies in the location of the storage reserves. In the axillary type the reserves are developed below the growing point of next season's plant whereas in the axial type they accumulate at the base of the current season's plant. There is comparable variation in corm development in the astelic, apically rooting corms of Irideae. Thus the *Ferraria* corm is derived from the base of the flowering axis and is thus axial, whereas the *Moraea* corm is always derived from an axillary bud at the base of the flowering stem (Lewis 1954a, Goldblatt 1990a). The relative advantage of the one type of corm development over the other is difficult

to fathom, but in *Micranthus* and *Moraea*, both with axillary corm development, several corms rather than a single daughter corm may develop in a growing season, facilitating vegetative reproduction.

Corms of Crocoideae vary in size, shape, number of internodes, and longevity (Lewis 1954a). Those of *Dierama*, *Pillansia*, and *Watsonia* species are large, often persistent (thus not completely resorbed annually), and comprise several internodes. More common in Crocoideae are corms that are replaced annually, and these tend to be smaller and have a variety of distinctive tunics, often of fine, netted fibers, thickened claw-like fibers, or unbroken layers of various texture. Roots are produced randomly from the lower part of the corm in most Crocoideae, but in *Afrocrocus*, *Geissorhiza*, *Hesperantha*, *Syringodea*, most species of *Romulea*, and a few of *Crocus*, the roots emerge from a basal ridge or ring of tissue (De Vos 1977, Goldblatt 1982a). The corms of these genera (except *Crocus*) are further specialized in having tunics of woody, concentric or overlapping layers and in being composed largely of one or few internodes. *Lapeirousia* and a few species of *Hesperantha* and *Romulea* have a bell-shaped corm with a flat base and new roots that arise from the periphery of the flat base.

## FLOWERING STEM

An erect flowering stem bearing several to a few leaves with blades of decreasing size, or sometimes just sheathing leaves (which often more or less resemble bracts), is common throughout the family. Produced annually, the stem is often branched but may be simple, or unbranched. In several genera the stem is very short and then often entirely subterranean, as in *Crocus, Duthieastrum, Syringodea,* and some species of *Babiana, Hesperantha, Ixia, Lapeirousia, Romulea, Tritonia* (all Crocoideae), and several species of *Iris, Moraea,* and *Olsynium* (Iridoideae). Stems are generally round in cross section, termed terete or centric, but they are compressed and ovoid in cross section or substantially flattened and winged in species of *Aristea* (Aristeoideae), *Neomarica* and *Sisyrinchium* (Iridoideae), and *Freesia viridis, Lapeirousia, Radinosiphon, Savannosiphon,* and a few species of *Gladiolus* (Crocoideae).

Woody, persistent stems are produced by the evergreen, shrub-like genera *Klattia, Nivenia,* and *Witsenia* (Goldblatt 1993a). Woody tissue is rare in the monocots, and its occurrence in some Iridaceae is exceptional. The woody tissue is produced by what is termed anomalous secondary growth, quite different from the pattern in most woody plants in which a continuous ring of dividing cells, the cambium, develops between the phloem and xylem. In Iridaceae a secondary thickening meristem, developed at the outer periphery of the central vascular region, produces radial files of secondary tissue, resulting in thickening of the stems, which live for many years and in some species may become several centimeters in diameter, sturdy enough in older plants to be climbed by a child.

## LEAVES

The basic and most common leaf type consists of a sheathing base that encloses the stem and a unifacial blade oriented edgewise to the stem (exemplified in the bearded *Iris* and cultivated *Gladiolus*). The leaf sheath is either open or closed, that is, with the margins united around the stem so that the sheath forms a tube enclosing a portion of the stem. In genera with corms or bulbs, each shoot is enclosed by one to three basal, entirely sheathing leaves, thus without blades, termed cataphylls. These usually extend a short distance above ground level and may have a somewhat membranous texture. Cataphylls may be ephemeral or persistent, then accumulating as a fibrous neck around the underground part of the stem. In *Moraea* the cataphylls of several species form a distinctive fibrous network around the lower part of the solitary foliage leaf. The basal portion of the cataphylls that surround the new corm develop into corm tunics.

Foliage leaves typically have a flat blade, or lamina, with a series of parallel veins, and typically the two leaf surfaces are identical, hence the term isobilateral (examples of leaf sections in Figure 2). This distinctive leaf type has been compared to the phyllodes of *Acacia* species, which are flattened, leafy, isobilateral leaf stalks, by the British plans anatomist Agnes Arber, who investigated the nature of the leaf blade in the Iridaceae. Arber (1921) proposed that the unifacial leaf so characteristic of the family evolved through congenital fusion of the upper halves of a channeled or longitudinally folded blade. A prominent central vein, often called a pseudomidrib (to distinguish it from the midrib in bifacial leaves) is characteristic of most Crocoideae, except *Pillansia* and the mature leaves of species of *Dierama,* and some Iridoideae (*Neomarica, Trimezia*). Leaf shape ranges from linear to lanceolate or occasionally ovate and the leaves are usually erect or sickle-shaped but occasionally prostrate. Pleated leaves without distinct midribs are found in *Babiana, Savannosiphon, Zygotritonia,* some species of *Crocosmia* (Crocoideae), and the genera of Iridoideae: Tigridieae.

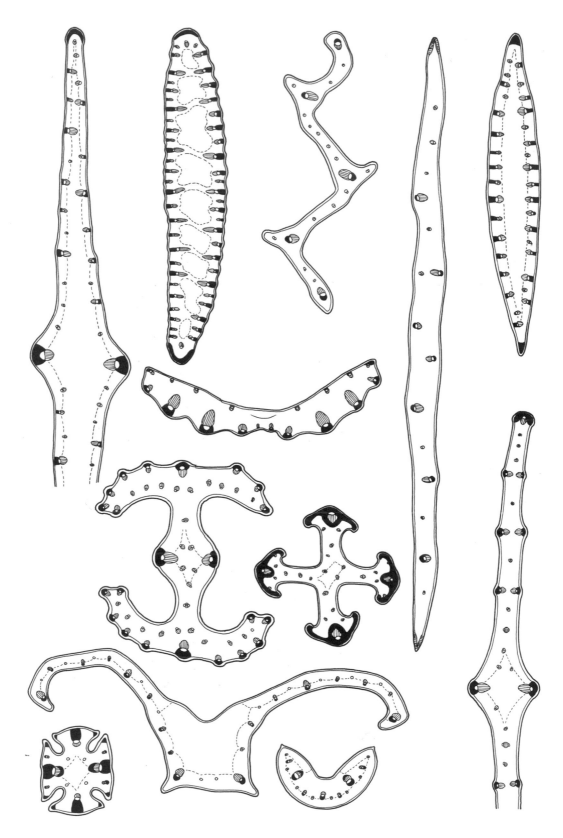

**Figure 2.** Leaf anatomy of (top row, left to right) *Ferraria crispa, Iris grant-duffii, Tigridia dugesii, Aristea alata,* and *Nivenia inaequalis,* (middle, left, above, right) *Gladiolus gracilis, Moraea verecunda,* and *G. cylindraceus,* (bottom row, left to right) *Romulea eburnea, Crocus vernus, Syringodea bifucata,* and *G. carmineus* (all much enlarged, not to scale).

Among the genera of subfamily Iridoideae, *Iris* subgenera *Scorpiris* (*Juno*) and *Xiphium*, and the largely African genus *Moraea* (all subfamily Iridoideae), have leaves with bifacial, dorsiventral leaf blades, usually channeled or sometimes flat. These leaves are interpreted as extended sheaths (Arber 1921) and in *Moraea* have a short, often conspicuous, flattened unifacial apex, perhaps the vestige of the ancestral unifacial blade. Among Crocoideae, *Crocus* and *Syringodea* have channeled to flat leaf blades, thus morphologically dorsiventral. The *Crocus* leaf blade typically has a prominent ridged keel and a central band of transparent tissue on the upper (adaxial) surface (Figure 2). This band is essentially a window that allows the maximum amount of light to penetrate into the deeper layers of leaf tissue where photosynthesis occurs.

Leaves that are rounded in cross section occur in species of genera that otherwise have either unifacial leaf blades (*Bobartia, Geissorhiza, Gladiolus, Hesperantha, Olsynium, Pseudotrimezia, Trimezia*) or bifacial leaf blades (*Iris, Moraea*). Distinctive leaves that are square in cross section are characteristic of *Iris* subgenus *Hermodactyloides* (the *Reticulata Iris* species) and *I. tuberosa*. In *Devia, Romulea*, and species of *Geissorhiza, Gladiolus*, and *Tritonia* the leaf margins or midribs, or both, are strongly raised or thickened, giving rise to leaves of unusual shape in transverse section (Figure 2): X-shaped if only midribs are raised, or H-shaped if the margins alone are raised. Sometimes both midribs and margins are so heavily thickened that the leaf appears to be a solid slender cylinder. Four narrow, obscure, longitudinal grooves are, however, always present, two on each half of the leaf. This leaf type is ancestral for *Romulea*.

Leaves in Iridaceae are typically hairless but are often softly hairy in *Babiana* and a few species of *Geissorhiza, Gladiolus, Hesperantha, Romulea* (Crocoideae) and *Moraea* (Iridoideae) among others. Undulate to twisted blades occur in species of *Geissorhiza* and *Moraea*, and undulate leaf margins characterize a few species of *Freesia, Ixia, Tritonia* (Crocoideae), and *Moraea*. The more or less terete leaf of *M. tortilis* is coiled helically, thus resembling a corkscrew, a truly remarkable looking organ. In *Geissorhiza* section *Geissorhiza*, species of *Gladiolus* section *Hebea*, and *Lapeirousia* subgenus *Lapeirousia*, the leaves are conspicuously multiribbed.

Most species have several or an indeterminate number of leaves, but in several lineages the leaf number is reduced and constant. Thus the majority of *Moraea* species have a single long-bladed foliage leaf. Many species of *Geissorhiza, Gladiolus, Hesperantha*, and *Lapeirousia* have only one basal leaf and one or two additional, partly sheathing cauline leaves. In some African genera and a few in South America, the leaves are produced at different times from the flowers. Such hysteranthous leaves (produced after flowering) are best known in *Gladiolus*, where they are typically produced after flowering on separate shoots (Goldblatt and Manning 1998). Hysteranthous leaves are also found in *Tritoniopsis* and species of *Moraea* and *Watsonia*, where flowering is delayed to such an extent that the leaves are withered by the time the flowers appear. This adaptation permits plants to bloom in the dry season, while leaf production takes place when conditions are suitable for vegetative growth.

The ecological significance of the unifacial leaf in the Iridaceae has long intrigued scientists; Gibson et al. (1988) speculated that the evident increase in flexural stiffness of the leaf is a function of its internal mechanics. While this may be true it does not satisfactorily explain its ecological advantage. Molecular studies dating the origin of the family in the Cretaceous, some 80 million years ago (Goldblatt et al. 2002a) and placing the origin in Australia–Antarctica, raise a second interesting possibility. Assuming a truly temperate origin for the family at high latitudes (where the supercontinent was positioned at that period), the erect, unifacial leaf has the effect of maximizing incident sunlight while the sun is at low levels in the sky. In this interpretation, the fan of isobilateral leaves acts to orient one or other of the identical leaf faces at right angles to the sun. This particular leaf form can thus be considered to be a preadaptation in the family to life in a Mediterranean climate, where the sun is invariably lower in the sky in winter during the wet, growing season. This may partly account for the radiation of Iridaceae in the Cape region of South Africa and the Mediterranean basin. Reversals to the bifacial and horizontally oriented leaf in both regions, respectively in the large genus *Moraea* and some species of *Iris* (Iridoideae), and in *Crocus* and *Syringodea* (Crocoideae), however, still require an explanation.

The development of the isobilateral leaf also allows for the elaboration of ribs or wings of sclerenchymatous thickening at both poles of the paired vascular bundles and at the leaf margins, enabling the enormous range of leaf forms that characterize Crocoideae in the Cape region, most conspicuous in *Geissorhiza* and *Gladiolus*. Although such elaborated leaves are developed throughout the sub-Saharan African members of the subfamily, they are predominantly associated with those found on nutrient-poor, so-called oligotrophic soils or heavily mineralized soils. Extensive areas of such sandy, nutrient-poor soils occur in the southwestern Cape, derived from quartzitic sandstone rocks, especially those of the Cape System, hence the large number of such modified leaves there. These soils are poor in certain minerals essential to plant growth, especially nitrogen and phosphorus. The production of carbohydrates, derived from atmospheric carbon dioxide though photosynthesis, is under no such constraint, and plants of nutrient-poor soils often have a carbohydrate surplus. The deposition of large amounts of carbon-rich tissue consisting of fibrous cells with carbon-rich woody walls is one way of sequestering excess carbohydrates in these habitats (Stock

et al. 1972). These adaptations may also have been selected through other environmental pressures, most probably in response to increased moisture stress, likely to be experienced by plants growing on porous, well-drained soils or in windswept situations. The elaborations of the margins and central veins not only increase mechanical support to the leaves, thus reducing the likelihood of damage due to wilting, but provide grooves on the leaf surfaces that are relatively sheltered from the elements and in which the stomata may be located, thus reducing water loss through them during transpiration when carbon dioxide is absorbed by the plant and oxygen eliminated into the atmosphere.

Similar thickened leaves with narrow grooves separated by massively thickened margins and midribs are also developed in areas of tropical Africa where the soils have unusually high proportions of heavy or toxic metals, including cobalt, copper, nickel, and uranium, the salts of which limit the ability of roots to absorb nutrients. These soils, like those of the Cape region, also retain moisture poorly and support very sparse vegetation because of their toxic character and low water-retention properties. They thus constitute a difficult environment for plant survival. Heavily thickened and fibrotic leaves are produced in *Gladiolus* and *Lapeirousia* in these habitats in Congo, Zambia, and Zimbabwe, a striking parallel development to the leaves of Iridaceae on sandstone soils in southern Africa.

The development of centric leaves, either round or oval in cross section, is a comparable adaptation, and such leaves often have shallow grooves alternating with thickened areas above the vascular traces. Again, stomata are often confined to the grooves, thus minimizing water loss during transpiration. The southern African *Bobartia*, a genus largely of nutrient-poor, sandstone soils, has such leaves, as does the Brazilian *Pseudotrimezia*, again a genus of similarly nutrient-poor, quartzitic soils. Scattered species in several other genera, including *Trimezia* in South America and *Aristea, Hesperantha,* and *Moraea* in southern Africa, have similar leaf adaptations in species on sandy, well-drained and nutrient-poor soils.

## SEEDLINGS

The structure of the seedling in the Iridaceae is remarkably diverse (Tillich 2003). In contrast to other, even larger families of monocots, including the orchids (Orchidaceae) and the grasses (Poaceae), which are uniform for seedling morphology, genera of Iridaceae show a bewildering range of variation. Most genera but relatively few species have been examined; nevertheless, initial results suggest that the various seedling types are often characteristic of different genera, tribes, or subfamilies.

Seedlings of Patersonioideae and Nivenioideae are compact and have a short cotyledon (embryonic leaf), the base of which sheathes the first leaves. *Aristea* is similar but develops a short, sheath-like outgrowth of the cotyledon, a coleoptile, regarded as a specialized character. Seedlings of *Diplarrena* and Sisyrinchieae are not much different from the ancestral *Patersonia* type, but the cotyledon is elongated and carries the seed above ground level. In Trimezieae and Tigridieae the seeds remain belowground and a well-developed sheathing coleoptile emerges above the surface. Irideae are diverse, and *Iris* particularly so, but the seed typically remains belowground. A compact seedling with a short cotyledonary sheath and one or more cataphylls characterizes *Bobartia* and *Dietes*. Seedlings of *Moraea*, however, seem to be more specialized by possessing an elongate coleoptile and, occasionally, a cataphyll. The seedling of the closely related genus *Ferraria* also has a well-developed coleoptile (Boyd 1932) and thus accords with the pattern in *Moraea*. Some *Iris* species, including *I. missouriensis* and *I. domestica* (= *Belamcanda*), have seedlings like those of *Bobartia* and

*Dietes,* thus with a cotyledonary sheath, occasionally with one or more cataphylls. Other species, including the *I. reticulata* and *I. xiphium* groups, however, have well-developed coleoptiles and, sometimes, as in *I. tuberosa* (= *Hermodactylus*), a cataphyll. The latter seedling type is present in both bulbous and rhizomatous species. Too few species of this large genus have been examined to determine whether there is any correlation with seedling structure and subgeneric classification.

Seedlings of Crocoideae are, if anything, even more diverse than those of *Iris.* Most genera have the ancestral type of compact seedling with a short cotyledonary sheath but with the addition of one or more cataphylls. Exceptions are *Gladiolus* and *Melasphaerula* (Gladioleae), which have an elongate, tubular cotyledon and lack cataphylls. A few Croceae also have an elongate tubular cotyledon, including *Hesperantha* and *Radinosiphon,* but *Crocus* and *Romulea* have the elongate cotyledon combined with a well-developed sheathing cataphyll. *Tritoniopsis,* the only genus of Tritoniopsideae, has seedlings closely resembling the apparently specialized *Crocus* and *Romulea* type. Presence of a cataphyll in Crocoideae evidently correlated with presence of a corm, and the absence of cataphylls in the seedlings of a few genera is probably derived. These genera do have sheathing cataphylls in mature plants.

The ecological significance of the different seedling types is not clear. Certainly within Crocoideae it appears that the presence of seedling cataphylls is associated with the development of a corm and its associated advantages, but this is clearly not the case in those rhizomatous genera of Iridoideae that also develop cataphylls at the seedling stage. The presence of a coleoptile is possibly easier to understand since it is correlated with burial of the seed, which has obvious adaptive value as a means of escaping predation and desiccation.

## INFLORESCENCE

The flowers are collectively arranged in two fundamentally different kinds of inflorescences in the Iridaceae. Simple or branched spikes, inflorescences of sessile flowers, occur in all Crocoideae. In other subfamilies the basic inflorescence units are umbel-like monochasial cymes called rhipidia, which are enclosed in enlarged, opposed, more or less leafy bracts called spathes.

### Rhipidia

Rhipidia are somewhat compressed laterally and consist of several to only two usually pedicellate flowers, or rarely a single flower (sessile flowers occur in several species of *Moraea*, notably the *Galaxia* group and some species of the *Hexaglottis* group), each subtended by a membranous, two-keeled, apically forked bract, except for the outermost, which is subtended by the inner of the two spathes, is usually green, and never forked at the tip. The outer spathe is interpreted as the bract subtending the entire inflorescence. Rhipidia are generally borne singly at the ends of the main and lateral branches, and occasionally the branches are short or vestigial, notably in most species of the *Hexaglottis* group of *Moraea* in which the lateral rhipidia are sessile, thus spicate in arrangement. In *Neomarica* and most species of *Bobartia* and *Orthrosanthus* the rhipidia are clustered apically or laterally on the stem, and their arrangement often appears complex. In subfamilies Aristeoideae, Geosiridoideae, Nivenioideae, and Patersonioideae the rhipidia are compound, comprising two partly fused rhipidial units, termed binate rhipidia (Weimarck 1939). Flower number per binate rhipidium is often two (*Klattia*, *Witsenia*, species of *Nivenia*) or even one (some *Nivenia* species). In several species of *Nivenia*, flowering stems bear many binate rhipidia in a corymb-like arrangement, while in *Klattia* they are arranged in laterally compressed heads enclosed in enlarged, often colorful, subapical leaves.

The arrangement of binate rhipidia can take on diverse forms in *Aristea* and the Nivenioideae. Flowering axes with multiple branches have the appearance of open-branching panicles in species such as *A. bakeri* and *A. inaequalis*, while in *A. capitata* the branches are short and confined to the upper part of the axis, resulting in a dense terminal cluster of flowers borne in dozens of individual binate rhipidia. In *Klattia* the binate rhipidia are sessile and crowded at the top of the flowering stems, in effect forming a head, or capitulum. In several *Nivenia* species the entire inflorescence consists of a highly branched flowering axis in which binate rhipidia are terminal on branches that all reach the same height, essentially resembling a corymb. In several of these species the individual binate rhipidia actually bear just one flower each and their true nature as binate rhipidia can only be determined by examining the bracts and spathes, of which there is one each for each subunit of the rhipidium.

The spathes enclosing rhipidial inflorescences are obscure in most species of the comparatively unspecialized genera *Libertia* and *Orthrosanthus*. In a few species of *Aristea* and *Nivenia* the flower bracts much exceed the spathes and are distinctively dry and wrinkled, and sometimes fringed or lacerate. Flowers of each rhipidium open centripetally (successively from outer one toward the center), and the pedicels are extended sequentially so that usually just one flower from any rhipidium is open at a time. Contractile pedicels are found in *Moraea* section *Acaules*, in which the ovary is withdrawn into the lower part of the inflorescence after fertilization. The spathes tend to be short, leathery, and partly dry in *Aristea* and *Orthrosanthus*. In some *Iris* and *Moraea* species the spathes often become dry and membranous, notably late in the flowering season.

In the *Gynandriris* group of *Moraea* the spathes are largely transparent with only the areas above the veins pigmented. The rhipidia sometimes have only a single flower, for instance in *Iris* section *Oncocyclus, Moraea cooperi,* and in a few other species, and their interpretation as rhipidia rests on comparison with related species within their respective genera. In the taxonomically isolated *Isophysis* (Figure 10) the solitary flower is enclosed in large, opposed bracts that we infer are homologous with spathes, which begs the question: Are the solitary flowers of *Isophysis* borne in rhipidia? This seems likely, and a rhipidial inflorescence, sometimes consisting of a single flower, is probably ancestral for the Iridaceae.

## Spikes

In Crocoideae the individual flowers are always sessile and subtended by two opposed bracts, an outer, or abaxial bract, and an inner, or adaxial bract. The inner bract is typically smaller than the outer and also usually forked at the tips and two-veined or two-keeled, but in *Tritoniopsis* (Figure 18) the inner bract is a single structure with no prominent veins and is larger than the outer bract. In light of the position of *Tritoniopsis* at the base of the phylogenetic tree for Crocoideae, this bract type can be interpreted as ancestral for the subfamily. The inner bract is sometimes deeply divided (species of *Watsonia*) or even completely so (*Babiana* section *Babiana*), so that in effect, the species of section *Babiana* have two inner bracts. In light of the condition in the rest of the subfamily, completely divided inner bracts must be seen as derived and highly specialized. This peculiar adaptation serves no obvious function.

The flowers of most Crocoideae are aggregated in spikes and arranged spirally, especially when the flowers are radially symmetric. When bilaterally symmetric the flowers are usually borne on one side of the inflorescence or occasionally in two opposed ranks (*Watsonia, Micranthus,* a few species of *Gladiolus*). The spikes are erect or bent abruptly forward (inflexed) at the base, thus leaning slightly forward, except in *Dierama* in which they are usually nodding or drooping, hanging downward (i.e., pendent) on slender, wiry peduncles (examples in Figures 40–45). The shape, texture, and size of the bracts are important taxonomic characters in Crocoideae and especially valuable at the generic level. Green, soft-textured, somewhat leafy bracts are typical of most species of *Geissorhiza, Gladiolus, Hesperantha,* and *Melasphaerula.* In *Romulea* the firm-textured bracts usually have dry, papery to somewhat wrinkled edges, especially the inner one. Dry, more or less translucent, membranous to papery bracts characterize *Dierama, Ixia, Sparaxis,* and *Tritonia,* and in *Dierama* and *Sparaxis* they are, in addition, conspicuously wrinkled. In *Tritoniopsis* and *Zygotritonia* the bracts are relatively short and leathery to dry. Distinctive, fleshy outer bracts with smooth or sometimes lightly serrated keels are characteristic of several species of *Lapeirousia* subgenus *Lapeirousia.*

In *Pillansia* (Figure 22) and many species of *Lapeirousia* the inflorescence resembles a panicle rather than a spike. In both genera, however, the inflorescence is best interpreted as a highly branched flowering stem, the terminal branches of which are spikes. In both genera the individual flowers are still sessile, as they are in a spike. Reduced inflorescences are found in several genera. In *Romulea* and *Xenoscapa* the flowers are single on short to long stalks and are best interpreted as solitary on branches of the flowering stem (Figures 31, 33). The spike axis may be subterranean when the flowers first open in *Romulea,* several species of *Lapeirousia* and *Hesperantha,* and always so in *Duthieastrum* and the trio of related genera *Afrocrocus, Crocus,* and *Syringodea* (Figures 34–36, 42). In most of these genera, as well as in *Romulea,* the flowering stems are raised aboveground as the capsules ripen, but in *Syringodea* the basal portion of the ovary elongates, contributing to the raising of the ovary (De Vos 1974). The subterranean nature of the inflorescence in *Crocus, Duthieastrum,* and *Syringodea* makes its interpretation difficult, but it seems best to treat them as branched spikes with a single flower per branch.

Phylogenetic studies of the Iridaceae (Souza-Chies et al. 1997, Reeves et al. 2001, Goldblatt et al. 2006) show subfamily Crocoideae to be immediately related to clades that have rhipidial inflorescences, specifically binate rhipidia. The origin of the spike in the Iridaceae has long defied satisfactory explanation; Weimarck (1939) postulated that the spike was ancestral to the rhipidium, which then arose through condensation of the spike axis. Molecular studies show that the reverse is true, for it is the spike that is derived from ancestors with binate rhipidia. We infer that the individual flowers on the spike represent reduced binate rhipidia that are sessile on an elongate flowering axis. Comparable arrangements of binate rhipidia that form compound spike-like arrangements are common in *Aristea,* and as outlined above, other types of compound inflorescences of binate rhipidial units occur in Nivenioideae, where they may form heads (*Klattia*) or flat topped corymb-like structures (*Nivenia*). Notably, single-flowered binate rhipidia are found in several species of *Nivenia* and sometimes in *Aristea singularis.* The paired bracts subtending each flower in a spike thus may be homologous with the two spathes, of a one-flowered binate rhipidium.

The origin of bilaterally symmetric flowers in Iridaceae appears to have accompanied the evolution of the spike in Crocoideae, presumably since this inflorescence allowed the flowers to face sideways rather than upward. Lineages of Iridaceae with zygomorphic flowers have a significant advantage over those with actinomorphic flowers in number and the rate at which they are able to exploit different pollination systems (Goldblatt and Manning 2006). This may go some way to accounting for the rapid and extensive radiation undergone by Crocoideae in Africa, where the subfamily originated, and hence the greater representation of the entire family Iridaceae there.

## FLOWER

Flowers of nearly all Iridaceae are perfect, that is, they are bisexual, with functional male and female organs. The flowers have petaloid sepals (calyx units) and petals (corolla units), collectively called tepals because they do not differ in texture or color. These are arranged in two whorls or rings of three, an inner and an outer whorl, and there are only three stamens, each inserted opposite an outer tepal. An inferior ovary consisting of three fused carpels is present in all genera except *Isophysis,* which has a superior ovary and partly for this reason is segregated in its own subfamily, Isophysidoideae. The taxonomic isolation of the genus and its ancestral position with respect to the rest of the family is amply supported by molecular DNA evidence.

Flowers that last more than one day typically display closing movements, the tepals unfolding and closing again at specific times of the day. Thus flowers pollinated by diurnal insects or birds open for all or part of the day but close at night, whereas those pollinated by night-flying moths usually open in the late afternoon or evening and close again at specific times before daybreak. Especially notable for precisely timed opening movements are species of *Gladiolus* and *Hesperantha* (Goldblatt and Manning 2002, Goldblatt et al. 2004c). *Hesperantha* species show particularly complex opening and closing patterns: diurnal opening is usually restricted to part of the day, morning or afternoon, whereas evening flowers open at specific times before or after sunset and close again in early or late evening. These closing movements not only prevent access to flowers by potential pollen or nectar thieves at certain times but also protect the flowers from the elements, especially pollen-damaging moisture (Vlok 2005). During unusually cold or wet weather, flowers will also close at times when they are normally open. They also create new niches for species that are able to partition the day and evening hours so precisely.

## Tepals

The tepals are free in *Isophysis,* united at the very base in *Aristea* and *Geosiris* (Aristeoideae), and usually free in subfamily Iridoideae. The flowers are radially symmetric in all subfamilies except Crocoideae and one genus of Iridoideae, the Australian *Diplarrena,* in which bilateral symmetry is developed and the flowers face sideways. In several species of *Moraea* (especially the *Galaxia* group) and a few species of *Bobartia* a floral tube is present. These tubes are closed at the apex and their function is to raise the flower above the bracts and inflorescence spathes, and in the *Galaxia* group also above the ground. Most species of *Iris* have a true perianth tube, which may be several centimeters long, reaching a maximum of 20 cm in *I. unguicularis.*

The tepal whorls are either subequal (especially *Orthrosanthus* and *Sisyrinchium* and its allies) but are dimorphic in *Libertia* and many other Iridoideae (e.g., *Iris, Moraea, Trimezia*). The outer tepals are smaller than the inner in *Libertia* (or occasionally vestigial) but are more often larger than the inner and usually provided with nectar guides. The smaller inner tepals are sometimes erect (many *Iris* species, a few species of *Moraea*). In a few species the inner tepals may be much reduced and curved downward (*Iris* subgenus *Scorpiris*) or three-lobed, bristle-like, or absent (species of *Moraea* and the genus *Patersonia*). The tepals in Irideae and Tigridieae are often differentiated into upper and lower portions, the lower portion called a claw. The claws, especially of the inner tepal whorl, are often hairy or variously marked and spotted, and sometimes glandular. In *Iris* subgenus *Iris* the outer tepals have the nectar guide covered with long multicellular hairs, the beard.

In Crocoideae, in contrast, a true perianth tube is always present, and this is usually well developed. The ancestral condition for the subfamily is evidently a bilaterally symmetric flower, and this is characteristic of most genera (Davies et al. 2004). Radial symmetry is secondary in the subfamily and has arisen independently various times in species scattered through several genera that have ancestrally bilaterally symmetric flowers. Radially symmetric flowers also characterize several specialized genera, most of them having underground stems, and there is a clear correlation between the stemless habit and radially symmetric flowers. In genera with bilaterally symmetric, bilabiate (i.e., zygomorphic) flowers the stamens are unilateral and arcuate (e.g., *Babiana, Freesia, Gladiolus, Tritoniopsis, Watsonia*). In such flowers the uppermost tepal is typically enlarged and often hood-like, and the lower three tepals together form a lip, which often functions as a landing platform for pollinating insects. In extreme examples of zygomorphy, often associated with bird pollination, the tube may be slender and cylindric below and abruptly expanded, curved, and broadly cylindric above. In bird-pollinated species there is a tendency for the enlargement of the upper tepal, often with an associated reduction of the lower tepals, notably in *Chasmanthe* and species of *Gladiolus*. In many genera of Crocoideae the perianth tube may be greatly elongated, sometimes reaching 15 cm in some species. Such long-tubed flowers are associated with pollination by long-proboscid flies (Nemestrinidae, Tabanidae) or sphinx moths (Sphingidae).

The development of a perianth tube in Nivenioi-deae and Crocoideae greatly increases the amount of nectar that could be offered to potential visitors. A longer tube also allows the flower to select among floral visitors by excluding those with insufficiently long mouthparts. This has enabled members of these two subfamilies to exploit several pollination systems that are poorly or totally unrepresented in the other subfamilies, including pollination by birds, butterflies, moths, and long-proboscid flies (Goldblatt and Manning 2006; Table 4).

## Androecium

The male part of the flower, or androecium, consists of three stamens, each inserted opposite an outer tepal. Each stamen consists of a stalk, the filament, and the pollen-bearing organs, the anthers. Filaments are typically thread-like and are either free, joined to the base of the outer tepals, or variously inserted within or at the mouth of the perianth tube when a tube is present. Often the tube widens into a throat above the point of insertion. *Diplarrena* is unique in the Iridaceae in having just two stamens with the abaxial (lower) one reduced to a vestigial bristle. The filaments are partially united in a few species of Crocoideae, notably *Ixia* section *Ixia*, and in many genera of Iridoideae. Filaments are partially united in most *Moraea* species and tribe Sisyrinchieae, for which this is a defining character. In *Tigridia*, several other genera of Tigridieae, and some *Moraea* species the filaments are fully united. The resultant filament column may be smooth and cylindric, enlarged below, and sometimes papillate to lightly hairy, notably in the *Homeria* group of *Moraea* and *Sisyrinchium* subgenus *Sisyrinchium*. In tribe Trimezieae and species of tribe Tigridieae with free stamens the filaments are extremely thin, weak, and do not support the anthers, each of which is attached to the abaxial surface of a style branch. The filaments are extremely short in *Cobana* and virtu-

ally obsolete in the *Sessilanthera* group of *Tigridia*. An odd feature of *Diplarrena* and several species of *Geissorhiza* is that the filaments are of different lengths, and in the latter genus one filament is sometimes shorter than the other two. *Nivenia inaequalis* (a species included in the past in *N. argentea*) also has this curious feature, and in the flowers of this species the shorter filament does not project beyond the mouth of the perianth tube so that one anther is hidden within the tube.

The anthers are two-lobed and four-celled, the cells being the sites of pollen development. In most Iridaceae the anther lobes split longitudinally toward the outside of the flower, a condition called extrorse. Anthers are typically oblong to linear and attached to the filament close to the base (basifixed) or shortly above the base (subbasifixed). Their lower tips sometimes diverge, giving the anther the appearance of an arrowhead. The tissue between the two anther lobes, or connective, is narrow but often bears a small extension, or mucro, at the apex. In several Neotropical genera (e.g., *Alophia*, some *Cypella* species) the anthers are unusual in being fiddle-shaped (pandurate) with a broad connective narrowest in the center and the anther lobes split laterally. In some species of *Ferraria* the two anther lobes diverge from the base and are held together at the tips where they are attached to the filament apex. Splitting of the anthers through apical pores occurs in four Madagascan species of *Aristea*, the *Sessilanthera* group of *Tigridia*, and the Central American *Cobana guatemalensis*. Presence of porose anthers were in part the reason for their segregation as the separate genera *Cobana* and *Sessilanthera*. In *Ixia scillaris* and its immediate allies in section *Dichone* the anthers split incompletely from the base and in some of the species of the section are bent at right angles just above the base.

In many Crocoideae the stamens are asymmetrically disposed and unilateral, usually suberect and arching forward with parallel, contiguous anthers held more or less horizontally and facing the lower tepals (e.g., species of *Babiana, Gladiolus, Watsonia*). Alternatively, the stamens arch downward with the anthers horizontal or suberect and facing the dorsal tepal (species of *Geissorhiza, Hesperantha, Watsonia*). As a result of arching and slight twisting of the filaments, the anthers in species with unilateral stamens end up facing the center of the flower at maturity but face outward in the bud stage, reflecting the ancestral extrorse condition.

The reduction in stamen number to three in the family, versus six in all related families, can be regarded as an essential first step leading toward the precise placement of pollen on the body of a floral visitor, thus promoting the development of specialized pollination systems in the Iridaceae. Among the sub-Saharan African members of the family, fully 95% of the species rely on specialized pollination systems (Goldblatt and Manning 2006). This is an important consideration in explaining the enormous radiation of the family there.

## Gynoecium

The female part of the flower, the gynoecium, consists of three fused carpel units, each consisting of a locule containing ovules, and a stalk terminating in tissue that receives the pollen, the stigma. Fusion of the carpel units has yielded an ovary consisting of three compartment or locules. The ovules are arranged in pairs within the locules and are attached to the central axis of the ovary along a band of highly vascularized tissue, the placenta. This axile placentation is found in all Iridaceae except *Iris tuberosus*, in which the locules of the ovary are confluent and the ovules are attached to placental tissue on the outer walls of the ovary. The presence of a unilocular ovary with parietal placentation was the reason for placing this *Iris* species in the separate genus *Hermodactylus*.

The ovary is superior in *Isophysis* but inferior in all other genera, thus with all other floral parts attached to the axis above it. The ovary bears a single style at its apex. Typically globose to oblong, the ovary is strongly three-lobed to three-angled in cross section in several Iridoideae and in *Melasphaerula* (Crocoideae). In the *Gynandriris* group of *Moraea* and in several species of *Ferraria* the upper part of the ovary is sterile and forms an elongated tube, or beak, which raises the flower above the inflorescence spathes.

The style is slender and more or less filiform but always divided and elaborated above in a variety of ways, often characteristic of a subfamily, tribe, or genus. The nature of the style branches is thus important for understanding relationships within the Iridaceae, something that was appreciated by early botanists who developed classifications of the family. Simple, slender style branches, stigmatic along the upper surface or near the tips, are presumably ancestral and occur in *Isophysis*, most Crocoideae, and *Nivenia* (Nivenioideae). In the two other genera of Nivenioideae, *Klattia* and *Witsenia*, the styles are minutely trifid apically. Minutely lobed styles are also characteristic of *Aristea* section *Racemosae*, but in other species of *Aristea*, as well as in *Geosiris aphylla* and *Patersonia*, the style divides into three broad, fringed lobes that are papillate and stigmatic over their entire surface.

In contrast, Iridoideae have hollow style branches that often arise below the level of the anthers, a feature characteristic of Sisyrinchieae and some Irideae, notably *Bobartia*. In most genera of other tribes of Iridoideae the style branches are usually complex structures, either flattened tangentially (species of Irideae) or thickened and compressed radially, in either case bearing paired apical, fleshy or petal-like appendages. Most striking is the development in Irideae of tangentially flattened, petaloid style branches, characteristic of *Iris*, for example. Here, each of the three broad style branches divides apically into paired appendages, called crests, above a transverse stigmatic lobe. The condition is similarly developed in *Dietes* and most species of *Moraea*. This elaborate structure is progressively reduced in species of the *Galaxia* and *Homeria* groups of *Moraea* into short but tangentially compressed and bilobed style branches, stigmatic at their tips. In the southern African *Hexaglottis* group of *Moraea* the style divides shortly above the base into three branches, each in turn immediately forked into two long filiform and horizontal, apically stigmatic arms. A convergent modification is found in the North American *Nemastylis*. In a few southern African species of *Moraea* the style branches are thread-like and lie alternate to the stamens, an apparent reversal to the ancestral state for the subfamily.

In New World Iridoideae elaborate style branches are present in several genera, including *Cypella*, *Neomarica*, and *Trimezia*, in which they are thickened rather than flattened and petaloid. Distal to the transverse stigma lobes are paired, acute crests and sometimes a second pair of crest-like appendages produced from the edges of the stigma lobes. Variation in the stamen–style branch apparatus in the New World Iridoideae is considerable. The *Cypella* type, in which the stamens have weak filaments and the anthers are loosely attached to the abaxial side of the style branch, is most likely ancestral. The pattern is progressively modified in various genera. In *Tigridia* and close allies the filaments are united into a tube and each style branch is divided nearly to the base, with the paired arms extending outward on either side of the opposed anther. The style branches are simple and filiform in *Eleutherine* and several species of *Calydorea* and extend between the anthers, a feature interpreted as a secondary reversal to the apparently ancestral state as represented in *Sisyrinchium* and its allies. In some species of *Cipura* (e.g., *C. paludosa*) the style branches are

barely developed and a thickened style bears three stigmatic lobes at its apex. The several, mostly small, genera of Tigridieae are defined largely by various configurations of the style branches and the way they are associated with the stamens.

The position of the style arms opposite or alternate to the anthers was regarded as important in some early classifications of Iridaceae and was used to separate *Sisyrinchium* from closely related genera of Iridoideae as a separate subfamily, Sisyrinchioideae. The character has no fundamental significance and is the result of a small twist in the style branch just above the style apex, which occurs after the flower opens. During early development of the flower the style branches lie opposite the stamens and only later come to lie alternate to the stamens, then extending between the filaments or bases of the anthers.

In Crocoideae, the level of division and orientation of the style branches are often characteristic. *Hesperantha* is distinguished from the allied *Geissorhiza* largely by its long, spreading style branches that divide at the apex of (rarely within) the perianth tube. *Gladiolus* is distinguished by enlarged and bilobed style branch apices. Several genera, including *Freesia*, *Lapeirousia*, *Romulea*, *Savannosiphon*, and *Watsonia*, have deeply bifurcate and recurved style branches. In *Crocus* the style branches are particularly variable and may be short to long, simple, bifurcate, or multifid, and sometimes distally flattened as in the cultivated saffron crocus and its close allies. In *Ixia* the style is typically well exserted from the tube but divides at the mouth in several species, including those of subgenus *Dichone*, in which the style branches are involute (or longitudinally rolled), tubular, and stigmatic at the apices rather than conduplicate (or longitudinally folded), channeled, and stigmatic along the margins. In a few isolated species of *Geissorhiza*, *Hesperantha*, *Ixia*, *Romulea*, and *Watsonia* the stamens and the style branches are completely included within the perianth tube. The significance of this unusual adaptation is presumed to be related to the pollination biology of these species but has yet to be established.

The stigmas or stigmatic surfaces of the style branches are of the dry type in all Iridaceae (Heslop-Harrison and Shivanna 1977), as it is in all related families. In contrast, members of the related order Liliales have wet-type stigmas. Finger-like, unicellular papillae are found on the stigma surface of the few species examined for the feature, and this appears to be a family characteristic. The entire stigma is covered by a cuticle layer, which pollen tubes penetrate after germinating. The pollen tubes grow though a layer of mucilage produced by secretory cells lying beneath the cuticle. The tubes grow though the mucilage layer along the style branches and into the stylar canal, never penetrating cellular tissue, until they finally reach the ovules (Clarke et al. 1977).

## Nectaries

Septal nectaries, located in slender pockets in the radial walls, or septa, of the ovary, may be an ancestral feature of the Iridaceae. They are found in Nivenioideae (Goldblatt 1993a), all Crocoideae that produce nectar, and in *Diplarrena* in the Iridoideae (Daumann 1970, Rudall et al. 2003). These nectaries open to the exterior through narrow ducts at the top of the ovary close to the base of the style and opposite the inner tepals and can be sometimes be recognized using a 10× hand lens as dark spots on the ovary surface. *Isophysis* lacks nectaries, as does *Geosiris* and all but a single species of *Aristea*.

Instead of septal nectaries, most Iridoideae have nectar glands on the surface of the tepals or perianth tube, so-called perigonal nectaries. Such nectaries are present in the tribes Irideae, Trimezieae, and Tigridieae of the subfamily and are also found in one species of *Aristea, A. spiralis.* In the predominantly

Old World tribe Irideae they are usually located at the base of the outer tepals and sometimes also at the base of the inner tepals. In the New World tribes Trimezieae and Tigridieae the nectaries are usually located on the inner tepals and occasionally also on the outer tepals (Molseed 1970). These glandular areas may consist of true sugar-secreting nectaries or may comprise oil-secreting glands, called elaiophores (Vogel 1974, Simpson and Neff 1981). These oil-secreting glands usually consist of unicellular, club- to cushion-shaped hair-like structures, or trichomes. The glandular trichomes are often concentrated on the middle or lower part of the inner tepals and are concealed by folds or pockets of the tepal surface, or they may be fully exposed. The crowded glandular hairs on the filaments of some South American species of *Sisyrinchium* also produce oil, but the scattered club-shaped hairs in other species of the genus do not.

## FRUIT AND SEEDS

In nearly all genera of Iridaceae the fruit is a loculicidal capsule, a fruit type that is dry when the seeds are mature and splits open along the along a suture in the center of each of the three locules. Capsules range from more or less globose to oblong or cylindric and are often three-lobed and sometimes three-angled in cross section. Capsule walls range in texture from leathery through firm and cartilaginous to hard and woody, and are beaked in many species of *Iris* and some of *Ferraria* and *Moraea*, thus with a sterile terminal prolongation. In the *Gynandriris* group of *Moraea* the sterile upper part of the ovary remains as an elongated beak, and a beak of similar origin is characteristic of several species of *Ferraria*. The beak results from the persistence of the tubular sterile upper portion of the ovary, the latter of course enabling the ovary to lodge deeply within the spathes, thus enjoying their protection from predation or the reach of egg-laying seed parasites.

In several less specialized genera, the central axis of the ovary separates from the inner walls, or septa, when the capsules split and remains as a rigid spike in the center of the fruit. The feature is found in all Nivenioideae. Curiously, in all these examples the capsules are hard and woody.

*Syringodea* is exceptional in the way that its capsules split open. Instead of opening when dry, the reverse occurs, and the capsules open in wet weather when rain can wash the seeds out of the locules. When the weather is dry the capsules close, protecting any remaining seeds until it rains again.

In species of *Dietes* the woody capsules may split open only at the apex and do not split open at all in *D. butcheriana*. In this species the capsules release their seeds only as the walls decay, months after the seeds have reached maturity. Capsules of *Aristea* are unusually variable and together with the seeds form the foundation of an infrageneric classification. Capsules of section *Pseudaristea* of the genus are cylindric, deeply three-lobed, and split open tardily, months after ripening, while those of sections *Aristea* and *Racemosae* have wide, extremely thin, radially oriented wings. In *Hesperantha* section *Radiata*, capsules split open only near the apex, whereas in *Gladiolus* the capsules open unusually widely, exposing the winged seeds to the wind, the means by which they are dispersed.

Seeds range from many to several to two (some species of *Aristea*) or just one (*Klattia, Witsenia,* most *Nivenia*) per locule. The seeds are typically dry and hard, usually light to dark brown, and have a smooth outline (without primary sculpturing). The shape of individual epidermal cells of the seed coat or testa (secondary sculpturing) is often distinctive and is usually domed (technically colliculate), sunken (foveolate), or rarely with a short projection on the surface of each cell (tuberculate). In *Crocus* there is considerable variation in the surface cells, which may be shallowly domed, strongly

domed, papillate, or finger-like (digitiform; Baytop et al. 1975, Mathew and Brighton 1977). A smooth, glossy seed surface is characteristic of several genera of Crocoideae section Croceae, including *Dierama, Duthieastrum, Ixia, Tritonia,* and *Sparaxis.* In these seeds the surface cells lack visible outlines and are considered highly specialized. Such seeds appear to remain viable for several years, significantly longer than seeds of species with thinner coats.

Seeds of most Iridaceae are relatively large and more or less globose to somewhat angled by pressure or are shaped like segments of an orange, sometimes called prismatic. In *Micranthus* and some species of *Thereianthus* of the Crocoideae the seeds are narrow and spindle-shaped. Seeds of many species of *Sisyrinchium* are unusual in being blackish and having a deep, wide depression on one side; sometimes the depression may so large as to encompass more than half the diameter of the seed. In many Crocoideae the end of the seed distant from the micropyle is flattened or somewhat collapsed. Flattened, disk-like, vertically compressed seeds are found in *Diplarrena, Moraea* subgenera *Grandiflora* and *Monocephalae,* and some species of *Iris.* These disk-like seeds may be thin and aerodynamic or have a corky surface that allows them to float, thus aiding dispersal along streams or running water. In *Iris* series *Hexagonae* the large seeds have a rough corky coat, adapted for distribution by water. The outer layers of the seed coat in *Iris pseudacorus* (series *Laevigatae*) is shaped into a flattened corky float while the seed body itself is globose.

In *Klattia, Nivenia,* and *Witsenia* the seeds are shield-shaped and tangentially compressed. Seeds of *Aristea* species are especially variable and include rounded to lightly angled forms with a regular sculpturing; columnar, three-angled seeds with a fringe of papillae at the top and bottom edges; and peculiar radially flattened seeds, kidney-shaped in outline with or without a fringe of papillae. In

*Gladiolus* the seeds have a wide membranous circumferential wing that is an outgrowth of the outer integument and raphe. The wing tissue is soft and consists of dead, inflated cells separated by large intercellular spaces. In many species of *Watsonia* the seeds have two rigid wings at opposite ends or a single wing either at the distal end or surrounding the whole seed. Wing-like ridges on the angles of the seeds are also weakly developed in some species of *Hesperantha*. The large seeds of *Tritoniopsis* have an elaborately sculptured testa. A moderately developed spongy testa is characteristic of several species of *Moraea* subgenus *Vieusseuxia* (e.g., *M. villosa*). A somewhat net-like sculpturing pattern characterizes seeds of the South American genera *Solenomelus* and *Tapeinia*.

Seeds with fleshy appendages, loosely called arils, are rare in the family but occur in the genus *Iris*, where white or yellow bodies are found in sections *Hexapogon*, *Oncocyclus*, *Psammiris*, *Pseudoregelia*, and species of section *Limniris* and subgenera *Scorpiris* (*Juno*) and *Hermodactyloides* (*Reticulata*; examples in Figure 46). Arils have various origins, but in *Iris* they arise from the seed coat layers around the micropyle (the exostome) and are technically called caruncles, or from the raphe, when they are termed strophioles. A few species of *Crocus* also have seeds with whitish, fleshy outgrowths, in this case evidently arising from the raphe, but they are often loosely called caruncles (Mathew 1982). In other *Crocus* species the raphe may form a prominent ridge or wing, and the chalazal end may develop into a prominent lobe (also sometimes referred to as a caruncle). White, fleshy seed appendages typically contain fatty or waxy material and are often referred to as elaiosomes, literally fat bodies. They usually signal that the seeds are dispersed by ants, and this is reported to be the case in *Crocus* species with white, fleshy seed appendages. *Iris* seeds with white or yellow fleshy outgrowths are likewise assumed to be ant dispersed, but we know of no observations confirming this function.

A pale yellow or whitish elaiosome containing copious lipid is present in several species of *Patersonia*. A whitish waxy aril is developed on the funicle of the seeds of *Aristea singularis* but in no other species of the genus (Figure 14).

A few species, mostly of forest habitats, have red, orange, or yellow seeds, among them *Chasmanthe* (Crocoideae) and *Iris foetidissima*, *Neomarica variegata*, and *Libertia* species (Iridoideae). In *C. aethiopica* the outer layers of the seed coat itself are somewhat fleshy when first exposed, but the seed coast is always dry in *C. floribunda*. In *I. foetidissima* and *N. variegata* the red fleshy tissue encloses the entire seed and is sometimes called a sarcotesta. Species with red or orange, fleshy seeds are presumably dispersed by birds. In the East Asian *I. domestica* (= *Belamcanda*) the ripe seeds are smooth, spherical, and glossy black. They remain attached to the dry placentas of the ovary long after the capsule has split open and collectively resemble a blackberry (hence on of its common names, blackberry lily). Seeds of *Babiana* are dark brown to blackish and stand out starkly against the pale inner surface of the capsule. In *Crocosmia aurea* the inner surface of the open capsule is often orange, which we speculate draws the attention of birds to the dark seeds, collectively rather blackberry-like in appearance. The exposed bright orange seeds of *Chasmanthe floribunda* also resemble a berry and like those of *Crocosmia aurea* offer no nutritive material to birds that may be tricked into eating them, thus dispersing them when they are eliminated.

In several genera of Crocoideae the vascular trace to the ovule is pinched out from the surrounding tissue and becomes excluded from the seed during development, typically persisting as a thread-like structure lying above the raphe. Ovular trace exclusion appears to have occurred in two lineages

(Goldblatt et al. 2004b). In *Crocosmia* and *Devia* (tribe Freesieae), which have wrinkled seeds with prominent cell outlines, the seed epidermis in the area above the ovular trace is little modified. In the other group, which includes *Chasmanthe, Dierama, Duthieastrum, Ixia, Sparaxis,* and *Tritonia* of tribe Croceae, the cells above the vascular trace are small and unthickened, unlike the surrounding epidermal cells, and the vascular bundle is thus cut off from the seed as they dry out and shrivel.

## INTERNAL ANATOMY

Distinctive elongate styloid crystals of calcium oxalate are present either in specialized cells, called idioblasts, in the mesophyll tissue of leaves and stems or in cells of the outer vascular bundle sheath of leaves and other organs of most genera and species, including the primitive genus *Isophysis* (Isophysidoideae; Goldblatt et al. 1984, Rudall 1995). They are, however, absent from all but one of 20 species of *Sisyrinchium* examined and are also lacking in the related *Olsynium*. Styloids are present in the flowering stem and rhizome of the achlorophyllous saprophyte *Geosiris* but not in its scale-like leaves. Many genera contain tannin in occasional mesophyll or epidermal cells, particularly in the sheathing leaf base.

Xylem vessels, which are a specialized type of water-conducting tissue comprising large-diameter cells with perforated end walls, are largely restricted to the roots. Less specialized vessels with scalariform perforation plates (usually more than 25 perforations) are reported for *Aristea*, the woody *Klattia,* and *Nivenia, Witsenia,* the Australasian *Patersonia,* and *Geosiris,* as well as in *Isophysis*. Numerous other genera examined by the plant anatomist Vernon Cheadle (1963) have vessels with both scalariform perforations and the more derived, simple type of perforation plates. In the great majority of species the conducting tissue in stems and leaves contains only unspecialized, narrow-diameter, water-conducting cells, called tracheids, with the exception of two of five species of *Sisyrinchium* examined.

The food-conducting tissue in vascular plants, the phloem, comprises sieve elements and their associated companion cells. The sieve elements contain small organelles, or plastids, of various types often characteristic of families or even orders of plants. Iridaceae appear to be have P-type sieve tube plastids of the typical monocot type, containing only wedge-shaped protein crystals, as reported in a single species each of *Crocus, Gladiolus, Moraea,* and *Orthrosanthus* (Behnke 1981). Plastids of *Nivenia corymbosa* belong to a subtype with additional, less densely packed crystals.

## Roots

Roots have a clearly defined rhizodermis surrounding the ground tissue, or cortex, within which is located the central vascular tissue, or stele. The epidermis is often replaced in older roots by an exodermis, formed by lignification of outer layers of the cortical cells. The cortex is sometimes further divided into inner, middle, and outer regions based on cell width and size and frequency of intercellular spaces, the innermost cells being the smallest.

Root contraction in specialized contractile roots is accomplished by active radial growth of middle and outer cortical cells in a discrete part of the root, causing the root to shorten and the cortical tissue to collapse or buckle. The central vascular area of the root is bounded by an endodermis, the tissue that controls the movement of substances into and out of the stele, and recognized by the thickened and lignified radial and inner tangential walls. Immediately within the endodermis are usually one, or occasionally as many as three, layers of thin-walled cells, the pericycle, from which lateral roots arise. Phloem strands alternate with protoxylem (the first xylem cells produced during development, composed of cells of small diameter) strands in a ring within the pericycle, and wide metaxylem vessels are arranged in a ring surrounding a central parenchymatous or lignified pith.

## Stems

As in the stems of most monocots, the ground tissue, or cortical region, is bounded on the outside by an epidermis or secondarily by a periderm, and by an inner region consisting of closed vascular bundles scattered in a ground tissue of thin-walled parenchyma cells. In many perennating organs, particularly corms, which have an enlarged cortex, the ground tissue contains numerous starch grains. In rhizomes the central vascular region is sometimes bounded by a lignified endodermal layer, although the presence of this layer is variable, and it is always absent in *Dietes, Neomarica,* and *Trimezia* (Rudall 1984). In flowering stems there are several layers of thick-walled cells at the outside edge of the central vascular region, presumably increasing the rigidity and strength of the stem.

The primary vascular bundles are randomly oriented within the central region of the stem, usually larger toward the center. In underground stems the central phloem tissue of each vascular bundle is most commonly completely surrounded by xylem tissue, a condition termed amphivasal, almost to the stem apex, although occasionally (e.g., in rhizomes of species of *Iris, Neomarica,* and *Trimezia,* and in many flowering stems) they are mainly collateral, with the xylem restricted to just the outer side of each bundle.

Rhizomes in Iridaceae typically have a pericyclic primary thickening meristem near the stem apex, initiating root primordia and a limited amount of stem vasculature (Rudall 1984). In species of *Orthrosanthus* the primary thickening meristem is extensive, producing a network of vascular tissue, termed a pericyclic vascular plexus. A secondary thickening meristem, similar to that in the monocots *Aloe* (Asphodelaceae) and *Dracaena* (Ruscaceae), is responsible for later thickening of the stem diameter in Nivenioideae. The secondary thickening meristem produces radial chains of individual or linked vascular bundles in the erect stems of the woody South African genera *Klattia, Nivenia,* and *Witsenia* (Scott and Brebner 1893, Adamson 1926) and the woody rhizomes of some species of the herbaceous *Patersonia* (Rudall 1984).

Corms, characteristic of Crocoideae, are essentially shortened or contracted rhizomes that are replaced annually, and they usually have the anatomy typical of rhizomes. While corms of Crocoideae have an organized central stele of vascular tissue, those of *Ferraria* and *Moraea* have scattered vascular bundles that diverge and branch through the corm tissue. The corms of the Crocoideae comprise one to several internodes, mostly the latter, but those of those of *Moraea* invariably consist of just one swollen internode.

## Leaves

Epicuticular wax platelets, often quite characteristic of higher taxonomic ranks, are of the *Convallaria* type. These irregularly shaped scales of wax oriented at right angles to the surface, characteristic of the Lilianae, are reported for a few species of Iridaceae (Barthlott and Frolich 1983). Cuticular striations are rare. The outer cell layer of the leaf, or epidermis, consists of a layer of cells that are most commonly elongated along the long axis of the leaf and are longer in areas above vascular tissue than between this tissue. The cell walls have either straight sides or, in most Crocoideae, deeply undulating radial walls, a distinctive feature of the subfamily. In some genera of Tigridieae the normal epidermal cells are interspersed with small groups of large (bulliform) cells. Outgrowths, or papillae, on the surface of the epidermal cells are frequent in Crocoideae, each epidermal cell usually with two or more papillae in a single row (e.g., in species of *Gladiolus* and *Ixia*). Surface papillae are less common elsewhere in the family, and then there is usually just one per epidermal cell (e.g., in species of *Iris*). The epidermal cells along the leaf margins develop into a fringe of short hairs, sometimes called trichomes, in many genera.

Stomata, or pores in the leaf surface, facilitate gas exchange and are often evenly distributed in the areas of the leaf blade between the veins. In some species of *Crocus* and *Iris*, stomata are confined to one surface, and where leaves have distinct ridges or marginal thickenings the stomata are typically restricted to the sunken or unthickened areas. Particularly unexpected is the differentiation of the leaf surfaces in some *Iris* species (e.g., series *Californicae*) which have developmentally isobilateral leaves (leaves in which both surfaces are identical). The leaves in these species arch toward the ground and only the lower surface bears stomata (Wilson 1998). In this way they behave functionally more like dorsiventral leaves with distinct upper and lower surfaces. As in most other Asparagales, the stomata in Iridaceae lack subsidiary cells, except in *Dietes* and *Diplarrena* (Rudall 1983), where subsidiary cells are formed by oblique divisions of neighboring cells. Stomata are sometimes slightly sunken and usually have only an outer cuticular ridge, but in a few genera (e.g., *Diplarrena*, *Pillansia*) both inner and outer cuticular ridges are developed. Some genera (e.g., *Dietes*, *Libertia*) have a raised rim around the stomatal aperture. These specializations do not seem to correlate with phylogenetic relationship and are more likely a result of ecological or physiological selection in these genera.

The anatomy of the leaf margins, in particular the distribution of wall thickenings in the epidermal and subepidermal layers, is often characteristic of genera (Rudall 1995) and is a useful character for assessing generic relationships (Figure 3). *Neomarica*, for example, has very thick walled marginal epidermal cells whereas *Dietes*, *Ferraria*, and *Iris* have a strand of thick-walled sclerenchyma cells beneath an unthickened epidermis. In Tigridieae the marginal epidermis is thin-walled and a sclerenchyma strand in present below the margins in some species, absent in others. In Crocoideae the marginal sclerenchyma strand is typically associated with a marginal vein (e.g., *Gladiolus*, *Ixia*, *Watsonia*). Several genera of Crocoideae lack submarginal sclerenchyma but have instead thick-walled, columnar epidermal cells at the margins. These genera include *Chasmanthe*, *Sparaxis*, all but two species of *Tritonia* (all tribe Croceae), and the genera of tribe Freesieae (*Crocosmia*, *Freesia*, *Xenoscapa*). Only *Pillansia* appears to lack cellular differentiation along the margins as well as lacking submarginal sclerenchyma. In *Isophysis* both thick-walled, columnar epidermal cells and subepidermal sclerenchyma are present at the leaf margins. *Patersonia* and Nivenioideae have leaf margins like those of *Dietes* and *Iris*, thus with thin-walled epidermal cells and a strand of sclerenchyma beneath the epidermis. Leaves of some species of *Patersonia* have a peculiar lignified raised marginal ridge not found elsewhere in the family. The leaf margins of *Aristea* depart from the pattern among the unspecialized genera of the family in lacking a strand of sclerenchyma beneath the marginal epidermis, and the epidermal cells themselves are columnar and have much thickened walls much like the pattern in some Crocoideae. In *Aristea*, however, the epidermal cells decrease substantially in size toward the tips of the margins, with the result that margins taper to a very sharp edge.

The tissue within the leaf, the mesophyll, also often consists of cells characteristic of groups of species or genera. In most species of Crocoideae the mesophyll cells are elongated along the horizontal axis of the leaf, a condition rare elsewhere in the family. In *Sisyrinchium* subgenus *Sisyrinchium*

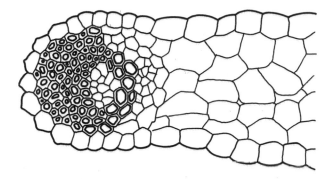

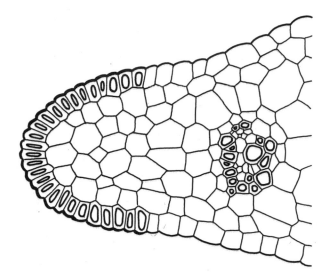

**Figure 3.** Leaf margin anatomy of subfamily Crocoideae: (above) *Tritoniopsis* sp., with unthickened marginal epidermal cells and marginal vascular bundle, the phloem cap extending to the epidermis, (below) *Crocosmia* sp., with thick-walled marginal epidermal cells and submarginal vascular bundle not associated with the leaf margin (much enlarged).

(= subgenus *Bermudiana*) the outer layers of mesophyll cells are elongated at right angles to the surface and are oval in both transverse and longitudinal section, whereas in species of subgenus *Echthronema* the mesophyll cells are longitudinally elongated and are lobed in longitudinal section (Rudall et al. 1986). In thick leaves of many genera only the outer two or three layers of mesophyll contain chloroplasts, thus are green, and the central cells are large and colorless. In leaves of *Crocus* the characteristic translucent (or apparently white) band along the central adaxial surface is the result of the presence of large colorless

cells below the epidermis (Rudall 1995). A longitudinal band or translucent tissue is also present in a few species of *Moraea,* and this seems to function as a window, allowing light to penetrate deeper within the leaf, allowing more efficient photosynthesis.

Vascular bundles in the sheathing leaf base are most commonly arranged in a single row, with their xylem poles situated on the outer edge toward the adaxial (outer) epidermis, but in *Dietes* there is also an extra row of bundles immediately within the adaxial epidermis (Rudall 1983), and in some species of *Neomarica* an extra row within the abaxial epidermis. In both cases the extra bundles are composed almost entirely of sclerenchyma. The leaf blade (Figure 2) in genera with unifacial leaves has vascular bundles either in two rows with xylem poles toward the leaf center, or in one row with alternating orientation, or more rarely in one row with groups of three to five bundles alternating in orientation across the leaf, as in Tigridieae, which have pleated leaves. In some species of several genera of Tigridieae the angles of the folds are extended into ridges or wings each with its own vascular bundle (Rudall 1991).

In terete or cylindrical leaves, such as those of species of *Bobartia* (Strid 1974) and several other genera, the vascular bundles lie in a single ring around the edge of the leaf, with xylem poles toward the center. In *Crocus* leaves, which have a central keel on the abaxial (lower) surface and two lateral arms, vascular bundles are in one row in the arms, all similarly oriented, and extend around the projecting edge of the keel. Leaves of many genera have a single bundle near one leaf margin oriented at right angles to the rest, which is continuous with the median bundle of the bifacial sheathing leaf base.

Vascular bundles may have an inner sheath and an outer sheath, as in many monocots. The outer sheath usually consists of one layer of small, thin-walled parenchyma cells that are sometimes indistinct from the surrounding mesophyll cells. The cells of the inner sheath, when it is present, are sclerenchymatous, with thickened, woody walls and are often discontinuous, although in a few genera, such as *Libertia,* the vascular bundles may be completely enclosed in sclerenchyma. In most cases sclerenchyma is confined to the phloem pole of the vascular bundle, although in species of *Sisyrinchium* subgenus *Sisyrinchium* and the small allied genera *Olsynium* and *Solenomelus,* sclerenchyma is confined to the xylem pole (Rudall et al. 1986). In some species of *Patersonia* the phloem is completely surrounded by sclerenchyma, and in some species of *Bobartia, Dietes,* and *Moraea* the phloem tissue is interspersed with fibers (Rudall 1983). Occasionally, sclerenchyma may be completely absent (e.g., species of *Sisyrinchium*). Vascular bundles may either be separated from the epidermis by one or more layers of mesophyll cells, or linked to it by a sclerenchyma cap or girder, this feature usually being characteristic of a species or group of species.

## Seeds

Seed anatomy is known in the family mainly as a result of the studies of Huber (1969), Manning and Goldblatt (1991), and Goldblatt et al. (2004b). The subject is important because seed structure is very conservative and differences thus assume considerable significance for systematic and evolutionary considerations. Both an outer integument, which becomes the testa in the mature seed, and inner integument, which becomes the tegmen, are usually present. The outer integument typically consists of four to six cell layers but only three in Nivenioideae and just two in *Aristea* and *Geosiris.* In most Iridaceae the outer epidermis is pigmented with brown material, the tannin phlobaphene. In *Klattia, Nivenia,* and *Witsenia* the outer epidermis lacks pigment and is transparent, and in the latter two genera the outer epidermis is usually partially

exfoliated at maturity. In some species of *Syringodea* the outer integument is also crushed at maturity (De Vos 1974). Both the outer and inner epidermis of the outer integument usually remain more or less intact at maturity. In *Watsonia* the outer integument forms a palisade-like layer around the seed body. The outer epidermal cell walls are smooth and often domed. Papillae are occasionally developed in species of *Romulea,* where they are short, and in species of *Crocus,* where they may be very long.

Strongly thickened radial and inner walls are common, but heavily thickened outer walls are present in those Crocoideae that have smooth hard seeds (e.g., *Dierama, Ixia, Sparaxis, Tritonia*). The tissue between the outer and inner epidermis usually consists of well-preserved cells often with brown-colored phlobaphene. The inner layer regularly disintegrates in *Cipura, Orthrosanthus, Sisyrinchium,* and many Crocoideae. In *Watsonia* the inner layer contains one to three cell layers with extraordinarily thick walls, with interiors packed with calcium oxalate styloid crystals. The inner epidermis often consists of cells with a fluid content of lipid nature, either clear or forming red-brown masses. The lipid layer is often two-layered in Crocoideae and two- to several-layered in *Iris* and its allies. Cells of the inner epidermis are inflated and protrude inward in *Libertia* and *Orthrosanthus.*

The inner integument, or tegmen, usually consists of a strongly flattened outer and a well-preserved inner epidermis that contains pigmented material. In *Aristea, Klattia, Nivenia,* and *Witsenia,* where the outer integument is only two- or three-layered, the outer epidermis of the tegmen is well developed and sometimes thickened and unevenly enlarged, with the result that the seed coat becomes undulate at maturity. The cells of the inner epidermis of the tegmen are often enlarged and bladder-like, and they impart a wavy sculpturing to the surface of the endosperm. In a few genera, notably *Orthrosanthus* and *Libertia,* and in some Crocoideae, the inner and outer layers form a more or less homogeneous structure.

Cells of the endosperm have heavily thickened walls of hemicellulose and contain the protein storage product aleurone as well as oil bodies. Starch is occasionally present, for example, in *Geosiris* and the African *Radinosiphon* (Crocoideae), in which a limited number of globose grains are present in the mature seed. Cell walls usually have large simple or weakly bordered pits (2–)4–10 μm wide. In many Crocoideae the walls are less heavily thickened and pits often lacking except in the central part of the endosperm. The embryo is usually one- to two-thirds as long as the endosperm, straight, and spindle-shaped. The embryonic leaf (cotyledon) is terminal and the terminal bud (the plumule) lateral. Dwarf embryos less than one-third as long as the endosperm are found in *Aristea* (Aristeoideae), *Nivenia* (Nivenioideae), and *Patersonia* (Patersonioideae), most likely the ancestral condition in the family. The condition in *Isophysis* is unknown.

## Embryology

Like seed anatomy, embryology is a very conservative character and often varies little even between plant families. Unfortunately, the field is not much studied today, and most of what we know dates from investigations done no later than the first half of the 20th century and is not always reliable because the identity of plants examined may be suspect, as may be the very detailed microscopic observations. The anther wall consists of four layers. Beneath the (1) outer epidermis there is a well-developed (2) inner layer of cells with elaborately thickened walls, the endothecium, which is believed to be responsible for facilitating the splitting of the anther at maturity. Internal to the endothecium is an (3) inner layer several cells thick that becomes crushed at maturity, and finally a (4) tapetum, responsible for producing nutrients for the new pollen grains, lining the interior of the anther locules. The wall thickenings of the endothecial cells assume a variety of distinct shapes that may be characteristic of tribes or subfamilies. The endothecial thickenings are U-shaped in *Isophysis,* Aristeoideae, Nivenioideae, Patersonioideae, and Iridoideae (Sisyrinchieae), and this thickening type is most likely ancestral in the family. Basal fusion of the thickening in Nivenioideae set this subfamily somewhat apart, and Patersonioideae are unique in the family in having base-plate-type thickenings, a feature uncommon in flowering plants. This is a specialized type of the U-shaped thickening. Helical thickenings characterize Crocoideae and Iridoideae, excepting Sisyrinchieae (Manning and Goldblatt 1990).

The tapetum is of the secretory type, and the cells are generally binucleate. The process of development of the microspore (the male reproductive cell of a plant, containing the sperm) or pollen grain is successive in *Geosiris* but simultaneous in *Sisyrinchium, Iris* species, and several genera of Crocoideae that have been studied (summarized by Rübsamen-Weustenfeld et al. 1994). The condition in *Isophysis,* Aristeoideae, Nivenioideae, and Patersonioideae is unknown. Microspore tetrads are isobilateral or tetrahedral. Pollen grains are normally two-celled.

Typical of most flowering plants, the ovule has two integuments and is primitively anatropous (straight) but is campylotropous (curved) in Crocoideae. Ovules are usually semicrassinucellate, thus with only one or two layers of peripheral cells surrounding the megaspore mother cell. The micropyle may be formed only by the inner integument, or by both integuments. A cushion of elongate, palisade-like cells is present on the funicle at the mouth of the micropyle, called the obturator (Steyn 1973), facilitates the passage of the pollen tube from the ovary chamber into the ovule itself.

The archesporial cell produces a parietal cell, which may form one or two layers of parietal tissue, but in *Sisyrinchium* the parietal cell degenerates without further division. In contrast, in the only two genera of Tigridieae known embryologically (*Eleutherine* and *Gelasine*) the archesporial cell functions directly as the megaspore mother cell, and these species are thus tenuinucellate. The primary sporogenous cell forms a linear or T-shaped tetrad, and embryo sac development is of the *Polygonum* type. The outer integument is usually several cells thick, and the inner integument two cells thick for most of its length. In *Crocus* and *Romulea* the nucellus disintegrates before fertilization so that the synergids extend into the micropylar canal. In Crocoideae a large refractive hypostase (a disk of lignified tissue) at the chalazal end of the embryo sac is formed from the nucellus and surrounds the antipodal cells (e.g., Rudall et al. 1984). The antipodal cells are generally large and persistent in Crocoideae, and relatively smaller in Iridoideae, and there are records of the proliferation of the antipodals (Haeckel 1930). The polar nuclei often fuse at an early stage before fertilization to form a fusion nucleus, which is usually closely associated with the antipodals. The two synergids have a filiform apparatus and are sometimes hooked.

The type of endosperm formation, often an important character for higher-level classification, is helobial in *Geosiris* and *Isophysis* (Rübsamen-Weustenfeld et al. 1994) but evidently nuclear in other genera examined, including one species of *Aristea* (Aristeoideae) and the few genera of Iridoideae and Crocoideae known (Wunderlich 1959). In helobial endosperm formation the first cell division produces two very unequal cells, followed by cell wall formation. The smaller of these two cells may be overlooked, hence endosperm formation can erroneously be identified as nuclear, in which no cell walls at all are produced after the nucleus divides. Embryogeny is poorly known but appears to conform to common patterns found in the flowering plants. There is insufficient information available for the family to draw any conclusions as to evolutionary trends or generic relationships.

## Pollen

The structure of pollen grains is highly conserved and is often a very fundamental feature, thus important for understanding evolutionary patterns. Pollen grains rarely vary within a species and not often within a genus or tribe, and when they do they assume considerable significance. They are unusually varied in the Iridaceae, far more so than in most monocots. As a result they have been used in conjunction with other characters to understand relationships at levels from subfamily to genus. The most important pollen features, the sculpturing of the exine, or outer wall of the pollen grain, and the type and number of the apertures, or germination zones on the grains, vary a great deal and yield a wealth of useful data for evolutionary studies. Grains are normally shed singly and are ellipsoid to spherical, and monosulcate (with a single, furrow-like aperture located at the distal pole) in most genera and species. Exceptionally, the pollen grains in *Aristea ecklonii*, *A. ensifolia*, and *A. pusilla* are shed in tetrads, a character confirming the close relationships of these three species within the genus.

The exine is primitively tectate (with an outer layer separated from the inner by a series of columnar thickenings), with reticulate, or net-like, sculpturing of the tectum, a condition believed to be ancestral in the monocots. *Isophysis* (Isophysidoideae) and most Aristeoideae, Nivenioideae, and Iridoideae have the ancestral pollen type in which the lumina of the reticulum are usually nearly equal but sometimes markedly unequal, as in *Ferraria* species (De Vos 1979). Lumina vary considerably in size and in some species are so small that the exine is described as microreticulate (with lumina less than 0.5 μm in diameter). Several species of *Aristea* have a rugulate (irregularly perforated) to areolate (perforations crushed and angular) exine. *Diplarrena* and the two species of *Patersonia* examined have an intectate exine (i.e., with the outer tectum so disrupted and reduced as to be essentially lacking) composed of scattered warty clumps, called verrucae, supported by short, small columns. Most members of the largest subfamily, Crocoideae, have a very different exine with an unbroken surface interrupted by small perforations, thus termed perforate. The exceptions in the subfamily are *Micranthus* and *Thereianthus racemosus*, which have reticulate exine grading to perforate at the aperture margins. The unusual exine in these species is associated with the ring-like apertures, quite different from those typical for the subfamily, and is secondarily derived.

The intine, the cellulosic inner layer of the wall of the pollen grains, is reported to be unusually thick (Heslop-Harrison 1977) in the family. This feature has been confirmed for *Aristea*, in which transmission electron microscope studies show particularly thick intine below the apertures, also notable in having a conspicuous microtubular structure (Suárez-Cervera et al. 2000) throughout the region of the aperture.

While monosulcate apertures of the type found in most monocots are most common in the Iridaceae, several other aperture types occur in several genera. *Aristea* is especially diverse in pollen morphology. Species of section *Aristea* have trisulcate (with three apertures) to spiraperturate (with a single helical aperture) grains, while in section *Eucapsulares* species have grains with the aperture largely to completely obscured by exine. Transmission electron microscopy shows that the apertures, recognized by very thick intine traversed by microtubules, are zonasulculate (forming a continuous ring around

the grain) or disulcate (with two furrows at opposite sides of the grain). Subgenus *Pseudaristea* has dizonasulcate apertures, thus with two ring-like furrows at opposite ends of the grains. Section *Racemosae* of subgenus *Aristea* has monosulcate pollen grains of the ancestral type for the subfamily. *Diplarrena* and the two species of *Patersonia* examined have inaperturate grains, thus completely lacking apertures in the exine.

In Crocoideae two evidently related genera of the subfamily, *Cyanixia* and *Zygotritonia* of tribe Watsonieae, both from tropical Africa, have trisulcate pollen grains, with three furrows. The tropical African *Savannosiphon*, with a single species and also Watsonieae, has grains that lack a discrete aperture and have been described as polyaperturate, though the exact nature of the aperture in these grains remains uncertain. Most other genera and species of Crocoideae have the single aperture traversed by two parallel bands of exine that run almost its entire length. The bands are interpreted as an operculum (Goldblatt et al. 1991), the function of which is to aid in the opening and closing of the aperture. In *Freesia viridis*, all *Ixia* species, and few of *Romulea* and *Thereianthus* the operculum consists of a single band or is somewhat disorganized. Two species of *Geissorhiza*, *G. heterostyla* and *G. inflexa*, also have unusual grains with multiple apertures and without the conventional two-banded operculum. *Crocus* has either inaperturate or spiraperturate pollen, while *Syringodea* pollen is inaperturate. *Afrocrocus*, a genus separated from *Syringodea* in this volume, has trizonasulculate grains with one central and two lateral ring-like furrows, a unique feature for the family (Figure 34).

Among the Iridoideae, the genus *Tigridia*, which now includes *Ainea*, *Fosteria*, *Rigidella*, and *Sessilanthera*, has disulculate pollen grains, thus with two parallel, longitudinal furrows but asymmetrically placed so that both furrows can be seen from one side of the grains but with no furrow evident from the opposite face. The type species of *Cardiostigma*, a small genus of species of Mexico, has been shown by DNA sequence data to be nested in the *Tigridia* group, and it has unique pollen grains with a single zonasulculate aperture displaced toward one pole of the grain (A. Rodríguez 1999). One species of the *Cardiostigma* group, *C. hintonii*, however, has disulculate grains of the *Tigridia* type and evidently does not belong with the rest of the group.

In a few genera of the subfamily, including some species of *Dietes* and *Iris*, grains are zonasulculate (Goldblatt and le Thomas 1992). *Cipura* is particularly variable, with different species having monosulcate, disulcate, or trisulcate pollen. In most species of *Iris* subgenera *Scorpiris* (*Juno*) and *Nepalensis* the grains themselves are spherical and have unconventional apertures (Schulze 1971). In *Iris* subgenus *Hermodactyloides*, pollen grains range from monosulcate to zonasulcate, or the entire grain may have hexagonal aggregations of exine regularly placed around the grain separated by a nonexinous aperture, a condition that defies available terminology (Zmarzty in Mathew 1989). *Moraea* species essentially have fairly typical reticulate exine, but there is a tendency in the genus for the exine to become beaded (termed retipilate or clavate) through reduction of the walls that form the reticulum. A more thorough survey of the pollen of both *Iris* and *Moraea* may yield useful information about relationships within these two large genera.

## CHROMOSOMES

Both chromosome number (Tables 2, 3) and size vary considerably in the Iridaceae (Goldblatt 1971a, 1982c, Kenton and Heywood 1984, Kenton et al. 1990, Goldblatt and Takei 1997), and the patterns of variation are often correlated with morphological variation. Chromosome size is, of course, a reflection of genome size, which in turn reflects not the number of genes but the way they are packaged within the chromosomes. Patterns of chromosome variation change in fairly predictable ways and sometimes provide valuable insights into evolutionary changes in groups of genera or within genera. As a result, the study of chromosomes has been the subject of considerable research. Chromosome number has been especially helpful in providing a set of characters independent of morphology that have often been invaluable in determining and refining the circumscription of genera. It has also been useful in understanding species relationships in genera that vary in their chromosome features.

Small chromosomes, such as found in Aristeoideae, Nivenioideae, and most Crocoideae, are probably ancestral. Genomes in these subfamilies are of the order of 0.6 picograms (pg) in diploid *Gladiolus* to 1.01 pg in *Pillansia*, which is polyploid (Goldblatt and Takei 1997). Other Crocoideae examined for genome size fall within this range. In contrast, most Iridoideae have medium-sized to large chromosomes. For example, diploid species of *Moraea* have genomes in the range 3.74–6.81 pg. *Iris* species have the largest chromosomes, and *I. histrio* has a genome size of 12.14 pg. Two exceptions among the Iridoideae are *Libertia* and *Orthrosanthus*, in which the chromosomes are very small. Chromosome and genome size is often fairly constant in genera and tribes, but even gross differences between taxa, as has been noted in *Sisyrinchium* (Kenton et al. 1987), may have no significance for systematics. The chromosomes of *Isophysis* are unfortunately unknown so that we cannot speculate on ancestral chromosome numbers or genome size in the family.

*Aristea* (Aristeoideae) and the woody *Nivenia*, *Klattia*, and *Witsenia* (Nivenioideae) have a basic chromosome number $x = 16$ (Table 2). Among

**Table 2.** Chromosome numbers in Iridaceae (see Table 3 for Crocoideae). Numbers in parentheses after the genera indicate number of species counted out of the total in the genus; parenthetical numbers in the basic chromosome number column $x$ indicate secondary base numbers. Triploids, unless known to be stabilized, and B chromosomes are not included in the table.

| Iridaceae | Basic and diploid numbers | |
| --- | --- | --- |
| | $x$ | $2n$ |
| subfamily Patersonioideae | | |
| Patersonia (6/21) | ?11 | 22, 42, c. 62 |
| subfamily Aristeoideae | | |
| Aristea (12/c. 55) | 16 | 32, 64 |
| subfamily Geosiridoideae | | |
| Geosiris (0/2) | uncounted | |
| subfamily Nivenioideae | | |
| Klattia (1/3) | 16 | 32 |
| Nivenia (4/11) | 16 | 32 |
| Witsenia (1/1) | 16 | 32 |
| subfamily Iridoideae | | |
| tribe Diplarreneae | | |
| Diplarrena (2/2) | 16 | 32 |
| tribe Sisyrinchieae | | |
| Libertia (5/c. 12) | 19 | 38, 76, 112 |
| Olsynium, including Phaiophleps (5/c. 12) | 10 (9, 8, ?11) | 20, 22, 40, 60, 18, 96 |
| Orthrosanthus (4/9) | ?9 (?12, 10) | 54, 40, 84, 50 |
| Sisyrinchium (40/c. 140) | 9 (8, 5, 17) | 18, 36, 72, 16, 32, 48, 64, 96, 34 |
| Solenomelus (1/2) | ?8 | 48 |
| Tapeinia (0/1) | uncounted | |
| tribe Trimezieae | | |
| Neomarica (4/12) | ?9 (8) | 18, 16, 32 |
| Pseudotrimezia (1/12) | ?8 (or 16) | 32 |
| Trimezia (5/20) | ?14 (13, 10, or 20) | 28, 26, 52, 40, 60, 80 |
| tribe Tigridieae | | |
| Alophia (3/5) | 14 | 28 |
| Calydorea, including Catila (4/10) | 7 | 14, 28, 42 |
| Cipura (4/9) | 7 | 14, 28 |
| Cypella (5/c. 30) | 7 (5) | 14, 28, 10 |
| Eleutherine (2/2) | 6 | 12 |
| Ennealophus, including Tucma (3/5) | 7 | 14 |
| Gelasine (2/c. 6) | 7 (6) | 14, 12 |
| Herbertia (4/7) | 7 | 14, 28, 42 |
| Hesperoxiphion (3/4) | 7 | 14 |
| Larentia (1/c. 4) | 7 | 14 |
| Mastigostyla (3/c. 20) | 14 | 28 |
| Nemastylis (3/4) | 7 | 14, 28, 56 |
| Tigridia, including Ainea, Cobana, Fosteria, Sessilanthera (18/55) | 14 | 28 |
| tribe Irideae | | |
| Bobartia (8/15) | 10 | 20 |
| Dietes (6/6) | 10 | 20, 40, 60 |
| Ferraria (12/14) | 10 | 20, 40, 60 |
| Iris, including Belamcanda, Hermodactylus (185/250) | ? (many diploid numbers; both polyploidy and dysploidy are frequent) | |
| Moraea, including Galaxia, Gynandriris, Homeria (32/198) | 10 (9, 8, 7, 6, 5) | 20, 40, 18, 16, 12, 24, 48, 10 |

unspecialized genera of Iridoideae, *Diplarrena* also has $x = 16$, but in Sisyrinchieae *Libertia* has $x = 19$, and *Orthrosanthus* probably $x = 9$. *Olsynium* may have an ancestral base number $x = 10$, and *Sisyrinchium* probably $x = 9$, but both genera have other base numbers (in *Sisyrinchium*, $n = 8, 17, 6, 5$). *Sisyrinchium* also frequently exhibits polyploidy (doubling of the chromosome complement), especially in the North American species. *Libertia* is characterized by extensive polyploidy. Among New Zealand species, ploidy levels range from $2x$ to $12x$ ($2n = 228$), and the single South American species counted is tetraploid ($2n = 76$). In Irideae, *Bobartia*, *Dietes*, *Ferraria*, and *Moraea* have an ancestral base number $x = 10$, evidence that they constitute a single lineage. The remaining genus of the tribe, *Iris*, is so variable cytologically that its ancestral base number is uncertain. Diploid numbers range from a low of $2n = 16$ to a high of $2n = 88$, occasionally even higher, and polyploidy is frequent in the genus. The most common numbers, not necessarily ancestral, are $2n = 24$ and 20.

Extensive stepwise decrease in number (dysploidy) has occurred in *Moraea*, in which haploid numbers range from $n = 10$ through 5, with $n = 6$ the most common number in the genus, including the *Gynandriris*, *Hexaglottis*, *Homeria*, and *Vieusseuxia* groups, each of which has a distinctive karyotype. While the frequency of polyploidy is generally low in Irideae, *Iris* excepted, *Ferraria*, with 12 species counted, has *F. crispa* and *F. schaeferi* with only tetraploid and hexaploid populations, and two more species have diploid and tetraploid races. The two Eurasian species of the *Gynandriris* group of *Moraea* are tetraploid, $2n = 24$, marking them as cytologically derived, while among the southern African species of the group, five are diploid and one polyploid. In the *Hexaglottis* group two species of the six are exclusively tetraploid. In the *Galaxia* group three species of the 15 counted have diploid

and polyploid races, and one species in only known from tetraploid populations. Several species of the *Homeria* group are also polyploids based on $x = 6$. Five species have both diploid and tetraploid races, but three species are tetraploid, and *M. flaccida* has tetraploid and hexaploid populations. Among the remaining species of *Moraea* polyploidy is rare, and just two species of 50 counted have exclusively polyploid populations.

Particularly interesting in the *Homeria* group are *Moraea demissa* with $2n = 10, 9$, and 8, and *M. flavescens* with $2n = 9$. Both are autogamous and are chain- or ring-forming complex heterozygotes, while *M. pallida*, $2n = 12$ and 8, also has autogamous, complex-heterozygote-forming populations (Goldblatt 1981). Remarkable as this reproductive mode is in the family, it also occurs in the South American *Gelasine elongata*, in which chromosomes form rings at meiosis (Kenton and Rudall 1987). *Iris* has considerable polyploidy as well as dysploidy with $x = 12$ and 10 the most common base numbers. Matching chromosome number against the molecular phylogenies available does not help establish a base number for the genus.

Among the New World Iridoideae, Trimezieae are poorly known cytologically, and base numbers in *Neomarica* and *Trimezia* include $x = 10, 9, 8$, and 7. *Pseudotrimezia* may have $x = 8$ (or 16; Chukr and Giulietti 2001), but only one species has been counted. In the bulbous genera, tribe Tigridieae, $x = 7$ is evidently ancestral and strongly conserved. Most species of *Tigridia* (including *Ainea*, *Fosteria*, and the *Sessilanthera* group) as well as the related *Alophia* are polyploid with $n = 14$. Reports of diploidy, $n = 7$, in Mexican species of *Tigridia* are probably based on misidentification, but the only counts for South American species currently included in this large genus are diploid (Kenton and Heywood 1984). Departures from $x = 7$ in Tigridieae are restricted to *Eleutherine*, $x = 6$, and one species of

**Table 3.** Ancestral, basic, and diploid numbers in Crocoideae. Numbers in parentheses after the genera indicate number of species counted out of the total in the genus; parenthetical numbers in the basic chromosome number column *x* indicate secondary base numbers. B chromosomes are not included.

| Crocoideae | Basic (ancestral) and diploid numbers | |
| --- | --- | --- |
| | *x* | *2n* |
| tribe Tritoniopsideae | | |
| Tritoniopsis, including Anapalina (6/24) | ?16 (15) | 32, 30 |
| tribe Watsonieae | | |
| Cyanixia (1/1) | 10 | 20 |
| Lapeirousia (32/42) | 10 (9, 8, 6, 5, 4, 3) | 20, 18, 16, 12, 10, 8, 6 |
| Micranthus (3/3) | 10 | 20 |
| Pillansia (1/1) | 10 | 40 |
| Savannosiphon (1/1) | 8 | 16 |
| Thereianthus (3/8) | 10 | 20 |
| Watsonia (30/51) | 9 | 18 |
| Zygotritonia (1/4) | 7 | 14 |
| tribe Gladioleae | | |
| Gladiolus, including Homoglossum (75/262) | 15(14, 13, 12, 11) | 30, 60, 90, 120, 28, 26, 24, 22 |
| Melasphaerula (1/1) | 10 | 20 |
| tribe Freesieae | | |
| Crocosmia (6/8) | 11 | 22 |
| Devia (1/1) | 10 | 20 |
| Freesia, including Anomatheca (12/15) | 11 | 22 |
| Xenoscapa (1/2) | 11 | 22 |
| tribe Croceae | | |
| Afrocrocus (1/1) | 11 | 22 |
| Babiana, including Antholyza (22/c. 90) | 7 | 14 |
| Chasmanthe (2/3) | 10 | 20 |
| Crocus (79/c. 85) | ?6 (many base numbers recorded including much polyploidy, sometimes within a species; Mathew 1982) | |
| Dierama (7/44) | 10 | 20 |
| Duthieastrum (1/1) | 10 | 20 |
| Geissorhiza (43/c. 85) | 13 | 26, 39, 52 |
| Hesperantha, including Schizostylis (30/c. 80) | 13 (12) | 26, c. 50, c. 72–76 |
| Ixia (14/c. 67) | 10 | 20, 40 |
| Radinosiphon (1/2) | 15 | 30 |
| Romulea (c. 80/c. 92) | 13 (12, 11, 10, 9) | 26, 28, 24, 22, 20, 18, 30, 52, 78 |
| Sparaxis, including Synnotia (10/16) | 10 | 20, 40 |
| Syringodea (5/6) | 6 | 12 |
| Tritonia (15/30) | 11 (10) | 22, 20, 44 |

*Gelasine, G. elongata,* likewise *n* = 6, and a species which forms complex heterozygotes. In *Cypella* most species have *x* = 7, but *C. coelestis* (= *C. plumbea*) has *n* = 5.

Most Crocoideae have relatively small chromosomes, and this large subfamily is variable cytologically (Table 3). Nevertheless, a single base number is characteristic of most genera or groups of genera. *Gladiolus* and *Radinosiphon* have *x* = 15; *Hesperantha* and *Geissorhiza, x* = 13; *Afrocrocus, Crocosmia, Freesia, Tritonia,* and *Xenoscapa, x* = 11; *Dierama, Duthieastrum, Ixia,* and *Sparaxis, x* = 10; *Watsonia, x* = 9; and *Babiana* and *Zygotritonia, x* = 7. *Crocus* and *Romulea* have extensive dysploidy, but either *x* = 14 or 13 may be basic for *Romulea* (De Vos 1972). Chromosome numbers in *Crocus* are startlingly variable—diploid numbers range from 2*n* = 6 to 30, but the base number in the genus is uncertain. The closely allied *Syringodea* clearly has *x* = 6, giving rise to the hypothesis that species of *Crocus* with this base number are ancestral and that higher numbers are derived via polyploidy and lower numbers by dysploid reduction.

Dysploidy has also been reported for several tropical African species of *Gladiolus* (Goldblatt et al. 1993), in which numbers range from the ancestral *x* = 15 through *n* = 14, 12, and 11. In contrast, the southern African species are remarkably constant cytologically, all having *x* = 15. Polyploidy occurs in only a few species of this large genus, notably in the widespread *G. dalenii,* in which tetraploid and hexaploid races predominate, but isolated diploid populations are recorded. The distinctive base number in *Gladiolus* provided evidence for the inclusion in *Gladiolus* of genera such as *Anomalesia, Homoglossum, Kentrosiphon,* and *Oenostachys,* which have the same base number and identical derived seeds but flowers very different from those of typical *Gladiolus.* No ancestral base number has been postulated for Crocoideae, but the base of *x* =

16 in *Tritoniopsis* make this number likely ancestral for the entire subfamily. Significantly, Nivenioideae, sister clade to Crocoideae, also have *x* = 16. For the Iridaceae as a whole, *x* = 10 is most likely ancestral, given the base numbers *x* = 10, 19, 9, and 16 (polyploid based on 8) in the least specialized genera. A base number *x* = 16 for Crocoideae would mark the entire subfamily as paleopolyploid.

In Watsonieae, *Micranthus, Pillansia,* and *Thereianthus* have *x* = 10 and a distinctive karyotype, with a pair of conspicuously longer chromosomes. *Pillansia* is paleotetraploid and thus has a diploid number 2*n* = 40. *Watsonia* has *x* = 9 and a karyotype of two large chromosome pairs, suggesting its derivation from the *x* = 10 group by fusion of two chromosomes. *Lapeirousia,* evidently most closely related to *Watsonia,* has an unusual bimodal karyotype with one extremely large chromosome pair and seven to nine small pairs in most species. The genus may have *x* = 10 as the ancestral base. It exhibits a remarkable descending dysploid series in the tropical African section *Paniculata,* species of which have *n* = 8, 7, 6, 5, and 4, and secondary polyploid increase to *x* = 6. This is followed by a second dysploid decrease to *x* = 5, 4, and 3. The dysploid species with the latter numbers all have twice as much DNA per cell as those *n* = 8, 7, or 6, which confirms their polyploid origin and subsequent derivation through decrease in chromosome number by chromosome fusion (Goldblatt and Takei 1997). The southern African *L. bainesii,* with *n* = 3, has the lowest chromosome number in the family. Such patterns of chromosome change have led to a greater understanding of the evolution of these species.

Among the tropical African members of Watsonieae, *Cyanixia* also has *x* = 10, but its different karyotype suggests that it is not immediately related to the *Micranthus* group of the tribe. The remaining *Savannosiphon* has *x* = 8, and *Zygotritonia, x* = 7.

# PHYTOCHEMISTRY

Iridaceae contain a wider range of phenolic compounds than its related families (Williams et al. 1986). A few species contain proanthocyanidins and the flavonol myricetin, compounds that are otherwise characteristic constituents of woody flowering plants. Another apparently primitive feature is the occurrence of the biflavone amentoflavone, recorded in *Patersonia* and also present in *Isophysis*. Biflavones are rare in the monocots but common in gymnosperms. Their presence in *Isophysis* and *Patersonia* is strong evidence for the close relationship of these two genera. The major flavonoids of the leaf and flower of Iridaceae are flavone C-glycosides, recorded in 65% of the species studied, with two flavonols, kaempferol and quercetin, frequently present. Unusual 6-hydroxyflavones have been identified only in *Crocus,* a genus also characterized by the water-soluble yellow carotenoid compound, crocein, in floral tissues. Isoflavones, including irigenin, tectorigenin, and irisolone, otherwise unknown not only in the Iridaceae but in the monocotyledons, occur in *Iris* (including *Belamcanda,* now included in *Iris*). The unusual glucosylxanthone mangiferin occurs widely and sporadically in *Iris* and some *Moraea* species (especially the *Gynandriris* group; Iridoideae: Irideae), and in *Eleutherine, Gelasine,* and *Tigridia* (including species treated elsewhere as *Rigidella;* Iridoideae: Tigridieae). In Crocoideae, mangiferin has been reported only in one species each of *Crocus* and *Lapeirousia,* and the compound is lacking in several other genera of the subfamily that have been examined.

There is a fair correlation between the distribution of flavone C-glycosides and flavonols and the current subfamilial classification. Flavonols are frequent in *Aristea, Geosiris, Patersonia,* the genera of Nivenioideae, and in Crocoideae, which together form one of the two main clades of the family. These compounds are infrequent in the other major clade, the Iridoideae, and are absent from most genera of the subfamily, although flavonols occur in a few species of *Iris* and scattered species of *Cipura, Cypella* (Tigridieae), and *Moraea* (Irideae). The flavonoid compounds of *Diplarrena* conform most closely to *Dietes,* thus providing independent evidence of its relationship to that genus, and its position in subfamily Iridoideae.

Another surprising chemical marker for subfamily Iridoideae are *meta*-carboxy-substituted aromatic amino acids and γ-glutamyl peptides (Larsen et al. 1981). These compounds occur widely in the subfamily, though they have not yet been isolated from the few *Sisyrinchium* species examined for the compounds. γ-Glutamyl peptides have not been found in isolated species of *Bobartia, Libertia,* or *Orthrosanthus* so far examined. Thus γ-glutamyl peptides have been confirmed in most genera of Iridoideae excepting members of Sisyrinchieae, plus *Bobartia.* These compounds are uniformly absent in the many Crocoideae and Nivenioideae studied. *Isophysis* has not been examined. *Diplarrena,* only genus of Diplarreneae and sister to the remainder of subfamily Iridoideae, has not been examined for *meta*-carboxy-substituted aromatic amino acids or γ-glutamyl peptides.

Chelidonic acid, a common compound in the orders Asparagales and Haemodorales and also characteristic of Liliales, is poorly represented in Iridaceae. Cyanogenic compounds are rare but recorded in some groups within *Moraea* (notably the *Homeria* group). The structure of these compounds is similar to the cyanogenic glycosides found in the very poisonous *Scilla* and *Urginea* (Hyacinthaceae). Not surprisingly, the leaves and corms of the *Moraea* species are toxic to livestock and humans. The possibly toxic quinone plumbagin occurs in *Aristea* and in isolated species of *Sisyrinchium* and *Sparaxis.* Quinonoid pigments are also recorded in the bulb of *Eleutherine* and rhizome of *Libertia.*

Other chemical classes known in the family and especially in *Iris* include steroidal saponins (a heterogeneous group of slimy or slippery terpenoids characterized by their ability to foam in water), fructan storage carbohydrates, and hydroxycinnamic acid. The genus is also famous as the source of the triterpenoid compounds contained in orris root oil, the oxidation of which releases methylionones, which have the vivid odor of violets and are important in the fragrance industry.

# NATURAL HISTORY

Like the vast majority of plants, nearly all members of the Iridaceae are autotrophic, that is, they produce their own carbohydrates and proteins directly, fixing carbon in the air by photosynthesis, and using nitrates from the soil to produce the amino acids necessary for synthesizing proteins. This is in contrast to parasitic plants, such as the broomrapes (*Orobanche* species), that obtain some or all of their nutritional requirements from another plant, attaching themselves to the tissue of a host via specialized organs called haustoria. A third life form is saprophytism, in which a plant obtains some or all of its nutrition from symbiotic fungi in the soil or leaf litter. *Geosiris* (Figure 11) has just such a life history. Plants grow in moist forest habitats and have roots, stems, and flowers, but the leaves are reduced to colorless scales and the entire plant lacks chlorophyll. It is assumed, but by no means established, that the roots house species of fungi and that these organisms obtain their nutrition from decaying plant material, absorbing what remains of the carbohydrate and protein in the rotting tissue. Saprophytes, or more specifically mycosaprophytes (from the Greek word *mycos,* fungus), offer the fungus species a sheltered place to live in the cells of their roots in exchange for excess carbohydrates that

the fungal tissues accumulate. In the case of *Geosiris* this scenario is highly speculative, and there may be more to its life history than we assume at present.

Largely because of its unusual lifestyle, the familial position of *Geosiris* was for many years in dispute. The genus was referred to the family Burmanniaceae because all members of that family are saprophytes, lack leaves, and are nongreen plants, and it has also been assigned its own family, Geosiridaceae. Anatomical study (Goldblatt et al. 1987) showed that *Geosiris* has styloid calcium oxalate crystals that are typical of the Iridaceae in some of its tissues, has a flavonoid chemistry profile similar to many Iridaceae, and has an inflorescence and flower structure consistent with Iridaceae but not with Burmanniaceae, whose members never contain styloid crystals. Molecular studies using DNA sequences show conclusively that *Geosiris* does indeed belong within the Iridaceae, where its position in the evolutionary tree is closest to *Aristea* and *Patersonia* (Reeves et al. 2001).

## GROWTH STRATEGIES

Like nearly all geophytic plants, that is, those with underground storage and regenerative organs, most species of Iridaceae are deciduous, dying down to ground level in the dry season. The majority of deciduous species conform to a standard pattern of remaining dormant underground during the dry season and producing leaves and then an aerial flowering stem during the course of the wet season. Several genera are evergreen, including most of those on the lower levels of the evolutionary tree. Thus *Isophysis, Patersonia, Libertia, Orthrosanthus* as well as the fairly specialized tropical lowland genera *Neomarica* and *Trimezia* in South and Central America, the African *Bobartia* and *Dietes,* and many species of *Iris* remain green throughout the year. Whether evergreen or deciduous, flowering typically occurs after or during the period of peak vegetative growth and is also preceded by the development of a new bulb, corm, or rhizome at the base of the stem. By the time that the capsules with their complement of seeds develop, the new underground organ is mostly provisioned with food storage material. As the parts above ground dry at the end of the wet season, the bulb, corm, or rhizome matures and becomes dormant. The dry leaves and flowering stem are shed, and the plant enters a resting phase, with the tiny new growth point already formed and ready to sprout at the beginning of the next growing season. In Iridaceae the flowering shoot terminates the annual growth axis.

In southern Africa, southern South America, and southern North America, with their two opposed growing seasons—a wet summer in the eastern three-quarters of the subcontinents and a wet winter in the southwest—growth cycles in the flora occur at quite different times of the year. In the winter-rainfall zones, which occupy the southwestern portion of the subcontinents, winter rains usually begin in April or May in the southern hemisphere, October or November in the northern hemisphere. Most geophytes then commence their growth cycles. In the southern hemisphere, flowering may begin as early as May or June in a few species, mostly of desert areas with low rainfall, particularly in genera

such as *Babiana* and a few species of *Gladiolus.* More often, flowering commences in early August and lasts until October in the lowlands. At higher elevations in the mountains, flowering takes place later, sometimes as late as December, especially in Chile, where winter-growing species of the high Andes grow after temperature rises above freezing. Plants of wet montane habitats, including several *Gladiolus* species in southern Africa, are less immediately affected by the limitations of seasonal availability of water. They flower late in the season, in December and January. *Gladiolus sempervirens* is unusual for a species of the winter-rainfall region in that its flowering is delayed until March or April, the southern autumn months. Despite growing in a winter-rainfall and largely summer-dry climate, it grows in habitats that seldom, if ever, become completely dry, and the plants are evergreen, an interesting reversal to the ancestral condition in the family.

A similar pattern prevails in the Mediterranean Basin and Middle East, which also have a winter-wet and summer-dry climate. *Gladiolus* and *Iris* species of this region flower in late winter and spring, March–May, following a phase of vegetative growth. *Crocus* is the exception—plants flower before producing their leaves. This strategy is essential for dwarf plants that have underground stems and must display their blooms before the surrounding vegetation, grasses, and broad-leaved herbs begin their leaf growth and would hide the *Crocus* flowers. A significant number of *Crocus* species bloom in the autumn, the end of the dry season in the Mediterranean region. This strategy is highly specialized. Plants have completed their vegetative growth by early summer, and with the rest of the herbaceous vegetation their leaves are dry and have often disappeared. Flowers of stemless plants now have a second opportunity to make their appearance and be seen by pollinators. Flowering in the dry season after the leaves have died down, at a time unfavorable for vegetative growth, sometimes called hysteranthy (from the Greek, after flowering, referring to the leaves produced after the flowers). This strategy is also seen in sub-Saharan Africa, especially in the western southern African winter-rainfall zone. There, several species of *Gladiolus,* all species of the *Crocus*-like genus *Syringodea,* and a few isolated species of *Moraea* and *Romulea* have evolved this strategy. Flowering when few, if any, other plants are in bloom limits competition for visits by pollinators and enhances reproductive success. A second advantage is that seeds are produced at the beginning of the wet season and can germinate when conditions for germination and growth are optimal. Leaves of the autumn-flowering species are also produced when growing conditions are favorable, and underground organs can be quickly regrown and replenished after storage resources were consumed by the flowering and fruiting process.

The separation of flowering and leafing periods is not restricted to plants of winter-rainfall and summer-dry climates, but far fewer species have adopted this strategy in regions of summer rainfall and dry or frigid winters. Nevertheless, tropical Africa and America and parts of southern Africa all have their share of species that bloom before the onset of the rainy season. In fact, in many areas of Africa the so-called prerain flora is striking. The strategy permits the same benefits as in the winter-rainfall zone—flowers appear at a time when the surrounding vegetation is most sparse and they are thus most visible. *Gladiolus* species such as the tropical *G. atropurpureus* and *G. unguiculatus* are particularly successful and widespread species of the prerain flora. After flowering, the latter species produces new leaves from shoots on the same corm as the leafless flowering stems as the wet season progresses. This contrasts with the situation in *G. atropurpureus* and several other species of the genus (Goldblatt and Manning 1998) in which the short leaves on the flowering stem remain green and continue to photosynthesize as the wet season progresses, long after the ripe capsules have

released their seeds. The widespread tropical African *Moraea schimperi,* a species that extends from Ethiopia in the north to Zimbabwe in the south, follows the same strategy as *G. unguiculatus,* as does the even more widespread *M. stricta.* This plant, with a range extending from Ethiopia to South Africa, flowers among dry grass in spring, then produces its long, trailing, string-like leaves after the rains have begun. It is noteworthy that most summer-growing hysteranthous Iridaceae have such wide ranges, exceptional for the family. The growth strategy is highly specialized and evidently once evolved ensures the success of the species.

Separation of flowering and leafing phases is achieved in various ways among the different species in which it occurs. In the hysteranthous species of *Tritoniopsis* from the southwestern Cape, for example, elongation of the flowering stem is delayed long after the appearance of the basal foliage leaves. Thus the dried and withered remains of the leaves are attached to the base of the flowering stem. This is also the situation in the hysteranthous *Moraea* species of the summer-rainfall area, including *M. stricta.* In the winter-flowering species of *Syringodea* and *Crocus,* however, the flowers emerge above the ground on an elongated floral tube before the leaves are fully developed. In both of these growth strategies the leaves and flowers are borne on the same stem, or growth axis. A very different strategy has been developed in a few hysteranthous species of *Gladiolus,* among them *G. brevifolius* and is relatives. In these species the flowers and foliage leaves are produced on quite separate shoots, and the new corms thus form at the base of the leafing shoot only.

## FIRE AND THE FLOWERING RESPONSE

Fire is an important aspect of the ecology of the grasslands, savannas, and shrublands of the world and has profound effects on the plants of such habitats. The fire response is particularly striking in southern Africa, with its large flora of geophytic plants. The underground storage and regenerative organs of geophytes are ideally situated to survive the destructive effects of fire, and they are among the first plants to regrow after a bushfire, which typically occurs in the mid to later part of the dry season. As soon as the first rains fall, and sometimes even before then, new shoots of geophytes emerge from the ashes. While the seeds of trees, shrubs, and herbs germinate and grow slowly into new plants, the geophytes race to produce leaves and flowers. The first flowering season after a fire, spring in the winter-rainfall zone, summer in the summer-rainfall zone, is dominated by displays of blooming geophytes. The result of the mass flowering has several interesting consequences.

The first is massive seed production. Seed survival is also enhanced because seed parasites such as bruchid beetles cannot quickly take advantage of such an unanticipated increase in the seed supply. Seed mortality, resulting from the destructive effects of the seed-eating larvae, which infest developing capsules, is thus reduced. Reseeding is thus particularly effective after fires because not only are numerous seeds produced, but competition from the surrounding vegetation for light, water, and nutrients is minimized. In fact, fire results in an increase in the amount of nutrients available for plants that survive, as well as a new generation of seedlings. Seedling recruitment thus takes place in waves that coincide with fire periodicity.

Flowering of geophytes in the years following a fire decreases and sometimes ceases as the surrounding vegetation recovers and outcompetes them. Nevertheless, the geophyte flora persists underground for many years even though it may not flower for as many years as it takes until the next fire. *Gladiolus phoenix,* a plant of the mountains east of Cape Town, South Africa, is one of the most striking examples of this phenomenon. We discovered plants in seed late in the summer after a fire the previous year. Not recognizing the species, we returned to the site the next year a little earlier in the season, expecting to see the species in flower. We were astonished to find just a few leaves had been produced, and not a single plant had bloomed just one year after plants had flowered in mass. A few years later, after a fire in the same mountains, we finally saw the species in bloom and were able to identify it as new to science. Evidently, plants like *G. phoenix* produce assimilatory leaves that slowly accumulate food material in the corm until it reaches a critical size and is ready to bloom again when fire again sweeps through the vegetation.

Fire in such habitats is not merely a destructive force. It results in the creation of special ecological niches for species, and including ones that geophytes are ideally suited to exploit. Habitats that are regularly subjected to fire encourage the reproductive success of geophytes, and in vegetation types where fire is a normal part of the ecosystem, such as fynbos, grassland, and savanna, it allows for the evolution of species adapted to take advantage of the postfire niche. *Gladiolus phoenix* is just one of a long list of "fire plants," species that depend on fire to bloom and reproduce.

## REPRODUCTIVE BIOLOGY

Outcrossing is the normal mode of reproduction in the large, usually brightly colored, bisexual flowers of Iridaceae. The flowers are weakly to strongly protandrous, with pollen released some hours to 1–3 days before stigma surfaces become available for pollen deposition. Among the several genera that have been critically studied, the male and female phases of anthesis are most pronounced in *Gladiolus* and *Tritoniopsis*. In these genera the stigmatic surfaces are only available for pollen deposition 2 or 3 days after flowers open, by which time most of the pollen is normally removed by pollinator activity, thus preventing the clogging of the stigma by self pollen as well as increasing the likelihood of cross pollination (Goldblatt et al. 1998a, Goldblatt and Manning 1999, Manning and Goldblatt 2005). The incompatibility system is gametophytic, a condition in which rejection of self pollen occurs within the style or ovary, and late acting where known (Heslop-Harrison 1977, Heslop-Harrison and Shivanna 1977). Studies in Eurasian species of *Crocus* (Crocoideae) and *Iris tuberosa* (Iridoideae) confirm that incompatibility is expressed within the ovary. The ovarian grooves at the base of the stylar canal have enlarged epidermal cells that produce a floccular secretion that evidently provides discriminatory activity to incoming pollen tubes (Chichiricò 1996, Grilli Caiola and Brandizzi 1997). In some examples, self-incompatibility was expressed within the ovule, where fertilized embryos aborted early in their development, an indication of the expression of post- as well as prefertilization incompatibility. Studies of African *Moraea* species likewise showed that self-incompatibility was expressed within the ovary, often in the ovule, and not in the style (Goldblatt et al. 2005a).

Compatibility relations have been little studied in the family, but strong self-incompatibility prevails in *Iris* section *Oncocyclus* (Sapir et al. 2005) and *Moraea;* just a few of the latter are self-compatible and autogamous (Goldblatt 1981, Goldblatt et al. 2005a). Self-incompatibility also characterizes the crocoid genera *Crocus* and *Gladiolus* (Chichiricò 1996, Goldblatt et al. 1998a). Among other Crocoideae, *Babiana, Freesia, Hesperantha, Lapeirousia,* and *Sparaxis* have both incompatible and self-compatible species (Goldblatt et al. 1995, 2000, 2004c), but *Romulea* and *Watsonia* evidently show weak self-incompatibility in all species examined for the feature, and some flowers on an inflorescence will produce seeds by self-pollination if not cross pollinated (e.g., Horn 1962, De Vos 1972). In the mono-specific *Melasphaerula* a number of capsules, often with lower than normal numbers of viable seeds, are produced by selfing in plants from which insects are excluded (Goldblatt et al. 2005b), a pattern consistent with that reported in *Romulea* and *Watsonia.*

In addition to genetic incompatibility and temporal separation of male and female phases of the flowers, spatial separation of anthers and receptive stigmatic surfaces is common. Prime examples are the *Iris*-type flowers of *Dietes* and *Moraea,* as well as *Iris* itself, in which the stigmatic lobes are typically held well above the anthers. Species of series *Californicae* and *Sibiricae* studied by Lenz (1959) are reported to be self-incompatible but never set seed unless pollen is transferred by insects or manually. Spatial separation of anthers and stigmatic surfaces is also frequent in Crocoideae. In many members of the subfamily the style does not expand fully until some time after the pollen is shed, at which time the style branches extend beyond the anthers and only then become receptive, as they move forward or downward as, for example, in *Gladiolus* (Goldblatt and Manning 1998). In *Tritoniopsis* the receptive phase of the stigmatic surfaces is accompanied by recurving of the filaments away from the style branches so that the anthers are moved even farther from possible contact with the stigmatic areas (Manning and Goldblatt 2005). In older flowers of other genera, however, style branches may recurve and contact the anthers, facilitating self-pollination in self-compatible species if cross pollination has not already been effected.

A few species with specialized pollination systems show marked facultative autogamy, evidently a fail-safe mechanism. Thus among long-proboscid-fly-pollinated *Lapeirousia* species, *L. silenoides* is self-incompatible, but in the absence of active pollen transfer, *L. anceps, L. jacquinii,* and *L. oreogena* will still produce normal capsules with full complements of viable seeds by selfing (Goldblatt et al. 1995).

Similarly, most *Babiana* species do not normally produce seeds without cross pollination, but long-proboscid-fly-pollinated *B. tubiflora* is self-compatible, as is bird-pollinated *B. ringens* (Anderson et al. 2005), and both set seed when no external agent is available for pollen transfer. A similarly mixed compatibility system also characterizes *Sparaxis*. Among the long-proboscid-fly-pollinated species, *S. variegata* is self-incompatible while *S. metelerkampiae* is autogamous; among the bee-pollinated species, *S. caryophyllacea* and *S. galeata,* both of which have large, strongly scented flowers, are self-incompatible, but smaller-flowered and unscented *S. parviflora* and *S. villosa* are autogamous.

In *Moraea,* species like *M. albiflora* and *M. vegeta,* which have small, inconspicuous flowers, at least as compared with their immediate relatives, are also autogamous (Goldblatt et al. 2005a). Likewise, the complex heterozygote species *M. demissa, M. flavescens,* and *M. pallida* are autogamous (Goldblatt 1981). Chromosome rings produced at meiosis are assumed to maintain favorable gene linkages and ensure the maintenance of structural heterozygosity. Associated with complex heterozygosity, the most common diploid chromosome number in *M. demissa* and *M. flavescens* is $2n = 9$, whereas the basic number for the clade to which they belong is $2n = 12$. Nevertheless, these species do receive pollinator visits and may best be regarded as facultatively autogamous. Complex heterozygosity has otherwise only been reported in the Iridaceae in the South American *Gelasine elongata* (Kenton and Rudall 1987), another autogamous species.

The phenomenon of heterostyly, rare in the monocots, is known in Iridaceae only in the genus *Nivenia*. In this genus seven of the 11 species are distylous, that is, different plants have flowers with either long or short styles and complementary short or long stamens (Figure 15). In none of them, however, was an associated self-incompatibility system found (Goldblatt and Bernhardt 1990), otherwise common in distylous plants. This finding has been confirmed independently in one species, *N. binata* (M. Grantham, unpublished data). Nevertheless, the seven heterostylous species are evidently obligate outcrossers. Pin flowers, with long styles and short stamens, and thrum flowers, with long stamens and short styles, cannot self-pollinate due to spatial separation of the stigmatic surfaces and pollen-bearing anthers. Evidently, the spatial separation of pollen and stigmatic surfaces, combined with deposition of pollen on different parts of the pollinators, long-proboscid flies or large anthophorine bees, maintains outcrossing by placing pollen on the stigmatic surfaces of flowers with complementary style lengths.

In the absence of additional and more rigorous data, therefore, it seems reasonable to conclude that most Iridaceae with large, colorful flowers are outcrossers. Comparatively few species show facultative autogamy, and these are often characterized either by relatively small, dull flowers, or they have highly specialized pollinators and the autogamy is a fail-safe mechanism in the absence of their pollinator. Outcrossing is promoted by protandry (maturation of the anthers before the stigma is receptive) and spatial separation of pollen and stigmas, reinforced in many genera (and species) by genetic self-incompatibility. Self-incompatibility prevents pollination by other flowers on the same plant whereas protandry and spatial separation of anthers and stigmas serve to limit stigma clogging by self pollen before cross pollination takes place.

## POLLINATION BIOLOGY

The large variety of variously shaped and colored flowers found in the Iridaceae signal to the biologist that that family has an interesting natural history, for flowers are central to the life history and reproduction of plants (e.g., Vogel 1954). There is, in fact, often a close association between flower form and pollination system in plants, and Iridaceae, in particular, show very tight associations between the structure of their flowers and particular pollinators (Goldblatt and Manning 2006). Variation in floral features thus signals corresponding diversity in the ways in which flowers are pollinated. As a result of pollination studies conducted since the early 1990s, mostly in sub-Saharan Africa, the great majority of Iridaceae are now understood to be highly specialized in their pollinator relationships. Sexual reproduction in plants generally requires an external means of transfer of pollen, which contains the cell that gives rise to the sperm, to the female parts of the flower, ideally located on another plant. The pollen is deposited initially on the stigma, located above the ovary, which contains numerous egg-containing ovules. The means of pollen transfer from anther to stigma may be wind or even water but is most often an animal, usually an insect or bird, occasionally a mammal.

The reason for animal visits is the offer of a reward. The petals of a flower can thus be seen as advertisements to potential visitors. The nature of the reward varies but is often nectar, a solution of various sugars that is a source of energy, or sometimes the only food source, for the pollinator. Pollen is another common reward, used by bees and some wasps as food and more importantly to provision nests for larvae. Other rewards include nonvolatile oils, waxes, and other food bodies, or even scent compounds used by some bees as pheromones to attract mates. Nectar is the most common reward offered in the Iridaceae and is a valuable source of carbohydrates for various animals, including bees, flies, many other insects, and birds.

Nectar is itself variable in site of production, volume, sugar concentration, and in the types of sugars it contains. As discussed earlier, nectar in Crocoideae and Nivenioideae is produced by special glands, called nectaries, located within the walls, or septa, of the ovary, thus known as septal nectaries. In Iridoideae, in contrast, nectar is produced on surface glands on the tepals or within the floral tube, except for *Diplarrena,* which also has septal nectaries, evidently the ancestral state for the family.

Nectar volume correlates fairly closely with the size of the pollinator, thus the larger the agent, the greater the quantity offered. Volumes range from trace amounts, less than 5 microliters, in many bee-pollinated flowers, to over 100 microliters in the large, sunbird-pollinated flowers of *Watsonia* and *Witsenia.* Flowers pollinated by large, active, long-proboscid flies is intermediate in volume between the two extremes. Nectar concentration is more complex, but bee flowers generally offer nectar of relatively high concentration, and flowers pollinated by insects with narrow mouthparts generally have nectar of lower concentration, 12–20% sucrose equivalents for butterflies, 16–30% for long-proboscid flies. This is evidently because nectar of lower concentration is less viscous and thus easier to draw though a narrow proboscis of butterflies and long-proboscid flies. Flies that lap rather than suck nectar though long probosces can also consume very concentrated nectar. An unusual feature of two *Ferraria* species that are pollinated by wasps is the production of very dilute nectar, usually less that 10% and sometimes less that 5% sucrose equivalents. This has led to speculation that water is really the reward in these plants.

The proportions of constituent sugars in nectar—fructose, glucose, and sucrose—is partly a function of pollinator preference but more often simply a reflection of what a plant is able to produce (Table 4). Nectar with high proportions of sucrose is produced by almost all Crocoideae and Nivenioideae, irrespective of pollinator type. This is despite evidence of a preference by sunbirds for nectar with higher levels of glucose and fructose, the so-called hexose sugars. There are a few examples of species of Crocoideae and Nivenioideae that produce nectar with high hexose proportions, and most of these do indeed turn out to be pollinated by sunbirds, or more surprisingly by large butterflies, which are not especially noted for a preference for hexose sugars. The bird-pollinated genera *Klattia* and *Witsenia* are prime examples of taxa with hexose-type nectar, and the species of the bird-pollinated genus *Chasmanthe* are another.

In contrast to Crocoideae and Nivenioideae, nectar produced by African Iridoideae is typically dominated by the hexose sugars, fructose and glucose, irrespective of pollinator, yet sunbird pollination is rare in the subfamily (Table 4). Thus bees, flies, or wasps that pollinate species of Iridoideae find nectar of quite different sugar types from that in Crocoideae acceptable. Nectar sugars in non-African members of the Iridoideae are poorly sampled, but at least bee-pollinated *Sisyrinchium arenarium* from South America conforms to the African pattern, producing nectar with high levels of glucose and fructose. Nectar in two *Iris* species, however, shows a different pattern: *I. brevicaulis*,

a bumblebee-pollinated species, has sucrose-dominant nectar, as does the hummingbird-pollinated *I. fulva*. As hummingbirds are known to prefer sucrose-dominant nectar, the nectar in the latter should not be surprising, but we have no explanation for the nectar sugar ratio in *I. brevicaulis*. Too few *Iris* species are known for nectar sugars for much more to be said, but so far the pattern in this genus seems exceptional in its subfamily. In general, at least in the Iridaceae, nectar type appears largely the result of ancestry, that is, it follows the pattern in the subfamily to which the species belongs and only occasionally is it the consequence of selection due to pollinator preference.

Pollen, unlike nectar, is a nonrenewable resource and once removed from the flower cannot be replaced. It is also a very nutritious material, rich in protein and fat, and with significant concentrations of sugar, phosphate, and other minerals. Pollen eaten is pollen wasted, and its loss to the flower is a significant one. On the other hand, even the most specialized pollen-eating insects cannot groom every grain from their bodies, and the remaining pollen is thus available for pollination.

Floral oils are the third type of reward offered by some Iridaceae. These nonvolatile oils are produced in club-shaped epidermal cells on the tepals of many species of the New World tribes Tigridieae and Trimezieae and on the filaments of some South American *Sisyrinchium* species (Vogel 1974). Only one African species, *Tritoniopsis parviflora* (Crocoideae), is known to produce floral oils (Manning and Goldblatt 2002). Like pollen, the floral oils are believed to be used as food stores for larvae. Only a few specialized bee genera utilize floral oils, notably *Rediviva* (Melittidae) in southern Africa, *Macropus* (Melittidae) in the Old and New World tropics, and *Centris*, *Chalepogenus*, and *Tapinotaspis* (Apidae) in North and South America. *Tritoniopsis parviflora* is unusual among oil-producing flowers in also pro-

Table 4. Nectar characteristics of Iridaceae. The four nectar sugar ratio categories are those identified by Baker and Baker (1983). Exclusively beetle-pollinated species produce no nectar and are not included below.

| | Ratio of sucrose / glucose + fructose | | | |
|---|---|---|---|---|
| | <0.1 | 0.1–0.49 | 0.5–0.99 | >0.99 |
| Iridoideae | | | | |
| hummingbirds | 0 | 0 | 0 | 1 |
| bees | 11 | 1 | 0 | 1 |
| short-proboscid flies or wasps | 3 | 0 | 0 | 0 |
| Nivenioideae | | | | |
| sunbirds | 4 | 0 | 0 | 0 |
| bees | 0 | 0 | 1 | 0 |
| long-proboscid flies | 0 | 0 | 3 | 0 |
| Crocoideae | | | | |
| sunbirds | 4 | 3 | 5 | 23 |
| moths | 0 | 1 | 0 | 11 |
| butterflies | 0 | 3 | 2 | 5 |
| bees | 0 | 0 | 4 | 28 |
| long-proboscid flies | 0 | 1 | 1 | 48 |

ducing nectar, retained in a particularly short peri-anth tube. It thus also offers a reward to more common nectar-foraging bees as well, thereby helping to ensure its pollination throughout its range despite the local absence of oil-seeking *Rediviva* bees.

The vast majority of African Iridaceae are specialized for pollination by one or a few species of insects or other animals, and fully 95% of the species fall into this category (Table 5). Generalist species that are visited by a range of different pollinators, in contrast, are rare and account for less than 3% of species. Examples include the tropical African *Lapeirousia erythrantha* and *L. montana,* and the Western Cape *Nivenia parviflora, Sparaxis bulbifera,* and *S. grandiflora,* which are visited by small flies, a range of long- and short-tongued bees, and Lepidoptera, and also hopliine beetles in the case of the latter species. Such flowers are atypical of African Iridaceae in having a short tube (or nectar present in the top of the tube), multiple flowers open simultaneously, or occurring in dense populations that provide display, and with prominent anthers and pollen. It has been suggested that specialized pollination systems are most likely to develop under conditions when appropriate pollinators are predictably present (Stebbins 1970). The relatively long-lived nature of species of Iridaceae, their propensity for vegetative reproduction, and the relatively dispersed nature of flowering plants among the vegetation are all likely conditions favoring the development of specialist pollination strategies.

An unusual subtype of specialized pollination, bimodal pollination, has been identified in several African Iridaceae (Manning and Goldblatt 2005). Species with a bimodal pollination system, combining features of two distinct pollination systems, have been documented in several genera of Crocoideae, including *Tritoniopsis* (sunbirds and large butterflies, and bees and long-proboscid flies), *Ixia* and *Romulea* (bees and beetles), *Hesperantha* (bees and moths), and *Sparaxis* (beetles and horseflies).

## Bee Pollination

Bee-pollinated flowers display a great deal of diversity, for they may offer pollen, nectar, nonvolatile oils, or a combination of these. Pollen flowers in particular differ from nectar flowers in having the anthers fairly prominently displayed, either comparatively large in comparison to the rest of the flower or often on a column held well above the tepals. Bee pollination is the most common pollination system in Iridaceae and is developed in more than half the sub-Saharan African species. It seems likely that pollination by large bees foraging for nectar is the ancestral pollination system in the family, and it is certainly ancestral for Crocoideae, Nivenioideae, and probably Iridoideae. The genus *Aristea* is, however, largely pollinated by bees foraging for pollen, the only reward, for most *Aristea* species do not produce nectar. A similar pollination system is likely for *Patersonia,* which likewise does not produce nectar. A few species of the southern

**Table 5.** Taxonomic distribution of pollination systems in sub-Saharan African Iridaceae. Genera for which pollination has not been documented are not included in these statistics.

| Subfamily | Percentage of species with each pollination system | | | | | | | | |
|---|---|---|---|---|---|---|---|---|---|
| | Bee | Long-proboscid fly | Short-proboscid fly or wasp | Moth | Butterfly | Sunbird | Scarab beetle | Mixed/ generalist | Total |
| Iridoideae | 73 | 0 | 5 | 1 | 0 | 0 | 7 | 15 | 210 |
| Aristeoideae | 90 | 2 | 0 | 0 | 0 | 0 | 8 | 0 | 52 |
| Nivenioideae | 32 | 32 | 0 | 0 | 0 | 29 | 0 | 7 | 14 |
| Crocoideae | 47 | 16 | 0.1 | 9 | 2 | 10 | 6 | 10 | 820 |
| Total | 57 | 12 | 1 | 6 | 2 | 8 | 6 | 8 | 1,097 |

African section *Pseudaristea* of *Aristea* have, however, have evolved different pollination systems, notably using by hopliine scarab beetles, discussed in more detail later.

Flowers pollinated by large bees with nectar as the reward generally have a well-developed tube in which nectar is retained. The anthers and stigmatic surfaces, although held in a position such that a visiting bee will brush against them while probing the tube for nectar, are often concealed and typically have pollen colored to match the tepals, thus rendering it less conspicuous. Such bee flowers vary hugely in color but often have contrasting markings, so-called nectar guides, that guide the bee into the appropriate position to access the nectar, and contact the anthers and stigma. Bee flowers are also frequently pleasantly scented, often of rose or violet type odors. Best known for their lovely scent, most *Freesia* species are pollinated by bees foraging for nectar. Moth flowers are also scented, but their scents are richer and heavier, recalling lily or carnation. In contrast, flowers pollinated by long-proboscid flies, butterflies, and birds are hardly ever scented.

The radially symmetric flowers of most Iridoideae are pollinated by bees. Their radial symmetry is often more apparent than real, however, and many are functionally bilaterally symmetric. The flowers of *Iris* and many species of *Moraea*, for instance, function as meranthia, or compound flowers consisting of three separate pollination units, each of which appears to a bee as an individual, bilaterally symmetric or bilabiate flower. Each unit or meranthium consists of a platform provided by the limb of the outer tepal, an upright standard consisting of the style branch and its petaloid crests, and a gullet provided by the claw of the outer tepal and the closely opposed style branch. Bees, usually foraging for nectar, visit each meranthium as if it were a separate flower and probe the gullet for nectar located either at the base of the tepal (in most *Moraea* species) or within the floral tube (in *Iris*). As they probe the gullet they brush against the stigmatic lobe and against the concealed anther. Pollen carried by the visiting bee from a flower just visited thus brushes first against the sticky stigma. When it exits the flower, now carrying pollen from a new anther, the stigma lobe is pressed against the style branch and self-pollination is avoided.

This type of floral unit functions very much as do the bilaterally symmetric flowers of genera of Crocoideae such as *Gladiolus, Sparaxis, Tritonia,* and many others. In these flowers the three lower tepals have nectar guides and together form a lower lip-like landing platform, while an enlarged dorsal tepal arches forward over them, partly concealing the stamens. Bees climbing into a flower of this type extend their proboscis and tongue forward into the floral tube and in doing so their head and the dorsal part of the thorax unintentionally brush against the anthers, acquiring a load of pollen and depositing pollen from another flower on the stigmatic surfaces of the style branches. Some species have special adaptations to facilitate pollen deposition on a foraging bee. In some species of *Lapeirousia* and *Tritonia,* for example, each lower tepal bears a prominent median tooth, and a bee must climb over this barrier; as a result it is forced to brush against the anthers suspended above them. In *G. appendiculatus* and its close allies the anthers bear rigid, tail-like appendages that bar entry to the floral tube but when pushed backward by a foraging bee (or curious biologist) cause the anthers to tilt downward, brushing pollen onto the bee's body as it crawls deeper into the flower to forage.

Some 40% of African Iridaceae and most species of the genus *Iris* share this mode of passive pollination by large nectar-feeding bees, and we regard it as a specialized pollination system. Important pollinators in Africa are both sexes of adult anthophorine bees in the genera *Amegilla, Anthophora,* and *Pachymelus* as well as worker honeybees, *Apis mellifera,* all members of the family Apidae according to current classifications. In *Iris,* bumblebees, *Bombus* species, are the most common pollinators.

In *Bobartia* and species of the *Homeria* group of *Moraea* the anthers are prominent and held above the subequal, spreading tepals, and these species are pollinated by a variety of female bees foraging primarily for pollen, usually the sole reward. The perianth in such flowers is commonly bright yellow or white, colors that are highly reflective and thus easily visible, and the pollen is almost invariably yellow. Comparable flowers have evolved in Crocoideae, where several species of *Gladiolus* have radially symmetric flowers and prominent anthers, as do a few species of *Babiana* and most species of *Geissorhiza, Hesperantha, Ixia, Romulea,* and *Crocus.* Worker honeybees and females of other genera of Apidae, and other families of short-tongued bees, including Andrenidae (*Andrena*), Halictidae (*Patellapis*), Megachilidae (*Megachile*), and Melittidae (*Rediviva*), are major pollinators of these flowers. Species of the Eurasian *Crocus* are pollinated by female bumblebees, *Bombus* species, and despite their tubular flowers, nectar is either forced into the upper part of the tube, where it can readily be reached by bees with relatively short tongues, or no nectar is produced at all. Pollination by pollen-collecting bees is suspected for the small, radially symmetric flowers of genera such as *Libertia, Orthrosanthus,* and *Sisyrinchium,* but this remains to be documented. These genera do not produce nectar and are thus unlikely to attract visits from other insects. The New World genus *Olsynium* is also pollinated by female bees foraging for pollen, but at least two species of the genus, including the only North American representative, *O. douglasii,* also offer nectar. This last species is visited by a range of bees, including *Bombus* and *Osmia* spe-

cies. The provision of nectar in pollen flowers both increases and prolongs their attractiveness to visiting insects. The development of false pollen in the form of conspicuous yellow hairs, as are found at the base of the filaments of bee-pollinated *Romulea* and *Sisyrinchium* species, is another way in which bees may be encouraged to visit flowers even after all the pollen has been removed. This is especially relevant in long-lived flowers, and false pollen is therefore not common in the fugacious flowers of many Iridoideae.

Vibratile or buzz pollination is a specialized type of pollination by pollen-collecting female bees and is typically associated with anthers opening by small pores instead of along their entire length. This pollination system is uncommon in the Iridaceae and has only been confirmed for the southern African *Ixia scillaris,* in which anthophorine bees are responsible for the pollination of the species. Pollen is only released from the anthers when they are vibrated at high frequency by a visiting bee—watching these bees carefully, or rather listening to them, is fascinating. As a bee grasps the anthers it begins to vibrate it body and wings more rapidly, producing a higher-pitched sound, and a small cloud of pollen is suddenly released, which the bee then gathers up and deposits in its pollen baskets. Buzz pollination typically occurs in fairly small, radially symmetric flowers with spreading, subequal tepals. Four species of *Aristea* on Madagascar and *Cobana* and the *Sessilistigma* group of *Tigridia* in Mexico and Central America also have porose anthers, and we infer that they too are adapted for vibratile pollination. Both *Cobana* and *Sessilistigma* were recognized as separate genera, largely defined by their porose anthers and the associated radially symmetric spreading tepals. DNA sequence data show *Sessilistigma* to be nested in *Tigridia,* and its status as a separate genus must be seen as simply based on a novel pollination strategy.

In several species of *Sisyrinchium* from southern South America, nonvolatile floral oil is the primary reward for a variety of female bees, which are responsible for pollination in these species (Cocucci and Vogel 2001). Oil is produced in gold-tipped, club-shaped hairs crowded on the filament column. Many other New World Iridaceae also secrete floral oils, in this case from club-shaped hairs on the tepals. These hairs are usually crowded on parts of the claw of the inner tepals and are often protected by a fold of the tepal limb, which forms a sort of pocket covering the glandular zone. The role of these hairs in the Iridaceae was first demonstrated by the Austrian biologist Stefan Vogel in the 1970s, who showed that *Herbertia*, which he called *Alophia*, and *Eleutherine*, which he called *Sphenostigma*, produce floral oils and are pollinated by oil-collecting female bees. The same pollination strategy has been confirmed for *A. drummondii* in southern North America (Lee 1994). Species of several more New World genera also bear zones of elaiophore-like hairs on the tepals and almost certainly have this pollination system. The only African species that produces floral oils is *Tritoniopsis parviflora*, which is pollinated in part by the oil-collecting bee *Rediviva gigas*. The species is unusual among plants with oil-producing flowers in also providing nectar. Both oil and nectar therefore form the reward. This bimodal strategy ensures its pollination in the event that oil-collecting bees are locally absent. Just as in nectar-producing flowers, the sites of oil production ensure that bees will brush against anthers or stigmas, strategically positioned in relation to sites of oil secretion. A range of bee genera are responsible for pollination of those Iridaceae that produce floral oils; these include *Centris*, *Chalepogenus*, *Paratetrapedia*, and *Tapinotaspis*, all members of the family Apidae.

The characteristically dark-colored flowers of many species of *Iris* section *Oncocyclus*, a western and central Asian group, have evolved a particularly unusual pollination system. Studies of selected species in Israel show that large male bees, including *Anthophora* species, shelter in the gullet overnight. The flowers lack nectar and appear to depend entirely on these male bees for pollen transfer as they inspect various flowers before settling for the night (Sapir et al. 2005). The reward to these bees may not only be a secure site for shelter at night but a source of morning heat (Sapir et al. 2006). The dark-colored flowers absorb heat in the early morning hours and allow the bees to emerge from their shelter earlier than bees sheltering in pale flowers or in holes in the ground.

## Long-Proboscid Fly Pollination

While bee pollination is predominant throughout the Iridaceae, the subfamily Crocoideae displays a uniquely wide range of other pollination strategies compared to the remaining subfamilies. These include using long-proboscid flies, settling and hovering moths, hopliine beetles, large butterflies, and sunbirds (Table 5). In addition, most genera of Crocoideae display similar kinds of specialized flowers adapted to particular pollination systems, a feature that for many years caused confusion among systematists.

One of the most interesting of these is pollination by long-proboscid flies (Figure 4), defined as having proboscides at least 2 cm and up to 7 cm long. Thus the long-tubed, white or cream flowers with red markings of many species in several genera, including *Babiana*, *Geissorhiza*, *Gladiolus*, *Ixia*, *Lapeirousia*, and *Watsonia*, are all pollinated by the long-tongued flies *Moegistorhynchus* (= giant nose) or *Prosoeca* (Nemestrinidae) and *Philoliche* (Tabanidae; Plate 33). These flowers have slender tubes 25–100 mm long, hollow internally and containing nectar in the lower half, where it is accessible only to insects with proboscides that are narrow enough and long enough to reach it. Bees and other insects

**Figure 4.** Pollination by long-proboscid flies of the families Nemestrinidae and Tabanidae is important in African Iridaceae: (above) *Gladiolus angustus* and its pollinator, *Moegistorhynchus longirostris*, (below) *Romulea syringodeoflora* and an unnamed species of *Prosoeca*. There is always a close match between the lengths of the floral tube length and proboscis of a pollinating fly species.

may try to reach the nectar but fail and are discouraged from visiting additional flowers of this type. Generally, the floral tubes are somewhat longer than a fly's proboscis, encouraging the visitor to probe the floral tube as deeply as possible, thereby forcefully contacting anthers or stigmatic surfaces. That an insect's mouthpart should be a little shorter than the floral tube of the flower they pollinate was first hypothesized by Charles Darwin in 1862, commenting on pollination in long-spurred orchids, and later demonstrated experimentally.

Classic long-proboscid fly pollination has been known in a few species of western South Africa since the early decades of the 20th century, among them the long-tubed *Lapeirousia anceps,* which is pollinated by *Moegistorhynchus.* Only as a result of studies conducted since 1990, however, has it been shown that long-proboscid fly pollination is especially well developed in the Iridaceae and of major importance in the southern African flora, where more than 250 plant species are pollinated only by these insects. Some 25% of *Lapeirousia* species and about 20% of *Babiana* and *Hesperantha* species depend on one or more of these fly species for their seed production and long-term survival, while some 28 species of African *Gladiolus,* 10% of the species in the genus, are pollinated only by long-proboscid flies.

In the eastern half of the African subcontinent a series of pink-flowered species of *Gladiolus* and *Hesperantha* from temperate grasslands are pollinated by *Prosoeca ganglbauri* and *P. robusta,* while a few species of bush or forest habitats are visited by another nemestrinid fly, *Stenobasipteron wiedemannii.* Two of the species of *Hesperantha* pollinated by *P. ganglbauri* have taken this system one step further. They produce no nectar but their flowers are mimics, resembling closely enough those of nectar-producing *Gladiolus, Hesperantha,* and other species, that flies are duped into visiting the nonnectar-producing flowers as well, a system known as pollination by deceit.

Then, along the western coast and near interior of western southern Africa, a number of long-tubed flowers with red or violet flowers with white or yellow markings are pollinated exclusively by three different species of *Prosoeca,* most often *P. peringueyi.* These flies are strongly attracted to intensely pigmented flowers, mostly in the genera *Babiana* and *Lapeirousia* in the Iridaceae but also to similarly colored flowers in species of several genera of other families, most notably *Pelargonium* in the Geraniaceae (Goldblatt and Manning 2000c). These flowers thus form guilds, groups of organisms that utilize a resource, in this case a pollinator, in a similar way. While long-proboscid fly pollination is particularly common in southern Africa, we suspect it also occurs in East Africa as well because of the presence there of *Gladiolus* species with flowers of similar floral form and coloring.

Long-proboscid flies are particularly exciting pollinators, for they are large insects, often exceeding 2.5 cm long, with their prosboces permanently extended to two to three times their body length, even to c. 7 cm in *Moegistorhynchus longirostris.* They can be seen as the African equivalent of hummingbirds, which they resemble in their rapid, often noisy flight, and in vibrating their wings while visiting flowers, although they do not usually hover while feeding as hummingbirds do. Sadly these wonderful and highly specialized pollinators are slowly disappearing from their native habitats, and the plant species that are dependent on them for their pollination are thus becoming increasingly threatened.

## Other Types of Fly Pollination

Classic carrion-fly pollination, in which dull-colored or speckled flowers produce decaying and rotting scents and attract short-tongued dung, game, and flesh flies, is relatively rare in the Iridaceae. It is developed significantly only in the African genus *Ferraria* (Goldblatt and Manning 2006). Species like

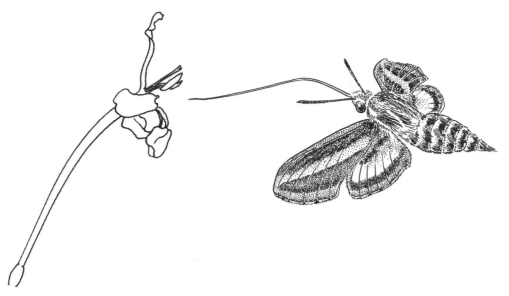

**Figure 5.** Pollination by night-flying Lepidoptera is important in several genera of Crocoideae: here, the white-flowered *Tritoniopsis nervosa* with its slender perianth tube, and the sphinx moth *Hyles lineata* with its proboscis extended before inserting it into the floral tube.

*F. crispa* and *F. foliosa* have dull yellow or brown flowers mottled with dark brown or purple that produce odors of rotting flesh. The flowers also produce concentrated nectar on the tepal claws that is lapped up by flies, attracted by the smell. As the insects crawl over the tepals, their backs become covered in the bright orange pollen produced by these *Ferraria* species. The only other species in the family known to be pollinated by such flies are *Moraea lurida* and *M. ochroleuca*. While *M. lurida* has the dull red flowers and the foul scent typical of this pollination system, *M. ochroleuca* has yellow or orange flowers with an odd scent of fermenting fruit. The flowers are visited by short-tongued flies but also by honeybees, and this species may have a truly bimodal pollination strategy.

## Moth Pollination

Pollination by settling moths, mostly in the families Drepanogynidae, Geometridae, and Noctuidae (Figure 5), occurs in a few species of *Babiana, Freesia, Moraea,* and *Tritoniopsis* but is particularly important in *Gladiolus* and *Hesperantha*. Moth flowers are almost always pale, mostly white or pale yellow, and open at night when they produce a rich scent. Settling-moth pollination is most common in *Hesperantha,* where 24 species, about one-third of the genus, have evening- or night-blooming flowers (Goldblatt et al. 2004c). In this genus, moth-pollinated flowers, usually white with red on the outside, actually close during the day, whereas bee-pollinated flowers in the genus, often pink or yellow, open in the morning and close in the evening. The single *Freesia* species inferred to be pollinated by moths is the green-flowered *F. viridis,* native to the western coast and interior of South Africa and Namibia. The curious, pale green flowers of this species are well camouflaged from day-flying insects and are sweetly scented only at night, a pattern frequent in moth flowers. Like a number of species with very specialized pollination strategies, *F. viridis* is self-compatible and facultatively autogamous.

Pollination by hovering sphinx moths (Sphingidae) or a mix of sphinx and large settling moths occurs in several *Gladiolus* species and is suspected for several more in tropical Africa, where few observations on pollination have been made. Sphinx moth pollination is also suspected for the five *Lapeirousia* species with perianth tubes in excess of 10 cm long (Goldblatt et al. 1995) and in the similarly long-tubed genus *Savannosiphon* of southern tropical Africa. Pollination by moths is known only among the Iridaceae in sub-Saharan Africa and is unlikely to occur elsewhere because tubular flowers occur almost exclusively in African members of the family, in subfamilies Nivenioideae and Crocoideae. It has been suggested that white-flowered *Crocus,* a Eurasian genus, in which all species have long tubes, may be pollinated by moths (Mathew 1981), but this is most unlikely. *Crocus* flowers close at night and many do not produce nectar.

## Butterfly Pollination

Pollination by large butterflies, as opposed to visits by smaller butterflies as part of a suite of generalist pollinators, is relatively uncommon but is known for several red-flowered southern African species of *Gladiolus* and *Tritoniopsis* as well as *Hesperantha coccinea* (formerly known as *Schizostylis;* Goldblatt and Manning 2002, Manning and Goldblatt 2005). The most important butterfly, especially in the southern African winter-rainfall zone, the Cape region, is the mountain pride, *Aeropetes tulbaghia* (Satyridae), or Cape Christmas butterfly because it emerges in mid-December. This swift-flying butterfly, with a wingspan of c. 10 cm, pollinates a range of summer- and autumn-flowering species in southern Africa mostly with large red flowers that produce quantities of nectar in the floral tube or spur (Plate 19). It is the sole pollinator of the red disa, *Disa uniflora* (Orchidaceae), which has the largest flower of any African orchid. *Aeropetes* has a strong innate attraction to the color red and is even attracted to hikers wearing red shirts or hats. Some orchids have capitalized on this by mimicking nectar-producing flowers of similar shape and color

but without providing nectar. Another species pollinated exclusively by large butterflies is *Crocosmia aurea,* which has large, nodding, radially symmetric orange flowers. The butterflies in this case are large, colorful swallowtails, *Papilio* species (Papilionidae), which hang upside down while they feed on nectar held inside the long perianth tube. As outlined earlier, butterfly flowers generally produce fairly dilute nectar, perhaps because more concentrated nectar is too viscous to be easily sucked though their very slender proboscis.

## Beetle Pollination

Pollination by hopliine scarab beetles (Scarabaeidae: Rutelinae: Hopliinae), commonly known in southern Africa as monkey beetles in allusion to the hairy bodies and long hind legs, is one of the more surprising pollination strategies in the Iridaceae (Plate 210). The role of hopliines in pollination in the large southern African flora was virtually unknown until the 1990s, but they are now understood to be the primary pollinators of numerous bulbous species, including the peacock *Moraea* species, *M. villosa* and *M. tulbaghensis* (Goldblatt et al. 1998, Steiner 1998). These initial studies were followed by a cascade of new observations on the importance of hopliines in pollination. Instead of nectar or pollen as the major reward, these beetles use brightly colored, dish- or shallow bowl-shaped flowers as sites for assembly, competitive behavior, mate selection, and copulation. They may also consume pollen, but this seems to be secondary to their main reason for visiting the flowers.

Many of the bulbous species adapted to hopliine pollination have brilliant orange, purple, and even red flowers with contrasting dark markings in the center, so called beetle marks. These flowers, large enough to accommodate two or more beetles at a time, have been described as exhibiting a painted bowl syndrome by the North American pollination biologist

Peter Bernhardt (2000). The preference of hopliine beetles for this type of flower seems to have driven selection in several genera of the Iridaceae, resulting in the plethora of brightly colored and often brilliantly marked flowers in the southern African winter-rainfall zone. The bright salmon-pink, orange, or dark blue flowers of species of *Ixia* and *Sparaxis* are especially good examples of beetle flowers. The dark marks in the center of these flowers often resemble the pollinating beetles with remarkable fidelity and are assumed to encourage visits by additional hopliines. Experiments with model flowers (Nänni in Goldblatt and Manning 2006) show that about twice as many hopliines will visit marked versus unmarked decoys. Hopliine pollination is now understood to be one of the more important pollination strategies in the winter-rainfall zone of southern Africa. It is particularly common in *Ixia*, in which some 20 species, representing around 33% of the genus, are pollinated exclusively by hopliines, and another four or five are pollinated by these beetles in combination with bees or other insects. Similarly, 14 species of *Moraea*, at least eight of *Romulea*, and a few of *Geissorhiza* and *Hesperantha* are pollinated only by hopliines, and another 30 species of *Moraea* and 16 of *Romulea* are pollinated by a combination of pollen-collecting bees and hopliines. A small group of closely related *Aristea* species in section *Pseudaristea* is also adapted to hopliine pollination, and their flowers often have unusual beetle markings. In *Aristea biflora* the tepals have transparent, window-like areas of tissue near the base that appear dark when viewed from above, while in *A. lugens* the entire outer tepal is brown or blackish in color and the inner tepals are blue or white (Figure 13). Because hopliines favor radially symmetric flowers, relatively few species in genera where bilaterally symmetric flowers are ancestral are adapted for hopliine pollination. Nevertheless, hopliines pollinate several species each of *Babiana*, *Sparaxis*, and *Tritonia*, in which hopliine pollination

is associated with the development of radial symmetry. In *Babiana* the dark beetle marks are often provided by the stamens rather than pigmented areas on the tepals, and in a few species the anthers have enlarged connectives to maximize the area of dark color.

A comparable syndrome of beetle pollination is found in the Mediterranean and Middle East, where similar floral adaptations occur in some species of *Anemone*, *Ranunculus*, and *Tulipa*. Quite different types of beetles are responsible for pollination in that part of the world, a remarkable example of convergent evolution. No Iridaceae are known to be pollinated by beetles there.

## Bird Pollination

Bird pollination, mostly by sunbirds, *Nectarinia* species (Nectarinidae), has evolved in eight of the 29 genera of Crocoideae, all of them in sub-Saharan Africa (Goldblatt et al. 1999). As is usual throughout the world, bird-pollinated flowers are mostly red to orange, mostly without contrasting markings and fragrance, and have a long perianth tube with the anthers well exserted from the flower. The flowers also produce large quantities of nectar as the reward for visiting birds. Often these species also have particularly sturdy stems on which the birds perch while feeding, and flowers with short lower tepals so that they are able to access the floral tubes without hindrance. Sunbird pollination is best developed in *Gladiolus* and *Watsonia*, where is has evolved independently in several lineages in southern and tropical Africa. Bird-pollinated species were often segregated by past systematists into separate genera because their extremely modified flowers concealed their true relationships. Such false genera included *Anomalesia*, *Antholyza*, *Homoglossum*, *Kentrosiphon*, and *Oenostachys*, all of which are now included in *Gladiolus*. The floral adaptations for bird pollination in *Oenostachys* (the name means wine-colored branch) are unusual—the flowers themselves are fairly small and pale-colored, and the colors that attract birds are provided by the dark red, enlarged bracts. Other African genera in which bird pollination has evolved include all three species of *Chasmanthe* and a few species of *Babiana*, *Crocosmia*, and *Tritoniopsis*, all from southern Africa. Bird pollination in the two species *Tritoniopsis burchellii* and *T. triticea* is unusual in that these flowers are shared with large butterflies. Both sunbirds and butterflies successfully pollinate their flowers, and it is not unusual to see both pollinators active on flowering populations of these species.

Among the three genera of Nivenioideae, sunbird pollination is the norm in *Klattia* and *Witsenia*. Both genera produce large quantities of relatively dilute nectar containing fructose and glucose but lacking sucrose.

Bird pollination is rare in the Iridaceae elsewhere in the world, but hummingbirds are the main pollinators of the North American *Iris fulva* and four species of *Tigridia* in Mexico. The flowers of *I. fulva* are unusual for the genus in being dark red, in having the outer tepals and the closely opposed style branch forming long gullets, and in lacking scent. They also produce unusually large amounts of nectar of low sugar concentration. Most other *Iris* species have scented flowers and secrete fairly small quantities of very sweet nectar.

The flowers of the bird-pollinated *Tigridia* species are so unusual that they were at first placed in a separate genus, *Rigidella*. Unlike most bird flowers, *Tigridia* species have no perianth tube, and nectar is instead retained in deep pockets in the tepals. The flowers are, however, the anticipated bright red, and the anthers are also well exserted, as is typical of most flowers adapted for bird pollination. The true relationships of the species of *Rigidella* were first established by crossing experiments, for *Rigidella*

species can be crossed with *T. pavonia*, an indication of close relationship. True intergeneric crosses cannot be made in the Iridaceae. Later, DNA sequence data showed the *Rigidella* species to be nested within *Tigridia*, and probably not all of them immediately related to one another (A. Rodríguez 1999), suggesting that bird pollination evolved independently at least twice in this genus. In *Gladiolus*, bird pollination most likely evolved seven times among the southern African species and once, or possibly twice, among those in tropical Africa. Repeated evolution of bird pollination within a genus seems not to be especially unusual in the Iridaceae, but the multiplicity of its evolution *Gladiolus* is quite remarkable.

## Wasp Pollination

Uncommon in the Iridaceae, only a few species of southern African *Ferraria* are known to have flowers exclusively adapted for pollination by wasps (Goldblatt and Manning 2006). The system is poorly known worldwide and needs more study. In *Ferraria*, radially symmetric flowers with a faint, somewhat unpleasant, but hard to define scent, and dull-colored flowers with dark speckles or streaked markings are visited exclusively by fairly large flower wasps (Vespidae: Masarinae) and mason wasps (Vespidae: Eumeninae). The tepals form a fairly deep cup containing very dilute nectar of less than 10% sucrose equivalents and even as low as 3%. The low sugar concentration has led to speculation that water may be the real reward. The only other Iridaceae known to be visited by wasps are species of *Moraea* with dull brownish flowers, such as *M. inconspicua*, but these observations require confirmation and more critical investigation.

## THE STEMLESS HABIT

Much has been made of the stemless habit, or acaulescence, a condition fairly widespread in the Iridaceae. Instead of flowers produced on aerial flowering stems, flowers are borne on a short underground stem, with the ovary either underground (the phenomenon of geoflory) or borne at or shortly above the ground level (called basiflory). In many of these species the tepals, style, and stamens are raised above the ground on an elongate perianth tube. The Eurasian genus *Crocus*, with 80 species, is the classic stemless member of the family, but the condition has evolved repeatedly in subfamily Crocoideae in sub-Saharan Africa. An underground ovary occurs in *Babiana bainesii* and *B. hypogaea* and in all species of the genera *Afrocrocus, Duthieastrum,* and *Syringodea.* More commonly than an underground ovary is one borne at ground level, and this occurs in a few species of *Hesperantha, Ixia, Lapeirousia,* and in many species of *Romulea.* In subfamily Iridoideae the stemless condition is found in several species of *Iris,* a genus in which a perianth tube is usually developed. Best known in the genus are the reticulata irises (section *Reticulata* or subgenus *Hermodactyloides*), but other species also lack aerial stems, including winter-blooming *I. unguicularis,* which has a perianth tube up to 20 cm long. A perianth tube is rarely present in other members of Iridoideae, but in South America the genus *Olsynium* has a perianth tube, and a few species of *Olsynium,* once segregated in a separate genus *Chamelum,* are stemless, the reason for their recognition as a separate genus. Among African Irideae several species of *Moraea* have flowers borne at ground level or just below the ground, but most species of the genus lack a perianth tube, which places limitations on the development of acaulescence. The *Galaxia* group of *Moraea* has overcome the problem by developing a perianth tube, as has *M. longiflora.* In *M. ciliata* and its close allies, plants also lack an aerial stem, but the flowers are raised above the ground on a contractile pedicel. After flowering, the fertilized ovary is withdrawn by the contracting flower stalk back to ground level or slightly below ground.

Reasons for the production of flowers at ground level with the ovary underground are several (Burtt 1970). We suspect that the stemless habit may be linked to protection of the developing capsules from herbivory. Grazing of young, sweet, and nutritious capsules is a clear danger to reproductive success. We have often seen plants in early fruiting stages with the young capsules neatly nipped off by grazing buck. Another advantage to an underground ovary is protection from parasitism. Beetles of the family Bruchidae lay their eggs in ovaries and developing capsules, and the grubs hatch and feed on the enlarging ovules as they begin to develop into seeds. It is quite common to find many seeds in a capsule devoured by small beetle larvae, the seeds coats bearing a tiny hole where the young larva entered to slowly consume the seed contents. An ovary borne below ground suffers no such damage.

The acaulescent habit is particularly well developed in desert habitats and areas with cold climates, and at least in cold conditions the underground ovary, a reproductively critical organ, is sheltered from climate extremes by insulating layers of soil. In *Crocus,* a genus of montane habitats and Mediterranean climates, flowering occurs early in the season, often soon after snow cover has melted and long before grasses and other plants have put out new growth. This protection may be what allows high-mountain acaulescent species of *Hesperantha* in the high southern African Drakensberg and Roggeveld Mountains, and *Olsynium* in the higher Andes, to flower and reproduce early in the season. Small plant size in desert plants may have a different explanation. Sheer small size means lower water requirements, an important factor where moisture is a limiting factor for survival. A combination of some or all of these factors may be the ultimate explanation for the frequency of acaulescent species in particularly cold or arid climates.

Bearing capsules underground or close to ground level raises a new problem for the plant—seed dispersal. Seeds need to be dispersed away from the parent. This is solved in *Crocus* and most other acaulescent species by having the flower stalk elongate as the capsules ripen. By this time the seed coat has hardened, rendering the seeds safe from larval attack, and the hard seeds are no longer attractive to grazing animals. Seeds are either retained in the dry, open capsules or are shed onto the ground. Dispersal by seed-eating birds or rodents follows in the same way as for plants with aerial stems, as discussed later under Dispersal Strategies.

In *Syringodea*, capsules are raised to ground level by a novel adaptation—the base of the ovary elongates as the capsules ripen. The genus also has a novel means of capsule splitting—the capsule walls open in wet weather and seeds are washed out of the capsules by rain, exactly as they are in many desert succulents of the family Aizoaceae. In stemless *Lapeirousia* and the *Galaxia* group of *Moraea* the flowering stem elongates when the capsules are nearly ripe and the parts of the plant above ground are dry. The stem dries rapidly and breaks away from the corm with the result that a cluster of capsules and dry leaves is left loose on the ground, a perfect dry ball of plant material open to the elements.

In the *Aristea alata* group of species in southern and tropical Africa, plants produce normal aerial stems, inflorescences, flowers, and capsules, but occasionally, and we do not know the reason for this, they also produce a second set of short stems that bear flowers and then capsules at ground level. This phenomenon is not known in other Iridaceae, and we can only guess at its function. Possibly, as in many *Viola* species, the flowers borne at ground level are self-pollinated, whereas those borne on aerial stems are open-pollinated. Alternatively, seeds produced in the normal, aerial capsules are subject to parasitism while those borne at ground level are concealed and escape being parasitized. The result of this dual set of reproductive strategies is that seeds produced low on the ground are unlikely to be lost to herbivores or parasites but will be poorly dispersed, while those aerial seeds that are produced are likely to be more effectively dispersed, but fewer of them survive to maturity.

## DISPERSAL STRATEGIES

Seeds are normally the most important dispersal units in Iridaceae, but vegetative reproduction by the branching or dividing of rhizomes, corms, or bulbs is significant in many genera. In southern Africa, dispersal of corms by mole rats (Bathyergidae) is important, and some species are spread greater distances in this way than by seed. Mole rats store quantities of corms in storage compartments in their burrows for later consumption, and those that are overlooked remain to sprout the next growing season. Small basal or axillary cormlets borne along the underground part of the stem, common in many African Iridaceae, are often dispersed by mole rats while carrying larger corms to storage sites.

A few isolated species, sometimes polyploid and partly or entirely sexually sterile, produce numbers of cormlets at the aerial nodes of flowering stems and inflorescences, notably *Geissorhiza bolusii*, *Hesperantha coccinea*, *Sparaxis bulbifera*, and races of *Watsonia meriana*, including the plants sometimes called *W. bulbillifera* or *W. meriana* var. *bulbillifera*. This latter plant has a triploid genotype, thus is normally sexually sterile, but it occasionally produces viable seeds. In *G. bolusii* and *Micranthus alopecuroides*, tiny cormlets are sometimes formed on the spikes instead of flowers or else they develop after the flowers fade in place of developing capsules. All populations of *G. bolusii* examined for chromosome number are triploid—the species is not known to reproduce sexually—and some or all of the flowers on a spike may abort before anthesis. Despite this, the species is widespread and is most likely dispersed by birds gathering material for lining their nests.

In some genera of Crocoideae the seeds are retained on the open valves of the capsules for a time. Such seeds are typically glossy and reddish brown and are presumably attractive to seed-eating birds and rodents. These seeds may be regurgitated from the crop or pass unharmed through the digestive tract, protected by their smooth, hard, damage-resistant coats, to be effectively dispersed some distance from the parent plant. Some forest species of *Dietes* and *Libertia* have capsules that do not split open when ripe. The seeds are released gradually as the fruits rot on the stems or as they lie on the forest floor. Capsules of the *Gynandriris* group of *Moraea* likewise never split open and are retained within the transparent inflorescence spathes after the old flowering stems fall to the ground. Seeds are released after decay or abrasion by the hooves of animals.

Seed dispersal has not been investigated in any detail in the Iridaceae, but it is evident that genera vary in their seed form and associated adaptations for dispersal, although specializations for seed dispersal in most members of the family are limited. The globose to angular seeds of most genera apparently simply fall to the ground. Here they may be gathered by ants or small mammals and so dispersed short distances to nests or storage sites. Wind is a much more efficient means of seed dispersal, however, and numerous species and genera have fruits or seeds adapted for this mode of dispersal, particularly in semiarid southwestern Africa. In *Moraea ciliata* and its close allies, the *Galaxia* group of *Moraea*, and in some species of *Lapeirousia*, the whole plant may break loose and be dispersed by wind. In these species the small, rounded plant body acts as a sail, and plants may be blown some distance. The seeds

are eventually shed as plants blow about, or where they finally settle and decay. Thus we have occasionally seen small piles of dry, much decayed plants of *L. plicata* and *M. falcifolia* driven into crevices in rocks by the wind, far away from the sandy flats where they grew and flowered. In a few species of the *Gynandriris* group of *Moraea* the flowering stem and its branches become loosely coiled as they dry out, forming a rounded structure that can roll short distances. They may also become entangled in the feet of small antelope and so be unintentionally transported away from the site of the parent plant.

The discoid seeds some species of *Moraea* and the circumferentially winged seeds of *Gladiolus* are exceptionally buoyant and effectively dispersed by wind (Figure 6). The seeds of many *Tritoniopsis* species have a light, spongy seed coat, sometimes with small wings, and they are probably also dispersed by wind. We suspect that the lightweight, flat,

**Figure 6.** Broad wings aid in the dispersal of *Gladiolus* seeds (one shown above at the left, with its capsules below at the right) by wind, a possible factor in the wide distribution of the genus, which extends across Africa and Eurasia.

and very thin seeds of species of *Aristea* subgenus *Aristea* are also adapted for this type of dispersal. Most species of the subgenus also have prominently fringed margins that may increase their aerodynamic capabilities. Seeds of many species of *Watsonia* are also winged and are assumed to be wind-dispersed. Unfortunately, however, no observations of the efficacy of wind dispersal are recorded for any member of the family.

The orange, fleshy seeds of some species of *Chasmanthe* and *Libertia*, and *Iris foetidissima* and the Central American *Neomarica variabilis*, all species of forest or woodland, are presumably dispersed by birds. In *Crocosmia aurea* the rounded, blackish seeds are exposed when mature in capsules that are often flushed an orange color. The entire capsule and its seeds resemble a berry, and individual seeds may be eaten by fruit-eating birds despite the absence of a fleshy coat. Species in these genera are often more widespread than most other Iridaceae, quite probably because of their more efficient means of dispersal. *Crocosmia aurea*, for example, extends through sub-Saharan Africa from Eastern Cape Province, South Africa, through the woodlands and forests of eastern Africa and Angola to Cameroon and Central African Republic, one of the widest ranges of any member of the family. Other species of *Crocosmia* are restricted to southeastern Africa and individually have quite narrow ranges. The bright orange seeds of *Chasmanthe aethiopica* also contrast sharply against the purplish capsules walls, and we have observed red-winged starlings consuming them. Uniquely among the African Iridaceae, they do have a thin, watery seed coat.

There are few published observations on the role in seed dispersal of the aril, a fleshy outgrowth on the seed characteristic of several species of *Crocus*, *Iris*, and *Patersonia*, and *Aristea singularis*. Their whitish or yellow color suggests that they contain lipids and are thus elaiosomes, and that the seeds are

therefore ant-dispersed. Sernander, whose work was quoted by Ridley (1930), reported as early as 1906 that the seeds of *I. ruthenica*, which have a white elaiosome, are indeed dispersed by ants. Mathew (1982), who described the aril in *Crocus* species, mentioned that this structure is sticky when fresh. Ant dispersal has been reported for the arillate seeds of some *Crocus* species by Mathew. The distinctive, large seeds of the Algerian iris, *I. unguicularis*, are covered with glistening glands and are attractive to ants, which are their likely dispersal agents. For the species of *Iris* series *Californicae*, Lenz (1959) noted that despite the absence of visible arils or elaiosomes, their seeds are dropped on the ground from nodding capsules and are carried by ants to the entrances of underground nests, where they accumulate. The benefit to the ants is not evident.

Water dispersal is likely for a few species, usually those of moist habitats, either of ponds, marshes, or streamsides. Thus *Crocosmia pottsii* and *Hesperantha coccinea* (Crocoideae) have spongy seed coats that enable the seeds to float for a considerable time before becoming waterlogged and sinking. *Iris* species, including *I. pseudacorus*, also have seeds that float. Seeds of the latter species are reported to float for 18–24 months and after sinking rise to the surface again on germinating if not anchored by their roots in the soil (Ridley 1930). Water dispersal is also suspected for the genera *Nivenia* and *Witsenia*, which have an unusual spongy or folded seed surface that traps bubbles of air when wet, rendering them buoyant.

Reproduction by seed is, for most species in the family, of vital importance. Vegetative reproduction is for all but the few species mentioned of secondary significance. Many species, despite having bulbs or corms that have the potential of producing vegetative offsets, in fact do not normally increase their numbers except by seeds. Vegetative reproduction is a fail-safe mechanism, a way to ensure the survival of the parental genotype if disaster in the form of disease or predation strikes. But it is after all merely a means of producing clones. Sexual reproduction, in contrast, the result of mating of two different genotypes, produces offspring with new combinations of genes in each new plant, which is then subject to evolutionary selection. The fittest offspring survive to reproduce again, and this continuing cycle leads eventually to genetic and morphological diversification, and the evolution of new races, and ultimately new species.

## CLIMATE, HABITAT, AND SOILS

Iridaceae have a nearly worldwide distribution but are especially well represented in southern Africa and in temperate and highland South and Central America. This pattern is largely the result of the exceptional radiation that has occurred in the subfamilies Crocoideae and Iridoideae.

The monotypic *Isophysis,* sister to the remainder of the family, and thus marked as the most primitive living member of the Iridaceae, is restricted to sandy heathlands in western Tasmania. *Patersonia* (subfamily Patersonioideae) is centered in Western Australia but the genus occurs almost throughout Australia, and one or two species are found in the mountains of New Guinea, Borneo, and Sumatra. Species mostly grow on sandy, leached, and nutrient-poor soils. *Aristea* (subfamily Aristeoideae) is widespread in Africa and Madagascar but is centered in the mountains of western southern Africa, where well-drained and nutrient-poor soils predominate. *Geosiris* (subfamily Geosiridoideae) is endemic to the forests of central and western Madagascar, and survives by obtaining nutrient and carbohydrates from decaying leaf litter

The three genera of subfamily Nivenioideae are restricted to the southwestern Cape, South Africa, and are associated with rocky sandstone soils, sometimes in wet, marshy sites. The recurrent theme for all these genera is sandy habitats and nutrient-deficient soils, which are incidentally the most common soil types in Australia.

Subfamily Iridoideae comprises Irideae, which are largely Old World, including Australasia, with the exception of *Iris,* which also occurs in North America. Tribes Trimezieae and Tigridieae are exclusively New World, and tribe Sisyrinchieae largely so. *Sisyrinchium,* largest genus of Sisyrinchieae, extends throughout South and North America from Patagonia to Greenland. The occurrence of a species of Iridaceae in Greenland is especially notable. Of the other genera of Sisyrinchieae, *Solenomelus* is restricted to the southern Andes, and *Tapeinia* to southern Argentina and Chile. *Orthrosanthus* is the exception—it extends through the Andes into central America as far north as Mexico, but it also has four species in Australia. *Libertia* is found in Australia, New Guinea, New Zealand, and Andean South America, from Chile to Colombia. Lastly, *Olsynium* has one species in western North America and the remainder in South America, from Peru southward to Tierra del Fuego. One species of *Olsynium* is endemic to the Falkland Islands in the southern Atlantic Ocean.

In Irideae, *Iris,* largest genus of the tribe and of the family, is found exclusively in the northern hemisphere and is unusual in the Iridaceae in its radiation in centers like California–Oregon, China, Europe, and the Middle East. Four of the six species of *Dietes* are restricted to southern Africa, one extends from South Africa to Kenya and Uganda, and another is endemic to Lord Howe Island (Australasia). *Moraea,* the other large genus of Irideae, is mainly sub-Saharan African and centered in the southern African winter-rainfall region between southern Namibia and Port Elizabeth in South Africa. The genus extends though eastern southern Africa to Ethiopia, and one species occurs in Nigeria, a gap of more than 3,000 km. Two species of the *Gynandriris* group of *Moraea* are native to the Mediterranean and Middle East, but the remaining seven species of the group are restricted to southern Africa. That disjunct distance is even greater and is a striking example of long-distance dispersal in a family where dispersal distances are usually quite small and usually measured only in tens or occasionally hundreds of kilometers.

The remaining two tribes of subfamily Iridoideae, Tigridieae and Trimezieae, have radiated extensively in temperate South America, where there are a few small endemic genera (*Gelasine, Herbertia*), and in the Andes (*Hesperoxiphion, Mastigostyla*). A second New World center is in northern Central America and Mexico, where *Tigridia*, including *Ainea, Fosteria,* and *Sessilanthera,* is the most speciose genus there. The few species of *Tigridia* in the Andes and coastal Peru and Chile in South America almost certainly do not belong in *Tigridia,* but their relationships are uncertain. *Nemastylis* is shared between the southern United States, Mexico, and northern Mesoamerica. *Cypella,* one of the larger genera of Tigridieae, has a wide range across temperate South America, including the West Indies. *Herbertia* has a notable disjunction with several species in Uruguay, southern Brazil, and Chile, and one subspecies in the southern United States. We wonder if that disjunction is historically recent and the result of human activity in post-Columbian time.

Subfamily Crocoideae is largely African, and only *Crocus* has radiated significantly outside the continent, extending across Europe to the western Himalayas. *Gladiolus* and *Romulea* also occur in the Mediterranean and Middle East but have their center of diversity in the southern African winter-rainfall zone. Both, however, have species in tropical Africa where two genera of Crocoideae are endemic. *Zygotritonia* (four species) is largely West African, and *Savannosiphon* (one species) is restricted to southern Congo and countries to the east. The monotypic *Cyanixia* might also be considered tropical African, although it is native to the Indian Ocean island of Socotra. *Gladiolus* and *Lapeirousia* have also radiated extensively across tropical Africa, although both have more species in southern Africa. Whereas *Gladiolus* is most common in temperate eastern and southwestern southern Africa, *Lapeirousia* is most common in the semiarid west and southwest of the subcontinent. Some 75 species of *Gladiolus* are endemic to tropical sub-Saharan Africa, where they are concentrated in highland areas. Most Crocoideae, however, are centered in the winter-rainfall area of western southern Africa, including the southwestern Cape, Namaqualand, and the western Karoo of South Africa. These include the genera *Babiana, Geissorhiza, Ixia, Sparaxis,* and *Tritoniopsis. Dierama* (44 species) and *Radinosiphon* (two species) are exceptional in being concentrated in eastern southern Africa, where there has also been significant radiation in *Gladiolus, Hesperantha, Tritonia,* and *Watsonia.* These four genera are, however, most diverse and speciose in the winter-rainfall southwest. Notable disjunctions in Crocoideae include one species *Romulea* on Socotra. The nearest populations of *Romulea* occur in Ethiopia and northern Arabia. In *Hesperantha, H. petitiana* occurs on the East African mountains but has populations in the highlands of Cameroon, with a wide gap in its distribution across the Congo Basin.

One of the most striking aspects of the geography of the family is the occurrence in Australasia of all the primitive genera. *Isophysis,* sister to the rest of the family, is restricted to Tasmania; *Patersonia,* sister to the lineage leading to Crocoideae, is entirely Australasian; and *Diplarrena,* ancestral to the remaining Iridoideae, is endemic to eastern Australia and Tasmania. The presence of *Libertia* and *Orthrosanthus,* unspecialized genera of Sisyrinchieae, in Australasia and South America add to our perception that Australasia was the cradle of the Iridaceae. When the family diverged from its ancestors in the late Cretaceous, c. 80 mya, Australia was joined to South America via Antarctica, and these continents separated much later, c. 50 mya.

Iridaceae are mostly small plants and thus often found in open scrub, desert, or grassland. Members of the family also favor temperate climates, and the distribution largely follows these conditions. Thus species are concentrated in heathlands and shrublands in southern Africa and the Mediterranean. Iridaceae occur in similar vegetation types in Australia, Chile, and western North America, but they have diversified very little in these places. Many members of the family have also diversified in temperate grasslands, and species are found in the grasslands of southern South America, the Andes, and the highland grasslands of eastern Africa. Semideserts adjacent to these areas in temperate latitudes also have a fair representation of Iridaceae, notably the Middle East, and interior western southern Africa, including Namaqualand and the western Karoo.

Few Iridaceae grow in forest, but *Neomarica* occupies this habitat in South and Central America, and *Dietes* favors forested or bush habitats in Africa and on Lord Howe Island. Several species of *Iris* also grow in deciduous forest, blooming early in the spring before the canopy closes. In Africa several species of *Aristea* and *Crocosmia* favor forest margins. *Aristea ecklonii* and *A. ensifolia* are often found in deep shade of evergreen forest in Africa, and *A. cladocarpa* occurs in similar habitats in Madagascar. *Crocosmia aurea* also favors shady places, thus occurring in evergreen forest, forest margins, and along streamsides. The winter-rainfall species *Chasmanthe aethiopica* usually grows under shrubs and small trees.

Even fewer Iridaceae favor semiaquatic habitats, but *Iris pseudacorus* is one notable exception, and this Eurasian plant of ponds and streams has become a weed of similar habitats across North America. Its floating seeds make it easily dispersed from gardens and parks where it was originally planted as an ornamental. The African *Hesperantha coccinea*, better known to gardeners as the genus *Schizostylis*, is another aquatic member of the family. Plants favor streams and shallow pools but thrive in garden conditions. Also readily dispersed in water by its lightweight seeds, this plant must be regarded as a potential weed. South America also has at least one aquatic member of the family, the very attractive *Cypella aquatilis*.

## ECONOMIC IMPORTANCE AND ETHNOBOTANY

Iridaceae are primarily known today in horticulture, both for the cut-flower industry and for garden display. Most important in the florist trade are the numerous cultivars of *Gladiolus*, *Iris xiphium* (the Dutch iris of the florist trade), and *Freesia*, which are grown commercially in many parts of the world. Some *Crocosmia* cultivars are also becoming important in the cut-flower trade, but the genus is better known in gardens. *Gladiolus* has been grown in Europe since the late 18th century, and the first hybrids were made there between two winter-growing Cape species, *G. carneus* and *G. tristis*. This cross was made at the Colville Nursery in London, and the strain is still known in Europe as 'Les Colvilles'. Later hybridization was conducted at nurseries in Belgium and France. The hybrid strain called *G. ×gandavensis* was raised at Ghent, and so-called *G. ×lemoinei* and *G. ×nanceianus* were bred at the Lemoine nursery in Nancy, France, from crosses using summer-blooming *G. dalenii* (also known in the literature as *G. natalensis* and *G. psittacinus*), *G. oppositiflorus*, and *G. papilio*. The former, a taller, more robust species, is polyploid, and its characters predominate in the large-flowered modern cultivars, to the point that they are sometimes mistaken for that species. The dark, butterfly-like markings in some cultivars are due to the influence of genes of *G. papilio*, itself a particularly lovely plant.

Early *Freesia* breeding was conducted first by amateurs in England, using white-flowered and particularly fine-scented plants that were then considered to be *F. refracta*. Only years later was it realized that the white-flowered plants were an unnamed species, and it was called *F. refracta* var. *alba,* and then *F. alba*. Plants now in cultivation are believed to be the results of crosses with *F. alba* and the closely related, yellow-flowered *F. leichtlinii,* both highly scented. Pink and red color was obtained using appropriately colored forms of *F. corymbosa,* itself small-flowered and hardly fragrant but a tall plant with numerous flowers. Repeated crossing of attractive hybrid plants to one another has yielded the elegant cultivars of today. Despite these improvements, the wild species still have the strongest fragrance, and *F. alba* and *F. leichtlinii* remain worth growing in their own right.

Numerous species and cultivars of *Crocus, Crocosmia, Freesia, Gladiolus, Iris* (especially the bearded *Iris* cultivars and hybrids), and *Watsonia* are grown in gardens throughout the world, and trade in their corms, bulbs, and rhizomes is considerable. Less well known in gardens are *I. domestica* (= *Belamcanda chinensis*), *Tigridia pavonia,* and species of *Dietes, Ixia, Moraea, Sparaxis,* and *Tritonia,* although several species of these genera are available in the nursery trade. The semiaquatic *Hesperantha coccinea,* or *Schizostylis,* is particularly successful in mild, wet climates and is grown in gardens in western Europe and parts of North America in places very different from its native eastern southern Africa. *Dietes bicolor* and *D. grandiflora* are extensively used as street plantings in areas of mild climate and may be seen along highways in California as well as in their native South Africa. Also used as street plantings are several species of *Watsonia,* especially the white-flowered

*W. borbonica* subsp. *ardernei* (the *W. ardernei* of horticulture) and *Aristea capitata.*

Use of *Iris* in gardens dates from at least 1500 B.C.E., when plants were portrayed in tombs and temple decorations in Egypt. *Iris* is not native in Egypt and probably never was, so the plants must have been cultivated. *Iris* was also grown by the Romans simply for their decorative value. White, the color of mourning in Moslem countries, has led to the planting of white-flowered *I. albicans* on graves. Native to southern Arabia, the plant has been spread by humans widely through the Moslem world and can now be found from Morocco to Kashmir.

Apart from the cut-flower and nursery trade, species of the Iridaceae are commercially important for many other reasons. Saffron, that most expensive of all spices, is harvested from the style branches and stigmas of cultivated, autumn-flowering *Crocus sativus*. The plant is cultivated today in parts of Europe, the Middle East, and India for this spice. Even more widely cultivated in the past, the labor-intensive harvesting makes it no longer an economically viable crop in many countries. *Crocus sativus* is a triploid plant with a chromosome number $2n = 24$ and does not reproduce by seed, thus is propagated by corm divisions. Its wild ancestor, *C. sativus* var. *cartwrightianus,* also regarded as a separate species, *C. cartwrightianus,* is native to Greece and the Aegean islands (Mathew 1977, 1982). Most likely the original source of saffron, it was harvested at least as early as 1600 B.C.E. and was an important medicinal and dye plant in Minoan Crete and a valuable export. Style branches of other *Crocus* species also yield saffron, but the smaller flowers and style branches make their use too laborious. Nevertheless, in historical times *C. nudiflorus* was grown in southern Britain as a source of saffron. The town of Saffron Walden in Suffolk was named for the local cultivation of the spice there in the 16th century. The medicinal uses of saffron in the past are legion and, like many other natural remedies, appear contradictory. Saffron has been used therapeutically for some 90 different medical conditions, notably optical diseases, and for contraception and abortion (Ferrence and Bendersky 2004) and is reportedly useful for reducing arteriosclerosis. As little as 2 g can, however, cause serious side effects. The main active components of saffron—crocin, crocetin, picrocrocin, and safranal—are steroids and chemically resemble mammalian reproductive hormones, including progesterone, estrogen, and the prostaglandins. They have been shown to have significant physiological effects, and large quantities of the spice can be harmful. Low levels of cardiovascular disease in Spain may be attributable to the high consumption of saffron there. These chemicals are absent from other parts of the plant, and corms of *Crocus* species are reported to be used as a food in Syria (Maw 1886).

Today, saffron is largely used as a flavoring in both savory and sweet foods. Its use as a dye is much diminished because of its high cost. The stigmas must be harvested by hand, and some 100,000 flowers are needed to produce c. 0.5 kg of dry saffron. No wonder, then, that saffron costs $150 or more per ounce (29 g). In Spain, the world's most important source of saffron today, cultivated crocus thrives in La Mancha in fields poorly suited to alternative crops. Flowers are harvested from dawn to midmorning, ensuring that wind and sun do not damage the delicate style branches, which are then picked from the flowers indoors. Boiled flowers of the related *Crocosmia* produce a dye similar to that of saffron, and the generic name means "smelling of crocus" because flowers of *C. aurea* steeped in warm water are said to smell like saffron. Possibly, parts of these flowers also produce saffron-like compounds. They have never been used as a spice, nor as far as we have been able to determine are they

used in traditional healing in southern Africa, where they are native.

*Gladiolus dalenii*, common in tropical and southern Africa, is one of the few species of this large genus important to humans other than for ornamental value. Its corms are used in parts of West Africa and eastern southern Africa in preparations to cure both constipation and severe dysentery, and it is "highly esteemed in curing snake bites" (Irvine 1930). In West Africa, *G. dalenii* is reported to be cultivated on farms in the forest, where it was introduced from the savanna country to the north (Dalziel 1937). How much of its remarkable, nearly pan-African distribution is due to deliberate human activity may never be known. Corms of *G. dalenii* are used as food in upper Shaba Province, Congo, where the starchy but tannin-rich and bitter corms are boiled and then leached in water for a week before consumption. In southern Africa, *G. dalenii* is a common component of the native herbalist's pharmacopeia. Its use as a cold remedy is also documented (Watt and Breyer-Brandwijk 1962, Jacot-Guillarmod 1971). Corms of *G. candidus* are used as food in Dhofar, southern Arabia.

A strikingly ornamental plant, *Gladiolus dalenii* is widely cultivated, not only in its native Africa. A late-summer-flowering form from southern Africa is perhaps the best known in horticulture. More important than its value as a wild species for garden display is its the role as one of the parents in the original crosses that led to the development of the large-flowered *Gladiolus* hybrids, today one of the world's most important cut-flower crops.

Corms of many African Iridaceae were an important source of food for early humans, the !Kung and Khoi peoples, in southern Africa. The consumption of corms of several *Babiana* and *Lapeirousia* species today was undoubtedly preceded by wider use by indigenous people in the past. The corms of these genera lack the concentration of tannin that makes for a bitter, acrid taste. The early 19th century English traveler-explorer, William Burchell, described the use of corms of *B. hypogaea* as food in central southern Africa (Burchell 1824), and in times of famine corms of related *B. bainesii* as well as *L. erythrantha* still provide much valued sustenance in parts of tropical Africa.

Rock shelters of the !Kung and perhaps their predecessors are littered with corm coverings of two *Moraea* species, *M. fugax* and *M. lewisiae* (called *soet uintjie* in Afrikaans, i.e., sweet onion, the common name thus alluding to its palatability), providing convincing evidence of their past importance as food. An early synonym of *M. fugax* is *M. edulis*, which also testifies to its past value as food. Having tried them ourselves, we agree that the corms have a crunchy texture and quite pleasant chestnut-like flavor eaten raw. Both species are locally common in the southern African winter-rainfall zone, along the western coast and interior, and were most likely an important food for hunter-gatherers. Corms of these two species are occasionally eaten today but largely as a curiosity. The common name of *M. sisyrinchium* (= *Iris sisyrinchium*), the Barbary or Spanish nut, refers to the chestnut-like flavor of the corm, and this species must have been consumed in the western Mediterranean in past times, just as southern African species of the genus were eaten by indigenous people there. There is no evidence that *Moraea* species were ever cultivated as a food crop.

Many other *Moraea* species are toxic (Goldblatt 1981, van Wyk et al. 2002), to livestock and humans, and there are occasional deaths in southern Africa as the result of children eating corms of *M. bipartita*, *M. polystachya*, and perhaps other species. Toxicity evidently does not extend to porcupines and mole rats, which avidly consume corms of all African Iridaceae. The active toxic principle is a class of cardiac glycosides called bufadienolides, also present in the bulbs of some Hyacinthaceae. Poisoning by ingestion of leaves of several *Moraea* species, often common in pastureland, still accounts for deaths and debilitation in sheep and cattle across southern Africa and has an significant economic impact.

An unexpected use of some members of the Iridaceae is that of the rhizome of some bearded *Iris* species, especially the white-flowered cultivar of *I. germanica*, also known as *I. florentina*, and its close ally, *I. pallida*. These are the basis for the orris root industry in Tuscany. Orris root oil, used as a flavoring and in the perfume industry, has a scent resembling that of *Viola odorata*, and a tincture of orris root is sold as essence of violets. Small doses have in the past also been useful for treatment of chronic sinus congestion and asthma. Fresh rhizomes themselves are odorless; peeled portions of the rhizome are sun-dried and stored until the scent develops, usually many months later through oxidation of substances in the fresh rhizome. Powdered orris root was in the past used to scent linen, clothes, and even wigs. The use of orris root has a long history, and even in ancient Greece orris-scented oils were used to disguise body odors. Wine, too, was flavored with orris root (Baumann 1993).

The eastern North American *Iris versicolor* was one of the most valued Native American medicinal plants before the 20th century and was used variously as, among other things, a diuretic and vermifuge. Leaves of the western North American *I. tenax* yield a strong fiber used in rope for fishing nets and snares. Many other *Iris* species have been used by humans for various purposes, especially medicinally. Rhizomes of *I. foetidissima*, *I. pseudacorus*, and several other species yield strong purgatives and diuretics and are mildly poisonous. *Iris pseudacorus* yields a black ink and dye.

In South America some Iridaceae were also used by indigenous populations, and at least *Eleutherine bulbosa* (also known in the literature as *E. plicata*) is widely cultivated in the gardens of Native American tribes. Dispersed from its likely native eastern Peru throughout tropical South America and the West Indies, most cultivated plants are a sterile clone that can only be propagated vegetatively (Goldblatt and Snow 1991). Plants have also been introduced into tropical Asia and have there been adopted into the local pharmacopeia. The large red bulbs are unmistakable. Schultes and Raffauf (1990) and Vickers and Plowman (1984) document its various uses as a diuretic, a vermifuge, and a treatment for hemorrhage and open wounds. The active principles have not been investigated in any detail.

*Cipura paludosa* is another Neotropical species used for its medicinal properties and, like *Eleutherine bulbosa*, occurs almost throughout tropical South America, but whether introduced over part of its range is unknown. A decoction of the boiled bulbs is used to relieve diarrhea. Finely pulverized dried bulbs in syrup are used for heart ailments. Documented uses of *C. paludosa* include relief of inflammation, pain, digestive ailments, and more specifically bronchitis.

# EVOLUTION AND CLASSIFICATION

In classifications of the superorder Lilianae, in which the series of families with septal nectaries and often seeds that are blackish and phytomelan-encrusted have been accorded status as the order Asparagales, separate from Liliales, Iridaceae have historically been placed in either of these two large clusters of families. The family is readily distinguished from other related lilioid families by its three stamens, ancestrally unifacial leaves, and, except for *Isophysis,* an inferior ovary. Iridaceae were included by Dahlgren et al. (1985) in Liliales, close to Colchicaceae, on the basis of their extrorse anthers, seeds without phytomelan pigment that is characteristic of so many genera of Asparagales, mottled or patterned tepals, presence of perigonal nectaries, and nuclear endosperm development. Perigonal nectaries are, however, now known to be derived in the family, and septal nectaries are the ancestral state. Patterned tepals are also derived in Iridaceae, and helobial endosperm development appears to be characteristic of the lower Iridaceae. Thus the placing of Iridaceae in a narrowly circumscribed Liliales now appears to have little support and to have been based on a combination of derived characters found among a few specialized members of the family.

Despite the absence of the characteristic black pigment, phytomelan, in their seeds, assignment of Iridaceae to Asparagales is justified on the basis of the presence of septal nectaries in most lineages in the family despite weak support from external morphology or anatomy. A series of molecular gene sequence studies has now conclusively supported the location of Iridaceae in Asparagales (Chase et al. 2000, 2006). Sequences from several chloroplast genes and DNA regions, including *rbc*L and *trn*L–F, place Iridaceae close to but outside the core taxa of Asparagales, all of which have phytomelanous seeds. The molecular data place Iridaceae closest to a group of families, including Ixioliriaceae, a family with a single species, the central Asian *Ixiolirion,* the Australasian Doryanthaceae, another small family comprising two species, and the Tecophilaeaceae. Except for Doryanthaceae, these allied families do not have phytomelanous seeds. None of these related families is particularly closely allied to the Iridaceae, and their affinities to it were never predicted from morphological comparison. Evidently, Iridaceae diverged from a shared ancestral stock so long ago that only molecular data now carry information about familial relationships.

# EARLY CLASSIFICATIONS

With about 2,000 species distributed among some 66 genera, a natural classification of the family is an essential adjunct to making sense of its diversity, geography, and evolution. There is a long history of attempts to produce an infrafamilial classification of the Iridaceae, beginning in the 19th century.

The first classification of major significance was developed by the British botanists George Bentham and Joseph Dalton Hooker in 1883, who recognized three tribes: Irideae (which they called Moraeeae), Ixieae, and Sisyrinchieae. The latter was subdivided into four subtribes: Crocinae (as Croceae) for the *Crocus* group of acaulescent genera with corms and solitary flowers, Cipurinae (as Cipureae) for some of the bulbous New World genera, Sisyrinchiinae (as Sisyrinchieae) for the *Sisyrinchium* group of the New World and Australasia but including the southern Africa *Bobartia*, and Aristeinae (as Aristeae) for the Australasian *Patersonia*, the African *Aristea*, and the woody genera *Klattia*, *Nivenia*, and *Witsenia*. Irideae, comprising plants with rhizomes or bulbs, multiple, short-lived flowers in spathe-enclosed clusters (now called rhipidia), and stamens opposite the style branches, seemed a truly natural assemblage. Likewise, Ixieae, with a distinctive type of corm, long-lived flowers arranged in spikes, and stamens not obviously opposed to the style branches, appeared to represent a natural generic alliance. The Sisyrinchieae, however, although apparently well defined by their short-lived flowers in spathe-enclosed clusters (a feature of the Irideae) and stamens alternate to the style branches, included plants with rhizomes, bulbs, or corms (like those found in the Ixieae) and was even then an unnatural group of disparate genera, many not conforming to the tribal definition.

The German school of botany followed with an apparently novel classification in which Ferdinand Pax (1888), in *Die natürlichen Pflanzenfamilien*, recognized three subfamilies, Iridoideae, Ixioideae, and Crocoideae, the latter including the acaulescent genera *Crocus*, *Romulea*, *Syringodea*, and *Galaxia*. The congruence with the earlier Bentham and Hooker system is obvious. The major difference, however, was that most genera of Bentham and Hooker's tribe Sisyrinchieae were included within the Iridoideae, excepting tribe Croceae, which was elevated to subfamily rank. The important differences between *Crocus*, *Romulea*, and *Syringodea*, with their crocus-like basally rooting corms, long-lasting flowers, and free filaments, among other features, and *Galaxia*, with its apically rooting corm, short-lived flowers, and united filaments opposed to the style branches, was simply not appreciated at the time and overlooked in favor of the superficial similarity of their stemless growth form.

In the second edition of *Die natürlichen Pflanzenfamilien*, Friedrich Diels (1932) reverted to Bentham and Hooker's system, thus subdividing the Iridaceae into three tribes and no subfamilies. Of minor significance was the novel classification by John Hutchinson (1934), in which he divided the family into 11 tribes, with no subtribes and no indication of hierarchy among the tribes. Most notably, Hutchinson included the Tasmanian monospecific genus *Isophysis* and the only member of his tribe Isophysideae in his circumscription of the family. Until this time, *Isophysis*, with its superior ovary and completely free tepals, was regarded as a member of its own family, Isophysidaceae, and its close relationship to the Iridaceae was not always recognized, despite having isobilateral leaves and flowers with three stamens, the major specializations of the Iridaceae. This decision was endorsed by most later workers, notably Armen Takhtajan (1980), who assigned *Isophysis* to a subfamily Isophysideae, although he failed to provide the requisite formal Latin description to validate the name. Isophysidoideae has now been legitimized nomenclaturally (Thorne 2007).

All these classifications reflected some areas of broad agreement, particularly in recognizing the close relationship of genera with mostly short-lived, *Iris*-like flowers, *Dietes*, *Iris*, *Moraea*, and their ilk, as a natural alliance, either as subfamily Iridoideae or tribe Irideae. Likewise, genera with spicate inflorescences and long-lived flowers with a perianth tube were understood to constitute a natural lineage, usually called subfamily Ixioideae or tribe Ixieae. Controversy centered on how to deal with the acaulescent *Crocus* group, and those genera with simple, radially symmetric flowers borne in spathe-enclosed clusters, for convenience included in a tribe or subtribe Sisyrinchieae.

Difficulty was also evident in how to arrange the numerous genera of Ixioideae in natural groupings. Pax, rather ingenuously, divided the subfamily into three tribes, based on the symmetry of the flowers and the division of the style branches. His Ixieae included genera with radially symmetric flowers and undivided style branches; Gladioleae, those with zygomorphic flowers and undivided style branches; and Watsonieae, those with zygomorphic flowers and divided style branches. The arrangement, in hindsight, was inconsistent and largely unnatural. For example, there was no place for taxa with radially symmetric flowers and divided style branches, as in several *Lapeirousia* species. Likewise, apparently closely allied pairs of genera such as *Ixia* and *Tritonia* or *Sparaxis* and *Synnotia* (the latter now included within *Sparaxis*) fell in separate tribes.

## TWENTIETH CENTURY DEVELOPMENTS

The South African botanist Gwendoline Joyce Lewis (1954a), proposed a revised classification of the genera of Ixioideae. Using the tribe as the major infrafamilial rank, she accordingly recognized six subtribes in her Ixieae, one of which, the Watsoniinae, corresponded to Pax's Watsonieae, while the Romuleinae included Bentham and Hooker's Crocinae minus *Galaxia*, which Lewis convincingly showed belonged to tribe Irideae, close to *Moraea*. Other details of Lewis's classification are now of historical interest only, as is Goldblatt's even more finely subdivided tribe Ixieae (i.e., subfamily Crocoideae), with 10 subtribes. Of lasting value, however, was Lewis's careful analysis, based on corm and inflorescence structure, of Pax's genera of Crocoideae. She showed the subfamily to be artificial, with *Crocus*, *Romulea*, and *Syringodea* matching exactly the Ixieae, and *Galaxia* the Irideae. The acaulescent or stemless habit was demonstrated to be an independently derived feature and is actually one not limited in the family to these genera alone.

In the first modern treatment using methods of phylogenetic classification, in which relationships are assessed on the basis of derived (specialized) features only, Goldblatt (1990a) proposed a four-subfamily classification of the Iridaceae. The seemingly taxonomically isolated *Isophysis* was included within the Iridaceae, following Hutchinson's assignment of the genus to the family. In addition to the isobilateral leaves and three anthers, the genus was then known to share another derived feature with the remaining Iridaceae, the presence of styloid calcium oxalate crystals in its tissues. There is now no doubt that the genus is best regarded as belonging to the Iridaceae, and in Goldblatt's classification it constituted the monogeneric subfamily Isophysidoideae.

A second subfamily, Ixioideae, was recognized for the largely African cluster of genera with basally rooting corms, derived pollen features, and long-lived flowers with a perianth tube, usually arranged in a spike. The *Crocus* group was included here, following Lewis's conclusions, and is now firmly established as comprising highly specialized genera with underground stems and solitary flowers, otherwise sharing with Ixioideae all its significant specializations. The name Crocoideae was subsequently discovered to be an earlier name for the subfamily when combined with Ixioideae and thus has nomenclatural priority over the better-known name Ixioideae. *Galaxia*, last member of Pax's small subfamily Crocoideae, is now included in the large African genus *Moraea* and thus firmly placed within subfamily Iridoideae. Goldblatt's classification placed the sisyrinchioid genera within Iridoideae, as Sisyrinchieae, thus enlarging this subfamily as first suggested by Pax.

The classification also united the southern African woody genera, with *Aristea* and the Australasian *Patersonia*, in a fourth subfamily, Nivenioideae, corresponding to Bentham and Hooker's subtribe Aristeinae. The leafless, nongreen Madagascan saprophyte *Geosiris*, often thought to belong to a separate family, Geosiridaceae, or even to belong to the Burmanniaceae, was also added to this subfamily. It shares with the remaining Nivenioideae ancestrally blue flowers and rhipidial flower clusters arranged in pairs (so-called binate rhipidia). Except for the leaves, lacking in the genus, *Geosiris* has the critical familial characters of the Iridaceae, namely, elongate calcium oxalate crystals in stem and flower tissues, an inferior ovary, and flowers with three stamens.

The major infrafamilial rank of subfamily, rather than tribe, seems most useful for a hierarchical classification of a family as large as the Iridaceae, and is followed today by botanists. It reflects the major clusters well and allows for the recognition of smaller groupings, tribes, within the larger subfamilies.

This classification broadly agrees with older systems in the recognition of Crocoideae for genera with flowers in which the tepals are united below in a perianth tube, that secrete nectar from septal nectaries, and that are mostly sessile and arranged in a long spike. A second major cluster of genera and

species, subfamily Iridoideae, is likewise congruent with earlier classifications, with minor changes. This group encompasses *Iris* and its largely African relatives, *Dietes, Ferraria,* and *Moraea,* plus several New World genera with bulbous rootstocks and pleated leaves, and a second smaller group with rhizomes, the best known of which are *Neomarica* and *Trimezia.* The feature that unites the Iridoideae, at least in this sense, is the more or less petaloid nature of the style branches and their close association with the stamens, each anther usually appressed to a style branch.

Whereas these broad divisions were now well established, less consensus was evident in relation to the rest of the family. Several of the remaining genera, including *Sisyrinchium* and its immediate allies, plus *Libertia, Orthrosanthus,* and the southern African *Bobartia,* share an unusually short style and long tubular style branches that extend between the stamens. In addition, all have simple, radially symmetric flowers that lack conventional septal or perigonal nectaries and, except for *Bobartia,* filaments that are partly to completely united. Most older classifications thus combined these genera in a tribe or even subfamily, but Goldblatt (1990a), noting similarities in the basic tubular structure of the style branches to those of many Iridoideae, placed the genera in tribe Sisyrinchieae within Iridoideae. The affinities of the Australian *Diplarrena* remained in doubt. This unusual genus, with only two stamens, has inflorescences like those of the Iridoideae but the septal nectaries characteristic of Crocoideae and some Nivenioideae in the sense of Goldblatt.

## DNA Sequences and Classification

Molecular studies using DNA sequences, usually of chloroplast genes, have now resolved much of the uncertainty about the broader generic relationships in the family. The first of these studies, by Tatiana Souza-Chies and coworkers (1997), showed that

Goldblatt's classification, based on anatomy and morphology alone, was substantially correct. The problematic *Sisyrinchium* group of genera nested within a larger, natural group composed of genera assigned to Iridoideae; *Isophysis* was indeed an isolated lineage and sister to the rest of the family; and *Crocus* and its acaulescent relatives nested within genera assigned to Ixioideae. The molecular results showed one disturbing feature: Crocoideae (= Ixioideae) nested with the genera assigned to Nivenioideae, apparently conflicting with Goldblatt's original circumscription of the subfamily. A refinement of the classification of the family in this area seemed called for. The Souza-Chies study did not include *Diplarrena* or *Geosiris*, so the relationships of these genera remained to be resolved.

A more extensive molecular study of the family by Gail Reeves and colleagues (2001), using DNA sequences from four chloroplast regions, confirmed all of the Souza-Chies findings. It also showed that *Diplarrena* occupied an ancestral position at the base of the Iridoideae, thus sister to the remaining members of that subfamily. *Geosiris* did indeed belong within the Iridaceae and was most closely related to *Aristea*. This puzzling genus was thus correctly included in the Iridaceae by Goldblatt (1990a). The disturbing earlier finding that Crocoideae nested within Nivenioideae was also confirmed. There is only one satisfactory classification, based on evolutionary relationships, that resolves this situation if Crocoideae are to be maintained as a separate subfamily. *Aristea, Geosiris,* and *Patersonia* must each assigned their own subfamilies (Aristeoideae, Geosiridoideae, and Patersonioideae), and the circumscription of Nivenioideae is restricted to include only the three woody southern African genera.

Reeves's molecular study and later work also provided guidelines for a tribal classification of subfamily Iridoideae, a major evolutionary branch of the family comprising some 815 species in 29 genera (Figure 7). The rather odd genus *Diplarrena* is sister to the rest of the subfamily and thus merits is own tribe, Diplarreneae, as does the African group of genera plus *Iris*, as Irideae. The southern African *Bobartia*, long thought to be allied to *Sisyrinchium*, was convincingly shown to be allied to the African *Dietes* and thus belongs in Irideae. The removal of *Bobartia* to Irideae may appear surprising since its flowers so closely resemble those of *Sisyrinchium* but is more understandable when its basic chromosome number, $x = 10$, unusual hairy pedicels, and free filaments as well as its geographical isolation from *Sisyrinchium* and its immediate relatives are taken into account. The largely African *Dietes* is the only other genus of Iridaceae with hairy pedicels that also has $x = 10$. The similar flowers of *Bobartia* and Sisyrinchieae must therefore be seen as convergent developments, derived independently from more complex types of flowers.

The remaining genera of the *Sisyrinchium* group are a natural assemblage, now treated as tribe Sisyrinchieae (Figure 7), sister to the remaining New World genera, which are currently assigned to two additional tribes, the rhizomatous Trimezieae and the bulbous and pleated-leaved Tigridieae. Generic circumscription within these two tribes remains a vexing problem, and there is little current agreement about how many genera should be recognized and what characters are important for their definition. We believe there should be fewer than the 15 that we continue to recognize (Table 1), some based on fairly trivial variation in the structure of the stamens and style but little else. Molecular analysis (A. Rodriguez 1999, Rodriguez and Sytsma 2006) has already shown that several have no merit. At least *Fosteria, Rigidella,* and *Sessilanthera*, for example, are nested in the largely Mexican *Tigridia* and represent different pollination strategies within that genus, notably buzz pollination for *Sessilanthera* and bird pollination for *Rigidella.*

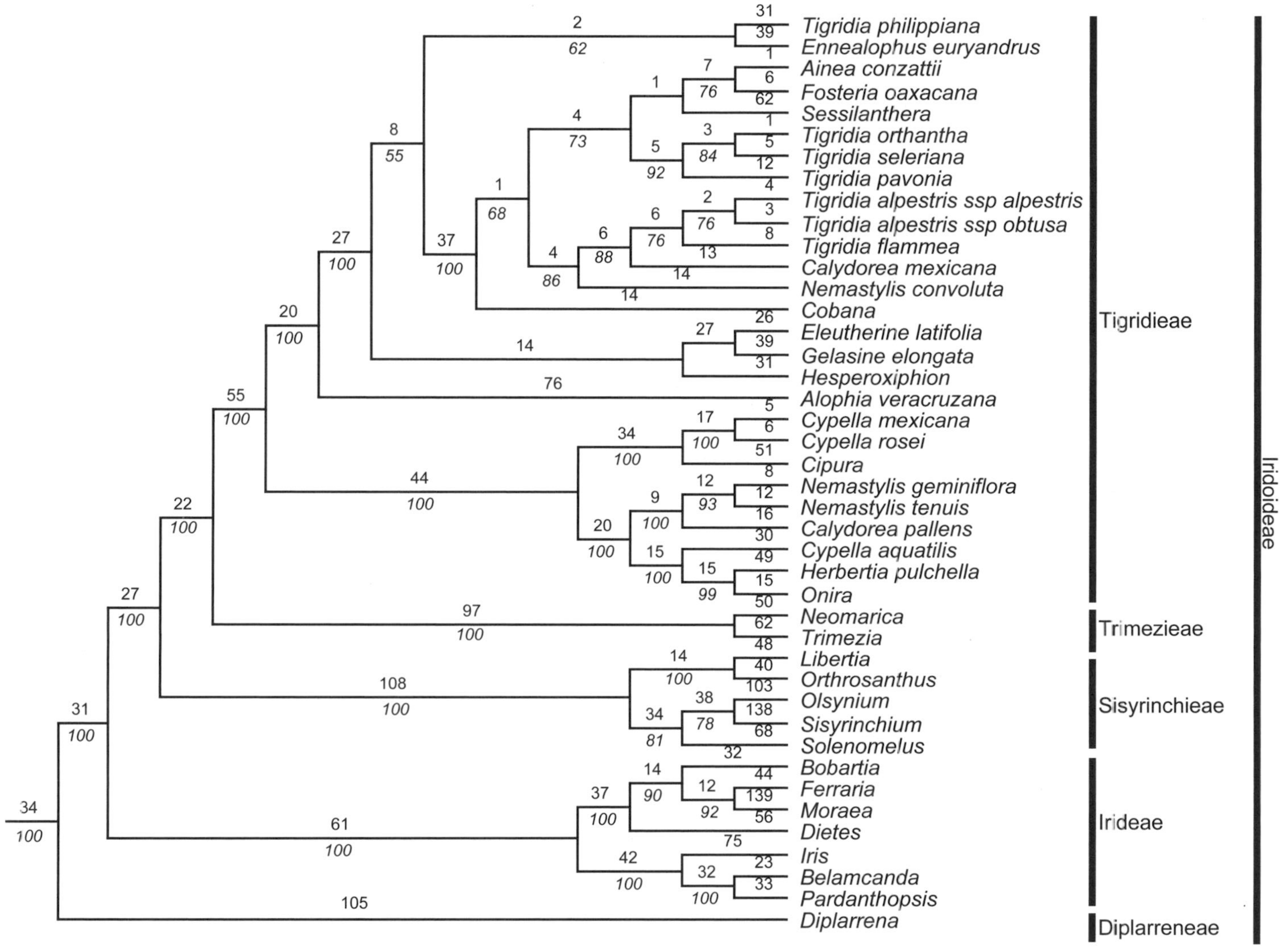

**Figure 7.** Generic phylogeny of Iridaceae subfamily Iridoideae based on six plastid DNA regions (Goldblatt et al., unpublished).

Ancestral characters for the Iridaceae as a whole are now seen to be their isobilateral leaves, possession of styloid calcium oxalate crystals, and radially symmetric flowers arranged in rhipidia and enclosed in large, opposed, spathe-like bracts. The flowers have free tepals, are typically stalked, and are raised sequentially out of the sheathing spathes. The ancestral pollen grains have a reticulate exine. The ancestral rootstock is a rhizome, but bulbs have evolved in Tigridieae and within *Iris,* while characteristic apically rooting corms are found in *Ferraria* and *Moraea.* Septal nectaries are also ancestral for the family but are suppressed in several genera, notably *Aristea* and *Patersonia.* In Iridoideae only the primitive *Diplarrena* has septal nectaries; other genera have nectaries located on the tepals (called perigonal nectaries) or no nectaries at all. Perigonal nectaries have evolved independently in one species of *Aristea, A. spiralis.* The inferior ovary, long thought to be a derived character for the family, is now also understood to be ancestral and shared with the related Doryanthaceae and Ixioliriaceae.

Relationships among the 29 genera of subfamily Crocoideae have the subject of endless and unsatisfactory speculation, and numerous tribal or subtribal groupings, or both, have been proposed for the alliance in the past. As just shown, the genera are united by their unusual and derived inflorescence, usually a spike, with stalkless flowers surrounded at the base of the ovary by a pair of bracts. In several genera the flowers are borne singly on the flowering stems but are still surrounded by a basal pair of bracts, even in acaulescent genera like *Crocus.* In addition, the flowers have a distinct perianth tube and are ancestrally zygomorphic and bilaterally symmetric but secondarily radially symmetric in several genera and species. The floral nectaries, when present, are always septal, and the style branches, although variously developed, are always slender. Apart from their specialized floral features,

Crocoideae also have a corm, which produces roots from the base, unlike the apically rooting corms of some Iridoideae. Pollen grains are likewise distinctive, having a basically tectate-perforate exine and an aperture with one or two exine bands that comprise an operculum, quite different from the rest of the family. The subfamily also has anatomical specializations, including the wavy-walled epidermal cells with multiple surface papillae, and elongation of the internal leaf tissue parallel to the long axis.

Crocoideae are relatively homogeneous, which has made understanding of relationships within the subfamily so difficult. Molecular analysis has finally provided independent evidence for relationships within the subfamily. The resulting classification recognizes five generic groupings as tribes (Goldblatt et al. 2006). The southern African genus *Tritoniopsis* is taxonomically isolated and is sister to the remaining genera, making necessary its placement in a monogeneric tribe Tritoniopsideae. The remaining genera are dispersed among the tribes Croceae, Freesieae, Gladioleae, and Watsonieae (Figure 8). The genera of each tribe and their geographical distribution are shown in Table 1.

Among the surprises delivered by the molecular study of Crocoideae is that *Gladiolus* is most closely related to the monospecific southern African *Melasphaerula,* an alliance never before proposed and one that receives no apparent support from morphology. The two genera are the only members of tribe Gladioleae. Equally surprising is that *Crocosmia* is most closely related to *Freesia* and not, as long believed, to *Chasmanthe* and *Tritonia.* The strange Cape genus *Pillansia,* which had seemed so unusual anatomically and in its inflorescence that it had been treated as a separate subtribe or tribe (Lewis 1954a, Goldblatt 1990a), is closely allied to *Thereianthus* and *Watsonia* and must be included within Watsonieae. This tribe is one that was recognized early on because of the unusual divided style branches of most of its

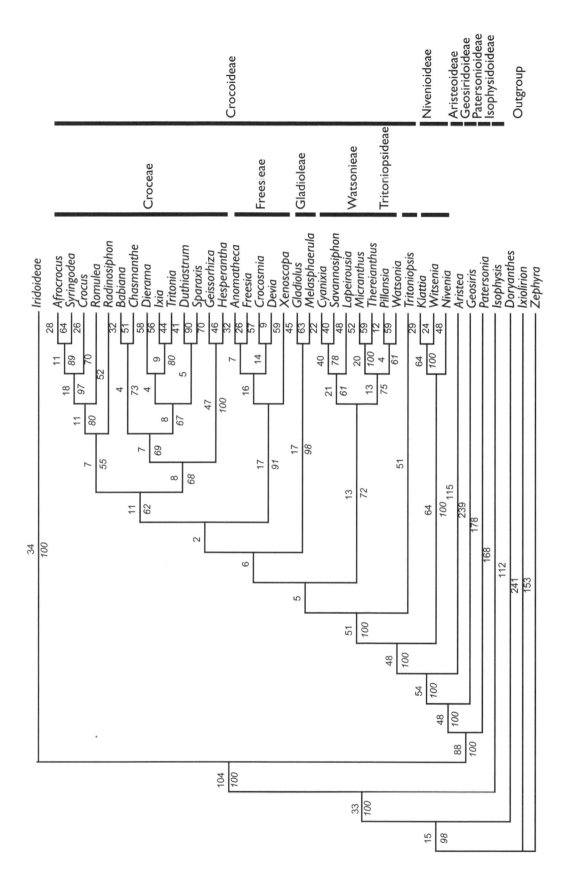

**Figure 8.** Phylogeny of Iridaceae, showing the relationships of *Isophysis*, *Patersonia*, *Geosiris*, and *Aristea* to the subfamilies Nivenioideae and Crocoideae, based on six plastid DNA regions.

genera, a feature only weakly developed in *Pillansia*. Watsonieae also include the tropical African genera *Savannosiphon* and *Zygotritonia*, the latter with a completely undivided style, and the Socotran *Cyanixia*, long known as *Babiana socotrana*. This plant is not allied to the southern African *Babiana*, but it remained for molecular analysis to demonstrate its correct status within Crocoideae, where it is now treated as a separate genus. Tritoniopsideae and Watsonieae are unusual among Crocoideae in having axillary corm formation as opposed to the axial corms that characterize the rest of the subfamily. *Freesia* and *Xenoscapa*, which are also characterized by divided style branches, are not related to the *Watsonia* group but constitute a quite separate lineage that together with *Crocosmia* and *Devia* are now included in their own tribe, Freesieae.

The remaining Crocoideae fall in the large tribe Croceae (Figure 8), which includes the largely acaulescent genera *Crocus*, *Romulea*, and *Syringodea* as well as *Babiana*, and a cluster of genera with unusual, smooth seeds with the vascular trace to the ovule excluded, among them *Dierama*, *Ixia*, *Sparaxis*, and *Tritonia*.

## Paleogeography and Diversification

There are, unfortunately, no reliably identified fossils of the Iridaceae of any significant age, and the age of the family must be determined using the molecular clock. This relies on the premise that random changes in noncoding regions of DNA take place at a constant or predictable rate. Calibrated either directly against the fossil record for a family or indirectly against the known age of other plant families (Wikström et al. 2001), the molecular clock has provided an estimate of c. 80 million years for the age of the Iridaceae (Goldblatt et al. 2002a). This places the origin of the family in the later Cretaceous, during the age of the dinosaurs, which ended abruptly c. 60 mya. The oldest lineages in the family,

subfamilies Isophysidoideae, Iridoideae: Diplarreneae, and Patersonioideae, probably diverged from shared ancestors in Australia–Antarctica 70–65 mya, when map of the world was very different from today (Figure 9). Immediately related to subfamily Patersonioideae, Geosiridoideae and Aristeoideae must have reached Africa–Madagascar via short-distance dispersal across the proto–Indian Ocean c. 55 mya, at a time when India had moved north away from western Australia, but distances between these landmasses were much shorter than today (compare the world's continents at 100 mya and 60 mya). Iridoideae, which are present in Africa, Asia, and South America, probably reached Asia and Africa at about the same time.

South America most likely remained connected to Antarctica until the mid Oligocene, c. 30 mya. At that time the Antarctic was not yet glaciated and formed a single continent continuous with Australia. South America still shares two genera, *Libertia* and *Orthrosanthus*, with greater Australasia (Australia, New Guinea, New Zealand), which remained a continuous landmass with Antarctica until c. 50 mya, South America separating from Antarctica well into the Oligocene, perhaps until 30 mya, and sharing some elements of their floras until then. Only after South America moved north and the connection to Antarctica was severed did the South American and Australasian floras evolve in complete isolation.

Much more recently, the linking of South America with North America via the Panama island arc was achieved by the mid-Miocene, but the direct land connection of South and North America was established only in the Pliocene. Thus, at least short-distance migration of southern lineages of Iridoideae, including *Neomarica* and *Orthrosanthus*, was possible after c. 26 mya but direct migration was possible only for the last 5 million years. The ancestors of the *Tigridia* lineage that radiated in Mexico diverged from South American ancestors c. 20 mya

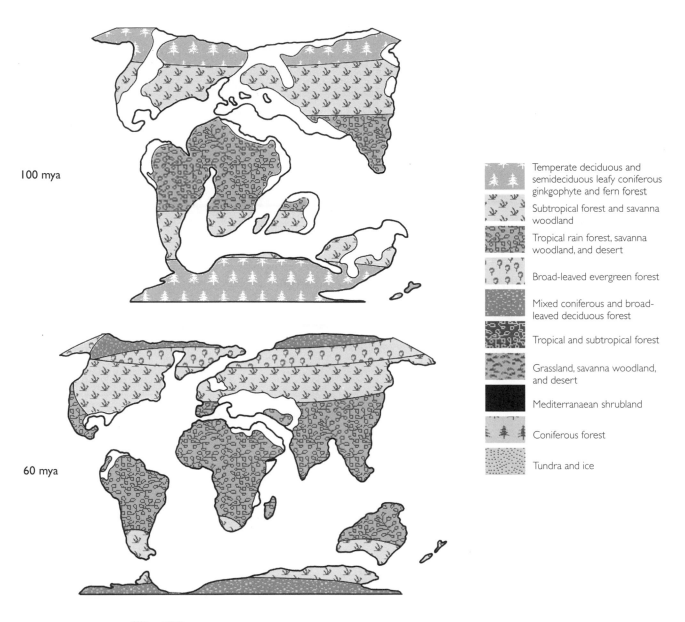

100 mya

60 mya

present

Temperate deciduous and semideciduous leafy coniferous ginkgophyte and fern forest

Subtropical forest and savanna woodland

Tropical rain forest, savanna woodland, and desert

Broad-leaved evergreen forest

Mixed coniferous and broad-leaved deciduous forest

Tropical and subtropical forest

Grassland, savanna woodland, and desert

Mediterranaean shrubland

Coniferous forest

Tundra and ice

**Figure 9.** Changes in world vegetation over the past 100 million years: (top) paleovegetation of the mid-Cretaceous (100 mya; modified from Saward 1992, Upchurch et al. 1998, Beerling and Woodward 2001), (middle) of the Eocene (60 mya; modified from Frakes et al. 1992, Wolfe 1985), (bottom) of today (modified from Miami Museum of Science 1997). Paleoprojections from Cox and Moore (2000). Unshaded portions of landmasses represent epicontinental seas.

and so must have dispersed from the south via island hopping across the proto-Caribbean. The *Tigridia* relative *Alophia* most likely reached Mexico and southern United States via short-distance dispersal across islands in the Caribbean, but *Herbertia,* otherwise only in temperate South America, must have reached the southern United States via long-distance dispersal relatively recently. Only subspecies *drummondii* of *H. lahue* occurs north of the equator, and it is hardly distinguishable from subspecies *amoena*. *Olsynium,* disjunct between Andean and temperate South America and northwestern North America, likewise, must have reached its northern stations via long-distance dispersal.

The great African radiation of the Iridaceae dates from the mid-Miocene (12–5.5 mya), although its roots lie in the mid-Oligocene. At that time the African climate was becoming increasingly dry and seasonal. Impetus for the explosive radiation of the family came from two sources. First, major continental uplift took place, especially in the southeast, accompanied by the spread of drought-adapted vegetation across the interior of the region at the expense of woodland and wet forest. Second, extreme seasonal aridity was established along the southwestern coast of southern Africa. Until the Oligocene the Iridaceae must have comprised mostly woodland and forest-margin species, like *Aristea* and *Dietes,* but contraction of forest as a result of aridification made available vast areas for the diversification of plants suited to open-canopy woodland and a seasonally dry climate, while new niches were available in a more rugged landscape with topographic relief. Subfamily Crocoideae, with some 1,100 species, that is, over half the total Iridaceae, radiated explosively after the end of the Miocene, although the genera themselves appear, according to the molecular clock, of mid- or late mid-Miocene age, 18–10 mya.

The deterioration of the African climate is linked to the development of the cold Benguela Current off the western coast of southern Africa, a result of the establishment of circum–Antarctic Ocean circulation and the glaciation of Antarctica. The Benguela Current brings cold Antarctic water north along the western coast of the continent, reducing the moisture content of the air above the ocean. Associated high pressure along the coast limits summer rainfall from the southeastern trade winds that bring rain to the southeastern coast and interior. This geological background set the scene for major radiation of the Iridaceae in southern Africa, especially in the winter-rainfall zone of the subcontinent, the Cape region and its surroundings. Diversification of genera gathered impetus as complete summer drought and a winter-rainfall climate regime became established in the Pliocene, after c. 5.5 mya. That climate is particularly difficult for most plants to adapt to, so that species and genera adapted for summer growth became increasingly rare, opening up niches for those lineages that could cope with the stresses associated with summer drought and a cool growing season in the winter and spring. Iridaceae and other families with underground storage organs were one of the life forms that thrived under these conditions.

# SYSTEMATICS OF THE IRIS FAMILY

## IRIDACEAE

Jussieu (1789)

Perennial evergreen or deciduous herbs, rarely annuals or shrubs with anomalous secondary growth. ROOTSTOCK a rhizome, bulb, corm, or when shrubs, a woody caudex, when annuals rootstock lacking. LEAVES basal and cauline, sometimes lower two or three without blades, with sheathing stem base and reaching shortly aboveground (thus cataphylls); mostly in two opposed ranks, bases usually overlapping and clasping the one above, sheaths of foliage leaves open or closed, usually contemporary with flowers, occasionally produced later, rarely already dry at flowering, occasionally leaves of flowering stem with reduced to entirely sheathing blades, then foliage leaves sometimes produced from separate shoots; blades either unifacial and oriented edgewise to stem, parallel-veined, without or with a distinct central vein, surface plane or pleated or occasionally oval to round in section; or bifacial and oriented with adaxial surface facing stem, then channeled to flat and usually without a median vein; margins plane or sometimes undulate to crisped, sometimes thickened and fibrotic or raised into wings held at right angles to surface. FLOWERING STEMS aerial or subterranean, simple or branched, round in section or compressed,

then often angled or winged. INFLORESCENCE either composed of umbellate monochasial cymes (rhipidia) enclosed in opposed leafy to dry bracts (spathes) with flowers usually pedicellate, sometimes sessile, each flower within rhipidium subtended by one bract; or flowers sessile, subtended by a pair of opposed bracts and solitary or in a spike. FLOWERS bisexual, with a petaloid perianth of two whorls of three tepals each, rarely inner whorl suppressed, radially or bilaterally symmetric, then usually bilabiate, variously colored, often with contrasting markings; scented or unscented; TEPALS usually large and showy, free or united below in a tube, whorls equal or unequal, when zygomorphic posterior tepal usually largest and inclined to hooded, lower three often smallest and with contrasting markings (nectar guides); tube when present straight or curved, cylindric or funnel- to trumpet-shaped. STAMENS three (two in *Diplarrena*), arising at base of outer tepals, or in the tube, symmetrically disposed or unilateral and arcuate or sometimes declinate; filaments filiform, free or partly to completely united; anthers two-thecous, usually extrorse and splitting longitudinally, occasionally splitting at apex or base; pollen monosulcate, trisulcate, zonasulculate, dizonasulculate, spiraperturate, or inaperturate, operculate or not, exine reticulate to areolate or minutely but conspicuously dotted. OVARY inferior (but superior in *Isophysis*), three-locular with axile placentation (rarely one-locular with parietal placentation); ovules anatropous (straight) or campylotropous (curved), many to few, in two rows per locule, rarely in one; STYLE filiform, usually three-branched, sometimes simple, or three-lobed, style branches either filiform to distally expanded, sometimes each divided in upper half and stigmatic toward apices, or branches thickened or flattened and petaloid, stigmas then abaxial below apices. FRUIT a loculicidal capsule, rarely not splitting open at maturity, firm to cartilaginous, occasionally woody, xerochastic (splitting open when dry) or rarely hygrochastic (moisture-responsive); SEEDS globose to angular or discoid, sometimes broadly winged, usually dry, rarely seed coat fleshy or an aril present, rugulose or smooth, shiny or matte; endosperm hard, with reserves of hemicellulose, oil and protein; embryo small.

## Key to Subfamilies of Iridaceae

1 Ovary superior; flowers without nectaries; inflorescence a solitary flower borne within opposed large green bracts; tepals free to the base; style dividing into three short lobes apically ...................... Isophysidoideae (p. 91)

1' Ovary inferior; flowers with or without septal nectaries or perigonal nectaries or oil glands; inflorescence either a umbellate clusters (rhipidia) enclosed within large, usually green bracts (spathes) or a spike with flowers sessile; tepals free or variously united; style various............................................. 2

2 Flowers sessile and subtended by a pair of opposed bracts, usually arranged in a spike or solitary on branches; tepals always united in a tube below; flowers lasting at least 2 days; style dividing into filiform branches, rarely simple; rootstock a corm producing roots

from the base; pollen grains usually with perforate scabrate exine, rarely exine reticulate; pollen grain apertures usually with operculum unless zonasulculate; nectaries septal.......................... Crocoideae (p. 113)

2' Flowers in umbellate clusters (rhipidia) enclosed by a pair of opposed leafy bracts (spathes), rarely solitary on the peduncles or plants acaulescent but then style either dividing below the anthers into tangentially compressed, petal-like branches or dividing below or above the base of the anthers and obscurely three-lobed apically, the lobes entire or fringed, individual flowers pedicellate, sometimes sessile; rootstock a woody caudex, a rhizome, a corm rooting from the apical bud, or a bulb; flowers with the tepals free to basally connate, or united in an extended tube; lasting a single day or 2 or more days; nectaries septal or perigonal or oil glands present ...................... 3

3 Rhipidia never united in pairs; style dividing below the level of the anthers into three branches, these either filiform, extending between the stamens, or thickened or flattened and lying opposite the stamens, usually each terminating in paired appendages (style crests); nectaries or oil glands when present perigonal ...................... Iridoideae (p. 195)

3' At least the terminal rhipidia united in pairs (binate); style notched or divided apically into three lobes, occasionally forming filiform branches; nectaries when present septal........ 4

4 Plants evergreen shrubs with woody aerial stems; rootstock a woody caudex; individual flowers sessile and the tepals always united in a well-developed tube and lasting at least 2 days ...................... Nivenioideae (p. 104 )

4' Plants perennial, either with aerial stems not woody or acaulescent, sometimes evergreen; rootstock a rhizome or corm; individual flowers stalked or sessile, the tepals free, basally connate, or united in a tube; lasting a single day and deliquescing on fading ...................... 5

5  Plants achlorophyllous, saprophytic and leaves reduced to small scales ...........................
......................... Geosiridoideae (p. 95)

5'  Plants green, autotrophic, and leaves present and well developed ............................... 6

6  Tepals shortly connate basally; inner tepal whorl well developed; filaments free; style apically notched or lobed, the lobes sometimes fringed; flowers pedicellate, the pedicel sometimes very short............. Aristeoideae (p. 98)

6'  Tepals united in a tube included in the bracts; inner tepal whorl minute; filaments partly to completely united; style with three deeply fringed lobes; flowers sessile.......................
.......................... Patersonioideae (p. 93)

## Subfamily **Isophysidoideae** Takhtajan ex Thorne (2007)

TYPE: *Isophysis* T. Moore

Evergreen perennials with a creeping rhizome. LEAVES unifacial, sword-shaped, without a midrib, forming a two-ranked fan. FLOWERING STEM unbranched. INFLORESCENCE a single flower enclosed in paired, opposed leafy spathes (a single-flowered rhipidium homologous to that in Iridoideae?). FLOWERS long lasting, radially symmetric, nectaries lacking; TEPALS free, spreading. STAMENS free; filaments straight, flattened below; anthers linear, loculicidal, extrorse; pollen monosulcate, exine reticulate. OVARY superior; style slender, dividing into three short branches. CAPSULES more or less woody; SEEDS angular. BASIC CHROMOSOME NUMBER unknown. Genus one, species one.

## *Isophysis* T. Moore (1853: 212)
Plate 1; Figure 10

TYPE: *I. tasmanica* (W. J. Hooker) T. Moore

ETYMOLOGY: from the Greek *iso,* equal, and *physis,* bladder, possibly referring to the three equal compartments of the capsule, somewhat swollen in the middle

SYNONYM: *Hewardia* W. J. Hooker (1852), illegitimate name, not *Hewardia* J. Smith (1841), type: *H. tasmanica* W. J. Hooker = *Isophysis tasmanica* (W. J. Hooker) T. Moore

REVISIONARY ACCOUNTS: Stones and Curtis (1969, 2: 84, pl. 40), Cooke (1986, 46: 4–5)

Small evergreen perennials with a thick creeping rhizome. LEAVES several in a two-ranked fan, leathery, the margins thickened and hyaline, without a midrib; leaf margins with specialized thick-walled columnar epidermal cells and with a subepidermal fiber strand. FLOWERING STEM erect, lightly compressed, unbranched. INFLORESCENCE a single terminal flower enclosed in paired, opposed, large leafy spathes. FLOWERS radially symmetric, long lasting, half-nodding, dark red-purple or yellow, without nectar; TEPALS free, subequal, lanceolate, spreading, recurving distally. STAMENS symmetrically disposed, free; FILAMENTS straight, slightly wider and flattened below; ANTHERS linear-oblong, splitting longitudinally. OVARY superior; STYLE short with thick, recurved stigmatic branches. CAPSULE narrowly ovoid, woody; SEEDS reportedly angular. BASIC CHROMOSOME NUMBER unknown. Species only *Isophysis tasmanica,* local in the mountains of western Tasmania, in heathland on sandy soils.

*Isophysis* has the outward appearance of a typical member of the Iridaceae and differs mainly in having flowers with an inferior ovary. The leaves are unifacial, isobilateral, and sword-shaped, and they lack a central vein as do so many other Iridaceae. The plant tissues also have styloid crystals of the type characteristic of the family and lacking in all closely related families. Likewise, the flowers

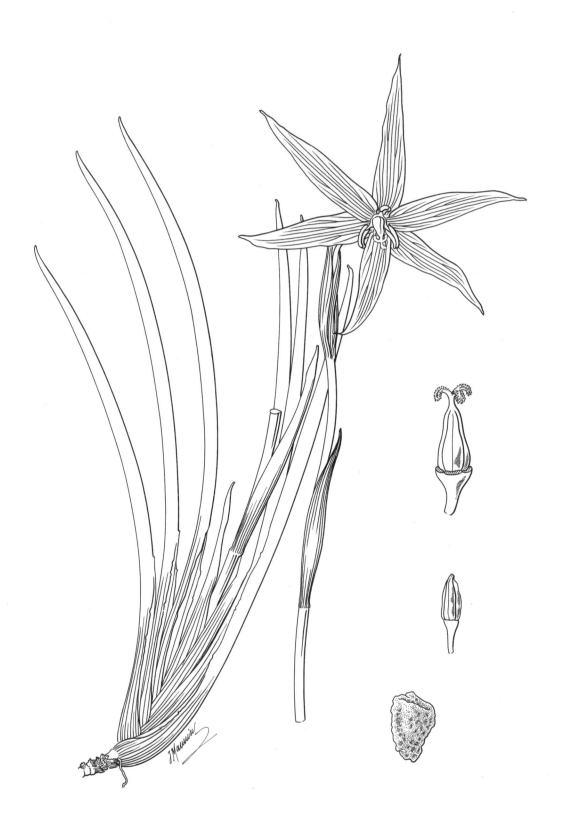

**Figure 10.** *Isophysis tasmanica* (×1) with ovary and style branches (right, above, ×3), capsule (middle, ×1), seed (bottom, ×12).

conform to the Iridaceae in having petaloid inner and outer tepal whorls and three stamens, inserted opposite the outer tepals. The flowers also have the single style and prominent style branches that characterize most Iridaceae. Apart from the superior ovary, unique in the family, the flowers of *Isophysis* lack nectaries of either the ancestral septal type or the perigonal nectaries typical of subfamily Iridoideae (Goldblatt 1990a). The leaf anatomy is unusual for the family in having the leaf margin cells columnar and with thickened radial walls, while the submarginal cells have thick walls but are not associated with a marginal vein (Rudall 1995).

The large, yellow or dark red, half-nodding flowers of *Isophysis* are solitary and borne at the apex of unbranched stems. Each flower is enclosed in a pair of large, opposed, leafy bracts. The flower bud is exserted from the bracts on long pedicels in much the same way as in many *Patersonia* and Iridoideae. We tentatively regard the inflorescence of *Isophysis* as a single-flowered rhipidium. That the flowers are solitary makes it impossible to determine whether the inflorescence of *Isophysis* is really a modified rhipidium and thus a form of the inflorescence type most likely ancestral for the Iridaceae.

Xylem anatomy provides equivocal information about the relationships of *Isophysis*. As in just a few relatively unspecialized genera of the Iridaceae, the vessel elements in the roots have scalariform perforation plates, considered primitive. Other Iridaceae with such vessel elements are *Aristea*, *Geosiris*, *Patersonia*, and the woody genera *Klattia*, *Nivenia*, and *Witsenia* (subfamily Nivenioideae in the sense of Goldblatt 1990a).

The several similarities that *Isophysis* shares with the Iridaceae make it clear that the genus is best regarded as a member of this family and not, as suggested in the past, Liliaceae in the broad sense, nor is it worthy of recognition as a separate family, Isophysidaceae. Its superior ovary has made it seem likely that *Isophysis* is primitive in the Iridaceae, and this assumption is supported by studies of DNA sequences (Reeves et al. 2001). An inferior ovary characterizes all the families immediately related to Iridaceae, suggesting that the superior ovary in *Isophysis*, far from being an ancestral and primitive condition, in fact represents a unique specialization for the genus. There is, however, no longer any question that *Isophysis* is correctly treated as a member of the Iridaceae and that it is fairly isolated taxonomically and evidently the most primitive living member of the family. Preliminary dating of the phylogenetic tree for the family suggests that *Isophysis* lineage diverged from the ancestral stock of the Iridaceae c. 70 mya, that is, in the later Cretaceous, a time when Australia and Antarctica were still joined to South America and this supercontinent had a common flora. In this context, *Isophysis* may be seen as an ancient, isolated relic.

## Subfamily **Patersonioideae** Goldblatt, new subfamily
TYPE: *Patersonia* R. Brown

*Plantae perennes vivaces, rhizomatis vel caudicibus lignosis, foliis unifacialibus sine vena media, inflorescentia rhipidio binato spathis foliatis incluso, floribus fugaceis actinomorphibus sine nectariis, tepalis patentibus in tubo connatis, filamentis parte vel tota connatis, antheris loculicidalis extrorsis, pollinis inaperturatis exinis verrucatis, ovario inferiore style gracile ad apicem diviso in lobis fimbriatis triis, capsulis sublignosis, seminibus angulatis.*

Evergreen perennials with a creeping rhizome or a woody caudex. LEAVES unifacial, without a midrib. INFLORESCENCE a binate rhipidium enclosed in paired, opposed leafy spathes. FLOWERS fugacious, lasting a single day, radially symmetric, without nectaries; tepals united in a tube, spreading. STAMENS with the filaments partly to entirely united; anthers loculicidal, extrorse; pollen inaperturate (but poorly known), exine verrucate. OVARY inferior; style slender, dividing into three fringed lobes. CAPSULES more or less woody; SEEDS angular. BASIC CHROMOSOME NUMBER $x =$ ?11. Genus one, species 21.

*Patersonia* R. Brown in Ker Gawler
(1807: pl. 1,041)
Plate 2
Conserved name
TYPE: *Patersonia sericea* R. Brown
ETYMOLOGY: named in honor of William Paterson (1755–1810), plant explorer and first Lieutenant Governor of New South Wales in Australia
SYNONYM: *Genosiris* Labillardière (1805, 1: 13, pl. 9), rejected name, type: *G. fragilis* Labillardière = *Patersonia fragilis* (Labillardière) Aschers & Graebner
REVISIONARY ACCOUNT: Cooke (1986, 46: 13–26)

Small to medium-sized perennials or evergreen undershrubs with woody rhizomes, sometimes with secondary growth. LEAVES sword-shaped to linear; leaf margins with subepidermal sclerenchyma strands and often with marginal ribs. STEM unbranched, terete. INFLORESCENCE a binate rhipidium, the spathes often leathery, sometimes pubescent. FLOWERS sessile, radially symmetric, fugacious, shades of blue to violet, rarely yellow or white; PERIANTH TUBE long, without nectar; TEPALS unequal, the outer large, spreading, the inner vestigial. FILAMENTS partly to entirely united; ANTHERS erect, not reaching the style apex. OVARY spindle-shaped, included in the spathes; STYLE prominently three-lobed, the margins entire or fringed. CAPSULES cylindric to narrowly ovoid, included in the spathes; SEEDS angular to ellipsoid, sometimes arillate. BASIC CHROMOSOME NUMBER $x =$ ?11, also 10.

Species 21, mostly Australian and centered in Western Australia but also at high elevations in the mountains of New Guinea, Borneo, and Sumatra.

Most species of *Patersonia* are seasonal perennials with creeping rhizomes, producing leaves and flowers in the cool, wet Australian winter and spring. The flowers are borne on unbranched flowering stems in unusual, biseriate inflorescences (binate rhipidia) of the type found in a few other genera, including *Aristea, Geosiris,* and the woody southern African *Klattia, Nivenia,* and *Witsenia.* In *Patersonia* the large rhipidial spathes enclose the flower buds and floral bracts, concealing the complex nature of the inflorescence. In most of the other genera that have binate rhipidia the spathes tend to be shorter, and the biseriate nature of the inflorescence is usually easy to see. A few species of *Patersonia* have a somewhat different growth habit. They are evergreen and have long-lived, twiggy stems that make the plants, in effect, small shrubs. The inflorescences and flowers are identical in all significant respects to those of the perennial species.

The flowers of *Patersonia* species all have a subsessile ovary, and the perianth has a long tube held within the spathes that apparently serves primarily as a pseudopedicel to elevate the flowers above the spathes. The outer tepals are large and outspread, and the inner are much smaller than the outer, usually vestigial and reduced to tiny cusps or completely lacking. The filaments are united in a tube around the lower part of the slender style, which terminates in three broad, fringed stigma lobes, recalling those of the African *Aristea.* Like *Aristea* and *Geosiris,* the flowers of *Patersonia* are fugacious and deliquescent on fading, and are usually blue, but *P. pygmaea* has bright yellow flowers. Pollen of the genus is poorly known, but at least some species of *Patersonia* (including *P. sericea*) have specialized inaperturate pollen grains with a vermiform or intectate (i.e., with the outer tectum so disrupted and reduced as to be essentially lacking), verrucate exine (Goldblatt and Le Thomas 1992, Furness and Rudall 1999). This is unusual in Iridaceae and needs further investigation. If characteristic of the entire genus it tends to confirm its taxonomic isolation.

Anatomically, the leaves of *Patersonia* conform to the basic and ancestral pattern of the Iridaceae in having a strand of submarginal sclerenchyma and unspecialized marginal epidermal cells. Like *Aristea, Isophysis, Geosiris,* and the woody genera, the roots of *Patersonia* have xylem vessels mostly of the unspecialized type, with scalariform perforation plates. Flavonoid chemistry of the genus is unusual. Its flavonoid compounds are mostly biflavones, not common in other monocot families and occurring in the Iridaceae possibly also in some of the woody southern African genera (Williams et al. 1986) and *Isophysis.*

It is clear from the foregoing that *Patersonia* shares some several features with the African genera of Nivenioideae, but most of these similarities are ancestral and do not signify close relationship. At least compared to *Isophysis,* the fugacious flower, the blue-pigmented perianth, and the binate rhipidial inflorescences appear derived and are grounds for assuming an immediate relationship with Nivenioideae. The presence of secondary wood in the rhizomes of some species of *Patersonia* has also been seen as evidence of a possible relationship between the genus and the woody southern African *Nivenia* and its allies, which have secondary growth in both the rootstock and aerial stems. On the basis of these several shared specialized features, *Patersonia* was included in subfamily Nivenioideae by Goldblatt (1990a). Sequences of several chloroplast DNA regions provide further evidence for the relationships of *Patersonia, Aristea, Geosiris,* and the woody genera, but this lineage also includes subfamily Crocoideae. *Patersonia* falls at the base of the lineage, suggesting that it is phylogenetically isolated. We now segregate the genus in a separate subfamily, Patersonioideae. Using the molecular clock for dating the age of genera of the Iridaceae, *Patersonia* evidently diverged from ancestral stock of the family c. 55 mya, thus in the early Eocene.

The geography of *Patersonia* is interesting, for although often considered an Australian genus, where is shows moderate adaptive radiation, one species occurs on New Guinea and the larger East Indian islands of Borneo and Sumatra. While its ancestors are all Australasian, *Patersonia* is sister to an entirely Afro-Madagascan lineage, the Aristeoideae, Nivenioideae, and Crocoideae.

The fugacious, blue, or rarely yellow flowers of *Patersonia* produce no nectar and thus are pollen flowers. Pollen is prominently displayed on exserted anthers. In the absence of published observations of pollinator activity, we assume pollination by female bees foraging for pollen for nest provisioning.

## Subfamily **Geosiridoideae** Goldblatt & J. C. Manning, new subfamily
TYPE: *Geosiris* Baillon

*Plantae perennes saprophyticae, rhizomatis, foliis reductis squamiformibus, bifacialibus sine vena media, inflorescentia rhipidio binato spathis foliatis incluso, floribus fugaceis actinomorphibus sine nectariis, tepalis patentibus in tubo brevi connatis, filamentis liberis, antheris loculicidalis extrosis, pollinis monosulcatis exinis reticulatis, ovario inferiore stylo gracili ad apicem diviso in lobis fimbriatis triis, capsulis sublignosis, seminibus parvissimis.*

Plants perennial, achlorophyllous saprophytes with a creeping rhizome. LEAVES reduced to small scales, unifacial, without a midrib. INFLORESCENCE units binate rhipidia enclosed in paired, opposed leafy or dry spathes, often many units per flowering stem.

FLOWERS fugacious, lasting a single day, radially symmetric, without nectaries; tepals united basally, spreading. STAMENS with the filaments free; anthers loculicidal, extrorse; pollen monosulcate, exine reticulate. OVARY inferior; style slender, dividing into three fringed lobes or barely notched at the tip. CAPSULES more or less woody; SEEDS minute, dust-like. BASIC CHROMOSOME NUMBER unknown. Genus one, species two.

*Geosiris* Baillon (1784, 2(146): 1,149–1,150)
Plate 3; Figure 11
TYPE: *Geosiris aphylla* Baillon
ETYMOLOGY: from the Greek *geos,* earth, compounded with *Iris,* thus a member of the *Iris* family, alluding to its low growing habit
REVISIONARY ACCOUNTS: Perrier de la Bâthie (1946, 45: 2), Goldblatt (1991: 45)

Small, achlorophyllous, saprophytic herb with stems produced from a short, thick, underground rhizome. LEAVES reduced to membranous scales only on the flowering stem, basal leaves lacking. STEM rounded, simple or branched, bearing scale-like leaves. INFLORESCENCE a binate rhipidium distorted by crowding of numerous flowers, binate rhipidia few to several; SPATHES submembranous and translucent, the margins ultimately becoming irregularly torn, sheathing the flower buds and membranous floral bracts. FLOWERS radially symmetric, lasting less than a day, perianth twisting spirally on fading and persisting on the capsules, sessile, blue to mauve or white, sweetly scented, evidently lacking nectar; TEPALS basally connate for up to 1.5 mm, subequal or the inner three slightly larger, lanceolate to ovate or the outer obovate-spathulate, spreading horizontally. STAMENS diverging or erect and more or less appressed to the style; FILAMENTS free; ANTHERS oblong, extrorse. OVARY ovoid, included in the bracts; STYLE slender, erect, becoming eccentric with age, dividing apically into three short, narrow or broad lightly fringed stigmatic lobes. CAPSULES ovoid, sessile, capped by the remains of the perianth; SEEDS minute, numerous, ovoid, surface reticulate and shallowly ridged. BASIC CHROMOSOME NUMBER unknown.

Species 2, *Geosiris aphylla* and a second species still to be described, restricted to central and eastern Madagascar and Mayotte in the Comoro Islands, in shade on the forest floor in leaf litter.

*Geosiris* is the only genus of the Iridaceae lacking chlorophyll and is therefore saprophytic rather than autotrophic, though this remains to be studied in any detail. The leaves are reduced to small scales appressed to the stem, which is usually branched and terminates in a dense cluster of blue to violet or white flowers. The crowding of the flowers makes the inflorescence difficult to interpret, but it is clear that the flowers are virtually sessile and arranged in two series separated by larger bracts than those subtending the individual flowers. The flowers are short-lived, lasting less than a day, and they deliquesce on fading. Their significant features are the very short perianth tube, erect stamens, and slender style that becomes eccentric with age, and of course the inferior ovary. The style terminates in three fairly broad, fringed lobes in the Madagascan *G. aphylla,* very much as in many species of *Aristea,* but in an undescribed species from Mayotte in the Comoro Islands the style divides into three minute lobes. Unlike other Iridaceae, the ovules are borne on a branched placenta. After the perianth collapses, it dries out and remains attached to the top of the developing fruit in exactly the manner it does in several other genera of the family, including most significantly *Aristea.* The ovules mature into minute, almost dust-like seeds. This is a common feature of parasitic or saprophytic plants that rely on wind dispersal to reach suitable new habitats. The small pollen grains have a reticulate exine and a

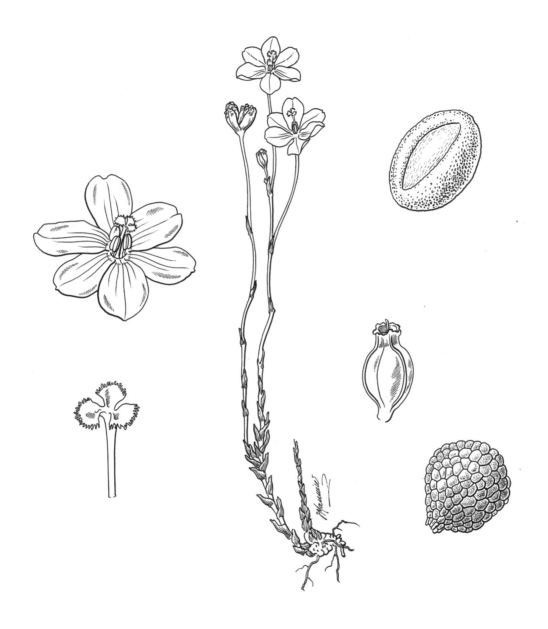

**Figure 11.** *Geosiris aphylla* (×1) with flower (left, above, ×2.5), detail of style (below, ×25), pollen (right, above, ×1,000), capsule (middle, ×4), and seed (below, ×25).

single elliptic aperture, the ancestral type of pollen in the family.

Because it is leafless and lacks chlorophyll, the relationships of *Geosiris* have long been puzzling—the genus has variously been placed in the Iridaceae, the Burmanniaceae, a family of exclusively nongreen saprophytic plants, or in its own family, Geosiridaceae. The three stamens inserted opposite the outer tepals, the inferior ovary, and the presence of styloid crystals in some of its tissues correspond exactly with the three most important diagnostic features of the Iridaceae, and Goldblatt et al. (1987) concluded, based on morphological and anatomical evidence, that *Geosiris* belongs in the Iridaceae. It is, however, the only nonphotosynthetic genus in the family and the only genus with minute, almost dust-like seeds. Within the Iridaceae, the fugacious blue flower with a vestigial perianth tube, long style with short, fringed stigma lobes, and biseriate inflorescence recall *Aristea* in particular, but these characters are all basic for the lineage and thus are not informative about relationships within it. Sequence analysis using four separate plastid DNA regions (Reeves et al. 2001) confirms the affinities of *Geosiris* within the Iridaceae and shows the genus to be sister to *Aristea,* which together with the woody genera *Klattia, Nivenia,* and *Witsenia* and subfamily Crocoideae form a clade.

## Subfamily **Aristeoideae** Vines (1895: 569)
TYPE: *Aristea* Aiton

Evergreen perennials with a creeping or erect rhizome. LEAVES unifacial, without a midrib. INFLORESCENCE units binate rhipidia enclosed in paired, opposed, leafy or dry spathes, often many units per flowering stem. FLOWERS fugacious, lasting a single day, radially symmetric, without nectaries or with perigonal nectaries (only *Aristea spiralis*); tepals united basally, spreading. STAMENS with the filaments free; anthers loculicidal and extrorse or porose; pollen variable, most commonly monosulcate, zonasulculate, or dizonasulcate, exine reticulate, microreticulate, or rugulate. OVARY inferior; style slender, dividing into three entire or fringed lobes or apically three-notched. CAPSULES more or less woody; SEEDS angular, triangular-columnar, or lamellate. BASIC CHROMOSOME NUMBER $x = 16$. Genus one, species c. 55.

## *Aristea* [Solander in] Aiton (1789, 1: 67)
Plates 4–9; Figures 12–14
TYPE: *Aristea africana* (Linnaeus) Hofmannsegg
ETYMOLOGY: from the Greek *arista*, an awn, a dry, acute-tipped, bract-like structure, as in the fringed spathes and bracts (of the type species)
SYNONYM: *Cleanthe* Salisbury (1812, 1: 312), type: *C. lugens* (Linnaeus fil.) Steudel = *Aristea lugens* (Linnaeus fil.) Weimarck
REVISIONARY ACCOUNTS: Weimarck (1940a, entire genus), Vincent (1985, eastern southern African species), Goldblatt (1991, Madagascan species; 1996a, tropical African species), Goldblatt and Manning (1997a, species of section *Pseudaristea*; 1997b, species of section *Racemosae*)

Evergreen perennials with creeping or erect rhizomes. LEAVES unifacial, sword-shaped to linear or terete, in two ranks, crowded basally; leaf margins often translucent, with specialized thick-walled columnar marginal epidermal cells and lacking subepidermal marginal fiber strands, blades terete in a few species. FLOWERING STEM rounded to compressed, or flattened and strongly winged, variously branched or simple, bearing reduced leaves below or leafless except for a subterminal leaflet. INFLORESCENCE a binate rhipidium, with two to several flowers; binate rhipidia single to many, either terminal on main and secondary axes or axillary, often sessile; SPATHES green or partly to entirely

**Figure 12.** (left) *Aristea ecklonii* (×1), (center) *A. torulosa* flowering stem (×1), (upper center) *A. capitata* flower (upper right, ×0.8) with stigma (below, much enlarged), (right) *A. abyssinica* fruiting plant (×1).

**Figure 13.** *Aristea* flowers: (top left) *A. lugens,* (top right) *A. cantharophila,* (top right) *A. biflora,* (bottom left) *A. teretifolia* (all ×1).

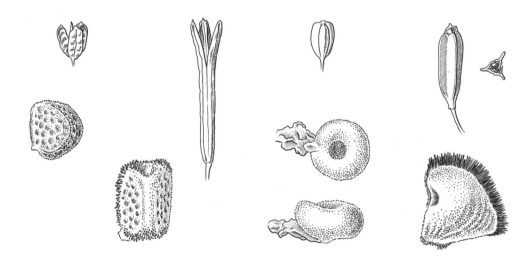

**Figure 14.** *Aristea* capsules and seeds: (left to right) *A. anceps, A. cistiflora, A. singularis, A. rigidifolia* (capsules, above, ×1, and seeds, below, ×12).

membranous or dry, the margins entire, fringed, or becoming irregularly torn; floral bracts similar to the spathes but often smaller. FLOWERS usually fugacious and lasting less than a day, usually a single morning, often subsessile, radially symmetric, usually pale to dark blue with a pale throat, occasionally mauve, lilac, or white, rarely with contrasting markings (subgenus *Pseudaristea*), the perianth twisting spirally on fading and persisting, scentless, nectar produced in *Aristea spiralis* from perigonal nectaries; TEPALS united basally for 1–2 mm, the outer somewhat to much smaller than the inner, ovate or obovate, spreading, or rarely suberect. STAMENS symmetrically or slightly eccentrically disposed, suberect; FILAMENTS free, unequal in *A. inaequalis;* ANTHERS oblong to linear, usually splitting lengthwise, or only at the tips in four Madagascan species. OVARY ovoid to oblong or cylindric, three-lobed; STYLE filiform, eccentric, minutely three-fid or with three entire or fringed stigmatic lobes. CAPSULES ovoid or oblong to cylindric, three-lobed, or broadly three-winged, subsessile or stalked, the dry perianth usually persisting on the capsules, sometimes with the central axis separating from the septa. *Seeds* angular to rounded, shortly cylindric, or radially compressed and disk-like, bearing a white elaiosome in one species, many to only two (or one) per locule, often with foveolate sculpturing or more or less smooth, when flattened the margins often papillate. BASIC CHROMOSOME NUMBER $x = 16$. Species c. 55, widespread across sub-Saharan Africa and Madagascar, extending in Africa from Senegal and Ethiopia in the north to the southwestern tip of the continent, with diversity increasing toward the south; most speciose in the southern African winter-rainfall zone.

Although one of the least variable of the larger genera of the Iridaceae in its flower morphology, *Aristea* is remarkably diverse in other features. Most species have deep blue flowers with broad, spreading, subequal tepals, a rudimentary perianth tube, straight, divergent stamens, and a slender, eccentric style. An unusual feature of *A. inaequalis* (section *Racemosae*) is its unequal stamens. The flowers of this species face to the side, and the lower (abaxial) filament is longer than the two upper filaments. Four species of *Aristea* in Madagascar stand out in having porose anthers, which release the pollen though small apical slits, unlike the longitudinal splitting of the anthers of other species. Most species of subgenus *Pseudaristea* have lilac, pale blue, or cream to white flowers, often with the tepals marked with areas of dark pigmentation. In *A. biflora* the outer tepals have translucent, window-like patches of tissue at the lower margins that appear dark when viewed from above. The distinctive *A. lugens* has blackish outer tepals much smaller than the inner and are held more or less erect. *Aristea nigrescens* has the open flowers uniformly colored, but the buds, showing the outside of the tepals, are black. The specializations are linked to the unusual pollination biology of the group (see below).

In contrast to the comparative uniformity of its flowers, *Aristea* is remarkably variable in its pollen morphology, capsule shape, and seed structure and number, features that do not vary in most other genera. The ancestral or primitive capsule appears to be uniformly ovoid with brittle walls, and the basic seed shape is lightly angular (Figure 14). These unspecialized capsules contain several seeds per locule, and the seeds have a foveolate (pitted) surface pattern. Such capsules occur in most species of subgenus *Eucapsulares.* In subgenus *Pseudaristea* the capsules are elongate and deeply three-lobed, with thick, leathery to woody walls that take several months to split open and shed their seeds. Subgenus *Aristea* has prominently three-winged capsules, with the locules radially compressed so that the capsules have three narrow, vertical lobes. The seeds are in consequence flattened, and in section *Aristea* there only one or two per locule but two to as many as 12 per locule in section *Racemosae.* In these seeds the margins are usually papillate or fringed, sometimes appearing almost hairy. *Aristea singularis,* also subgenus *Aristea,* departs from the norm in having rounded seeds with a sunken chalazal end and a fleshy white aril, a feature unique among African Iridaceae. The aril probably contains food attractive to ants, which we assume disperse the seeds. Ant-dispersed seeds are common in many plant families in the southern African winter-rainfall zone.

The capsule and seed variation is complemented by the variation in pollen. Species of subgenus *Eucapsulares* have, with few exceptions, pollen grains with microreticulate to rugulate exine. Except in the taxonomically and geographically isolated *Aristea latifolia,* the disulcate or zonasulcate apertures are covered with exine. Pollen grains are shed singly except in three species of the subgenus, the *A. ecklonii* group, in which pollen is usually shed in tetrads. In subgenus *Pseudaristea* the pollen grains have reticulate exine and unique two-zonasulcate apertures while sections *Racemosae* and *Singulares* of subgenus *Aristea* have monosulcate pollen grains with reticulate to rugulate exine, more or less typical of the monocots in general. In section *Aristea,* pollen grains are unusually large and have apertures best described as trisulcate to spiraperturate; the confluent apertures divide the exine into three or more separate plates. The correlation between capsule shape, seeds, and pollen morphology has led to the classification of *Aristea* into three subgenera (Goldblatt and Le Thomas 1997). Previously, *Aristea* was treated as comprising eight sections by the Swedish botanist Henning Weimarck (1940a), whose classification was based largely on capsule and seed morphology, unfortunately not then fully known.

Other important variation in *Aristea* includes inflorescence and leaf morphology. The inflorescence units of the genus, binate rhipidia, are arranged on the flowering stem in a variety of ways, often distinctive, to form compound inflorescences, sometimes called synflorescences. In section *Aristea* the inflorescence is dichotomously branched with all the binate rhipidia stalked. *Aristea singularis* (section *Singulares*) is unique in having nodding inflorescences. In many other sections the lateral binate rhipidia are sessile and are typically so in subgenus *Pseudaristea* and several species of subgenus *Eucapsulares. Aristea capitata* has a crowded inflorescence with short lateral branches clustered toward the stem apex, giving the entire structure a columnar appearance (Plate 6).

The range of *Aristea* across Africa and Madagascar closely follows the infrageneric classification. Subgenus *Eucapsulares* has one species, *A. latifolia,* in the southern African winter-rainfall zone, and the remaining 26 species largely restricted to areas of summer rainfall. It is the only section represented in tropical and eastern southern Africa and Madagascar, which has seven species, six of them endemic. A few species of section *Eucapsulares* extend southward for a short distance into the winter-rainfall part of southern Africa. *Aristea nana* and *A. pusilla* are centered in the southern Cape, while *A. ensifolia* is restricted to the evergreen forests of the winter-rainfall zone. Subgenus *Aristea* (c. 20 species) and subgenus *Pseudaristea* (nine species) occur exclusively in the winter-rainfall southwest. Most species of the last subgenus are ecologically unusual for the genus in favoring lowland habitats on clay soils and thus occur in the local shrubland called renoster-veld, unlike the montane species, which grow in chaparral-like fynbos heathland.

Pollination biology appears fairly uniform as might be expected given the similarity of the flowers of so many species. The only reward offered by the blue-flowered species is pollen, which is gathered by a variety of bees, both solitary and social. The flowers open shortly after sunrise on warm days and soon after that the anthers split open to expose their pollen. Bees quickly take advantage of this food source, and by 8:30 a.m. on warm days, later on cool or cloudy days, all pollen is removed. The flowers generally last until shortly after 1:00 p.m. and then wilt and rapidly collapse. A range of bees successfully pollinate these flowers, including *Amegilla*, *Anthophora*, and *Xylocopa* species, the honeybee *Apis mellifera* (all Apidae), and various species of Halictidae and Andrenidae. A second pollination strategy, restricted to subgenus *Pseudaristea*, involves hopliine scarab beetles. The flowers of the species that attract hopliine beetles open later in the day than those of bee-pollinated species and last until the late afternoon. Not only are the flowers of these species pale bluish, lilac, or cream, but they often have discrete dark markings, and the anthers are larger than elsewhere in the genus and are usually orange, an unusual color shift. Species of hopliine beetles congregate on these flowers to feed on pollen, compete for mates, and engage in copulation. As they crawl around the flowers they become liberally dusted with pollen, which is readily brushed onto a receptive stigma of another flower, thus effecting cross pollination. The dark markings on these flowers are thought to be beetle marks, that is, signals that attract beetles to the flowers, perhaps in search of mates.

One species of subgenus *Pseudaristea*, *Aristea spiralis*, exhibits yet another pollination strategy. The large flowers face to the side and have unusually long stamens. It is the only species of *Aristea* that produces nectar, a reward attractive to long-proboscid horseflies, of which *Philoliche rostrata* is the only recorded visitor. As a fly forages for nectar it becomes dusted with pollen on the abdomen. The pollen is readily transferred to the stigmas of other flowers that they visit.

Although seemingly unspecialized in many floral and vegetative features, much of the apparent simplicity is now known to be secondary, and *Aristea* has several unusual features. These include leaf margins without a subepidermal fiber strand, the latter character evidently ancestral in the family. Instead, the leaves have a derived marginal epidermis composed of columnar cells with thickened walls. A curious feature of the margins is that the epidermal cells decrease in size toward the margin tip. As a result, the margins taper to a very fine edge. The seed coat epidermis has papillate cells on the margins in most species of subgenera *Aristea* and *Pseudaristea*, a feature unique in the family. The flowers also lack septal nectaries, the presence of which is most probably ancestral for the Iridaceae. Septal nectaries are present in the three genera of Nivenioideae, in all Crocoideae, and in *Diplarrena* (subfamily Iridoideae), and their absence in *Aristea*, far from being a primitive condition, is best interpreted as a later loss, probably connected with a shift from nectar to pollen as the floral reward. It is uncertain whether the absence of a fully developed perianth tube is derived or not. The blue flowers contain an unusual pigment, plumbagin, not recorded elsewhere in the Iridaceae, although the pigment in flowers of the closely related genus, *Geosiris*, is unknown. DNA sequence analysis of plastid genes shows *Aristea* to be the sister clade to the woody Cape genera plus the entire subfamily Crocoideae. *Aristea* and the three woody genera share the same basic chromosome number $x = 16$, but no other nonmolecular character appears to be unique for these four genera. Molecular evidence, less reliable for saprophytes, shows *Geosiris* to be sister to the *Aristea*–woody genera–Crocoideae clade.

Taxonomically isolated within the Iridaceae, *Aristea* is here regarded as comprising the sole genus of subfamily Aristeoideae. In flower and fruit morphology it resembles the achlorophyllous, scale-leaved saprophyte *Geosiris*, the flowers of which are smaller and the minute seeds of which are borne on branched placentas. *Aristea* has also been associated with the Australasian *Patersonia* and, historically, with *Nivenia*, species of which were often assigned to *Aristea* when first described. The similarity actually ends with their actinomorphic, blue flowers with spreading tepals and in the case of *Nivenia* their shared southern African distribution. All these genera were included in an enlarged subfamily Nivenioideae by Goldblatt (1990a), but DNA sequences show the relationships to be less close than supposed (Reeves et al. 2001).

A few species of *Aristea* are known in cultivation, mostly in specialist collections. *Aristea capitata* (long known as *A. major* or *A. thyrsiflora*) is an important exception. It responds well to garden situations and to a variety of soil conditions, and it is much used in parts of South Africa as a plant for large borders, groupings of native plants, and even in street plantings. The plants have numerous flowers crowded on columnar inflorescences carried on stems up to 1.2 m high. The flowering season lasts for about a month, usually late October to the end of November. A form with pale pink flowers is also known. The fruiting stems also make attractive accents as the capsules turn from green to reddish brown. *Aristea capitata* is best grown from seed or small plants in pots. Mature plants seldom transplant successfully. *Aristea ecklonii* is also cultivated widely and has become naturalized in tropical parts of the world, including western India. It sets seed without cross pollination and is a potential weed.

The large-flowered species *Aristea bakeri, A. bracteata*, and *A. rigidifolia*, all tall plants c. 1 m high and producing numerous flowers, should be tried as garden subjects. *Aristea rigidifolia* has the largest flowers in the genus, almost 4 cm in diameter. Only *A. capitata* is regularly available in the horticultural trade, either from specialist seed distributors or from the Botanical Society of South Africa. The particularly striking lowland species *A. biflora* and *A. lugens* respond poorly to cultivation, and both flower well in the wild only after fire.

## Subfamily **Nivenioideae** Schulze ex Goldblatt (1990a)

TYPE: *Nivenia* Ventenat

Evergreen woody shrubs with a woody underground caudex, the stems with anomalous, monocot-type secondary growth. LEAVES unifacial, without a midrib. INFLORESCENCE units binate rhipidia enclosed in paired, opposed, leafy or dry spathes, the units variously aggregated into pseudocorymbs, racemes, or heads. FLOWERS long lasting, radially symmetric, with septal nectaries; tepals united in a tube below, spreading or upright above. STAMENS with the filaments free; anthers loculicidal and extrorse; pollen monosulcate, exine reticulate. OVARY inferior; style slender, apically three-notched or dividing into three slender branches. CAPSULES more or less woody; SEEDS tangentially compressed, shield-shaped. BASIC CHROMOSOME NUMBER $x = 16$. Genera three, species 15.

## Key to Genera of Nivenioideae

1  Inflorescence compound, forming a compressed head enclosed by enlarged green or colored leaves; perianth tube shorter than the linear, spathulate tepals .......... *Klattia* (p. 108)
1'  Inflorescence either compound, forming branched panicles or corymbs, or flowers borne in isolated pairs, enclosed in green or brown spathes; perianth tube shorter or longer than the oblong to ovate tepals ................. 2
2  Flowers shades of blue; tepals patent, not bearing soft, relatively long hairs on the outside; stamens and/or style well exserted from the flower, species often heterostylous ...... *Nivenia* (p. 105)
2'  Flowers green to blackish with the tepals yellow on the reverse; tepals remaining closed during flowering, densely velvety outside; stamens included in the flower .................
.................................... *Witsenia* (p. 110)

*Nivenia* Ventenat (1808, 5: no. 1)

Plates 10–14; Figure 15

TYPE: *Nivenia corymbosa* (Ker Gawler) Baker

ETYMOLOGY: named for James Niven, Scottish botanist employed in the late 18th and early 19th centuries to collect plants in southern Africa; Niven was one of the first people to collect the genus and was responsible for the introduction of *Nivenia* into the British Isles and thence to western Europe

REVISIONARY ACCOUNTS: Weimarck (1940b), Goldblatt (1993a: 51–99); see also Goldblatt and Manning (1997c), Manning and Goldblatt (2007)

Evergreen shrubs or subshrubs, sometimes forming cushion-like tufts, with a woody underground caudex. STEMS few to many, upright or inclined, compressed, becoming rounded below, brittle and woody (with secondary growth), marked with leaf scars, the main axes simple, branched, or bearing spur shoots. LEAVES sword-shaped, crowded apically, in a two-ranked fan; leaf margins with subepidermal fiber strands. INFLORESCENCE usually compound, composed of paired (binate) rhipidial units, these two- or one-flowered; synflorescence either in racemose or corymbose arrangement, occasionally inflorescence a single binate rhipidium; SPATHES leathery to more or less dry, lanceolate to ovate-truncate, long or short; floral bracts usually longer than the spathes, membranous to dry, brown or silvery, smooth or wrinkled. FLOWERS sessile, radially symmetric, salver-shaped, pale to deep blue, often pale in the tube, some species heterostylous, plants then either with long style and short stamens (pin morph) or long stamens and short styles (thrum morph), unscented, containing small amounts of nectar from septal nectaries; PERIANTH TUBE well developed, cylindric, short to long; TEPALS subequal, lanceolate to ovate, spreading or shallowly cupped. STAMENS erect, in some species dimorphic and then either short and barely exserted from the tube (pin flowers) or well exserted (thrum flowers); FILAMENTS, one shorter than the others and included in the tube in one species; ANTHERS oblong, submedially fixed, sometimes blue. OVARY globose, locules usually with two ovules, up to six ovules in one species; STYLE filiform, dividing into slender, recurved branches or shortly three-notched, in dimorphic species reaching to just below the mouth of the tube (thrum flowers) or well exserted (pin flowers). CAPSULES ellipsoid, more or less woody, with the central axis separating from the septa; SEEDS tangentially compressed and shield-shaped, one, occasionally two, per locule, as many as six in *Nivenia levynsiae*, the surface irregularly sculpted, the testa often partly exfoliated. BASIC CHROMOSOME NUMBER $x = 16$. Species 11, restricted to the southwestern Cape, South Africa, on rocky sandstone soils and rock outcrops in fynbos vegetation, from near sea level to 1,500 m.

Ranging from tall shrubs up to 2 m high to low cushion plants only 15–20 cm tall, all *Nivenia* species are evergreen, woody-stemmed plants with blue flowers, usually of a very intense hue. The flowers, usually salver-shaped, with a slender cylindric tube and horizontally spreading tepals, are borne in binate rhipidial units that have either two or, by reduction, only one flower in each binate unit. The binate rhipidia are, however, usually arranged in a compound structure (a synflorescence), either a branched racemose panicle, the apparent ancestral condition, or in flat-topped panicles, sometimes with more than 120 flowers per synflorescence (Goldblatt 1993a). Only *N. fruticosa* has an inflorescence consisting of just a single binate rhipidium. *Nivenia levynsiae* is unusual in having a cupped perianth and a short perianth tube, and the synflorescence is reduced to just one or two binate rhipidia per branch.

Unusual in the Iridaceae, seven of the 11 species of *Nivenia* are heterostylous, and individual plants produce flowers with either short or long styles and correspondingly long or short stamens. In short-styled individuals the style reaches the mouth of

**Figure 15.** *Nivenia stokoei* with capsules (two at center left) (×1), bracts (three at center right: floral bract, left, and inner and outer spathes, right; ×1.5), detail of stigma (upper left, ×10), and seed (lower left, ×8), (lower right) *N. parviflora* flowering branch and half-flowers of short- (above) and long-styled (below) morphs (×1.2).

the tube or is shortly exserted, and the filaments are long so that the anthers are held well above the style apex. The opposite holds for the long-styled morph, which has an elongate style that is well exserted from the tube and short filaments, the result being that the anthers lie close to the mouth of the tube. The function of heterostyly is to promote outcrossing, thus maintaining genetic diversity. Morphological heterostyly is usually accompanied by genetic incompatibility between members of the same style morphs, but the presence of genetic incompatibility has not been confirmed for *Nivenia.*

Like the other woody genera, *Nivenia* has anthers with unusual endothecium cells in the anther—the cells have U-shaped thickenings joined together on the inner periclinal walls (Manning and Goldblatt 1990).

Seeds of *Nivenia* are unusual in the Iridaceae in their tangentially compressed, shield shape and in having a transparent testa and an undulate tegmen that gives the seed surface a roughly wrinkled appearance. Because of the differential growth of the tegmen, some cells of the testa become exfoliated during seed maturation. Most species of the genus have just one seed per locule of the capsule, and it is rare for more than one locule per capsule to have a mature seed.

*Nivenia* is closely related to the two other shrubby Cape genera, *Klattia* and *Witsenia*, which have the same growth form, capsule morphology, similar tangentially compressed, shield-shaped seeds, and basic chromosome number $x = 16$. The stems are truly woody and quite brittle, and exhibit the modified type of secondary growth characteristic of those monocots that have secondary growth. Curiously, the stems are compressed and elliptic in transverse section when young but become rounded with age due to differential growth of the cambium layer. The woody stems arise from a woody underground caudex, a rootstock that is remarkably resistant to fire. New stems regenerate from this base after being burned in the frequent fires that occur in the Cape mountains where they grow. Vegetatively, *Nivenia* is distinctive among the shrubby genera in having the sword-shaped leaves rather crowded at the branch tips, thus forming small fans. The leaf anatomy shows a strand of fibers below the marginal epidermis, an ancestral feature in the Iridaceae, and an unusual feature, the presence of scattered strands of fibrous tissue in the leaf tissue.

Apart from the incontestably close relationships of *Nivenia* to *Klattia* and *Witsenia*, the genus shows similarities to the Australasian *Patersonia* (Manning and Goldblatt 1990, Goldblatt 1993a), which also has a woody caudex, similar (but not identical) U-shaped anther endothecial thickenings, and the same leaf margin anatomy. Evidence from four plastic DNA regions shows *Nivenia* to be sister to the remaining two woody genera; these three together form a clade that is sister to subfamily Crocoideae.

The pollination biology of *Nivenia* shows unexpected diversity for so small a genus. The shorter-tubed species are pollinated primarily by *Amegilla* bees (Apidae) with tongues c. 10 mm long. In contrast, the several long-tubed species are pollinated by long-proboscid flies of the genus *Prosoeca* (Nemestrinidae) with prosboces exceeding 20 mm (Goldblatt and Bernhardt 1990). The reward in both cases is nectar, small quantities of which are secreted into the base of the perianth tube of all *Nivenia* species. The nectar is produced from septal nectaries that open into the perianth tube at the apex of the ovary, thus at the base of the style. Heterostyly in *Nivenia* functions simply by the differential placement of pollen on the bodies of visiting insects, either on the frons (for long-styled morphs) or on the lower thorax and abdomen (short-style morphs). Pollen is thus positioned to be placed on the stigmas of the complementary style morph when the insect visits other flowers.

While largely favoring open rocky slopes, two species, *Nivenia corymbosa* and *N. dispar,* occur in riverine bush or forest margins not far from perennial streams, and *N. parviflora* and *N. levynsiae* grow in rock crevices rather than in open ground. The last, as well as *N. fruticosa,* are cushion plants that form low, rounded tufts.

*Klattia* Baker (1877: 109)
Plates 15–16; Figure 16
TYPE: *Klattia partita* Ker Gawler ex Baker
ETYMOLOGY: the name celebrates the 19th century German botanist Friedrich Wilhelm Klatt, who made a life-long study of the Iridaceae
REVISIONARY ACCOUNT: Goldblatt (1993a: 99–117)

Evergreen shrubs with a woody underground caudex. LEAVES sword-shaped, crowded apically, and forming a two-ranked fan, the upper leaves below the inflorescences broad and pale green or dark red. STEMS upright or inclined, few to many, compressed, becoming rounded below, brittle and woody (with secondary growth), marked with leaf scars, the main axes simple or few branched. INFLORESCENCE compound, composed of several two-flowered binate rhipidia crowded at the stem apex, enclosed below by enlarged leaves, individual binate rhipidia subtended by short bracts; spathes and floral bracts membranous, the bracts two-keeled, shorter than the spathes. FLOWERS radially symmetric, sessile, red, yellow, or purplish black, with pale claws, unscented, with nectar produced from septal nectaries; PERIANTH TUBE cylindric, short, filled to overflowing with nectar; TEPALS linear-spathulate, much exceeding the tube, with linear claws and more or less spoon-shaped limbs. STAMENS free; FILAMENTS flattened below, filiform above; ANTHERS linear, subbasifixed, the connective pouched below around the filament apex, split-

ting longitudinally. OVARY globose, domed above the insertion of the tepals, enclosing enlarged septal nectaries, locules with two ovules; STYLE filiform, reaching to just below or just beyond the tepal apices, shortly three-notched apically. CAPSULES ellipsoid, more or less woody, with the central axis separating from the septa; SEEDS tangentially compressed and shield-shaped, one per locule, smooth, the surface cells plane, elongated. BASIC CHROMOSOME NUMBER $x = 16$. Species three, South Africa, local in the mountains of the winter-rainfall zone in the southwest, on rocky sandstone slopes.

*Klattia* species are moderate-sized woody shrubs of the same general appearance as the better known genus *Nivenia* except that the leaves are larger and the terminal leaves form enlarged, highly colored, sheathing bracts enclosing the flowers. Both the woody stems, elliptic in transverse section when young and becoming round with age, and the fan-like cluster of leaves at the stem apices are exactly like *Nivenia*. Like *Nivenia, Klattia* species have small ovoid capsules containing tangentially flattened seeds. The inflorescence and the flowers are, however, very different. The individual inflorescences of *Klattia* are two-flowered binate rhipidia, but the flowers are grouped into a compound head of several binate rhipidial units. The flowers themselves have a fairly short perianth tube and extremely long, linear-spathulate tepals that are spooned near the tips. Each flower is enclosed in short membranous bracts, while the binate rhipidia are subtended by larger leafy spathes, and the entire flowering head is tightly enveloped in enlarged, colored leaves. A flowering branch thus resembles a large paintbrush and, indeed this type of inflorescence is referred to as a brush type by pollination biologists. The leaves clasping the inflorescences are yellow in *K. flava,* pale greenish cream in *K. partita,* and bright red in *K. stokoei,* and evidently advertise the flowers to pollinators from a distance.

**Figure 16.** *Klattia stokoei* (×1) with (bottom left) flower and bracts (outer, left, and inner, right) (×1), (center left) stigma (×20), (upper right) anther (×5), (lower right) capsule (×1), and seed (inner and outer surfaces, ×4).

Together with the other woody Iridaceae, *Nivenia* and *Witsenia*, *Klattia* forms a well-supported clade sister to subfamily Crocoideae. *Klattia* and *Witsenia*, both of which have unusual apically notched styles, are believed to be immediately allied, thus comprising a clade sister to *Nivenia*.

*Klattia* flowers are adapted for pollination by sunbirds, and we have seen two common sunbirds, the malachite and orange-breasted sunbirds, actively visiting *Klattia* species. The reward for visiting sunbirds is nectar, which the flowers of *Klattia* species produce in ample quantities. The nectar has a low sugar concentration (Goldblatt 1993a), a feature typical of bird-pollinated flowers. The nectar sugars also conform to a common pattern in plants pollinated by sunbirds in Africa: they have exclusively pentose sugars, fructose and glucose, a marked difference from the nectar of insect-pollinated *Nivenia* and most members of subfamily Crocoideae, which have sucrose-rich nectar and often very low quantities of fructose and glucose. As in *Nivenia*, nectar is produced in septal nectaries and is secreted into the perianth tube through pores at the base of the style. The septal nectaries are very large in *Klattia* species so that the upper part of the ovary is swollen and protrudes into the base of the floral tube. The enlarged ovary may be related to the need for the production of large quantities of nectar. The amount of nectar is so large that it fills the perianth tubes of individual flowers and often spills into the space formed by the sheathing leaves, excess nectar sometimes leaking out between these upper leaves and dripping down the stems below the flower heads.

Like the other woody genera, *Klattia* species occur on rocky sandstone mountain slopes in the Cape region of South Africa. Plants favor slightly wetter sites in this area of predominantly winter rainfall. The entire range of *Klattia* extends from the Bain's Kloof Mountains and the Cape Peninsula in the west to the Langeberg near Riversdale in the east, a distance of little more than 200 km. The single record from the Cape Peninsula has never been confirmed, and the genus may be extinct there. The altitudinal range of *Klattia* is generally 250–1,200 m but somewhat lower along the southern coast east of Cape Town.

## *Witsenia* Thunberg (1782: 33)

Plate 17; Figure 17

TYPE: *Witsenia maura* (Linnaeus) Thunberg
ETYMOLOGY: named after Nicholas Witsen, counselor to the Chief Magistrate of Amsterdam and a patron of botany; Witsen financed the botanist Carl Peter Thunberg's travels to South Africa and Japan and was rewarded in this commemoration
REVISIONARY ACCOUNT: Goldblatt (1993a: 117–126)

Evergreen shrub with a woody caudex. LEAVES sword-shaped, crowded apically, in two ranks. STEMS upright or inclined, compressed, becoming rounded below, brittle and woody (with secondary growth), marked with leaf scars, the main axes simple, sparsely branched. INFLORESCENCE compound, the upper lateral branches short, terminating in shortly stalked binate rhipidia, subtended by large green bracts, collectively forming a pseudopanicle; binate rhipidia each two-flowered, spathes large, pale green, leathery, floral bracts membranous, shorter than the spathes. FLOWERS radially symmetric, sessile, long-lived, tubular, greenish and black with the upper half of the tepals yellow outside, tepals remaining erect throughout flowering, unscented, with nectar produced from septal nectaries; PERIANTH TUBE elongate, widely cylindric; TEPALS obscurely clawed, the reverse of the limbs velvety hairy. STAMENS free, enclosed in the flower; FILAMENTS inserted at the mouth of the tube, flattened, reaching to about the middle

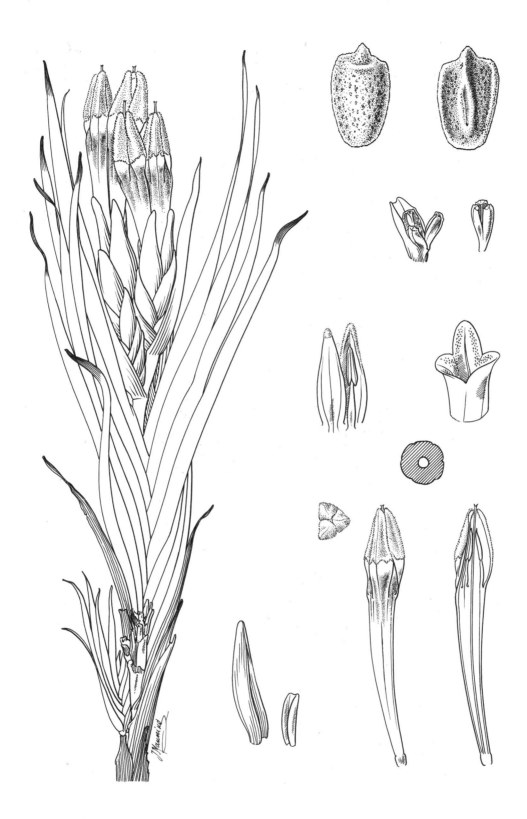

**Figure 17.** *Witsenia maura* with (lower right, left to right) flower (top view), side view, and half-flower, (bottom) bracts (outer, left, and inner, right (×1), (right, top to bottom) seed (inner and outer surfaces, ×4), capsules (×1), detail of tepals and stamen (left, ×2), and stigma (right, ×20; transection of style shaded).

of the tepal limbs; ANTHERS oblong, pseudobasifixed, the connective pouched below around the filament apex, splitting longitudinally. OVARY globose, domed above the insertion of the tepals, enclosing enlarged septal nectaries, locules with two ovules; STYLE filiform, shortly exserted from the flower, shortly three-notched apically. CAPSULES narrowly ovoid, more or less woody, with the central axis separating from the septa; SEEDS tangentially compressed and shield-shaped, one per locule, smooth, the surface granulate, the testa often partially exfoliated. BASIC CHROMOSOME NUMBER $x = 16$. Species only *Witsenia maura*, South Africa, along the southern coast from the Cape Peninsula in the west to the Langeberg near Swellendam in the east, favoring seeps and marshes in peaty sandstone soil from near sea level to elevations of over 1,200 m.

Growing from a sturdy underground caudex, plants produce several fairly slender stems that ultimately reach a height of up to 3 m as they compete for light among dense, shrubby vegetation. Plants resprout readily after fire and regrow rapidly from the rootstock. The stems are woody and have anomalous secondary growth typical of the monocots that produce secondary wood. As in the two other woody genera, *Klattia* and *Nivenia,* the stems are elliptic in section when young, later becoming rounded through the differential growth of the cambium. Also like *Klattia* and *Nivenia,* the leaves are grouped along the upper part of the stems in a more or less fan-like fashion. The leaves have strands of sclerenchyma below the marginal epidermis and scattered strands of sclerenchyma in the mesophyll, also conforming in these features to the pattern in *Klattia* and *Nivenia.*

The flowers are borne on closely branched, compound panicles, and, as in the other woody genera, the individual inflorescences are two-flowered binate rhipidia. The long-lasting flowers remain on the stems after fading, and the paired nature of the individual flower clusters is obvious for weeks after they have opened. The flowers are tubular, and the fairly short tepals remain closed over the top of the tube throughout flowering. The tepals are fairly firm in texture, and access to all but the strongest flower visitors is prevented. The tepals are unusual in the Iridaceae in having a dense velvety outer surface, providing the yellow tepal color. The perianth tube is deep green grading to almost black. When the flowers are receptive, the long style emerges from between the tips of the contiguous tepals and the minute stigmatic lobes diverge. The capsules and general seed shape is exactly like that in *Klattia* and *Nivenia.* The seed surface is, however, distinctive, the epidermal cells of the seed coat being transparent and partially exfoliated. *Witsenia* appears fairly unspecialized in its overall morphology, particularly in the branched, panicle-like compound inflorescence, but the large leathery bracts sheathing the flowers, the long perianth tube, and the closed tepals are highly specialized features. Pollen of *Witsenia* is unusual—the monosulcate grains with reticulate exine have large ball-like blobs on the surface, called gemmules, unique among the woody genera.

Within the tightly knit group of woody genera, *Witsenia* appears to be most closely related to *Klattia* (Goldblatt 1993a), the two together forming a clade sister to *Nivenia.* Both *Klattia* and *Witsenia* have unusual, apically notched styles, flattened filaments, and anthers attached to the filaments by a pouch-like pocket at the base of the anther connective. The long-tubed flowers produce large quantities of nectar and are adapted for bird pollination. The malachite sunbird, *Nectarinia famosa,* has been recorded visiting flowers, presumably in search of nectar. The nectar volume, up to 900 microliters per flower, is remarkable. The nectar is composed almost solely of the pentose sugars fructose and glucose, as is that of closely related *Klattia,* a feature consistent with pollination by sunbirds.

**Plate 1.** The red-flowered form of *Isophysis tasmanica* growing in heathland in western Tasmania (photo J. Bruhl).

**Plate 2.** *Patersonia occidentalis,* a native of Western Australia.

**Plate 3.** *Geosiris* flowering in leaf litter in eastern Madagascar (photo B. Cooke and D. Du Puy).

**Plate 4.** Flowering after a wildfire at Highlands, near Caledon, South Africa, *Aristea bakeri* makes a brilliant display of blue, contrasting with orange-flowered *Watsonia schlechteri.*

**Plate 5.** The extremely rare *Aristea bicolor* has unusual transparent windows at the base of the tepals, beetle marks that are believed to attract hopliine beetles, their pollinators.

**Plate 6.** *Aristea capitata* has the typical deep blue flowers of the genus but borne on crowded compound inflorescences.

**Plate 7.** The highly branched *Aristea inaequalis* of western South Africa has the typical blue flowers of the genus but is unique in having stamens of unequal length, one longer than the other two.

**Plate 8.** The only species of *Aristea* that produces nectar, *A. spiralis* is adapted for pollination by long-proboscid flies. Plants flower well only after wildfires, as here on Lion's Head in Cape Town, South Africa.

**Plate 9.** *Aristea torulosa,* a widespread southeastern African species of montane grassland, extends from coastal South Africa to Tanzania.

**Plate 10.** The shrubby *Nivenia inaequalis* in full flower in the Rooiberg in the Little Karoo, South Africa.

**Plate 11.** The woody shrublet *Nivenia levynsiae* is an evergreen cushion plant restricted to outcrops of sandstone rocks in the mountains near Betty's Bay, South Africa.

**Plate 12.** *Nivenia parviflora,* native to the Little Swartberg in southern South Africa, is a pollination generalist, visited by bees, short-proboscid flies, and butterflies, here with *Vanessa cardui* foraging for nectar

**Plate 13.** Mounds of *Nivenia stokoei* bushes in fynbos vegetation at Highlands, near Caledon, South Africa.

**Plate 14.** With the largest flowers in the genus, *Nivenia stokoei* is striking in bloom in late summer, the hottest time of the year in western South Africa.

**Plate 15.** *Klattia partita,* with nearly black flowers, in the Langeberg of South Africa.

**Plate 16.** Red bracts and flowers characterize sunbird-pollinated *Klattia stokoei,* a narrow endemic of the mountains east of Cape Town, South Africa.

**Plate 17.** *Witsenia maura,* a shrub of marshy habitats, has yellow, black, and green flowers.

**Plate 18.** With 24 species, *Tritoniopsis* is a small genus of the Cape region of South Africa. Red- and orange-flowered *T. antholyza* favors sunny stony slopes.

**Plate 19.** The brilliant scarlet flowers of *Tritoniopsis burchellii* have a bimodal pollination system that includes sunbirds and the satyrid butterfly *Aeropetes tulbaghia*.

**Plate 20.** *Tritoniopsis caffra,* native to the southern coast of South Africa, flowering well after a bushfire the previous summer.

**Plate 21.** In contrast to the red-flowered species of the genus that are pollinated by butterflies and sunbirds, *Tritoniopsis lata* has flowers with a short perianth tube and is attractive to large bees.

**Plate 22.** *Tritoniopsis nervosa,* with its white, richly scented flowers, is a moth-pollinated species; the flowers remain open and scented at night.

**Plate 23.** *Tritoniopsis parviflora,* with its bizarrely colored yellow and brown flowers, is the only African species of Iridaceae that produces floral oils to attract oil-collecting bees, but it also produces sugary nectar as a backup pollination strategy when oil-collecting bees fail to visit.

**Plate 24.** The numerous pink flowers borne on branched stems make *Tritoniopsis ramosa* of South Africa's Western Cape a charming plant. Like most other members of this genus, it blooms in summer in this area of winter rainfall and dry, hot summers.

Plate 25. The genus *Cyanixia*, with just one species, *C. socotrana*, is restricted to the Indian Ocean island of Socotra; note the pleated leaf blades (photo W. Wranik).

Plate 27. The common Cape species *Lapeirousia corymbosa* has striking blue flowers with central white markings.

Plate 26. Western South African *Lapeirousia anceps*, a plant of sandy habitats, has one of the longest floral tubes of any Iridaceae and is adapted for long-proboscid fly pollination.

Plate 28. *Lapeirousia fabricii* is another western southern African species with long-tubed flowers, also adapted for pollination by long-proboscid flies.

Plate 29. *Lapeirousia jacquinii*, an early-flowering species of western South Africa.

**Plate 30.** The acaulescent *Lapeirousia montana* is a local endemic of the semiarid western Karoo of South Africa.

**Plate 31.** *Lapeirousia oreogena* has brilliant, deep violet flowers with contrasting white triangular markings. It is a wonderful subject for container culture.

**Plate 32.** *Lapeirousia silenoides*, native to Namaqualand in western South Africa, favors rock crevices, where its tasty corms are safe from hungry porcupines and baboons.

**Plate 33.** The long-tubed flowers of *Lapeirousia silenoides* are avidly visited by the long-proboscid fly *Prosoeca peringueyi*, one of the few insects able to reach the sugar-rich nectar held deep within the flower.

**Plate 34.** *Lapeirousia verecunda*, of clay slopes in Namaqualand, South Africa, is highly desirable for the garden.

**Plate 35.** Restricted to the sandstone mountains east of Cape Town, South Africa, *Pillansia templemannii* flowers only after bushfires and then appears in mass on the bare slopes.

**Plate 36.** The brilliant orange flowers of *Pillansia templemannii* are borne on crowded, highly branched flowering stems, very different from the simple spikes of its relatives.

**Plate 39.** The minute blue flowers of *Micranthus junceus* are borne in a congested, two-ranked spike and despite their small size are visited by a surprising array of insects, all competing for a drop of nectar.

**Plate 37.** With its purple flowers, *Thereianthus minutus* makes a charming picture on the seeps and stream banks where it grows in the mountains of southwestern South Africa.

**Plate 38.** *Thereianthus spicatus* is one of the more common species of this small genus of the Cape region of South Africa.

**Plate 40.** *Watsonia angusta,* one of several sunbird-pollinated species of this southern African genus, here with a pair of orange-breasted sunbirds perched on a spike.

Plate 41. Named in error for the Isle de Bourbon, now Mauritius, *Watsonia borbonica* is actually native to the southwestern corner of South Africa. Like many plants from this part of the world, it flowers best after a bushfire and then can cover the hill slopes with pink blooms.

Plate 43. Native to eastern coast of South Africa, *Watsonia densiflora* is a summer-blooming plant of open grasslands.

Plate 42. *Watsonia coccinea* is a diminutive species of this genus of mostly tall plants.

Plate 44. *Watsonia latifolia*, so named for it particularly broad leaves, is native to eastern South Africa and Swaziland. The red flowers have the classic form of bird-pollinated Iridaceae.

Plate 45. *Watsonia schlechteri*, a summer-blooming species of the southern African winter-rainfall zone, growing within sight of the Atlantic Ocean among clumps of grass-like Restionaceae (see also Plate 4).

**Plate 46.** *Watsonia strubeniae*, a species of Mpumalanga Province in eastern South Africa, reaches over 1 meter in height in highland grassland.

**Plate 47.** The delicate pink flowers, surrounded at the base by dry, light brown bracts, of *Watsonia strubeniae* are borne in masses on the branched stems and make the species a very desirable garden subject.

**Plate 48.** Another bird-pollinated species of the genus, *Watsonia tabularis* is a narrow endemic, restricted to the Cape Peninsula of South Africa.

**Plate 49.** A genus of more than 260 species, *Gladiolus* displays a marvelous range of flower types, most adapted for specialized pollination systems. *Gladiolus alatus* flowers, although red, which usually signals bird pollination, have short tubes and are pollinated by large bees.

**Plate 50.** One of c. 10 Eurasian species of *Gladiolus*, *G. atroviolaceus*, here in Armenia, has unusual flowers with five tepals forming a prominent lower lip; the small dorsal tepal is relatively inconspicuous (photo M. Tomiyama).

**Plate 51.** *Gladiolus brachyphyllus* is a dry-country species, restricted to lowland bushveld in eastern southern Africa.

**Plate 52.** *Gladiolus carinatus,* renowned for the wonderful scent of its blue or yellow flowers, is a favored cut flower in the countryside around Cape Town, South Africa—one flowering stalk will fill a house with a rich, violet-like odor.

**Plate 53.** The New Year lily of the mountains of the Cape region of South Africa, *Gladiolus cardinalis* flowers in December and January, at the height of the dry season. The species is restricted to damp cliffs and banks of perennial streams and waterfalls.

**Plate 55.** The rare *Gladiolus cataractarum* is restricted to cliffs in the Drakensberg in Mpumalanga Province, South Africa.

**Plate 54.** *Gladiolus carneus,* the painted lady, is a native of western South Africa, one of the first species to be used in hybridization experiments in Great Britain to produce a hardy garden gladiolus.

**Plate 56.** Very different from typical gladiolus, *Gladiolus cunonius* has flowers modified for sunbird pollination, hence the bright red color and the well-exserted anthers, which are held for protection from moisture under the spoon-shaped dorsal tepal.

**Plate 57.** Occurring across Africa from the Eastern Cape to Ethiopia and in the Arabian Peninsula, *Gladiolus dalenii* has the widest range of any member of the genus. Flowers vary from red with yellow markings to brown, yellow, and even pale green.

**Plate 58.** Variable in flower color, the marshland species *Gladiolus ecklonii* typically has tepals spotted a dark color on a red, pink, or cream background. The red-flowered form here, from Mpumalanga Province in South Africa, is particularly attractive.

**Plate 59.** Photographed in the fading sunlight, flowers of moth-pollinated *Gladiolus guthriei*, native to western South Africa, glow as the light shines through them.

**Plate 60.** The large pink flowers of *Gladiolus mortonius*, native to the coast and near interior of southeastern South Africa, are adapted for pollination by long-proboscid flies, hence its elongate perianth tube.

**Plate 62.** The green-flowered *Gladiolus pardalinus* flowers in spring, before the single long, hairy leaf is produced. The contrasting brown speckled markings recall the spotting on a leopard's coat, hence the specific epithet, *pardalinus*.

**Plate 62.** *Gladiolus quadrangulus* is closely related to *G. carinatus* (Plate 52) but differs from that and most other species of the genus in its radially symmetric flowers. The species is now seriously endangered as the wetland habitats close to Cape Town, South Africa, are drained for urban development.

**Plate 64.** One of a handful of Eurasian species of *Gladiolus*, *G. italicus*, here growing near Naples, Italy, used to be a common weed in wheat fields in southern Europe. The species is becoming less common today as modern agricultural practices eliminate weeds (photo M. Tomiyama).

**Plate 63.** Typical of bee-pollinated species of the genus, *Gladiolus rufomarginatus* is a local endemic of dry bushveld in Mpumalanga Province, South Africa, here with a pollinating insect, a large *Amegilla* bee.

**Plate 65.** *Gladiolus rhodanthus* is an example of an extreme local endemic—it is confined to cliffs on a few high mountains south of Worcester, South Africa.

**Plate 66.** Perhaps most unlike the typical *Gladiolus*, the gray-blue flowers of *G. stellatus*, of southern South Africa, are small and radially symmetric. A rich, *Freesia*-like scent more than makes up for its drab appearance.

**Plate 67.** Common in the dry interior of the southern African winter-rainfall zone, *Gladiolus venustus* is a charming garden or container subject and has deliciously scented blooms.

**Plate 68.** Perhaps the most wonderfully scented of all the species of the genus, *Gladiolus watermeyeri* has creamy green flowers marked with purple and yellow that are difficult to spot among the surrounding vegetation. The amazing floral scent usually signals its presence before the plants can be located.

**Plate 69.** *Melasphaerula ramosa*, so named for its highly branched flowering stems, producing a mass of tiny flowers, occurs on cool slopes throughout the southern African winter-rainfall zone.

**Plate 70.** Although deserving of horticultural attention, the individual flowers of *Melasphaerula ramosa* are themselves small and dull-colored, and are probably adapted for pollination by tiny flies.

**Plate 71.** The nodding, radially symmetric flowers of *Crocosmia aurea* are specialized in the genus and adapted for pollination by large butterflies.

**Plate 72.** Surprisingly, *Crocosmia aurea* is a plant of bush and forest habitats, very different from places that most species of Crocoideae prefer.

**Plate 74.** Native to the high Drakensberg of Lesotho and adjacent parts of South Africa, *Crocosmia pearsei* is seldom common and grows as scattered individuals rather than in the large colonies of its close relative, *C. paniculata.*

**Plate 73.** One of the parents of the *Crocosmia* cultivar 'Lucifer', *C. paniculata* is a plant of high-elevation grassland and has bright red or orange flowers.

**Plate 75.** The dusty pink flowers of *Devia xeromorpha,* the only species of this odd genus of the western Karoo of South Africa, are produced in the hot summer months of November and December.

**Plate 76.** One of the parents of the cultivated *Freesia, F. alba* is a native of sandy soils and rock outcrops on the southern coast of South Africa.

Plate 77. Winter flowering in its wild habitat in the winter-rainfall zone of South Africa, *Freesia caryophyllacea* has perhaps the finest scent of any species of the genus.

Plate 78. The species that contributed the pink color to the gene pool of the cultivated *Freesia, F. corymbosa* occurs in the wild in Eastern Cape Province, South Africa, in pink-, yellow-, or almost white-flowered populations.

Plate 79. *Freesia fucata* is a late-winter-flowering species of clay slopes near Worcester, South Africa.

Plate 80. Very different from the typical *Freesia* in its flowers, *F. grandiflora* is a summer-growing species of southern tropical Africa. The red flowers are completely unscented.

**Plate 81.** A plant whose affinities have long been misunderstood, tropical and southern African *Freesia laxa* has been treated as a species of *Anomatheca* or *Lapeirousia*. The red flowers are thought to be adapted for pollination by butterflies; a subspecies, not known in cultivation, has attractive white and blue flowers.

**Plate 84.** *Radinosiphon lomatensis* is native to the eastern highlands of southern Africa. The long-tubed flowers are pollinated by long-proboscid flies.

**Plate 82.** Largest-flowered species of the genus, *Freesia speciosa,* with its pale and deep yellow flowers, is a desirable garden subject, unfortunately not amenable to cultivation.

**Plate 83.** The dwarf species *Xenoscapa fistulosa* is widespread in winter-rainfall southern Africa and favors cool, south-facing slopes.

**Plate 85.** A true aquatic, *Romulea aquatica* grows in the few muddy seasonal pools found in the rolling clay slopes north of Cape Town, South Africa.

**Plate 86.** *Romulea atrandra* is native to the high escarpment of western and southern South Africa, where freezing temperatures and occasional light snow are common.

**Plate 88.** The red and black flowers of *Romulea monadelpha* are adapted for pollination by furry scarab beetles and closely resemble those of closely related *R. sabulosa* (Plate 91).

**Plate 87.** An unusually fine display of *Romulea cruciata* on a slope near Saldanha Bay, South Africa.

**Plate 89.** *Romulea kamisensis* of central Namaqualand in western South Africa is one of just four species of this genus of more than 90 species that has flowers adapted for long-proboscid fly pollination (photo L. J. Porter).

**Plate 90.** Like a river of vibrant red, *Romulea sabulosa* covers the ground in early spring on the Bokkeveld Escarpment in northwestern South Africa.

**Plate 91.** The black markings in the floral cup in *Romulea sabulosa* flowers signal beetle pollination; on warm days flowers of this plant teem with large, hairy, brown beetles looking for mates.

**Plate 92.** Fairly unusual in the genus, *Romulea leipoldtii* has sweetly scented flowers that complement the large yellow and white booms.

**Plate 93.** Honey-scented *Romulea schlechteri* grows on sandy flats north of Cape Town, South Africa; the species blooms in the wild only after bushfires that occur at irregular intervals.

**Plate 94.** *Romulea syringodeoflora* of the high Roggeveld Plateau in western South Africa is unusual in the genus in having a long, narrow perianth tube and horizontally spreading tepals.

**Plate 95.** Common in the western Karoo of South Africa, *Romulea tortuosa* has sweetly scented yellow flowers that carpet this arid land in early spring.

**Plate 96.** *Afrocrocus unifolius* flowers in late autumn or early winter soon after the first rains have fallen in the high interior of western South Africa.

**Plate 97.** *Syringodea longituba* is typical of this small southern African genus in its stemless growth habit and long-tubed flowers.

**Plate 98.** *Syringodea pulchella* flowers in the autumn in the semiarid Great Karoo, South Africa.

**Plate 99.** A favorite garden *Crocus, C. chrysanthus* is widely cultivated across the northern hemisphere for its bright yellow flowers, which appear at the end of winter.

**Plate 100.** *Crocus graveolens* in full boom in the western Tian Shan, near Tashkent, Uzbekistan (photo M. Tomiyama).

**Plate 101.** White-flowered *Crocus nevadensis* in bloom in early spring in the Sierra Nevada of Spain (photo M. Tomiyama).

**Plate 102.** *Crocus sativus,* with its enlarged orange style and style branches, is the source of saffron.

**Plate 103.** Large-flowered *Crocus vernus* is seen in gardens and parks across Europe and North America, where it is a favorite early spring plant.

**Plate 104.** White-flowered *Crocus sieberi* in bloom on Crete (photo M. Tomiyama).

**Plate 105.** The Turkish *Crocus speciosus* is unusual in the genus in its multifid style (photo M. Tomiyama).

Plate 106. With cheerful, pink flowers, *Geissorhiza bonaspei*, a narrow endemic, is found only on the Cape Peninsula, South Africa.

Plate 108. The long-tubed flowers of the western South African *Geissorhiza exscapa* are pollinated by long-proboscid flies.

Plate 107. *Geissorhiza corrugata*, named for its tightly wavy leaves, carpets the ground for miles in the semiarid western Karoo of South Africa in early spring.

Plate 109. Favoring sheltered places, *Geissorhiza inaequalis* is often found in seasonally moist ground below dolerite boulders in South Africa's western Karoo.

**Plate 110.** Few Iridaceae can match the brilliant scarlet flowers of the local race of *Geissorhiza inflexa* from the Tulbagh Valley in South Africa; elsewhere, the flowers of this species are pink or white.

**Plate 111.** The tiny *Geissorhiza ornithogaloides* has bright yellow blooms.

**Plate 112.** Restricted to the mountain slopes near Ceres, South Africa, *Geissorhiza silenoides* makes a brilliant display in the years following bushfires.

**Plate 113.** Known locally as "wine cups" in western South Africa, flowers of *Geissorhiza radians* are deep blue with a glistening red center edged with a white band.

**Plate 114.** Remarkable even for this genus of brilliantly colored flowers, *Geissorhiza splendidissima* of the western Karoo, South Africa, has glistening blue blooms with a dark central eye, yellow throat, and rich red-brown pollen.

**Plate 116.** Many species of *Hesperantha* have white flowers that remain closed during the day and only open in the later afternoon, when they produce a rich sweet scent; *H. cucullata* of the western Karoo, South Africa, seen here near sunset, is typical of the of these species.

**Plate 115.** The nodding white flowers of *Hesperantha bachmannii* open in late afternoon and remain open at night when their pollinators, settling moths, attracted by a rich scent and pale color, visit them to feed on nectar.

**Plate 117.** Close up, flowers of *Hesperantha cucullata* can be seen to have red pigmentation on the outside of the tepals, believed to function as camouflage, making them less visible to grazing animals when closed, as they are during most of the daylight hours.

**Plate 118.** Long known as the only species of the genus *Schizostylis*, *Hesperantha coccinea* is a semiaquatic plant of mountain steams in eastern southern Africa.

**Plate 119.** The common western South African *Hesperantha falcata* has white- and yellow-flowered races; blooms of the latter are open during the day and closed at night.

**Plate 120.** An unusual member of this African genus, *Hesperantha humilis* is a stemless species that produces its flowers in the winter months in high country in western South Africa.

**Plate 121.** The western South African *Hesperantha luticola*, a plant of shallow seasonal pools, has unscented white flowers with a dark central eye; the flowers are open during the day and are pollinated by bees.

**Plate 122.** Pink-flowered *Hesperantha pauciflora* of northwestern South Africa in full bloom.

**Plate 123.** The high Drakensberg species *Hesperantha scopulosa*, of cliffs and rock outcrops, is typical of the eastern southern African members of the genus in its pink flowers that open during the day and close at night.

**Plate 124.** *Hesperantha sufflava*, native to the rolling hills north of Cape Town, South Africa, prime wheat country, is reduced to a few small colonies on the outskirts of the town of Malmesbury.

**Plate 125.** *Hesperantha vaginata* of the Calvinia district in South Africa is one of a few beetle-pollinated members of this genus—the dark brown markings in the flowers mimic the beetles that pollinate them.

**Plate 126.** Exceedingly rare, *Babiana carminea* is known from a few limestone outcrops in the arid desert of southern Namaqualand in western South Africa—the stemless plants grow in rock crevices in virtually no soil.

**Plate 127.** Tall *Babiana ecklonii* favors rocky sandstone outcrops, where its corms are secure from predation. The species is a very desirable garden plant.

**Plate 128.** Western South African *Babiana melanops,* named for the dark central eye, has radially symmetric flowers adapted for pollination by scarab beetles.

**Plate 129.** One of several species of the genus with radially symmetric flowers, *Babiana papyracea* is a narrow endemic of the Bokkeveld Escarpment in northwestern South Africa.

**Plate 130.** Found in sandy coastal habitats in western South Africa, *Babiana ringens* has an unusual adaptation for a sunbird-pollinated plant—the flowering stem is modified into a sterile perch, and the flowers are borne on short branches at the stem base.

**Plate 131.** *Babiana rubrocyanea* grows in the same places as *Geissorhiza radians* (Plate 113), and its similarly colored flowers are a striking example of convergent evolution.

**Plate 132.** *Babiana sambucina,* a widespread species of winter-rainfall South Africa, has large, blue-gray to violet flowers marked with white, borne at ground level. The plant is named for its wonderful scent, said to be reminiscent of flowers of the European elderberry (the genus *Sambucus*).

**Plate 133.** The western South African *Babiana sinuata* favors dry, stony slopes and is unique in having the anthers joined together.

Plate 134. Western South African *Babiana spiralis*, named for its loosely spiraled leaves, grows in sandy ground in years places that have less than 25 cm of rain annually.

Plate 135. Bird-pollinated *Babiana thunbergii*, a species of the western southern African seashore, can reach up to 1 meter high when growing in bush.

Plate 136. Flowering in early winter when little plant collecting is undertaken, *Babiana torta* was for many years thought to be a rare species but is now known to be widespread in northwestern South Africa.

Plate 137. The long-tubed, white flowers of *Babiana tubulosa,* a species of coastal dunes in western South Africa, are adapted for pollination by long-proboscid flies.

Plate 138. One of the few yellow-flowered species of the genus, *Babiana vanzijliae* is restricted to the Bokkeveld Escarpment in northwestern South Africa.

**Plate 139.** Native to the Tulbagh Valley in western South Africa, *Babiana villosa* has deep red flowers and dark stamens, the latter beetle marks, believed to attract their pollinators, dark-colored hairy beetles.

**Plate 140.** The red, long-tubed flowers of *Chasmanthe* signal bird pollination; *C. aethiopica* of coastal bush and forest also has fleshy orange seeds, attractive to fruit-eating birds that disperse the seeds.

**Plate 141.** Widespread across winter-rainfall parts of South Africa, *Chasmanthe floribunda* has scarlet flowers, produced in the southern autumn.

**Plate 142.** A favorite of herbivorous mole rats that consume their starchy corms, white-flowered *Sparaxis bulbifera* produces numerous small cormlets at the nodes of the stem, a feature for which the plant is named. Too small to attract mole rats, the cormlets ensure survival of the plants.

**Plate 143.** *Sparaxis elegans,* once placed in the genus *Streptanthera* because of its coiled anthers, has populations of white or salmon flowers, with a dark central eye dotted with yellow.

**Plate 144.** A species of southwestern South Africa, *Sparaxis grandiflora* has four subspecies, each with differently colored flowers—subspecies *acutiloba* has bright yellow blooms.

Plate 145. Most unusual in the genus, *Sparaxis grandiflora* subsp. *grandiflora* has rich purple flowers, making it a desirable garden subject.

Plate 146. *Sparaxis tricolor* grows in dense colonies and has striking orange and yellow flowers. The species, known from a few small populations on the Bokkeveld Escarpment in northwestern South Africa, is one of the parents of the hybrid *Sparaxis*, or harlequin flower, grown in gardens.

Plate 148. *Duthieastrum linifolium*, the only species of this South African genus, is a stemless plant with long-tubed, yellow flowers produced in the autumn.

Plate 149. A favorite garden subject, *Tritonia crocata* has a radially symmetric perianth but anthers seemingly pointed in different directions, a feature that gave rise to the generic name, meaning weathervane.

Plate 150. A plant of the most arid part of the western Karoo in South Africa, *Tritonia florentiae* is a stemless plant with bright yellow flowers, unusual for the genus.

**Plate 147.** A common, almost weedy species of western South Africa, *Sparaxis villosa* has small purple and yellow flowers.

**Plate 151.** Like *Tritonia florentiae* (Plate 150), *T. karooica* grows in South Africa's arid western Karoo; the pale orange flowers are so well camouflaged they are more easily located by their strong odor of violets.

**Plate 152.** *Tritonia laxifolia*, a native of Eastern Cape Province, South Africa, has orange flowers typical of this genus of some 28 species.

**Plate 153.** Long-tubed *Tritonia pallida* blooms in the late spring in the Little Karoo in South Africa and can carpet the ground with its white flowers.

**Plate 154.** *Tritonia undulata*, long-known as *T. crispa*, one of several species of the genus pollinated by long-proboscid flies, is restricted to sandy soils in western South Africa.

**Plate 155.** Spring-flowering *Tritonia securigera* makes a fine show in the Little Karoo of South Africa in years when adequate rain falls in this semiarid area (photo L. J. Porter).

**Plate 156.** Close up, the characteristic ax-head-shaped teeth are visible on the lower tepals of *Tritonia securigera* flowers; this feature is found in many but not all species of the genus (photo L. J. Porter).

**Plate 157.** *Ixia acaulis* occurs in the same limestone habitat as *Babiana carminea* (Plate 126) and is the only acaulescent species of this genus of some 67 species.

**Plate 158.** The small pale pink or white flowers of *Ixia divaricata*, from the interior mountains of western South Africa, are pollinated by bees and lack the glamour of the beetle-pollinated species of this genus (photo L. J. Porter).

**Plate 159.** Striking in its white and purple flowers, *Ixia leipoldtii* is known in the wild today from one small population in the middle of a wheat field in the Little Karoo, South Africa.

**Plate 160.** The brown marking in the center of *Ixia maculata* flowers is thought to be a beetle mark, attracting their unusual scarab beetle pollinators.

**Plate 161.** Another beetle-pollinated species of the genus, *Ixia monadelpha*, like *I. maculata* (Plate 160), it is restricted to the southwestern corner of South Africa.

**Plate 162.** Making the best of two worlds, *Ixia tenuifolia* flowers have beetle marks and produce nectar so that their pollination is doubly secured. In the absence of scarabs, nectar-foraging flies and bees will accomplish pollen transfer in the species.

**Plate 163.** *Ixia versicolor,* restricted to the coastal hills and flats east of Cape Town, South Africa, is threatened with extinction as urban development expands with rapid growth of the human population.

**Plate 164.** Flowers of *Ixia viridiflora* are pale green or sometimes aquamarine, but always have a dark central eye, a beetle mark, marking this species as one more beetle-pollinated member of this genus.

**Plate 165.** *Dierama dissimile,* one of many attractive species of this African genus, is native to the southern Drakensberg of South Africa.

**Plate 166.** The large, nodding, white flowers of *Dierama luteoalbum,* endemic to the Midlands of KwaZulu-Natal, South Africa, make the plant a particularly desirable garden subject.

**Plate 167.** Eastern South African *Dierama mobile* shows clearly the fine, almost thread-like branches that bear the flowers, the feature responsible for the common name, hairbells.

**Plate 168.** *Diplarrena moraea,* one of two species of this Australian genus, has small zygomorphic flowers, unique in subfamily Iridoideae.

**Plate 169.** Native to the Transcaucasus, *Iris acutiloba* has the oddly colored flowers of section *Oncocyclus* but distinctive pointed tepals (photo M. Tomiyama).

**Plate 170.** *Iris albomarginata* has distinctive, thickened, white leaf margins in addition to the channeled leaves that are characteristic of the *Juno* irises (subgenus *Scorpiris*) as are the much smaller, reflexed inner tepals (photo M. Tomiyama).

**Plate 171.** *Iris atropurpurea* of Israel and adjacent Gaza has dark maroon flowers, a remarkable color even for section *Oncocyclus* (see Plate 169) (photo M. Tomiyama).

**Plate 172.** Middle Eastern *Iris bismarckiana* shows the strange coloration and patterning of most species of section *Oncocyclus* (photo M. Tomiyama).

Plate 173. *Iris domestica*, better known as *Belamcanda chinensis*, is probably native to northeastern China but has been cultivated for its medicinal value for millennia and has been dispersed across temperate and tropical Asia. Brought into garden cultivation in the West as an ornamental, it is becoming naturalized in North America.

Plate 174. The reason for the common name of *Iris domestica* in North America, blackberry lily, is obvious from the fruiting branch, with black seeds clustered above the valves of the open capsules (photo G. Yatskievych).

Plate 175. The curious coloring of flowers of *Iris elegantissma*, native to Turkey and Armenia, is typical of section *Oncocyclus*. Instead of a bright nectar guide, members of the section have darker marks on the outer tepals. Several species of the section have been found to be pollinated by male bees as they search for a secure place to sleep at night (photo M. Tomiyama).

Plate 176. One of the Louisiana irises (section *Limniris*, series *Hexagonae*), *Iris fulva* has unusual red flowers and is the only *Iris* species adapted for pollination by hummingbirds.

Plate 177. The dwarf *Iris loczyi* (subgenus *Limniris*), native to the high mountains of central Asia, here in the Tian Shan of Kazakhstan, has the narrow leaves of the *I. tenuifolia* group (photo M. Tomiyama).

**Plate 178.** Another species of section *Oncocyclus, Iris mariae,* a rare species of the Negev desert of southern Israel, makes a bright color splash among the sparse desert vegetation (photo M. Tomiyama).

**Plate 179.** *Iris missouriensis* (section *Limniris*), a widespread species of western North America, is shown here in full flower in the Colorado Rockies.

**Plate 180.** *Iris pallida,* with large flowers typical of section *Iris,* is the source of orris root, which has a violet-like perfume. Thought to be native to the eastern Adriatic coast, the species is naturalized in Italy, center of the orris root industry.

**Plate 181.** A wetland species, the Eurasian *Iris pseudacorus* makes a fine additions to the garden but is now a weed in North America.

**Plate 182.** The almost translucent, blue-gray flowers of *Iris regis-uzziae* (subgenus *Scorpiris*), named for the biblical King Uzziah of Judah, is native to southern Israel and Jordan (photo M. Tomiyama).

**Plate 183.** *Iris sibirica* is a well-known and loved garden plant.

**Plate 184.** *Iris tenax* (series *Californicae*), native to western North America, in bloom near Tillamook, Oregon.

**Plate 186.** Pale yellow flowers with dark marks at the base of the outer tepals are characteristic of the southern African *Dietes bicolor,* a plant now widely cultivated in gardens and street plantings. The genus differs from *Iris* mainly in having the tepals free to the base.

**Plate 187.** *Dietes grandiflora* has remarkably *Iris*-like flowers, complete with petaloid style branches bearing terminal crests, but the outer tepals are spreading rather than erect. An attractive garden subject, the flowers of *D. grandiflora* last 3 days, unlike those of its fellow species, which last just a single day.

**Plate 185.** The eastern North American *Iris versicolor* (section *Limniris*) is found in moist habitats from Canada to Texas. The rhizomes have been used medicinally for various diseases.

**Plate 188.** The small southern African genus *Bobartia* has just 15 species, all with similar flowers, with spreading, subequal tepals. The type species, *B. indica,* photographed here on the Cape Peninsula, South Africa, was so named because the first specimens known to science were mistakenly thought to have come from the East Indies.

**Plate 190.** Dull and bizarrely marked flowers mark the genus *Ferraria*. *Ferraria crispa,* of the western coast and interior mountains of South Africa, one of the more common species of this small genus, is often seen on rock outcrops along the coast.

**Plate 191.** Extremely rare *Ferraria ovata* is known from just three populations in Namaqualand in western South Africa. It was discovered in the 1790s by the Royal Botanic Gardens, Kew, plant collector Francis Masson and first placed in the genus *Moraea,* but when rediscovered in 1995 it was found to be an unknown species of *Ferraria*.

**Plate 189.** *Bobartia orientalis,* so named because it is the easternmost species of the genus, is native to the Eastern Cape Province, South Africa.

**Plate 192.** Most *Ferraria* species grow on sandy soils, but *F. schaeferi,* a true desert plant, takes this to the extreme, favoring sand dunes in the Namib Desert of southwestern Namibia and adjacent South Africa. The speckled flowers produce a strange scent that attracts various flies, their pollinators.

**Plate 193.** One of the few colorful species of the genus, *Ferraria uncinata* has blue to purple flowers edged with light brown.

**Plate 194.** *Moraea bella,* a species of central tropical Africa, is a plant of seasonally wet habitats, called dambos.

**Plate 195.** The propeller-like flowers of *Moraea knersvlaktensis* make a splash in the stony desert of the Knersvlakte in western South Africa, famous more for its diverse succulent flora than for its geophytes.

**Plate 196.** The poppy-like flowers of *Moraea insolens,* a species native to low mountain slopes near Caledon, South Africa, is on the verge of extinction.

**Plate 197.** The sticky substance on the branched stems mark *Moraea bituminosa* as a member of subgenus *Visciramosa,* all species of which occur in western South Africa.

**Plate 198.** Members of the *Homeria* group of *Moraea,* like the western South African *M. miniata,* have flowers lacking broad style branches, the stamens and style instead forming a column, just like those of the *Galaxia* group, but they have aerial stems. The white-flowered form of *M. miniata* (the name means orange) is rare and contrasts beautifully with the orange blooms of the daisy, *Gorteria diffusa,* in the background.

**Plate 199.** *Moraea elegans* has wonderfully marked flowers, an extraordinary scent of coconuts, and the reduced style branches that mark is a member of the *Homeria* group of the genus.

**Plate 200.** *Moraea fugacissima* of the *Galaxia* group of the genus grows in low tufts of needle-like leaves and has sweetly scented yellow blooms that last just a single day.

**Plate 201.** The *Iris*-like *Moraea muddii* (subgenus *Grandiflora*) is a species of montane grassland in eastern southern Africa.

**Plate 202.** *Moraea ochroleuca,* another species of the *Homeria* group of the genus, flowers well in the wild in western South Africa but is proving to be a good garden plant. The large flowers, produced in profusion, each last 3 days and have an odd but pleasing scent.

**Plate 203.** *Moraea pritzeliana,* a member of the *Gynandriris* group, is native to northwestern South Africa. The group has a disjunct distribution with several species in southern Africa and two in the Mediterranean Basin and Middle East.

**Plate 204.** *Moraea serpentina,* native to the western coast of South Africa, shows its *Iris*-like features: spreading outer tepal limbs bearing yellow nectar guides, erect inner tepals, and petal-like style branches topped by paired crests.

**Plate 205.** Diminutive *Moraea tricolor* is a stemless species of wet, sandy flats north and east of Cape Town, South Africa.

**Plate 206.** In favorable years *Moraea serpentina* covers acres of semidesert with its white, violet, and yellow flowers.

**Plate 207.** The endangered western South African *Moraea tulbaghensis* has orange flowers, the outer tepals of which have brilliant navy blue or emerald "beetle marks," marking it as a beetle-pollinated species.

**Plate 209.** *Moraea villosa* has a quintessential beetle flower; its strikingly marked flowers grace the fertile lowlands north of Cape Town, South Africa.

**Plate 210.** A flower of *Moraea villosa* and one of its beetle pollinators dusted with orange pollen show just how similar are the beetle marks on the tepals and a beetle itself. The yellow hairs at the base of the dark mark on the tepals appear to mimic pollen on the back of a beetle.

**Plate 208.** *Moraea versicolor,* native to the Cape Peninsula and the surrounding country in South Africa, is a member of the acaulescent *Galaxia* group and has simple style branches, a feature of the alliance.

**Plate 211.** *Libertia chilensis* flowers show the three large inner tepals, vestigial outer tepals (barely visible here), and basally united filaments that characterize the genus.

**Plate 212.** *Orthrosanthus monadelphus,* photographed at the northern end of its range in Costa Rica, grows in clearings and at forest edges in the cloud-shrouded high mountains of Central America and northern South America.

**Plate 213.** *Olsynium douglasii* flowers in early spring in the Columbia Gorge in Oregon and Washington State. Sometimes the plants grown in dense drifts, covering meadows with purple color.

**Plate 214.** The nodding flowers of *Olsynium douglasii* and their somber color must have provided the reason for its local common name, grass widow.

**Plate 215.** Eastern North American *Sisyrinchium atlanticum* has the small blue flowers typical of subgenus *Sisyrinchium.* Photographed here in Missouri, it is easy to see why the genus is widely known as blue-eyed grass (photo G. Yatskievych).

**Plate 216.** *Sisyrinchium scabrum,* a Central American species of this widespread genus, has a typical blue-eyed-grass-type flower.

**Plate 217.** Belonging to subgenus *Echthronema, Sisyrinchium chiricanum,* of Costa Rica and Panama, is an example of a yellow-eyed grass; species of this section have yellow flowers with the tepals spreading from the base, unlike the cupped tepals of section *Sisyrinchium.* The anthers have prominent brown tips, giving the flowers a distinctive appearance (photo L. J. Porter).

**Plate 218.** One of the most glamorous of the yellow-eyed grasses, *Sisyrinchium convolutum* produces masses of bright yellow blooms with a ring of brown in the center.

**Plate 219.** *Sisyrinchium mexicanum,* with fairly large flowers (for a *Sisyrinchium*), grows in moist habitats in the mountains of Arizona as well as Mexico (photo G. Yatskievych).

**Plate 220.** One of just two species of its genus, *Solenomelus pedunculatus,* native to the Andes of Chile, has bright yellow flowers with a prominent, thickened filament column.

**Plate 221.** *Trimezia steyermarkii* is the only native Central American species of this otherwise South American and West Indian genus. The coiled inner tepal limbs have a zone of oil glands at their bases.

**Plate 222.** *Neomarica coerulea,* now widely cultivated in the tropics, has large blue flowers borne on stems more than 1 meter high.

**Plate 223.** *Neomarica fluminensis,* native to coastal central Brazil, shows the characteristic broad, flattened, winged flowering stem and intricately marked tepals.

**Plate 224.** *Neomarica northiana,* the walking stick plant, because of its habit of rooting at the tops of the flowering stems as they lean over and touch the ground, is native to the Atlantic forests of Brazil.

**Plate 225.** *Cypella coelestis,* better known by the later name *C. plumbea,* is a species of wet habitats in northern Argentina and Paraguay (photo G. Roitman).

**Plate 226.** *Cypella unguiculata* has blue flowers, and long anthers that clasp the style branches; the inner tepals recall those of *C. coelestis* (Plate 225) with their recurving inner tepal limbs.

Plate 227. Flowers of *Cypella brasiliensis*, a rare native of southern Brazil, also placed in the genus *Kelissa*, have darkly spotted outer tepals and much smaller, yellow inner tepals, the limbs of which curl back in much the same manner as those of *C. coelestis* (Plate 226).

Plate 228. *Cypella herbertii*, from northern Argentina, has yellow flowers typical of section *Cypella*. The species has been in cultivation in Europe since the early 19th century, when plants that flowered in Great Britain were the basis for the new genus *Cypella*.

Plate 229. The half-nodding flowers of *Gelasine uruguaensis* have subequal, spreading tepals (photo G. Roitman).

Plate 230. *Herbertia quairemiana,* like the other four or five species of *Herbertia,* has blue to violet flowers with short inner tepals; a zone of crowded oil glands impart the intense dark color to the lower part of the inner tepals (photo G. Roitman).

Plate 231. *Nemastylis geminiflora,* one of five species of this genus of the southern United States and Mexico, has the largest blooms in the genus. The thread-like style branches extend horizontally between the bases of the large, upright anthers (photo G. Yatskievych).

Plate 232. The uniformly colored flowers, with subequal, spreading tepals, of *Tigridia latifolia* have sessile anthers, and in the past it was placed in the genus *Sessilanthera.* Note the contrast with the more elaborate flowers of *T. pavonia* (Plate 233), signaling quite different pollination systems (photo M. Boussard).

Plate 233. *Tigridia pavonia* or Aztec lily, a plant widespread in Mexico and Guatemala, with remarkably large flowers, has been cultivated at least since Aztec times. The bulbs are reported in early Spanish accounts of Mexican ethnobotany to have been eaten when cooked. Its original wild range is unknown.

Subfamily **Crocoideae** Burnett (1835)

TYPE: *Crocus* Linnaeus

SYNONYM: Ixioideae Klatt (1866), as subordo Ixieae

Deciduous or evergreen perennials with corms producing roots from below, rarely rhizomes. LEAVES unifacial, usually with a prominent midrib. INFLORESCENCE a spike or flowers single per branch, always subtended by a pair of opposed bracts at ovary base, thus without pedicels. FLOWERS long lasting, mostly zygomorphic, or radially symmetric, with septal nectaries; tepals united in a tube. STAMENS with the filaments free or united; anthers loculicidal and extrorse to latrorse; pollen usually monosulcate, rarely trisulcate or zonasulcate, exine usually perforate, rarely reticulate. OVARY inferior; style slender, dividing into three slender branches, rarely undivided. CAPSULES cartilaginous or woody; SEEDS angular to globose, winged in some genera. BASIC CHROMOSOME NUMBER $x = ?16$, with many other base numbers. Genera 29, species c. 1,010, in five tribes: Tritoniopsideae Goldblatt & J. C. Manning (2006; *Tritoniopsis*), Watsonieae Klatt (1882; *Cyanixia, Zygotritonia, Savannosiphon, Lapeirousia, Pillansia, Thereianthus, Micranthus, Watsonia*), Gladioleae Dumortier (1822; *Gladiolus, Melasphaerula*), Freesieae Goldblatt & J. C. Manning (2006; *Crocosmia, Devia, Freesia, Xenoscapa*), and Croceae Dumortier (1822; *Radinosiphon, Romulea, Afrocrocus, Syringodea, Crocus, Geissorhiza, Hesperantha, Babiana, Chasmanthe, Sparaxis, Duthieastrum, Tritonia, Ixia, Dierama*).

## Key to Genera of Crocoideae

1　Floral bracts membranous to dry and usually translucent to transparent with veins often darkly colored, occasionally outer bract solid below but never predominantly green; leaves never pleated .................................. 2

1'　Outer and inner bracts green to brown and dry, soft-textured or firm to leathery, rarely dry and often lacerate but then leaves pleated, sometimes inner bracts with broad membranous to dry margins ............................ 10

2　Plants acaulescent; leaves usually entirely bifacial, mostly channeled to adaxially grooved, sometimes terete; corm tunics woody or fibrous but then leaves always entirely bifacial ......... 3

2'　Plants with aerial stems or acaulescent but then leaves unifacial, oriented edgewise to stem, blades plane and linear to lanceolate or oval to terete in transverse section; corm tunics woody, or papery to fibrous ............................ 5

3　Corm tunics composed of fibrous or membranous layers forming a network; leaves bifacial with the abaxial (lower) surface elaborately ridged and usually with a prominent keel; upper surface of the leaf translucent in the midline ............................... *Crocus* (p. 165)

3'　Corm tunics composed of woody unbroken layers; leaves channeled and with abaxial (lower) surface rounded or leaves rounded in section distally; upper surface of the leaf not translucent in the midline ........................ 4

4　Corm strongly compressed; leaf solitary, round in section distally; capsules splitting open when dry .............................*Afrocrocus* (p. 160)

4'　Corm globose; leaves usually more than one, channeled or round in section distally; capsules splitting open when wet .... *Syringodea* (p. 163)

5　Leaves centric, oval in transverse section with four longitudinal grooves; flowers dusty pink, actinomorphic, with stamens rotated counterclockwise ........................... *Devia* (p. 147)

5'　Leaves flat or rarely centric, then solid or with four longitudinal grooves, but then stamens never twisted sideways; flowers variously colored, zygomorphic, with stamens unilateral, or actinomorphic but stamens never rotated counterclockwise ................................. 6

6   Bracts pale, dry, papery and crinkled or solid below, irregularly streaked with dark flecks or veins ................................................. 7

6'  Bracts pale or rust-brown, membranous or dry, then not papery and crinkled, sometimes streaked with dark flecks or veins............... 8

7   Flowers borne on wiry stems and usually nodding; leaves linear, narrow, tough and fibrotic, often without an evident central vein when mature; perianth always radially symmetric and usually nodding ................. *Dierama* (p. 193)

7'  Flowers borne on firm somewhat succulent stems and held upright or facing to the side; leaves lanceolate to linear, relatively succulent, and not tough and fibrotic; perianth radially symmetric or zygomorphic but never nodding ......................... *Sparaxis* (p. 181)

8   Flowers usually zygomorphic, with stamens unilateral or tepals actinomorphic but stamens irregularly spreading and style eccentric or stamens and style symmetrically arranged; stems firm and relatively thick, never wiry ............................... *Tritonia* (p. 186)

8'  Flowers either actinomorphic, with stamens erect and symmetrically disposed around a central style, or perianth regular but stamens unilateral with anthers drooping and with a right-angled bend near base; stems often more or less wiry, or plants acaulescent ............... 9

9   Stem usually aerial and more or less wiry, rarely plants acaulescent but then flowers not stalked below the ovary, stamens decurrent and leaves without a definite central vein; outer bract usually tridentate or denticulate; pollen grain apertures with a one-banded operculum ............................ *Ixia* (p. 189)

9'  Stem subterranean; flowers distinctly stalked below the ovary; outer bract acute; pollen grain apertures with a two-banded operculum ................. *Duthieastrum* (p. 184)

10  Style undivided; leaves pleated with a major vein at each fold ........... *Zygotritonia* (p. 120)

10' Style divided into three filiform branches, these sometimes additionally divided; leaves pleated, plane, or oval to rounded in section ........... 11

11  Style branches deeply divided, usually once, occasionally multifid ............................. 12

11' Style branches undivided or at most notched apically ............................................... 19

12  Leaves terete to oval in transverse section with narrow longitudinal grooves, or four-winged, or unifacial; corm tunics composed of brittle woody concentric layers; flowers actinomorphic, solitary on branches, not arranged in spikes or plants acaulescent ....................... *Romulea* (p. 157)

12' Leaves usually with plane blades, sometimes round in transverse section but then without longitudinal grooves; corm tunics of leathery to fibrous layers; flowers zygomorphic or if actinomorphic then arranged in spikes and plants never acaulescent ......................... 13

13  Corms bell-shaped, with a flat base; leaves plane or corrugate or pleated..... *Lapeirousia* (p. 124)

13' Corms globose to obconic, round at base .... 14

14  Flowers solitary on branches; leaves prostrate, soft in texture.................. *Xenoscapa* (p. 152)

14' Flowers arranged in erect or inclined spikes; leaves usually erect, occasionally prostrate, not noticeably soft in texture ........................ 15

15  Leaves pleated with a major vein at each fold; stamens and often style branches partly to fully included in the perianth tube ................ ............................. *Savannosiphon* (p. 123)

15' Leaves plane, ribbed or round in section but never pleated; stamens and style branches usually fully exserted from the perianth tube ................................................. 16

16  Spike inclined to horizontal with flowers borne on upper side; bracts green or dry above, then often dark brown at tips......... *Freesia* (p. 149)

16' Spike erect, flowers in two ranks or spirally arranged; bracts green or partly to entirely dry but then never dark brown at apices ..........17

17 Flowers small, shorter than 12 mm, crowded on dense, two-ranked spikes; bracts solid below with broad membranous margins ......................*Micranthus* (p. 133)

17' Flowers medium to large, usually at least 20 mm long, in dense or lax, two-ranked or spiral spikes; bracts without membranous margins..........18

18 Spike two-ranked; leaf blades plane, relatively broad, margins often moderately to strongly thickened; flowers never blue or purple, and perianth tube always curved, flowers thus facing to side ......................*Watsonia* (p. 135)

18' Spike spiral; leaf blades rounded in section or plane but then narrow and without thickened margins; flowers shades of blue to nearly white or purple; perianth tube straight, flowers facing upward ....................*Thereianthus* (p. 130)

19 Inflorescence a panicle, individual flowers always with a peduncle; flowers radially symmetric, bright orange...........*Pillansia* (p. 127)

19' Inflorescence a simple or branched spike, flowers sessile, rarely inflorescence reduced to a single flower; flowers actinomorphic or zygomorphic, variously colored................20

20 Inner floral bracts always substantially longer than outer and not notched or forked apically; leaves usually with more than one prominent vein, thus without a single central vein...........*Tritoniopsis* (p. 116)

20' Inner floral bracts usually shorter, sometimes about as long as the outer, always notched or forked at the tips, sometimes divided to the base; leaves usually with a single central vein unless pleated....................................21

21 Style branches dividing at apex of perianth tube or within tube, branches long and laxly spreading............................*Hesperantha* (p. 172)

21' Style branches usually dividing well above mouth of perianth tube, branches relatively short and spreading to recurved................22

22 Corm bell-shaped, with a flat base; ovary deeply three-lobed; perianth tube vestigial....................*Melasphaerula* (p. 142)

22' Corm more or less globose with a rounded base; ovary not deeply three-lobed ............23

23 Leaves several in a two-ranked fan, blades either plane or pleated but then leaves, stems, or bracts never pubescent; flowers blue or scarlet to orange or yellow; floral bracts short, more or less twice as long as ovary, green or dry, nearly equal .....24

23' Characters not combined as above.............26

24 Flowers zygomorphic, perianth tube narrow and cylindric below, abruptly expanded into a broad upper cylindrical part and pouched at base of upper part; seeds bright orange ......................*Chasmanthe* (p. 178)

24' Flowers actinomorphic or zygomorphic but then perianth tube not abruptly expanded at top of lower cylindric portion and upper part not forming a pouch at base; seeds brown to blackish............................................25

25 Stems aerial; flowers orange to scarlet; leaves plane or pleated; plants of southern and tropical Africa ......................*Crocosmia* (p. 144)

25' Stem subterranean; flowers blue; leaves pleated; plants of Socotra...............*Cyanixia* (p. 118)

26 Leaf blades pleated, sometimes more or less linear and striate; stems and/or leaves or bracts pubescent to pilose ..............*Babiana* (p.175)

26' Leaf blades plane, corrugated or rounded in transverse section with or without four longitudinal grooves; plants smooth, normally without hairs or other obvious surface irregularities, or sometimes pubescent on leaves and/or bracts ....................................27

27 Flowers actinomorphic or if zygomorphic then perianth actinomorphic and stamens unilateral

and declinate; corm tunics usually composed of hard, brittle woody layers, or fibrous in a few species; seeds globose to somewhat angular........................ *Geissorhiza* (p. 169)

27' Flowers usually zygomorphic, with tepals unequal and stamens unilateral and arcuate, rarely radially symmetric in a few species but then seeds winged; corm tunics composed of fibrous layers ......................................28

28 Style branches slender throughout; seeds globose; leaves soft-textured; stems lightly angled....................... *Radinosiphon* (p. 155)

28' Style branches expanded and bilobed at the tips; seeds usually with a broad circumferential wing, occasionally wing obsolete and seed irregularly angled to subglobose; leaves various, occasionally soft-textured; stem usually round in section, rarely angled to winged ....................... *Gladiolus* (p. 138)

*Tritoniopsis* L. Bolus (1929a)
Plates 18–24; Figure 18
Tribe Tritoniopsideae
TYPE: *Tritoniopsis lesliei* L. Bolus
ETYMOLOGY: the name, not particularly apt, alludes to the resemblance of the type species to the African genus *Tritonia,* with *opsis,* from the Greek suffix, meaning looking like
SYNONYMS: *Anapalina* N. E. Brown (1932: 274), type: *A. triticea* (Burman fil.) N. E. Brown = *Tritoniopsis antholyza* (Lamarck) Goldblatt; *Tanaosolen* N. E. Brown (1932: 262), type: *T. Tanaosolen nudus* N. E. Brown = *Tritoniopsis nervosa* (Baker) G. Lewis; *Exohebea* R. C. Foster (1939: 36), type: *E. parviflora* (Jacquin) R. C. Foster = *T. parviflora* (Jacquin) G. J. Lewis
REVISIONARY ACCOUNTS: Lewis (1959c: 355, revision of the *Tritoniopsis* group; 1960, revision of the *Anapalina* group), Goldblatt (1990c, reduction of *Anapalina* in *Tritoniopsis*), Manning and Goldblatt (2001a, review and description of three new species)

Deciduous or sometimes evergreen perennials with depressed-globose corms, rooting from below and axillary in origin, the tunics of matted, coarse to medium-textured fibers often in a dense mass. LEAVES several, the lower two or three cataphylls; foliage leaves several, mostly basal, in two ranks, with multiple main veins unless very narrow, the blades linear to sword-shaped, the basal longest, decreasing in size above, the margins plane, sometimes with a slender false leaf stalk abruptly expanded into the broad lamina, often partly or entirely dry at flowering. STEM round in section, simple or few-branched, leafy below or bearing dry scales. INFLORESCENCE a spike, the flowers two-ranked in bud, spirally arranged at maturity; BRACTS leathery, becoming dry and brown at flowering time, fairly short, the inner longer than the outer, the apex not forked. FLOWERS mostly zygomorphic, radially symmetric in *Tritoniopsis lesliei,* pink to purple or red, sometimes white, yellow, brown, or cream, the lower tepals usually with darker or lighter markings, sometimes scented, with nectar from septal nectaries; PERIANTH TUBE short to long, cylindric, funnel-shaped or narrow below and broadly tubular above; TEPALS subequal, or unequal with the dorsal largest, the lower tepals often forming a prominent lip and sometimes markedly clawed. STAMENS unilateral and arcuate or horizontal, rarely symmetrically disposed and erect; FILAMENTS slender, curving back after the anthers split; ANTHERS oblong to linear, sometimes with a short to long, sterile apex, splitting longitudinally. OVARY globose, sessile; STYLE filiform, the branches short and recurved, sometimes forked or shortly two-lobed at the tips. CAPSULES ovoid to globose, leathery, often somewhat to much inflated; SEEDS angled, sometimes winged on the angles, with a chalazal crest, irregularly sculpted, the coat somewhat spongy, surface cells prominent. BASIC CHROMOSOME NUMBER $x = 16$, also 15, and possibly 17. Species 24, South Africa, centered in the winter-rainfall southwestern

**Figure 18.** (bottom left) *Tritoniopsis lesliei* flower (×0.8), (lower left) *T. parviflora* flower (front and side views; ×0.8), (center) *T. toximontana* with (center left) flower (front and side views), capsule (upper right, ×0.8), and seed (top right, ×3), (center right) *T. triticea* flower (side view, ×0.8), (lower right) flowers, front and side views, of *T. caledonensis* (above) and *T. caffra* (below) (×0.8).

Cape but extending from Nieuwoudtville in the north to the Transkei in the east, mainly in stony sandstone-derived soils in fynbos.

*Tritoniopsis* is taxonomically isolated within Crocoideae and is readily distinguished by the short, leathery floral bracts, the inner floral bract longer than the outer, and the plane leaves with more than one main vein, thus lacking a definite midrib unless very narrow, then only one vein being developed. The flowers are extremely variable in form and color and provide no generic characters, but the stamens, initially parallel, have the curious habit of diverging from one another as the flower matures, and the anthers often have a prominent sharp apex, a short point, called an apiculus. In addition, in all species except *T. nervosa*, the tepals separate from one another in bud, well before the flowers expand, unlike all other Iridaceae, where the tepals remain joined up to and until the flower actually opens. The ecological significance of this odd feature remains to be explained.

Leaf anatomy, often helpful in determining relationships of genera in subfamily Crocoideae, is of the ancestral type, with subepidermal marginal sclerenchyma associated with a marginal vein and undifferentiated marginal epidermal cells. Corm development is axillary, and pollen grains are of the standard type for the subfamily, with an operculum of two exine bands in the aperture. One feature that seems to set *Tritoniopsis* apart in Crocoideae are the floral bracts, the inner of which is larger than the outer and not two-keeled or forked at the tip. Lewis (1954a) made a detailed examination of floral bract development and found it unique in the subfamily. This feature as well as the peculiar leaves with multiple major veins led her to place the genus in its own subtribe, Exohebeinae. At the time of Lewis's writing, *Anapalina* and *Exohebea* were regarded as genera apart from *Tritoniopsis*, the latter comprising only *T. lesliei*, unique in the alliance in having a radi-

ally symmetric perianth. *Anapalina* included species with large, bright red flowers with an elongate perianth tube, adapted for pollination by sunbirds, sometimes in combination with satyrid butterflies, while *Exohebea* comprised species with smaller flowers, most with short tubes and pollinated by bees. Lewis (1959c) later united *Exohebea* with *Tritoniopsis*, and Goldblatt (1990c) united *Anapalina* with *Tritoniopsis*.

It hardly needs repeating that *Tritoniopsis*, as currently understood, has species with a wide range of pollination systems. The short-tubed species are mostly pollinated by bees, and the long-tubed species either by moths or long-proboscid flies (Manning and Goldblatt 2005). The genus has the distinction of being the only one outside the New World with a species, *T. parviflora*, that secretes floral oils as a reward to pollinators; it is pollinated in part by an oil-collecting bee in the genus *Rediviva* (Manning and Goldblatt 2002). The red-flowered *T. lesliei*, which has salver-shaped, radially symmetric flowers, is probably pollinated by the butterfly *Aeropetes*. Red-flowered species with zygomorphic flowers may also be pollinated by *Aeropetes* or by sunbirds or both. Bird-pollinated flowers have evidently evolved at least three times in the genus. The light, spongy seeds with winged angles are wind-dispersed.

### *Cyanixia* Goldblatt & J. C. Manning in Goldblatt et al. (2004a: 529)

Plate 25; Figure 19
Tribe Watsonieae
TYPE: *Cyanixia socotrana* (J. D. Hooker) Goldblatt & J. C. Manning
ETYMOLOGY: named for the *Ixia*-like radially symmetric flower, combined with the Greek *cyanos*, blue

Deciduous geophyte with globose corms, axillary in origin and rooting from below, the tunics of coarse

**Figure 19.** *Cyanixia socotrana* with (bottom right) exploded view of spike with inner and outer bracts detached (×1), detail of stamens and style (upper left, ×4), and pollen (upper right, ×3,500).

fibers. LEAVES few, in two ranks, the lower two or three bladeless cataphylls, foliage leaves more or less sword-shaped to lanceolate, lightly pleated, with a major vein at each fold. STEM aerial, round in section, unbranched. INFLORESCENCE a few-flowered spike, the flowers spirally arranged; BRACTS green, soft-textured, the inner much shorter than the outer and forked apically. FLOWERS radially symmetric, long-lived, blue, presence of nectar unknown; PERIANTH TUBE elongate-cylindric and straight, widening slightly toward the apex; TEPALS nearly equal, spreading. STAMENS symmetrically disposed, upright; FILAMENTS parallel, exserted; ANTHERS exserted, linear, splitting longitudinally. OVARY globose, sessile; STYLE filiform, straight, exserted, dividing distally into three short, slender branches. CAPSULES unknown; SEEDS globose, lightly wrinkled, slightly flattened at the chalazal end, the surface cells domed to lightly tuberculate. BASIC CHROMOSOME NUMBER $x = 10$. Species only *Cyanixia socotrana* from the Indian Ocean island of Socotra.

After its discovery on Socotra in 1880, in the course of Isaac Bayley Balfour's pioneering exploration of that Indian Ocean island., the plant now called *Cyanixia* was first referred to the southern African genus *Babiana* ( J. D. Hooker 1881), apparently on the basis of a broad general similarity in plant form, especially the pleated leaves, and blue flower. Weak as these reasons were, Lewis (1959) included the species in *Babiana* in her monograph of that genus. More careful examination, however, reveals more differences than similarities. Corm development in *Cyanixia* is axillary, the plant is hairless throughout, the pollen grains are trisulcate, and the seeds are more or less globose, with the surface cells colliculate to slightly tuberculate (Goldblatt et al. 2004a). In addition, the basic chromosome number is $x = 10$. All these fundamental characters contrast with those of *Babiana*, in par-

ticular, its basic chromosome number $x = 7$ and the pear-shaped seeds with the surface cells covered by thick, smooth cuticle.

Molecular studies using the plastid gene *mat*K confirm that *Cyanixia* and *Babiana* are unrelated. The affinities of *Cyanixia* lie instead with those genera of subfamily Crocoideae that have axillary corm development, specifically with *Lapeirousia* and *Savannosiphon* of tribe Watsonieae, and probably also with *Zygotritonia*, a genus for which no DNA sequences are available. *Zygotritonia* also has axillary corm development, and it the only other genus in the subfamily that also has trisulculate pollen grains. *Savannosiphon* and *Zygotritonia* also have pleated leaves of relatively soft texture and that lack a central vein, thus very similar to those of *Cyanixia*. *Zygotritonia* differs from *Cyanixia* mainly in its zygomorphic flower and undivided style, the latter unique in Crocoideae, as well as in its basic chromosome number $x = 7$.

Although the pollination of *Cyanixia* is unknown, the radially symmetric flower, blue perianth, short perianth tube, and prominent anthers suggest a simple pollination system using female bees collecting pollen for nest provisioning. Whether the flowers produce nectar or not is unknown.

### *Zygotritonia* Mildbraed (1923: 230)
Figure 20
Tribe Watsonieae
TYPE: *Zygotritonia bongensis* (Pax) Mildbraed
ETYMOLOGY: named for the strongly bilabiate (zygomorphic) flower and the fancied resemblance to some species of the genus *Tritonia* (essentially only in the orange coloration of some species)
REVISIONARY ACCOUNTS: Stapf (1927, only *Z. bongensis,* as *Z. crocea*), Goldblatt (1989b)

Seasonal geophytes with globose corms, rooting from below and axillary in origin, with tunics of

**Figure 20.** (bottom left and top right) *Zygotritonia bongensis* capsule (×2) and flower (front and side views) (×2), (left) *Z. praecox* (×0.8) with bracts (inner, above, and outer, below; ×4), (right) *Z. nyassana* (×0.8) with seed (below, center, ×10).

coarse fibers. LEAVES few, the lower two or three bladeless cataphylls, foliage leaves lanceolate to linear, prominently multinerved, lightly pleated. STEM aerial, round in section, usually two- to four-branched, the branches diverging. INFLORESCENCE a spike, the flowers spirally arranged; BRACTS small, subequal, leathery, green. FLOWERS zygomorphic, long-lived, orange to scarlet, yellow, or white, evidently unscented, probably producing nectar from septal nectaries; PERIANTH TUBE short, narrowly funnel-shaped; TEPALS unequal, the dorsal largest, held apart, arching in a semicircle and hooded over the stamens, the lower three sharply bent outward above the base, forming a lip. STAMENS unilateral and arcuate; FILAMENTS slender, free; ANTHERS oblong, parallel, lying below the dorsal tepal, splitting longitudinally. OVARY globose, sessile; STYLE filiform, arching over the stamens, ultimately drooping downward, undivided, stigmatic apically. CAPSULE depressed-globose, broadly three-lobed, more or less woody; SEEDS large, globose to weakly angular, one or two per locule, flattened at the chalazal end, smooth, matte, the surface cells colliculate. BASIC CHROMOSOME NUMBER $x = 7$. Species four, in sub-Saharan tropical Africa, extending from Senegal in the west to southwestern Tanzania and Malawi in the east, mostly in open woodland.

Although clearly a member of subfamily Crocoideae and one of just a handful of genera of the subfamily that does not occur on southern Africa, *Zygotritonia* is an enigma. The round-based, tunicate corms, spicate inflorescence, and strongly zygomorphic, bilabiate flowers seem to conform with several genera of Crocoideae, and even the pleated leaves with multiple major veins are not particularly distinctive. Leaf anatomy shows that the leaf margins have a strand of marginal sclerenchyma associated with a marginal vein, and the marginal epidermal cells are not differentiated, the ancestral condition for Crocoideae. Yet the genus has several unexpected and ultimately puzzling features. Goldblatt and Manning (2004a) concluded that the corm development is axillary, a feature shared with seven other genera, six of them assigned to tribe Watsonieae. The style branches, often a useful guide to relationships, are unique within the subfamily in being undivided and apically stigmatic. The pollen grains have a perforate exine, typical of the Crocoideae, but the trisulcate aperture and absence of an operculum are unusual and known elsewhere in Crocoideae only in the Socotran genus *Cyanixia*. Chromosome number too, is unusual. The base number $x = 7$ suggests that *Zygotritonia* is an ancient diploid, whereas most other genera of the subfamily have higher base numbers, suggesting polyploid ancestry.

Although the southern African *Babiana* also has $x = 7$ and pleated leaves with marginal anatomy like that of *Zygotritonia*, it has apical corm development and pollen grains that are monosulcate and operculate, and there seems no strong reason to regard *Zygotritonia* and *Babiana* as closely allied. Despite its generic name, *Zygotritonia* does not seem to be related to *Tritonia* or any of the genera allied to that southern African genus. Genera allied to *Tritonia* typically have specialized leaf marginal anatomy with columnar marginal epidermal cells and without a submarginal sclerenchyma strand. *Tritonia* and its allies also have specialized seed morphology in which the raphal vasculature is excluded from the seed body during development.

We now believe that the relationships of *Zygotritonia* lie with genera of tribe Watsonieae, all of which share axillary corm development and mostly deeply divided style branches. Among these genera, *Cyanixia* and *Savannosiphon* have similarly pleated leaves, and *Cyanixia* has trisulcate pollen grains like those of *Zygotritonia*. Unfortunately, there is no information available from molecular sources relating to the relationships of *Zygotritonia*.

Little is known of the biology of *Zygotritonia*. The flowers are short-tubed and attract a range of small insects, including bees and wasps. The pollination strategy thus appears to be a generalist one. *Zygotritonia hysterantha* is unusual in producing flowering stems early in the growing season before the leaves emerge. Later, during the wet season, typical broad foliage leaves are produced, and these remain green and photosynthetic while the capsules and seeds mature. Flowering out of season also occurs in *Z. praecox*, which produces flowering stems at the beginning of the rainy season when the stems bear short-bladed or bladeless leaves. In this species no additional leaves are produced during the wet season. Flowering at a different time from the majority of the flora occurs in several genera of the Iridaceae and is particularly well developed in *Gladiolus*, both in tropical and southern Africa. The strategy is thought to lessen competition for light, water, and pollinators.

*Savannosiphon* Goldblatt & Marais (1979)
Tribe Watsonieae
TYPE: *Savannosiphon euryphylla* (Harms) Goldblatt & Marais
ETYMOLOGY: from the Greek *siphon*, tube, combined with savanna, for the long perianth tube and its distribution in the African savanna
REVISIONARY ACCOUNT: Goldblatt (1993b)

Deciduous geophytes with globose corms, rooting from below and axillary in origin, the tunics of fairly coarse, compacted fibers. LEAVES several, the lower two or three cataphylls, foliage leaves lanceolate, pleated, with a large vein at each fold, the lowermost leaf longest and inserted on the stem near ground level, upper leaves progressively smaller. STEM aerial, compressed and angled to winged, usually unbranched. INFLORESCENCE a few-flowered spike; BRACTS green and firm-textured, relatively large, usually overlapping, the outer slightly larger than the inner. FLOWERS more or less radially symmetric, long-lived, uniformly white, opening at nightfall and then sweetly scented, with nectar from septal nectaries; PERIANTH TUBE cylindric, extremely long; TEPALS subequal, the dorsal slightly inclined. STAMENS symmetrically disposed around the style and included in the upper part of the tube; FILAMENTS slender, short; ANTHERS linear, included or the apices exserted, with a short point, splitting longitudinally. OVARY globose, sessile; STYLE filiform, included in the tube, the branches usually forked for up to half their length, partly exserted from the tube. CAPSULES cartilaginous, oblong; SEEDS globose, flattened to concave at the chalazal end, smooth, matte, the surface cells lightly colliculate. BASIC CHROMOSOME NUMBER $x = 7$. Species only *Savannosiphon euryphylla*, widespread in southern tropical Africa, including southern Congo, Zambia, Malawi, Mozambique, and western Tanzania, occurring in woodland, often associated with termite mounds.

On initial examination, *Savannosiphon* appears unusual mainly in its highly specialized flowers, which have an extremely long perianth tube, white color, and stamens and style included in the mouth of the floral tube. The flowers are specialized for sphinx moth pollination and help little in understanding the relationships of this monospecific genus. The only aspect of the flower that seems unrelated to the pollination system is that the style branches are deeply divided, a specialization found in a limited number of genera of Crocoideae. *Savannosiphon* is also unusual vegetatively in having axillary corm development, in the compressed, angular stem, and in its broad, more or less pleated leaf blades. Anatomically, the leaves accord with Crocoideae in general, with the leaf margins having a strand of subepidermal sclerenchyma associated with the marginal vein, the ancestral condition in the subfamily. The pleated blades have a major vein at each fold of the pleated leaf surface, also the typical pattern for pleated leaves in Crocoideae. The seeds are round, with a flattened to concave chalazal end, and have colliculate epidermal cells. The axillary corm ontogeny and divided style branches accord particularly with tribe Watsonieae of the subfamily, and the foliage leaves not associated with the corm tunics, the compressed and angled stem, and the seed morphology suggest a close relationship with *Lapeirousia*. Only the round-based corms with fibrous tunics leave room for doubt that the genera are not immediately related.

Evidence from several chloroplast DNA regions confirm that *Savannosiphon* belongs in Watsonieae, showing that features such as axillary corm development, deeply divided style branches, and single basal leaf are important indicators of relationship (Goldblatt et al. 2006). The molecular evidence shows that *Savannosiphon* is sister genus to the Socotran *Cyanixia*, which we would not have predicted from morphology, but both genera do have similar corm tunics, corm development, and pleated leaves. *Cyanixia* does not have divided style branches, and its basic chromosome number $2n = 10$ differs from that of *Savannosiphon*, as do the pollen grains, which are trisulcate in *Cyanixia*, unlike the polyaperturate grains of *Savannosiphon*, which actually have an apparently disorganized pattern of exine and aperture. According to the molecular data, the two genera are together the sister clade to *Lapeirousia*, from which *Savannosiphon* was segregated in 1979.

Although the pollination of *Savannosiphon* has not been studied, the pure white flowers opening in the evening and then releasing a rich scent, coupled with the production of ample nectar held within a perianth tube up to c. 10 cm long, leave little doubt that the flowers are adapted for pollination by sphinx moths. The association of *Savannosiphon* with termite mounds bears investigation. There seems no obvious reason for this habitat preference, an unusual one for the family.

*Lapeirousia* Pourret (1788: 79)
Plates 26–34; Figure 21
Tribe Watsonieae
TYPE: *Lapeirousia compressa* Pourret = *L. fabricii* (Delaroche) Ker Gawler
ETYMOLOGY: named in honor of the Compte Philippe Picot de Lapeyrouse, patron of French science and contemporary of the abbé Pierre André Pourret, who described the genus
SYNONYMS: *Ovieda* Sprengel (1817: 258), illegitimate name, not *Ovieda* Linnaeus (1753), type not designated; *Peyrousia* Poiret (1826: 363), type not designated; *Meristostigma* A. Dietrich (1833: 293), type not designated; *Sophronia* Lichtenstein ex Roemer & Schultes (1817: 482), type: *S. caespitosa* Lichtenstein ex Roemer & Schultes = *Lapeirousia plicata* (Jacquin) Diels; *Chasmatocallis* R. C. Foster (1939: 40), type: *C. macowanii* R. C. Foster = *L. divaricata* Baker
REVISIONARY ACCOUNTS: Goldblatt (1972, southern Africa; 1990b, tropical Africa), Goldblatt and Manning (1992, additional species)

Deciduous geophytes with bell-shaped corms with a flat base, rooting from the lower edges and axillary in origin, the tunics of densely compacted fibers or woody. LEAVES several, the lower two or three bladeless cataphylls, foliage leaves linear to sword-shaped, plane with a definite midrib or closely pleated (rarely terete), then the lowermost longest and inserted on the stem near ground level, upper leaves cauline smaller. STEM sometimes entirely underground, or aerial, compressed and angled to winged, usually branched, sometimes repeatedly, then forming a flat-topped panicle. INFLORESCENCE either a simple or branched spike, sometimes much branched, forming a false panicle, with

**Figure 21.** (bottom left) *Lapeirousia fabricii* flower (side and front views; ×1), (left) *L. oreogena* flower (side and top views, ×1), (center) *L. arenicola* with flowers (front views), capsule (×1), and seed (×12), (bottom right) *L. pyramidalis* flower (side and front views, ×1).

sessile flowers, or flowers clustered at ground level in a basal tuft; BRACTS green and firm to soft-textured, the outer sometimes ridged, keeled, crisped, or toothed, the inner shorter than the outer and forked at the tip. FLOWERS radially symmetric or zygomorphic, long-lived, often salver-shaped, blue, purple, red, pink, or white, the lower or all the tepals usually with contrasting darker or lighter markings, sometimes sweetly scented, with nectar from septal nectaries; PERIANTH TUBE cylindric or funnel-shaped, short to extremely long; TEPALS subequal or unequal, with the dorsal enlarged. STAMENS symmetrically disposed or unilateral and arcuate; FILAMENTS slender, free; ANTHERS linear, splitting longitudinally, often purple or violet. OVARY globose, sessile; STYLE filiform, the branches usually forked for about half their length, occasionally entire or barely forked. CAPSULES membranous to cartilaginous, globose to oblong; SEEDS more or less globose, flattened at the chalazal end, smooth, matte, the surface cells usually colliculate, sometimes areolate. BASIC CHROMOSOME NUMBER $x = 10$, other base numbers 9, 8, 7, 6, 5, 4, 3. Species 42, sub-Saharan Africa from Nigeria and Ethiopia to South Africa, 35 in southern Africa and centered in the semiarid winter-rainfall zone in southwestern South Africa and Namibia, often in rocky habitats.

Flowers of *Lapeirousia* are extraordinarily variable in shape color and size so that the genus is most easily recognized by the flat-based, bell-shaped corms with hard, usually woody corm tunics. In addition, plants usually have compressed stems, sometimes angled to narrowly winged, and the style branches are deeply divided in all but a few species. Species of the largely tropical Africa subgenus *Paniculata* frequently have plane leaves, and the flowering stem forms a complex, branched, panicle-like inflorescence, rare in other members of the family. In contrast, species of subgenus *Lapeirousia* are more conventional in appearance, with a main axis

and short lateral branches, while a few species form a tuft at ground level. The subgenus is readily recognized by the tightly pleated leaf blades and often enlarged, fleshy bracts.

The axillary corm development and divided style branches of *Lapeirousia* place the genus firmly in tribe Watsonieae of subfamily Crocoideae. Morphology suggests no particular relationship within tribe. Studies using chloroplast DNA sequences confirm the tribal placement and in addition place *Lapeirousia* in a clade together with the tropical African genera *Cyanixia* and *Savannosiphon*, both monospecific. We assume that *Zygotritonia*, also tropical African, also belongs here, but the genus has not been studied at the molecular level.

Species of *Lapeirousia* favor relatively xeric habitats, even in areas of relatively high rainfall, and are most often found in shallow soils in rock outcrops. A few species favor deep, well-drained sands. The preference for rocky habitats is in part related to protection from predation, for the corms are edible and a favored food of baboons and porcupines. Corms were eaten by various indigenous peoples throughout its range and are still gathered by children in parts of Namibia.

The highly variable shape, tepal orientation, color, and scent characteristics of flowers of *Lapeirousia* species signal diverse pollination strategies. Major pollinators are bees, bombyliid flies, noctuid moths, and butterflies for short-tubed species; long-proboscid flies of the genera *Philoliche* (Tabanidae), and *Prosoeca* and *Moegistorhynchus* (Nemestrinidae) for species with long-tubed red, purple, or pink to cream flowers; and sphinx and other moths for species with pale, long-tubed, and fragrant flowers (Goldblatt et al. 1995). We assume the ancestral pollination system is the unspecialized one involving a range of bees, wasps, butterflies, and perhaps bee flies. Blue-flowered and short-tubed species of subgenus *Paniculata* across tropical and summer-rainfall southern Africa have this generalist pollination system, and their small blue flowers are visited by nectar-foraging insects as well as female bees foraging for pollen.

Along the western coast of southern Africa, subgenus *Lapeirousia* seems to have abandoned this pollination strategy, and species typically have flowers with an elongate perianth tube. Several species, including *L. silenoides,* with odorless purple-red or dark blue to violet flowers with white markings, are pollinated solely by the nemestrinid fly *Prosoeca peringueyi* or *P.* sp., which forage on the nectar held within the long floral tube and thus unavailable to insects with short mouthparts. Long-tubed species, including *L. fabricii,* with cream to pinkish flowers with red markings, are pollinated by another nemestrinid, *Moegistorhynchus longirostris,* or by the tabanid fly *Philoliche gulosa.* Long-tubed species with sweetly scented, white flowers, including *L. pyramidalis* and *L. odoratissima,* must be assumed to be pollinated by sphinx moths. These two species as well as the widespread tropical African *L. schimperi,* which also has long-tubed, white flowers, are the only species in the genus that have flowers open at night. The radially symmetric flowers of the southwestern Cape *L. corymbosa* and its close allies appear to be adapted for pollination by a range of insects, including bees, hopliine beetles, and bee flies.

One of just a handful of the genera of Crocoideae that is widely distributed across Africa, *Lapeirousia* extends from Nigeria and Ethiopia south to the southern tip of Africa. Its pattern of distribution differs, however, from that of the few other genera, *Gladiolus* and *Hesperantha* among them, that have both southern and tropical African species. While the latter are mostly found in the well-watered highlands of eastern Africa, *Lapeirousia* has a western distribution pattern, occurring in areas of dry climate. Thus the genus is particularly well developed along the dry western coast and near interior

of South Africa and Namibia. Elsewhere in Africa, species occur in local dry areas such as rock outcrops with thin, well-drained soils, or in deep sands.

*Lapeirousia* species are occasionally cultivated in specialist collections and are worth the effort to grow. Given a rich, well-drained soil and sufficient water, the winter-growing *L. corymbosa, L. oreogena,* and *L. silenoides* make wonderful displays in containers or in the rock garden. The tropical species, which are summer growing and dormant in winter, can be even more rewarding, for they are larger plants and produce large numbers of flowers, each lasting several days. They deserve to be tried in gardens, especially in areas of dry climate where water limits gardening activities, such as the southwestern United States and of course their native Africa.

### *Pillansia* L. Bolus (1915: 20)

Plates 35–36; Figure 22
Tribe Watsonieae
TYPE: *Pillansia templemannii* (Baker) L. Bolus
ETYMOLOGY: honoring the South African botanist Neville Stuart Pillans (1884–1964), who collected the species and drew the plant to the attention of Harriet Margaret Louisa Bolus, who described the genus
REVISIONARY ACCOUNT: Obermeyer (1962)

Evergreen geophyte with depressed globose corms, rooting from below and axillary in origin, past season's corms not resorbed, the tunics coarsely fibrous. LEAVES few, the lower two or three cataphylls, foliage leaves unifacial, without a definite midrib, linear, twisted, sometimes trailing, basal leaves one, sometimes two, with two or three small, cauline, leathery, and fibrotic, uppermost dry. STEM erect, repeatedly branched above, round in section, often warty. INFLORESCENCE a flat-topped panicle with each flower sessile; BRACTS leathery,

**Figure 22.** *Pillansia templemannii* (base of stem at lower left with portion of a leaf curling around the drawing) with (upper right) half-flower and bracts (inner, above, and outer, below), (bottom right) capsule (above, ×0.8) and seed (below, ×2), and (center) detail of style branches (×1.5).

green with reddish brown margins, glutinous on the inside, the inner about as long as the outer, clasping the ovary, multinerved apex entire. FLOWERS radially symmetric, long-lived, bell-shaped, orange, scentless, not closing at night, with traces of nectar from septal nectaries; PERIANTH TUBE short, funnel-shaped; TEPALS subequal, spreading. STAMENS symmetrically arranged; FILAMENTS erect, free; ANTHERS linear, splitting longitudinally. OVARY globose, sessile, covered in mucilage from the bracts; STYLE filiform, exserted, the branches slender, notched apically for one-quarter to one-third their length. CAPSULES subglobose, woody; SEEDS large, angular, with a chalazal crest, smooth and shiny, one to three per locule, the surface cells concave. BASIC CHROMOSOME NUMBER $x = 20$. Species only *Pillansia templemannii*, restricted to the coastal mountains of the Caledon district in Western Cape Province, South Africa, mostly in wetter sites on slopes at elevations of 300–700 m, also in marshes and seeps, and occasionally at low elevations not far from the coast.

*Pillansia* is readily recognized by the panicle-like, multibranched inflorescence of long-lived, bright orange, radially symmetric flowers, which are sessile and subtended by a pair of bracts. The central style is surrounded by the free stamens, and the slender style branches are divided at the tips. The flowers have the appearance of being completely unspecialized and have a short perianth tube and no obvious adaptation to a particular pollination system. The corm, which is typical of the Crocoideae, consists of several internodes and produces roots from the lower portion. The corm development is of the axillary type, typical of *Watsonia* and its allies. The pollen grains, too, are typically ixioid in having perforate exine and the aperture with a well-developed two-banded operculum. The capsules are unusually large, often c. 16 mm in diameter, to accommodate the large seeds, of which there are usually only one or two per locule, each up to 10 mm long. They are smooth and shiny, angular in shape, and have a prominent crest at the chalazal end. The glutinous secretion from the inner epidermis of the bracts is unique.

Affinities of *Pillansia* have long been puzzling because although the flowers and corm are typical of Crocoideae, the paniculate inflorescence, often regarded as primitive, is not. Another feature atypical of the Crocoideae is the leaf, which lacks a central vein and, equally puzzling, does not have anatomical specializations of the subfamily, lacking both a subepidermal sclerenchyma strand or columnar marginal epidermal cells, one or other of which occur in all other genera of Crocoideae. However, *Pillansia* has the sessile flower subtended by two bracts, a long-lived perianth, a perianth tube, basally rooting corm, operculate pollen grains, and perforate exine that are derived in the subfamily. The basic chromosome number $x = 20$ is polyploid. On the basis of these characters, *Pillansia* is clearly a member of the Crocoideae. But it has usually been regarded as an ancient relict polyploid, surviving in local equable sites in the southwestern Cape coastal mountains. *Pillansia* was believed to be close to the ancestral type of Crocoideae by Goldblatt (1990a), who assigned it to its own tribe, Pillansieae.

Chloroplast DNA sequence analysis indicates quite a different relationship for *Pillansia*, and it appears that the genus is not at all unspecialized nor taxonomically isolated within the Crocoideae. Instead, it is closely allied to *Micranthus* and *Thereianthus* in phylogenetic trees generated from sequences of some plastid DNA regions. In trees produced from the combined sequences, however, *Pillansia* is sister to *Watsonia*, and this pair is sister to *Thereianthus* plus *Micranthus*, a topology that has strong statistical support. The hypothesis that *Pillansia* is taxonomically isolated and unspecialized within Crocoideae must be abandoned. Instead, its apparently primitive features must be seen to represent secondary specializations, perhaps related to its habitat and pollination system. *Pillansia* is now understood to be a specialized genus of tribe Watsonieae, in which at least its axillary corm development and apically notched style branches are typical.

*Pillansia* was described only in 1915, very late for a plant with a geographical range as close as 50 km from Cape Town and growing not far from roads traveled by botanists since the 18th century. The erratic flowering and montane habitat provide part of the answer to this anomalous situation. The species was, however, gathered by Christian Friedrich Ecklon and Carl Ludwig Zeyher, who collected plants in southern Africa in the 1820s and 1830s. *Wredowia pulchra*, a name lacking a formal taxonomic description, was published by Ecklon in 1827, the first published record of the plant we now call *Pillansia*. Ecklon's name was never validated with a formal description and was not adopted by later botanists. When John Gilbert Baker first saw collections of the species, he called it *Tritonia templemannii*, named for the Cape Town nurseryman who had made the collection on which the name is based.

Typical of plants of the nutrient-poor soils of South Africa's Cape mountains, which are derived from quartzites and sandstones, *Pillansia* flowers only in the one or two seasons after fires, a common phenomenon in geophytes of such habitats. In the first year after a fire, flowering and fruiting are usually profuse, but the year following that, flowering is much reduced; flowers are rarely seen again until after the next fire, which may occur 5–25 years later. Pollination biology has not been studied in detail, but preliminary observations suggest that the flowers are visited, and presumably successfully pollinated, by a range of medium-sized bees, notably those in the family Halictidae, as well as by hopliine scarab beetles.

Attractive as *Pillansia templemannii* is, it has not been grown successfully in gardens. Plants tend to be difficult to establish from transplanted corms, and they grow slowly from seeds. In neither case have individuals flowered annually. Modern horticultural techniques, including fire simulation of the corms by smoked water treatment, may result in better success with growing the species.

*Thereianthus* G. J. Lewis (1941: 33)
Plates 37–38; Figure 23
Tribe Watsonieae
TYPE: *Thereianthus spicatus* (Linnaeus) G. J. Lewis
ETYMOLOGY: from the Greek *thereios*, summer, and *anthos*, flower
SYNONYMS: *Beilia* Ecklon ex Kuntze (1898: 305), superfluous, illegitimate name, type: *B. spicata* (Linnaeus) Kuntze = *Thereianthus spicatus* (Linnaeus) G. J. Lewis; *Watsonia* [rankless] *Beilia* Ecklon ex Baker (1877: 164), type: *W. punctata* Ker Gawler = *T. spicatus* (Linnaeus) G. J. Lewis
REVISIONARY ACCOUNTS: Goldblatt and Manning (2000a: 149–150), Manning and Goldblatt (2004)

Deciduous geophytes with globose corms, rooting from below and axillary in origin, the tunics fibrous. LEAVES few, the lower two or three cataphylls, foliage leaves plane or more or less rounded, the lowermost inserted on the stem above the corm, longest, blades linear or sickle-shaped, either with a definite midrib or with a few prominent veins, the margins usually prominently thickened, upper leaves progressively smaller than the basal. STEM usually unbranched, round in section. INFLORESCENCE a spike, flowers spirally arranged or more or less in two ranks when crowded, the entire spike loosely twisted; BRACTS firm-textured, short, often overlapping, green below, the apices dry and brown, or entirely dry, the inner two-nerved and forked at

**Figure 23.** (left) *Thereianthus montanus* with flower (front view and half-flower) and bracts (outer, left, and inner, right) (×0.8), and detail of stamens and style branches (×2), (right) *T. ixioides* flowering stem with flower (×0.8) and detail of stamens and style branches (×2), (lower right) *T. spicatus* capsule (above, ×3) and seeds of *T. bracteolatus* (left) and *T. minutus* (right) (×10).

the apex. FLOWERS zygomorphic or radially symmetric, long-lived, blue, purple, or white, the lower three tepals often with darker markings in the lower half, scentless, usually with nectar from septal nectaries, or without nectar; PERIANTH TUBE short to elongate, funnel-shaped or cylindric; TEPALS subequal, spreading or the dorsal arching over the stamens. STAMENS unilateral and arcuate or symmetrically arranged and central; FILAMENTS slender, free; ANTHERS linear, splitting longitudinally. OVARY globose, sessile; STYLE filiform, the branches slender, deeply divided and recurved. CAPSULES woody, ellipsoid to spindle-shaped; SEEDS angular-elongate with a chalazal crest or narrowly ovoid with a long, persistent funicle (*Thereianthus minutus*), smooth or wrinkled, matte, the surface cells areolate. BASIC CHROMOSOME NUMBER $x = 10$. Species eight, South Africa, restricted to the winter-rainfall zone of the southwestern Cape, mostly in nutrient-poor, stony, sandstone soils; two species, *T. juncifolius* and *T. minutus,* grow in seeps and along streams.

*Thereianthus* is typical of Crocoideae in its cormous rootstock, spicate inflorescence, tepals united below in a tube, and slender style branches. The genus is difficult to define, and it is not surprising that its component species were usually regarded as belonging to *Watsonia* subgenus *Beilia* until 1941, when it was described by South African botanist Gwendoline Joyce Lewis. *Thereianthus* shares with *Watsonia* the deeply divided style branches, often a reliable indicator of relationships in Iridaceae. *Thereianthus* differs from *Watsonia* in the small size of the plants and flowers, the blue to violet color of the flowers of most species, and more importantly, in its short, usually dry floral bracts and the insertion of the leaves on the stem above the corm (rather than on the corm itself). The latter feature differs from all other Crocoideae except *Micranthus,* which also has short, more or less dry floral bracts.

Chromosome numbers, not known to Lewis but now established for nearly all genera of the Iridaceae, support Lewis's decision to separate *Thereianthus* from *Watsonia*. While the latter has a basic chromosome number $x = 9$, *Thereianthus* has $x = 10$, a number shared with *Micranthus*. This suggests that their distinctive leaf insertion and similar floral bracts are true indications that these two genera are immediately related. Morphology points to a broader relationship of *Thereianthus* and *Micranthus* with *Watsonia,* which, like these two genera, has corms that are axillary in origin. Chloroplast DNA sequences confirm the sister relationship of *Thereianthus* and *Micranthus* but surprisingly show that their closest relative is not *Watsonia* itself but the clade that includes the sister pair *Pillansia* and *Watsonia.* Although this seems surprising at first and was not suspected from morphological or anatomical data, it makes sense from a cytological perspective, for *Pillansia,* although polyploid with $2n = 40$, otherwise has a karyotype like that of *Thereianthus* and *Micranthus.*

Pollen of *Thereianthus* appears to conform with that of other Crocoideae in both the perforate exine sculpturing and predominantly two-banded operculum. One species, *T. racemosus,* however, stands out in the genus in having reticulate exine, shared in the Crocoideae only with *Micranthus.* Pollen of the latter genus differs from all Crocoideae in its zonasulcate aperture.

Ecologically, *Thereianthus* species are unusual for plants restricted to areas of winter rainfall in that they flower mainly in the summer and seldom before November, which in the Cape region of South Africa is the beginning of summer. Such late flowering is unusual for small plants of the southern African winter-rainfall zone. Plants favor rocky sandstone slopes or wetter clay sites and are mainly montane in distribution. *Thereianthus minutus* and *T. juncifolius* occur in moist habitats, the former growing on wet, rocky pavement, often among clumps of moss. *Thereianthus juncifolius* grows in deeper soils in seeps or along streams and is most often seen after fire. Like other geophytes of nutrient poor soils, *Thereianthus* species flower in mass the season after a wildfire but thereafter only occasionally again until the next fire.

Like most genera of Crocoideae, even as small a genus as *Thereianthus* has diverse pollination biology. While this aspect of the genus has been little studied, hopliine scarab beetles are the only recorded pollinators of the short-tubed *T. racemosus*, in which the radially symmetric flowers are clustered at the spike apices. *Thereianthus longicollis* and *T. montanus*, which have flowers with a perianth tube more than 24 mm long, are probably pollinated by long-proboscid flies, either *Moegistorhynchus* or *Philoliche*. Flowers of the remaining species are most likely pollinated by bees or a combination of bees and other insect orders.

Little attempt has been made to grow species of *Thereianthus*. We suspect that plants will grow readily if treated in the same way as *Watsonia*. They will have to be treated as winter-growing plants and will require ample moisture during the growing season. After coming into flower in early summer, water should be withheld and the foliage allowed to dry back. Summer and autumn conditions must be dry except in *T. juncifolius* because of its habitat, stream banks and seeps. The blue flowers of most species would make an attractive display in the rock garden.

*Micranthus* (Persoon) Ecklon (1827: 43)
Plate 39; Figure 24
Tribe Watsonieae
Conserved name, not *Micranthus* Wendland; *Gladiolus* subgenus *Micranthus* Persoon (1805: 46)
TYPE: *G. alopecuroides* Linnaeus = *M. alopecuroides* (Linnaeus) Ecklon

ETYMOLOGY: from the Greek *micro*, small, and *anthos*, flower
SYNONYM: *Paulomagnusia* Kuntze (1891: 702), type: *P. alopecuroides* (Linnaeus) Kuntze (lectotype here designated) = *Micranthus alopecuroides* (Linnaeus) Ecklon
REVISIONARY ACCOUNTS: Baker (1896: 97), Goldblatt and Manning (2000a: 136–137)

Deciduous geophytes with globose corms, rooting from below and axillary in origin, the tunics coarsely fibrous. LEAVES few, the lower two or three cataphylls, foliage leaves either plane with a definite midrib and sickle-shaped or linear blades with the margins moderately to heavily thickened, or the blades terete and hollow, the lowermost inserted on the stem above the corm, longest, remaining leaves inserted above the ground and smaller than the basal. STEM simple or few-branched, round in section. INFLORESCENCE a congested, two-ranked spike; BRACTS firm-textured, short, overlapping, dry, and brown, with broad membranous margins, the inner forked apically. FLOWERS zygomorphic, long-lived, blue to violet or white, scentless, with nectar from septal nectaries; PERIANTH TUBE short, curving outward and more or less cylindric; TEPALS subequal, the dorsal arching over the stamens. STAMENS unilateral and arcuate, filaments slender, free; ANTHERS oblong, held under the dorsal tepal, splitting longitudinally. OVARY globose, sessile; STYLE filiform, the branches slender, deeply divided and recurved. CAPSULES woody, small, spindle-shaped; SEEDS cylindric, lightly striate and matte, the surface smooth. BASIC CHROMOSOME NUMBER $x = 10$. Species three, South Africa, restricted to the winter-rainfall zone of the southwestern Cape, on stony slopes, one species, *Micranthus junceus*, growing in seeps or seasonal marshes.

Species of *Micranthus* are readily recognized by their crowded, many-flowered spikes of tiny blue

**Figure 24.** *Micranthus alopecuroides* (×1) with capsules (upper left, ×5), half-flower and flower (upper right, ×4), bracts (lower right: inner, left, and outer, right; ×4), and seed (lower left, ×12).

or, rarely, lilac or white flowers. The dry floral bracts closely overlap one another, and the zygomorphic flowers are arranged in two opposed ranks. The flowers have a short, curved floral tube, a slightly larger, arching dorsal tepal and smaller lower tepals forming a lower lip. The stamens are unilateral and arcuate, and the style branches are deeply divided. The leaves are variable, either linear-lanceolate with a midrib (*M. alopecuroides*) or hollow and without a midrib (*M. junceus, M. tubulosus*). A few populations have narrow leaves with both the midrib and the margins heavily thickened, and these may represent an undescribed species. Variation in the flowers, apart from color, which ranges from pale to deep blue, or occasionally lilac or white, is virtually nonexistent.

The narrow, spindle-shaped capsules of *Micranthus* are elongate and do not readily split when dry, and the seeds are released as they slowly decay or are scorched by fire. The seeds have a unique, nearly cylindrical shape. Another unusual feature of *Micranthus* is the pollen—the grains are zonasulcate and have reticulate exine, grading to perforate close to the aperture. Most Crocoideae have monosulcate grains with a distinctive two-banded operculum, and perforate exine. There is no reason to doubt the subfamilial position of the genus, and the reticulate exine must be seen as a reversal to the ancestral condition.

The relationships of *Micranthus* lie with another South African endemic, *Thereianthus,* as discussed in detail under that genus. The two share the same chromosome number $2n = 10$ and karyotype, the basal leaf inserted on the stem above the corm, and short, dry floral bracts. The axillary corm development and deeply divided style branches are shared with other members of the tribe Watsonieae, to which *Micranthus* and *Thereianthus* belong. Chloroplast DNA sequences show an immediate, sister relationship between the two genera, which are together related to a clade consisting of two other Southern African genera, *Pillansia* and *Watsonia.*

Pollination in *Micranthus* is unspecialized. The unusually small blooms are visited by a range of insects, including bees, bee flies, butterflies, noctuid moths, and even wasps. *Micranthus* is not in cultivation but certainly should be grown in specialist collections in areas of mild winter climate and dry summers. Planted in masses, the plants would make a colorful display for several weeks as the numerous tiny flowers open sequentially.

*Watsonia* Miller (1759, 2: pl. 276)
Plates 40–48; Figure 25
Tribe Watsonieae
Conserved name
TYPE: *Watsonia meriana* (Linnaeus) Miller
ETYMOLOGY: named for William Watson, 18th century British botanist
SYNONYMS: *Meriana* Trew (1754: 11, pl. 40), rejected name, type: *M. flore rubello* Trew = *Watsonia meriana* (Linnaeus) Miller; *Lomenia* Pourret (1788: 74, pl. 5), type: *L. borbonica* Pourret = *W. borbonica* (Pourret) Goldblatt; *Neuberia* Ecklon (1827: 37), name invalid, without description
REVISIONARY ACCOUNT: Goldblatt (1989a)

Deciduous or sometimes evergreen perennials with depressed-globose corms, rooting from below and axillary in origin, the old corms often not resorbed, the tunics leathery, with age becoming fibrous. LEAVES several, the lower two or three cataphylls, foliage leaves lanceolate to sword-shaped, leathery and fibrotic, plane with a definite midrib, the margins and midribs often thickened and prominent, the cauline leaves smaller than the basal. STEM aerial, usually branched, round in section. INFLORESCENCE a several- to many-flowered, two-ranked spike; BRACTS firm, green or partly to completely dry at anthesis, the inner smaller, as long or longer

**Figure 25.** *Watsonia dubia* with corm (×0.8), detail of style branches (upper left, ×4), (top right) *W. aletroides* flower (×0.8), (right) *W. meriana* flower, half-flower, and bracts (outer, left, and inner, right) (×0.8), (bottom left) *W. vanderspuyiae* capsule (above, ×0.8) and seed (below, ×6).

than the outer, two-nerved and usually forked apically. FLOWERS zygomorphic (radially symmetric in *Watsonia marginata*), long-lived, pink, orange, or red, rarely cream to pale yellow, sometimes with contrasting markings on the lower tepals, scentless, with nectar from septal nectaries; PERIANTH TUBE slightly to strongly curved, the lower part cylindric, the upper part flared or broad and cylindric; TEPALS subequal. STAMENS symmetrically disposed or unilateral and then arching upward or downward; FILAMENTS slender, free; ANTHERS oblong to linear, splitting longitudinally. OVARY ovoid, sessile; STYLE filiform, the branches slender, forked for half their length and recurved. CAPSULES globose to oblong or elongate, sometimes spindle-shaped, leathery to woody; SEEDS large, angular or compressed and winged at the chalazal end or at both ends, matte, the surface cells areolate. BASIC CHROMOSOME NUMBER $x = 9$. Species 51, southern Africa, centered in the southwestern Cape, South Africa, but extending north into Namaqualand and east into the summer-rainfall zone of eastern South Africa, Swaziland, and Lesotho.

A relatively large genus, *Watsonia* can be recognized by its sturdy, erect spikes, often of numerous flowers, with firm bracts holding successive flowers facing in opposite directions, giving the spike a distinctive appearance. The flowers themselves are usually quite large and always have the slender style branches divided for half their length and recurved. With one exception the flowers are zygomorphic, usually with the tepals nearly equal but the perianth tube strongly curved and the stamens unilateral and either arching upward below the dorsal tepal or arching downward above the lowermost tepals. The large, somewhat flattened corms are axillary in origin, and the leaves have the marginal anatomy type ancestral in subfamily Crocoideae, with a pronounced sclerenchyma strand associated with a marginal vein. *Watsonia* has a unique basic

chromosome number in the subfamily, $x = 9$, and a karyotype with one large pair of chromosomes. The pollen grains are typical of Crocoideae, with perforate exine and a well-developed two-banded operculum. Seeds of many species of *Watsonia* are specialized in having the proximal and distal ends flattened and drawn into wing-like processes. In a few species the seeds may even have only one large distal wing. Winged seeds are found only in species of the southern African winter-rainfall zone, and it is here that most species occur and the diversity of the genus is greatest.

Flowers are usually either shades of pink or bright red to orange. Correlated with pink flower color is either a relatively short tube or a moderately long but narrow one. These flowers are adapted for pollination, respectively, by bees or long-proboscid flies. In contrast, red or orange flowers nearly always have a perianth tube narrow below and wide and tubular above, and they are pollinated by sunbirds (*Nectarinia* species). The wide part of the tube permits entry of the bird's bill to the flower, and the narrow part contains the nectar, accessible to the bird's tongue. Exceptional species are the eastern southern African *Watsonia latifolia*, which mostly has dark maroon flowers (but is still presumably pollinated by sunbirds), and *W. watsonioides*, which has small, pale yellow flowers over most of its range. This short-tubed species is also pollinated by bees. *Watsonia marlothii* of the Swartberg of the southern Cape, South Africa, has a long but rather narrow perianth tube, and it seems likely that its pollination system is shifting (or has shifted) from sunbirds to the large butterfly *Aeropetes*. A few species with pink, long-tubed flowers are pollinated by long-proboscid flies, notably *W. pauciflora*, pollinated by *Moegistorhynchus* sp. (Nemestrinidae).

The relationships of *Watsonia* lie with other genera of Crocoideae with similar deeply divided style branches and axillary corm development. These include *Lapeirousia, Micranthus, Thereianthus,* and *Pillansia,* though this latter genus, with an unusual panicle-like inflorescence, has style branches only shortly forked. Studies using chloroplast DNA confirm this relationship and furthermore show that *Pillansia,* which is monospecific, is the immediate sister genus of *Watsonia,* while *Micranthus* and *Thereianthus,* also immediately related, are the sister clade to *Pillansia* plus *Watsonia.* These four genera together with *Lapeirousia* and the tropical African *Cyanixia, Savannosiphon,* and *Zygotritonia* constitute the tribe Watsonieae. Basic chromosome number for the tribe is evidently $x = 10$, and *Watsonia* appears derived in having the secondary base $x = 9$.

*Watsonia* was for many years much misunderstood, and J. G. Baker, who revised the genus for *Flora Capensis* in 1896, admitted only 15 species to the genus, four of which are now regarded as belonging to *Thereianthus* and one to *Ixia.* Since that time, species were added rather piecemeal, most of them by the South African botanist H. M. L. Bolus. Several of Bolus's new species were described in collaboration with J. W. Matthews, the curator of Kirstenbosch Botanic Garden, Cape Town. Many species of *Watsonia* were cultivated there in the 1920s and 1930s, and even today *Watsonia* species are important subjects for spring and summer display. By 1975 the total species recognized in *Watsonia* had reached 72, but the taxonomy was in such confusion that it was impossible to name specimens with any confidence. A critical monograph of the genus by Goldblatt (1989a) reduced this number to 52, several of them new to science.

*Watsonia* species are widely cultivated in southern Africa and to some extent in Australia and New Zealand. Flowering somewhat later that most spring bulbs, they make very fine displays in October and November in southern hemisphere gardens and street plantings. Some excellent cultivars are also available, some with larger, longer-lasting flowers than the wild species. *Watsonia* species, including *W. marginata* and *W. meriana* (especially the bulbiliferous genotypes), are aggressive weeds in parts of Australia and are particularly difficult to eradicate. The white sport of *W. borbonica,* often called *W. ardernei* and an excellent garden subject, is locally naturalized in California, where it was introduced as a garden plant.

*Gladiolus* Linnaeus (1753: 36)
Plates 49–68; Figure 26
Tribe Gladioleae
TYPE: *Gladiolus communis* Linnaeus
ETYMOLOGY: from the Latin *gladiolus,* little sword, referring to the sword-shaped leaves, in fact, typical of most members of the *Iris* family
SYNONYMS: *Antholyza* Linnaeus (1753: 37), type: *A. cunonia* Linnaeus (lectotype designated by Hitchcock and Green 1929) = *Gladiolus cunonius* (Linnaeus) Gaertner; *Cunonia* Miller (1759, 1: 75; 1768), rejected name, not *Cunonia* Linnaeus (1759), type: *C. antholyza* Miller = *G. cunonius* (Linnaeus) Gaertner; *Anisanthus* Sweet (1830: 566), type: *A. splendens* Sweet = *G. splendens* (Sweet) Herbert; *Petamenes* Salisbury ex J. W. Loudon (1841: 42, pl. 8), type: *P. abbreviatus* (Andrews) N. E. Brown = *G. abbreviatus* Andrews; *Sphaerospora* Sweet ex Loudon (1841: 66, pl. 14), type: *S. imbricata* (Jacquin) Sweet ex Loudon = *G. italicus* Miller; *Acidanthera* Hochstetter (1844: 25), type: *A. bicolor* Hochstetter = *G. murielae* Kelway; *Ballosporum* Salisbury (1866: 142), type: *G. segetum* Ker Gawler; *Homoglossum* Salisbury (1866: 143), neither type nor constituent species indicated, type: *H. watsonium* (Thunberg) N. E. Brown, according to De Vos (1976), = *G. watsonius* Thunberg; *Hyptissa* Salisbury (1866: 142), type: *H. rosea* Salisbury, name invalid, identity uncertain; *Ophiolyza* Salisbury (1866: 142), lectotype designated by Goldblatt and Manning (1998): *G. alatus* Linnaeus; *Ranisia* Salisbury (1866:

143), type: *G. tristis* Linnaeus; *Symphydolon* Salisbury (1866: 142), type: *G. floribundus* Jacquin; *Oenostachys* Bullock (1930: 465), type: *O. dichroa* Bullock = *G. dichrous* (Bullock) Goldblatt; *Anomalesia* N. E. Brown (1932: 270), type: *A. cunonia* (Linnaeus) N. E. Brown = *G. cunonius* (Linnaeus) Gaertner; *Kentrosiphon* N. E. Brown (1932: 271), type: *K. saccatus* (Klatt) N. E. Brown = *G. saccatus* (Klatt) Goldblatt & De Vos; *Dortania* A. Chevalier (1937: 402), type: *D. amoena* A. Chevalier = *G. chevalieranus* W. Marais

REVISIONARY ACCOUNTS: Lewis et al (1972), Goldblatt (1996), Goldblatt and Manning (1998)

Deciduous geophytes (evergreen in *Gladiolus sempervirens*) with globose to depressed-globose corms, rooting from the base and axial in origin, the tunics leathery to papery or membranous to fibrous. LEAVES few to several, usually contemporary with the flowers, occasionally borne earlier or later than the flowers and on separate shoots, the lower three cataphylls, foliage leaves usually with a definite midrib, two to several, basal or some inserted above ground level, sometimes the blade reduced or lacking, thus the entire leaf partly to entirely sheathing, the blades linear to lanceolate, sometimes velvety or hairy, either plane and the margins, midrib, and sometimes other veins not or only lightly thickened and hyaline, or the margins or midrib strongly raised, sometimes even winged (thus H- or X-shaped in section), or the midribs and margins much thickened and the blade evidently terete but with four narrow longitudinal grooves. STEM terete or occasionally compressed and angled, simple or branched, often flexuose, occasionally scabrid to velvety. INFLORESCENCE a spike, the flowers usually secund, or in two ranks; BRACTS green, sometimes dry above, usually large, the inner slightly smaller than the outer and notched apically or entire. FLOWERS zygomorphic, or radially symmetric in a few species, funnel- to salver-shaped, or tubular, often bilabiate, the lower tepals usually with contrasting nectar guides, often closing at night, sometimes fragrant, with nectar from septal nectaries; PERIANTH TUBE obliquely funnel-shaped to cylindric; TEPALS usually unequal, the dorsal broader and arched to hooded over the stamens, the lower three narrower, sometimes clawed and shortly united. STAMENS unilateral, arcuate, ascending to horizontal, or symmetrically arranged; FILAMENTS filiform, free, sometimes lightly hairy; ANTHERS linear, splitting longitudinally, subbasifixed, rarely centrifixed with sterile tails, sometimes with a short point (some tropical species). OVARY globose, sessile; STYLE filiform, usually arching over the stamens, the branches expanded above and often bilobed apically. CAPSULES usually slightly inflated, often large, leathery, ovoid to ellipsoid; SEEDS discoid with a broad circumferential wing, rarely globose to angled, smooth, the surface cells colliculate on the seed body, foveolate on the wing. BASIC CHROMOSOME NUMBER $x = 15$, other numbers 14, 12, 11. Species c. 262, mainly sub-Saharan Africa and Madagascar, also Europe and the Middle East, c. 167 species in southern Africa, centered in the winter-rainfall zone of the southwestern Cape with secondary centers in the eastern African highlands and Shaba Province of Congo.

Second largest genus of the family after *Iris*, *Gladiolus* is one of few genera of Crocoideae that has radiated conspicuously outside the Cape region. The genus is strikingly variable in both floral and vegetative morphology, but most species have distinctive seeds with a broad circumferential wing and an ovoid, leathery, somewhat inflated capsule. The style is also unusual, having the branches expanded above into broad, bilobed tips. Despite the large size of the genus, pollen morphology is uniform, conforming to the basic monosulcate type with a two-banded operculum, ancestral for Crocoideae.

**Figure 26.** (bottom left) *Gladiolus lapeirousioides* flower (×0.8), (center left) *G. paludosus* with half-flower (×0.8), (top left) *G. bonaspei* flower (×0.8), (upper right) *G. carneus* seed (×2.5) and capsules (×1), (lower right) *G. uysiae* (×0.8), (bottom right), flowers of *G. brevitubus* (above) and *G. saccatus* (below) (×0.8), (bottom center) *G. oppositiflorus* flower (×0.8).

The basic chromosome number $x = 15$ indicates that the genus is paleopolyploid. Most species are diploid, $2n = 30$, but the almost pan-African *G. dalenii* (= *G. natalensis*) is heteroploid, with tetraploid, hexaploid, and occasionally diploid populations. A pattern of decreasing chromosome numbers has been recorded in tropical African species, in which haploid numbers of $n = 14$, $12$, and $11$ occur.

The large number of generic synonyms reflects the floral diversity in the genus. For example, long-tubed, white-flowered species with subequal tepals, once assigned to *Acidanthera*, reflect a typical adaptation to hawkmoth pollination. Likewise, species with long cylindrical tubes and red or orange pigmentation, variously included in *Anomalesia*, *Antholyza*, and *Homoglossum*, reflect adaptations to sunbird pollination. Despite the floral variation, plants included in these genera all have the identical winged seeds and the same basic chromosome number. A few species have seeds in which the wing is reduced or completely lost, for example, the southern African *G. pretoriensis* and the Eurasian *G. italicus*.

The affinities of *Gladiolus* have long been uncertain, although there has never been any doubt that the genus belongs in subfamily Crocoideae. Suggested allies have included *Babiana*, which has similar, apically bilobed style branches, and the eastern African *Radinosiphon*. This *Gladiolus*-like plant also has a basic chromosome number $x = 15$, and its long perianth tube resembles that in some *Gladiolus* species. Chloroplast DNA sequences surprisingly show that neither of these suggestions is correct. The genus most closely allied to *Gladiolus* is the monospecific *Melasphaerula* of the southern African winter-rainfall zone. Nothing in the morphology of the two genera suggests this relationship, which nevertheless receives strong statistical support. On this basis, *Gladiolus* and *Melasphaerula* are now regarded as the only two genera of tribe Gladioleae, a classification that reflects their taxonomic isolation from other genera.

*Gladiolus* has become a model genus for pollination studies. Nearly all species have specialized pollination systems that use a single group of insects or birds for pollen transfer. Most common in the genus is passive pollination by large anthophorine bees foraging for nectar, but some 29 southern African species have long-tubed white to pink flowers adapted for pollination by long-proboscid flies. Bird pollination is frequent in southern and tropical Africa, as is moth pollination by large settling moths or hovering sphinx moths. Several species with large, bright red flowers are pollinated by large butterflies, notably in southern Africa the satyrid butterfly *Aeropetes*. Radially symmetric flowers have evolved in a handful of species in both southern and tropical Africa and in Madagascar, and these appear mostly to be pollinated by female bees actively foraging for pollen. One species in southern Africa, *G. meliusculus*, has a bimodal pollination system that uses large bees or alternatively hopliine beetles. Matching pollination system to the phylogeny of the genus, we have concluded that shifts from the ancestral anthophorine bee pollination system have occurred repeatedly; thus long-proboscid fly pollination may have evolved independently 12 times in the genus, bird pollination at least seven times, and moth pollination at least three times (Goldblatt et al. 2001). Thus among the 167 southern African species, one shift in pollination system has occurred for every five species, a remarkable example of evolutionary adaptive radiation.

Floral diversity is matched by numerous vegetative adaptations, notably reduction in leaf number and development of winged midribs and or margins, or reduction of the entire leaf blade. In some species flowering occurs before the leaves are produced or after they have dried, thus achieving complete separation of the growth and reproductive phases of the life cycle. In these species, vegetative growth occurs in the favorable wet season, and flowering is delayed until the dry season when fewer species bloom, thus reducing competition for pollinators.

*Gladiolus* is one of the world's most important cut flowers, and cultivation of a range of hybrids for the florist trade is a multimillion dollar industry. Corms are also widely offered in the nursery trade. Breeding of the cultivated *Gladiolus* began in Great Britain in the early 19th century with the production of interspecific hybrids using Cape species, *G. cardinalis* and *G. tristis*. Additional species brought into cultivation later, including most importantly the tall, large-flowered *G. dalenii* (as *G. psittacinus* or *G. natalensis*), but also *G. oppositiflorus* and *G. papilio*, were added to breeding programs in France, Germany, and the United States in the later 19th and early 20th centuries. The vogue for *Gladiolus* cultivars approached tulipomania with eventually more than 30,000 cultivars being produced. Cross breeding and selection of new hybrid forms continues in the Netherlands, the United States, and elsewhere today (Goldblatt and Manning 1998). New strains are constantly being brought to market to satisfy the desire for new cut flowers by a market accustomed to novelty.

The genus also has more practical value as both food and medicine. Corms of *Gladiolus dalenii* are used as food in tropical Africa, and it is grown in small gardens. The corms are eaten as a porridge or vegetable after leaching in water to remove the bitter-tasting tannins. In Dhofar in southern Arabia, corms of *G. candidus* are likewise an important food source, probably less so today than in the past. The corms of *G. dalenii* are also used medicinally for a variety of ailments.

## *Melasphaerula* Ker Gawler (1803)
Plates 69–70; Figure 27
Tribe Gladioleae
TYPE: *Melasphaerula graminea* (Linnaeus fil.) Ker Gawler = *M. ramosa* (Burman fil.) N. E. Brown
ETYMOLOGY: named for the blackish, rounded cormlets crowded at the base of the corm, from the Greek *melas*, black, and *sphaerulos*, small sphere

SYNONYMS: *Phalangium* Burman fil. (1768: 3), illegitimate name, not *Phalangium* Miller (1754), type: *P. ramosa* Burman fil. = *Melasphaerula ramosa* (Burman fil.) N. E. Brown; *Diasia* de Candolle, (1803), type: *D. graminifolia* de Candolle = *M. ramosa* (Burman fil.) N. E. Brown; *Aglaea* Steudel (1821: 21), type: *A. graminea* (Linnaeus fil.) Steudel = *M. ramosa* (Burman fil.) N. E. Brown
REVISIONARY ACCOUNTS: Baker (1896: 115), Goldblatt and Manning (2000a: 136)

Deciduous perennials with a bell-shaped corm with a flat base, rooting from the base and axial in origin, the tunics woody to firm-papery and concentric. STEM aerial, terete, and wiry, with many spreading branches. LEAVES several, the lower two or three cataphylls, foliage leaves sword-shaped, with a definite midrib, in a two-ranked fan, relatively soft-textured. INFLORESCENCE a lax spike; BRACTS green, soft-textured, short, the inner shorter to about as long as the outer, notched apically. FLOWERS zygomorphic and bilabiate, cream to pale yellow, the lower tepals with darker median streaks, with either a sweet or a sour, musk-like scent, with nectar from septal nectaries; PERIANTH TUBE obsolete; TEPALS unequal, lanceolate, the tips attenuate, tapering to thread-like apices, the dorsal tepal largest. STAMENS unilateral and arcuate; FILAMENTS inserted in the mouth of the tube; ANTHERS parallel, held beneath the dorsal tepal. OVARY strongly three-angled, sessile, locules with two or three pairs of ovules; STYLE exserted, the branches filiform and recurved. CAPSULES three-angled, leathery, wider than high; SEEDS more or less globose, flattened at the chalazal end, mostly three or four per locule, rarely five or six, smooth, matte, the surface cells domed. BASIC CHROMOSOME NUMBER $x = 10$. Species only *Melasphaerula ramosa*, southern Africa, restricted to the winter-rainfall zone and extending from southwestern Namibia in the north to the Little Karoo and Bavi-

**Figure 27.** *Melasphaerula ramosa* with capsules (lower center left) (×1), flower (three-quarters view, left, and half-flower, upper right; ×3), and seed (lower left, ×8).

aanskloop Mountains in the south, mostly in sheltered, shady, and moist places.

The distinctive monotypic *Melasphaerula* has a unique combination of woody corm tunics, a short-tubed bilabiate flower, short filiform style branches, and few-seeded and winged capsules. The flowers are cream to pale yellow, with lanceolate-attenuate tepals each with a maroon to purple median streak. The perianth is bilabiate with a hooded dorsal tepal and longer lower tepals forming a lower lip. The dorsal tepal conceals short, unilateral, arcuate stamens and an arching style that exceeds the stamens, dividing into three filiform, recurved branches that curve well above the oblong loculicidal anthers. A feature of many populations of the species is a musky floral odor commonly associated with other small, cream or pale yellow flowers, for example, species of *Rhus*. Curiously, not all populations have this scent; sometimes the flowers a have a faint sweet odor.

Within the Iridaceae, such flowers are unusual, for the family typically has medium to fairly large, brightly colored flowers that attract larger insects, including apid and andrenid bees, long-proboscid flies, moths, large butterflies, hopliine beetles, and passerine birds. Our observations of *Melasphaerula ramosa* in flower at several sites in South Africa showed no evidence of these common pollinators, but the plants were actively visited by small March flies (Bibionidae; Goldblatt et al. 2005b). The cream to pale yellow flowers, often somewhat unpleasantly scented, are consistent with pollination by these small flies, which are attracted by sour and putrid odors and dull-colored flowers.

The relationships of *Melasphaerula* have always been puzzling, and on the basis of its woody corm tunics and soft-textured bracts the genus has been regarded as most likely related to *Geissorhiza* and *Hesperantha* (Goldblatt 1971a). Studies of plastid DNA sequences, however, show that it is most closely related to *Gladiolus*. The two genera show no close relationship to the remaining Crocoideae

and are placed together in tribe Gladioleae (Goldblatt et al. 2006).

## *Crocosmia* Planchon (1851)
Plates 71–74; Figure 28
Tribe Freesieae
TYPE: *Crocosmia aurea* (Pappe ex J. D. Hooker) Planchon
ETYMOLOGY: from the Greek *krokos*, saffron, and *osme*, odor, for the saffron-like fragrance of the dried flowers steeped in water
SYNONYMS: *Crocanthus* Klotzsch manuscript, cited in synonymy by Klatt in Peters (1864: 516), without description and an invalid name; *Curtonus* N. E. Brown (1932: 270), type: *C. paniculatus* (Klatt) N. E. Brown = *Crocosmia paniculata* (Klatt) Goldblatt
REVISIONARY ACCOUNTS: De Vos (1984, 1999: 129–138), Goldblatt et al. (2004b)

Deciduous geophytes with globose to depressed-globose corms, those of past seasons often not resorbed, axial in origin and rooting from below, producing thin rhizomes from the base in some species, the tunics firm-papery, sometimes becoming fibrous with age. LEAVES several, the lower two or three cataphylls; foliage leaves mostly basal and forming a two-ranked fan, lanceolate to sword-shaped, either plane with a definite midrib composed of more than one pair of veins or pleated with several equal veins, cauline leaves few and reduced. STEM aerial, round in section, simple to several-branched, sometimes repeatedly. INFLORESCENCE a two-ranked spike, sometimes one-sided, sometimes strongly flexuose, flowers usually many and crowded; BRACTS small, green, leathery, drying at the tips, the inner about as long as the outer and notched apically. FLOWERS zygomorphic, trumpet-shaped or radially symmetric, salver-shaped and nodding, shades of orange to red, the lower tepals sometimes with contrasting markings, unscented, with nectar from septal nectaries; PERIANTH TUBE cylindric or funnel-shaped, widening gradually and flared or tubular above;

**Figure 28.** *Crocosmia aurea* with (center) flower (front view and half-flower), (center right) bracts (outer, left, and inner, right), capsules (upper right, above, ×0.8), and seed (below, ×1.5), (top left) *C. mathewsiana* flower (half-flower and front view; ×0.8), (bottom right) *C. fucata* flower (top to bottom: side view, half-flower, and front view; ×0.8).

TEPALS equal or unequal, then the dorsal largest and often arching over the stamens. STAMENS unilateral and arcuate or symmetrically disposed and central; FILAMENTS free, slender; ANTHERS subversatile, linear, splitting longitudinally. OVARY globose, sessile; STYLE ascending to horizontal or central, the branches filiform or expanded apically, notched apically. CAPSULES globose, leathery, often warty above; SEEDS globose, two to four, sometimes as many as eight, per locule, brown or blackish, shiny and smooth when fresh, becoming wrinkled on drying, the coat initially fleshy in *Crocosmia aurea*, the surface cell outlines prominent, the ovular vascular trace excluded. BASIC CHROMOSOME NUMBER $x = 11$. Species eight, mainly eastern South Africa, with one species restricted to high elevations in Namaqualand, one shared with tropical Africa and north to Uganda and Cameroon, and one restricted to western Madagascar, mainly in grassland or forest, or along streamsides.

*Crocosmia* species have a diversity of leaf and floral form that make it difficult to distinguish them from related genera. Flowers are always shades of orange to scarlet, or yellow, but the form ranges from zygomorphic with a short funnel-shaped tube, weakly spreading tepals, and short stamens (*C. mathewsiana, C. pottsii*), or widely spreading tepals with long stamens (*C. masoniorum*), to a long cylindrical tube and well-exserted stamens (*C. fucata, C. paniculata*), and even radially symmetric and nodding with a narrow straight tube (*C. aurea*). Leaf morphology is also unusually variable, for while four species have plane, soft-textured leaves with a prominent central vein, the other four have firm, pleated leaves with prominent veins at the angles of the pleats. Both leaf types have similar marginal anatomy, with columnar marginal epidermal cells with thickened margins and lacking a marginal vein or strand of sclerenchyma. All the species share anthers with the filaments inserted above the base, the style branches notched to shortly divided, capsules often

wider than high, and the surface often lightly warty. Seeds also vary but always have the vascular trace to the ovule excluded and the surface lightly wrinkled and matte with the surface cell outlines prominent. Seed number, usually two per locule, is often considered taxonomically significant, but seed number ranges from one to three, rarely four, per locule in most species, with *C. pottsii* having up to eight seeds per locule. Seeds of *C. aurea* are unusual in having a fleshy outer surface when first released, and they are retained in the open capsules where their black color contrasts with the reddish inner surface of the capsule walls. Basic chromosome number in all species known for this character is $x = 11$.

The relationships of *Crocosmia* are controversial. The genus most closely resembles the larger southern and tropical African *Tritonia*, which has some 30 species, especially in its orange to red flowers and short floral bracts, and even in a few species in flower shape and leaf morphology. Indeed, some species of *Crocosmia* were until the late 20th century included in *Tritonia* or its synonym *Montbretia*. The orange-flowered species of *Tritonia* can be distinguished immediately by the yellow, tooth-like ridge on the lower tepals and the anthers attached to the filaments at their bases. Cytological and leaf and seed anatomical studies seemed to support the *Crocosmia–Tritonia* relationship, for both genera have a basic chromosome number $x = 11$ and the leaves have specialized anatomy with columnar marginal epidermal cells (Goldblatt 1971a, Rudall and Goldblatt 1991). Both genera also have seeds with the ovular vascular trace excluded (De Vos 1984). The morphological and anatomical similarities are, however, apparently misleading. Sequences from several chloroplast DNA regions show that *Crocosmia* is most closely related to the monospecific genus *Devia* (Goldblatt et al. 2006), a local endemic of the Roggeveld Plateau near Sutherland in South Africa, and together the two genera are related to the African genus *Freesia*, which has 15 species. The molecular data make the few differences between *Crocosmia* and *Tritonia* seem particularly significant. These include style branches undivided, capsules smooth, and seeds hard and shiny in *Tritonia* but style branches notched to shortly divided, capsules often lightly warty, and seeds wrinkled and matte with cell outlines prominent in *Crocosmia*. The latter features are shared with *Freesia*, which also has a basic chromosome number $x = 11$ and similar specialized leaf anatomy, but it does not have the ovular trace excluded, and it has smooth hard seeds rather different from those of *Crocosmia*. *Devia* also shares these features except for a derived basic chromosome number $x = 10$, and it agrees with *Crocosmia* in seed features. While the generic relationships of *Crocosmia* are by no means established with certainty, the weight of evidence now seems to favor the molecular data, and the genus has been included in tribe Freesieae while *Tritonia* resides in tribe Croceae.

Floral morphology is closely linked to pollination system (Goldblatt et al. 2004b). The flowers of the three species of *Crocosmia* are adapted for pollination by sunbirds (*Nectarinia* species), and like all bird-pollinated flowers they have reddish to orange pigmentation, long stamens, and an elongate, relatively wide perianth tube. The nodding flowers of *C. aurea* are pollinated by large butterflies as are those, we suspect, of *C. masoniorum*, which has upright, short-tubed flowers with well-exserted stamens. The remaining *C. mathewsiana* and *C. pottsii* have flowers adapted for pollination by large, long-tongued bees. The reward for insect and avian visitors is always nectar, retained in the lower part of the perianth tube.

Surprisingly for a comparatively small genus, *Crocosmia* has a remarkably wide geographic range and diverse ecology. One species, *C. fucata,* is a narrow endemic of streamsides in the high mountains of Namaqualand in the southern African winter-rainfall zone. The remaining species occur in eastern southern Africa, except for *C. aurea*, which extends from Eastern Cape Province in South Africa through southern tropical Africa to Uganda, northern Congo, and Central African Republic north of the equator. It is a forest and forest-margin species, often growing in dense shade. *Crocosmia mathewsiana* favors forest-margin habitats in the northern Drakensberg in South Africa while *C. pottsii* is a streamside plant. Both *C. masoniorum* and *C. pearsei* are montane species of rock outcrops and cliffs.

*Devia* Goldblatt & J. C. Manning (1990: 362)
Plate 75; Figure 29
Tribe Freesieae
TYPE: *Devia xeromorpha* Goldblatt & J. C. Manning
ETYMOLOGY: named in honor of the South African botanist and specialist in the Iridaceae, Miriam Phoebe De Vos
REVISIONARY ACCOUNT: Goldblatt (1999: 148–150)

More or less evergreen geophytes with depressed-globose corms, axial in origin and rooting from below, the tunics of coarse fibers accumulating in a dense mass. LEAVES several, the lower two or three cataphylls; foliage leaves mostly basal, linear, oval in transverse section, with a definite midrib and a second pair of veins on either side heavily thickened, the surface thus with two narrow longitudinal grooves on each surface, margins unthickened, edged by narrow grooves, dry or becoming dry at flowering time, cauline leaves few and reduced. STEM aerial, branched, round in section, sheathed below by a thick collar of coarse fibers. INFLORESCENCE a many-flowered, one-sided spike; BRACTS leathery, dry at anthesis, the inner about as long as the outer and notched apically. FLOWERS radially symmetric, long-lived, trumpet-shaped, pink, unscented, with nectar from septal nectaries; PERIANTH TUBE narrowly funnel-shaped; TEPALS subequal, suberect,

**Figure 29.** *Devia xeromorpha* (×0.5) with corm and flowering stem (×0.8), bracts (upper left: outer, above, and inner, below; ×3), flower (upper right: side and top views; ×2); transection of leaf (center right, ×20), and (below left) capsules (below, ×0.8) and seed (above, ×4).

enclosing the filaments. STAMENS symmetrically disposed, rotated counterclockwise; FILAMENTS slender; ANTHERS lying opposite the inner tepals, facing inward, splitting longitudinally. OVARY globose, sessile; STYLE eccentric, the branches short, notched apically. CAPSULES globose, cartilaginous, lightly warty above; SEEDS globose, flattened at the chalazal end, hard and shiny, one or two per locule, smooth, the surface cell outlines prominent, the ovular vascular trace excluded. BASIC CHROMOSOME NUMBER $x = 10$. Species only *Devia xeromorpha*, South Africa, a local endemic of the high rocky central Roggeveld Escarpment in the western Karoo, an area of predominantly winter rainfall.

Discovered only in the 1980s, *Devia* is a surprising plant for a member of the Iridaceae. It grows in dense clumps, and with its long, narrow, sharp-tipped leaves resembles nothing more than tussocks of the native grasses of the genus *Merxmuellera* among which they grow. Plants flower surprisingly late in the season, in November and December, long after the winter and spring rains have ceased. The small, relatively inconspicuous, dusty pink flowers are produced on slender spikes reaching 50–70 cm high, and the capsules and seeds ripen in the hot, dry, late summer. *Devia* is clearly a member of subfamily Crocoideae for it has long-lasting, sessile flowers with a well-developed perianth tube borne on spikes. The flowers are radially symmetric except that the style is twisted to lie off-center while the stamens are rotated counterclockwise, a feature unknown elsewhere in the family. The leaves are unusual in having a pair of narrow longitudinal grooves on each surface, and the margins have columnar epidermal cells with thickened walls. The more or less globose capsules are lightly warty and usually contain two rounded to lightly angled seeds that have the ovular vascular trace excluded.

When we first described *Devia* (Goldblatt and Manning 1990) we did not understand the nature of the excluded vascular trace and described the seeds as having a persistent funicle. Nevertheless, we concluded that *Devia* might be most closely related to *Crocosmia* despite its basic chromosome number $x = 10$, contrasting with $x = 11$ in the latter genus. Both the internal leaf anatomy and capsule and seed characters are consistent with those of *Crocosmia*. Sequences of several plastid DNA regions confirm the suggested relationship—*Devia* and *Crocosmia* are sister genera, together forming a clade sister to *Freesia* and *Xenoscapa*, and the four genera are now included in the tribe Freesieae of subfamily Crocoideae.

Little is known of the biology of *Devia* except for its habitat, rocky dolerite slopes on the cold, high Roggeveld Escarpment at close to 2,100 m in elevation. The area is one of the coldest parts of southern Africa, and winter temperatures often remain several degrees below freezing for weeks. The inconspicuous flowers are visited by long-proboscid bee flies (Bombyliidae), which may be their legitimate pollinators.

*Freesia* Klatt (1866: 672)
Plates 76–82; Figure 30
Tribe Freesieae
Conserved name
TYPE (conserved): *Freesia refracta* (Jacquin) Klatt
ETYMOLOGY: named in honor of Friedrich Heinrich Theodor Freese, a physician at Kiel, Germany, and friend of plant collector Christian Friedrich Ecklon, who proposed the name but without providing a description, as *Freesea;* the modern spelling was introduced by Friedrich Wilhelm Klatt when he formally named the genus
SYNONYMS: *Anomatheca* Ker Gawler (1804: 227), type: *A. juncea* (Linnaeus fil.) Ker Gawler = *Freesia juncea* (Linnaeus fil.) Klatt
REVISIONARY ACCOUNTS: Goldblatt (1972: 75–91, *Anomatheca* group; 1982b, *Freesia* group), Goldblatt and Manning (1995a)

Deciduous perennials with obconic corms, rooting from below and axial in origin, the tunics finely to coarsely fibrous, producing thin rhizomes from the base in some species. LEAVES several, the lower two or three cataphylls; foliage leaves unifacial, with a distinct midrib, in a two-ranked fan, the blades plane, firm or soft-textured, sometimes prostrate. FLOWERING STEM aerial, erect, or prostrate below, simple or branched, terete or compressed and angled. INFLORESCENCE a spike, flexed at the base, the flowers borne on the upper side; BRACTS green and leathery or soft-textured or pale and membranous, often brown at the tips, the inner shorter than the outer, notched apically. FLOWERS zygomorphic, salver-shaped or narrowly to widely funnel-shaped, white to yellow or pink to red, rarely greenish to brown, sometimes with contrasting darker markings on the lower three tepals, usually strongly and sweetly scented, nectar produced from septal nectaries; PERIANTH TUBE either slender and cylindric throughout or narrow below, widened into a narrowly or broadly flared upper part; TEPALS subequal or the dorsal larger and hooded. STAMENS unilateral and arcuate; FILAMENTS inserted at the base of the wide part of the tube; ANTHERS included or exserted. OVARY globose, sessile; STYLE filiform, the branches each deeply divided and recurved. CAPSULES more or less globose, cartilaginous, the surface usually papillate to warty; SEEDS globose, hard and shiny, smooth or lightly wrinkled, the raphe inflated in species related to *Freesia leichtlinii*, flattened or concave at the chalazal end. BASIC CHROMOSOME NUMBER $x = 11$. Species 15, mainly in the southern African winter-rainfall region, two species in eastern southern Africa and tropical Africa, one extending to Sudan. Most common on clay soils in renosterveld or karroid scrub. The two species of the summer-rainfall region occur in light shade in woodland or forest margins.

Well known in cultivation, *Freesia* is recognized primarily by the deeply forked style branches and the sharply inclined to horizontal spike. The flower form, a deeply cupped perianth with relatively short tepals, the dorsal erect to hooded and the lower three forming a lip, and intense fragrance are typical of the genus, but *F. verrucosa* and *F. laxa*, until 1995 included in *Anomatheca*, have a uniformly slender tube, horizontally spreading, red, pink, or whitish tepals with red makings, and a light or nonexistent scent. The tropical *F. grandiflora* also has red flowers with long filaments, and *F. viridis* has green flowers, both very different from the stereotypical *Freesia* flower. Other features characteristic of the genus are conical rather than rounded corms and fibrous netted corm tunics. Anatomically, the leaves have columnar marginal epidermal cells with thickened margins and lack a submarginal vein or sclerenchyma trace. Seeds of the genus have a smooth or slightly wrinkled surface without visible cell outlines. It was also thought for some time that seeds with an inflated raphe characterized the genus, but this feature is restricted to *F. refracta* and its allies. Basic chromosome number in *Freesia* is $x = 11$. The pollen is typical of subfamily Crocoideae except for the unusual *F. viridis*, which has a one-banded operculum rather than the usual two-banded one (Goldblatt and Manning 1995a).

While the genus is centered in the southern African winter-rainfall zone, *Freesia grandiflora* and *F. laxa* (the latter long known in horticulture as *Anomatheca* or *Lapeirousia cruenta*) range from eastern South Africa to tropical Africa. The unusual *F. viridis*, one of the most drought tolerant of the species, extends along the southern African western coast and interior from Mamre near Cape Town, South Africa, to southwestern Namibia. Leaves of the interior subspecies *crispifolia* are often prominent in heavily grazed areas; because of their extraordinarily bitter taste they are usually avoided by all

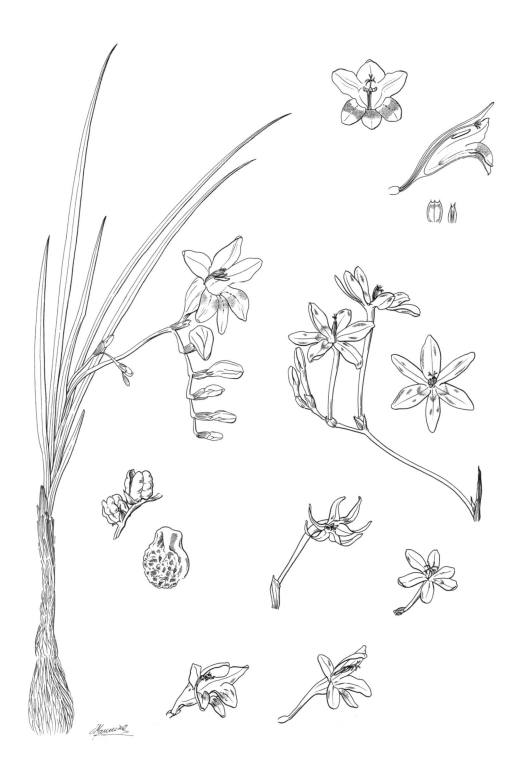

**Figure 30.** (left) *Freesia fucata* with capsules (above, ×0.8) and seed (below, ×4), (top right) flower (front view and half-flower), bracts (outer, left, and inner, right) (all ×0.8), (center right) *F. laxa* flowering branch and flower (front view, ×0.8), (bottom right) flowers of *F. viridis* (above left), *F. verrucosa* (above right), *F. refracta* (below left), and *F. sparmannii* (below right) (all ×0.8).

herbivores. The cultivated *Freesia* is derived from selections of the white-flowered southern Cape coastal species *F. alba* crossed with pale yellow *F. corymbosa* and *F. leichtlinii*. In the early horticultural accounts of *Freesia* these species and their hybrids were called *F. refracta*, in fact a very different species. This mistake has persisted even today, despite the error having been noted by N. E. Brown in 1935 in his now outdated revision of the genus. Fragrance in the cultivated *Freesia* is derived primarily from *F. alba* and *F. leichtlinii*, and crosses with other species usually have diminished scent. Perhaps most fragrant of all the species, the winter-flowering *F. caryophyllacea*, is otherwise a rather inconspicuous, low-growing plant.

The relationships of *Freesia* have long been puzzling. Because of the divided style branches it was often thought to be related to *Lapeirousia*, a widespread African genus, and several species were included in *Lapeirousia* subgenus *Anomatheca*, for example, by Baker (1896). *Anomatheca*, first described by Ker Gawler in 1804, was restored to generic rank by Goldblatt (1972). Seed and leaf anatomical studies subsequently showed that *Freesia* and *Anomatheca* are congeneric, and the two were united by Goldblatt and Manning (1995a) at the same time that the unusual *A. fistulosa* was transferred to the new genus *Xenoscapa*.

The possibility of a relationship between *Freesia* and *Lapeirousia* is now known to be untenable. The axial corm development and smooth seeds lacking surface cell outlines of *Freesia* are inconsistent with *Lapeirousia*, which has axillary corm development, seed surface cells with prominent outlines, and different leaf marginal anatomy. This led Goldblatt and Manning (1995a, 2000b) to suggest that *Freesia* might be allied to *Tritonia* and *Crocosmia*, with which the fundamental features of corm development and leaf anatomy are consistent. Sequences of several chloroplast DNA regions now show that

*Freesia* is immediately related to *Xenoscapa*. These two genera are together allied to *Crocosmia* and *Devia*, which have notched but not deeply divided style branches. The four genera are now regarded as comprising tribe Freesieae within subfamily Crocoideae (Goldblatt et al. 2006).

Pollination of *Freesia* has received little attention, but our own observations show that most species are pollinated by large anthophorine bees and *Apis mellifera* workers. *Freesia grandiflora* and *F. laxa* are most likely pollinated by large butterflies, and *F. viridis*, which has flowers that are usually scented at night, by moths. Thus even the relatively small genus *Freesia* shows marked diversity in its pollination ecology.

*Anomaza* Lawson ex Salisbury (1812: 323), a name without description and thus invalid, has been regarded as a synonym of *Anomatheca* (and thus now of *Freesia*), but the basionym of the type species, *A. excisa*, is *Ixia excisa*, a later synonym of *I. ovata* (now *Geissorhiza ovata*).

**Xenoscapa** (Goldblatt) Goldblatt & J. C. Manning (1995a: 172)
Plate 83; Figure 31
Tribe Freesieae
*Anomatheca* section *Xenoscapa* Goldblatt (1972: 88), type: *X. fistulosa* (Sprengel ex Klatt) Goldblatt & J. C. Manning
ETYMOLOGY: from the Greek *xenos*, strange, and *scapa*, flowering stem, for the unusual flowering stem, which bears a single flower on the main and lateral branches

Seasonal perennials with small globose corms, rooting from below and axial in origin, the tunics of fine fibers. LEAVES few, the lower two or three cataphylls, foliage leaves unifacial, two or three, with a definite midrib, prostrate, soft-textured, the margins with columnar epidermal cells. STEM short or long,

**Figure 31.** (left) *Xenoscapa fistulosa* with capsule (below, ×1.5) and seed (above, ×15), (right) *X. uliginosa* with capsule (bottom right, ×1.5) and stigma (×5).

erect, terete, often with one to three short branches. INFLORESCENCE of solitary, sessile flowers terminal on the axes; BRACTS green, leathery, the inner often slightly longer, or slightly shorter, than the outer, often notched apically. FLOWERS zygomorphic, tubular or salver-shaped, cream and sweetly scented or pink with contrasting markings on the lower tepals and odorless, with nectar from septal nectaries; PERIANTH TUBE cylindric and elongate; TEPALS subequal, spreading or the dorsal erect, slightly larger, and spoon-shaped. STAMENS unilateral and arcuate; ANTHERS exserted, parallel. OVARY globose, sessile; STYLE filiform, with short, deeply divided, recurved branches. CAPSULES oblong to cylindric, cartilaginous; SEEDS strongly angled, with a prominent chalazal crest, lightly wrinkled, matte, the surface cells tuberculate. BASIC CHROMOSOME NUMBER $x = 11$. Species two, in the southern African winter-rainfall zone of southern Namibia and western South Africa.

*Xenoscapa* species are small plants, rarely exceeding 10 cm, and more often only 3–5 cm high. The small, rounded corms have fine, fibrous tunics and produce roots from the base while the basal leaves are prostrate and soft-textured and have marginal epidermal cells columnar with thickened lateral and outer walls. The stems are unbranched or have one or two branches, which always bear only a single flower each. The inflorescence is nevertheless interpreted as a single-flowered spike. The seeds are angular and have a rough surface due to the strongly domed epidermal cells of the seed coat. Flowers of both species are zygomorphic and have a fairly long perianth tube, and in *X. fistulosa* the dorsal tepal is hooded over the stamens.

The relationships of *Xenoscapa* have long been puzzling. The taxonomic history of the widespread and locally common *X. fistulosa* reflects this uncertainty, for the species was first assigned to the genus *Ovieda* and later transferred to *Lapeirousia* by Baker (1877) when *Ovieda* was found to be a

later synonym for this genus. In 1972 the plant was referred to *Anomatheca* (Goldblatt 1972) after it became clear that it did not belong in *Lapeirousia*, a genus defined by its woody, bell-shaped corms. It seemed to accord with *Anomatheca* because of the shared fibrous corm tunics and forked style branches. Subsequently, *Anomatheca* was assigned to infrageneric rank in *Freesia*, but because *Xenoscapa* seeds differ fundamentally from those of *Freesia*, Goldblatt and Manning (1995a) argued against inclusion in *Freesia*, which has specialized smooth, round seeds, often with an inflated raphe, and warty capsules. The unusual branching pattern and smooth-walled, elongate capsules, the only obvious specializations in the genus, do not suggest any particular alliance, and *Xenoscapa* seems to be an isolated relic. Evidence from base sequences of chloroplast DNA shows that the genus is, in fact, closely allied to *Freesia* and *Crocosmia*, most likely sister to the remaining species of the other three genera included in tribe Freesieae. Both *Freesia* and *Xenoscapa* share derived, deeply forked style branches, and the entire tribe has specialized leaf marginal anatomy, with columnar epidermal cells and absence of a submarginal sclerenchyma strand.

*Xenoscapa fistulosa* is widespread in the southern African winter-rainfall zone and extends from southern Namibia into South Africa, where it occurs in Namaqualand, and through the western Karoo to the Little Karoo near Oudtshoorn. Plants favor seasonally damp, clay or granitic soils on south-facing slopes, often shaded for much of the day during the growing season. The second species, *X. uliginosa*, is a localized endemic of the high Kamiesberg of Namaqualand, where all known collections are from Sneeukop peak. Its long-tubed, pink flowers are pollinated by the long proboscid fly *Prosoeca peringueyi* (Nemestrinidae). The fairly small, whitish, fragrant flowers of *X. fistulosa*, which remain open at night, have the hallmarks of pollination by small moths.

*Radinosiphon* N. E. Brown (1932: 263)
Plate 84; Figure 32
Tribe Croceae
LECTOTYPE here designated: *Radinosiphon leptostachya* (Baker) N. E. Brown
ETYMOLOGY: from the Greek *radinosus*, slender, and *siphon*, tube, for the tubular flowers
REVISIONARY ACCOUNTS: Carter (1962), Goldblatt (1993b: 65)

Deciduous geophytes with globose corms, rooting from below and axial in origin, the tunics papery, becoming finely fibrous. LEAVES several, the lower two or three cataphylls; foliage leaves sword-shaped, plane with a definite midrib, mostly basal and forming a lax two-ranked fan, fairly softly textured. STEM aerial, simple or few-branched, compressed and angled. INFLORESCENCE a spike, the flowers facing to one side; BRACTS green, soft-textured, becoming dry apically, the inner shorter than the outer, notched apically. FLOWERS zygomorphic, long-lived, salver-shaped, pink to light purple, the lower tepals with nectar guides, unscented, with nectar from septal nectaries; PERIANTH TUBE cylindric, elongate; TEPALS subequal, the dorsal slightly larger and hooded, the lower tepals forming a lip. STAMENS unilateral and arcuate; FILAMENTS slender, free; ANTHERS parallel, linear-oblong, splitting longitudinally. OVARY globose, sessile; STYLE filiform, the branches slender, undivided, diverging. CAPSULES globose, cartilaginous; SEEDS globose, flattened at the chalazal end, few to several per locule, lightly wrinkled, matte, the surface colliculate. BASIC CHROMOSOME NUMBER $x = 15$. Species probably two, mainly montane, extending from Mpumalanga Province, South Africa, and Swaziland through eastern Zimbabwe, Zambia, and Malawi to southern Tanzania in rocky habitats, or short grassland and light bush.

Although a typical member of subfamily Crocoideae in its corm, its tubular, long-lived flower, and its perforate pollen grains with a two-banded operculum, there is little that distinguishes *Radinosiphon* as a genus, and its relationships have long remained obscure. It most closely resembles *Freesia* in general appearance, but the leaf anatomy is inconsistent with that genus. The leaf blades have a submarginal sclerenchyma strand and small, undifferentiated marginal epidermal cells, and this as well as the undivided style and base number $x = 15$ make a relationship with *Freesia* unlikely. An affinity with *Gladiolus* has seemed more plausible on the grounds of similar leaf anatomy and shared basic chromosome number, but the angled stems of *Radinosiphon* contrast with the rounded stems typical of *Gladiolus*. That *Radinosiphon* seeds are wingless, unlike typical *Gladiolus* seeds, also argues against a relationship with that genus, although seeds with vestigial wings are known in a few species of *Gladiolus*.

Studies using several chloroplast DNA regions provide a surprising result—*Radinosiphon* is sister genus to the clade that includes *Romulea* and the generic pair *Crocus* and *Syringodea*, all of which show a tendency to a stemless habit. Some other features are, however, consistent with this relationship—all have the same marginal anatomy (when leaves are unifacial), and the pollen grains are sulcate with a two-banded operculum, at least in *Romulea* (inaperturate pollen grains are typical of *Crocus* and *Syringodea*). Other features of *Romulea* and *Syringodea*, such as the woody corm tunics, and divided style branches in the former, must be viewed as specializations for those genera alone. Statistical support for this unexpected alliance is so strong that it is unlikely that the molecular data are providing a false signal of relationship.

There has long been confusion about the number of species in *Radinosiphon*. N. E. Brown (1932), who described the genus, recognized five species, four transferred from *Lapeirousia* and *Gladiolus*, and one new one. A review by Carter (1962) correctly transferred *R. leptosiphon* back to *Gladiolus*

**Figure 32.** *Radinosiphon leptostachya* with capsule (right, above, ×1) and seed (center right, ×12).

and placed three species in the synonymy of *R. leptostachya,* leaving *R. lomatensis* as the second species in the genus. *Radinosiphon leptostachya,* at least at its type population near MacMac Falls in Mpumalanga Province, South Africa, has relatively small flowers, typically two small seeds per locule (up to six per capsule), and is autogamous. This contrasts with plants matching larger-flowered *R. lomatensis,* which have up to eight seeds per locule (as many as 24 per capsule) and are pollinated by the long-proboscid fly *Prosoeca ganglbauri.* Provisionally, two species continue to be recognized in *Radinosiphon,* but we note that pollination, reproductive biology, and seed number per locule are unknown for most populations across its wide range from central Swaziland into tropical Africa as far north as Tanzania.

*Romulea* Maratti (1772: 13, pl. 1)
Plates 85–95; Figure 33
Tribe Croceae
Name conserved against *Ilmu* Adanson (1763)
TYPE: *Romulea bulbocodium* (Linnaeus) Sebastiani & Mauri
ETYMOLOGY: named for Romulus, one of the legendary founders of Rome, because a species of the genus is common in the Roman countryside
SYNONYMS: *Bulbocodium* Miller (1759: 160), type: *B. pedunculis nudis uniflorus, foliis subulatis longissimis,* illegitimate name, not *Bulbocodium* Linnaeus (1753; Colchicaceae), = *Romulea rosea* (Linnaeus) Ecklon; *Ilmu* Adanson (1763: 497, 566), rejected name, type not designated; *Trichonema* Ker Gawler (1802a), type: *T. cruciatum* (Jacquin) Ker Gawler = *R. cruciata* (Jacquin) Baker; *Spatalanthus* Sweet (1829a), type: *S. speciosus* Sweet = *R. monadelpha* (Sweet) Baker
REVISIONARY ACCOUNTS: De Vos (1972; 1983a: 10–73, southern African species), Manning and Goldblatt (2001b, sub-Saharan African species)

Deciduous perennials with asymmetric or bell-shaped corms, rooting from a circular or crescent-shaped basal ridge or around the basal edges and axial in origin, the tunics of hard woody, or rarely fibrous layers. LEAVES few to several, the lower two or three cataphylls, foliage leaves solitary or several, usually with a definite midrib, more or less filiform or cylindric, straight or twisted, occasionally hairy on the margins, usually the midrib and margins thickened, or the margins sometimes winged, the blade thus oval to terete in transverse section with two longitudinal grooves on each surface between the margins and midrib, occasionally up to eight-grooved or nearly plane with lightly thickened margins and midrib, rarely bifacial and channeled. STEM short, subterranean or aerial, occasionally hairy, usually branched, sometimes only below the ground, sometimes coiled in fruit. INFLORESCENCE composed of solitary flowers terminal on the branches; BRACTS green or membranous, the margins of the outer sometimes and of the inner always membranous to dry and pale or rusty, occasionally the inner completely dry, the inner usually acute, undivided apically. FLOWERS radially symmetric, long lasting, mostly bell-shaped, the cup deep or shallow, or salver-shaped, variously colored, often paler in the floral cup or throat, sometimes with darker markings, often with prominent dark veining on the outside; PERIANTH TUBE usually short and funnel-shaped, sometimes elongate and cylindric; TEPALS equal or subequal, usually ascending below and spreading above. STAMENS radially symmetric; FILAMENTS erect, more or less contiguous, occasionally united, often slightly swollen and hairy below; ANTHERS linear, diverging or contiguous, splitting longitudinally. OVARY globose, sessile; STYLE filiform, exserted from the tube, branching opposite or beyond the anthers, the branches usually divided for half their length, rarely multifid. CAPSULES oblong to subglobose,

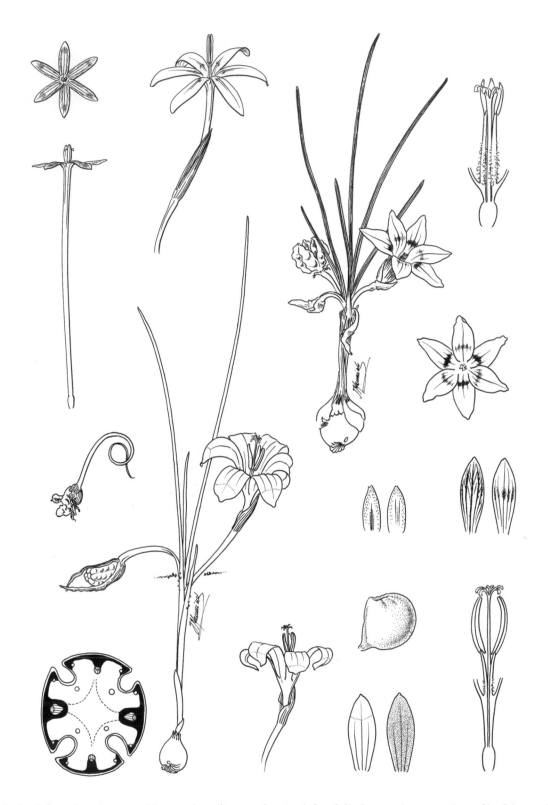

**Figure 33.** (below) *Romulea eburnea* with capsule split open (center left, ×0.8), (bottom) transection of leaf (lower left, ×25), flower (side view), detached tepals, showing lower surfaces (inner, left, and outer, right) (all ×0.8), detail of stamens and style (lower right, ×1.5), and seed (×10), (upper left) *R. hantamensis* flower (front and side views, ×0.8), (top center) *R. albiflora* flower (×0.8), (upper right) *R. collina* with flower (front view), bracts (inner, left, and outer, right), detached tepals, showing lower surfaces (outer, left, and inner, right) (all ×0.8), and detail of stamens and style (top right, ×3).

cartilaginous; SEEDS globose or lightly angled, flattened at the chalazal end, smooth, matte, the surface cells usually colliculate. BASIC CHROMOSOME NUMBER *x* = 14 or 13, other base numbers 12, 11, 10, 9. Species c. 92, widespread across Africa, southern Europe, and the Middle East but centered in the winter-rainfall zone of South Africa and with a secondary center in the western Mediterranean and Canary Islands.

*Romulea* species are readily recognized by their very short stems or stemless habit combined with slender, often almost needle-like leaves with four longitudinal grooves, two on each surface. Most species have relatively large flowers carried close to ground level and borne singly on the branches, several of which are produced by each plant. The flowers typically have a short perianth tube and are cup-shaped, with the stamens symmetrically arranged around the central style. The style branches are deeply divided, even multifid in some species. In addition to the habit, leaves, and flowers, the genus can often be recognized by the corms, which have woody tunics and are usually asymmetric with a rounded base, often with a crescent-shaped lateral ridge directed downward, a corm type that is typical of subgenus *Romulea*. In subgenus *Spatalanthus* the corm has a rounded or pointed base, and the tunics have fairly prominent basal teeth, directed downward or recurving to lie appressed to the corm base.

There are a fair number of exceptions to the norms for both subgenera. Several species have symmetric, bell-shaped corms (e.g., *Romulea discifera, R. hirsuta*), and a few species also have salver-shaped rather than bell-shaped flowers, notably *R. hantamensis* and *R. kamisensis*, accompanied by an elongate tube filled with nectar, in contrast to the trace amounts of nectar, or evident absence of nectar, in bell-shaped flowers. Even leaf form varies—the leaves of *R. barkerae* have two longitudinal grooves and a channeled upper surface while *R.*

*aquatica* and *R. multisulcata* have leaves round in section with multiple longitudinal grooves.

Both morphological and molecular data show *Romulea* close to the line that gave rise to *Crocus* and *Syringodea,* genera in which the stem is invariably entirely underground when the flowers open, the perianth tube is elongate, and the leaves are usually secondarily bifacial and flat or channeled. The asymmetric corms and woody tunics with the roots arising from a basal ridge suggest a common ancestry with *Geissorhiza* and *Hesperantha,* but this hypothesis is disputed by molecular data, which show that the immediate ancestor to the *Romulea–Crocus–Syringodea* clade is the eastern African *Radinosiphon,* a situation discussed in more detail under the latter genus.

Pollination biology of *Romulea* is surprisingly diverse for a genus with a fairly conservative flower structure (Goldblatt et al. 2002). Key to the floral biology of the genus is flower color and marking, and secondarily presence or absence of scent. Yellow, white, blue, or pink flowers with a yellow cup and small dark markings are often sweetly scented and are pollinated largely by a range of bees of different families. This pattern is particularly true in late winter and spring in the southern African winter-rainfall zone. Prime examples of such species are *R. flava* and *R. tortuosa*. In western southern Africa, later-flowering species like *R. komsbergensis, R. monadelpha,* and *R. sabulosa* have more brilliantly colored flowers, usually in shades of cherry red, scarlet, or bright purple, and have prominent dark markings in the floral cup. These flowers are unscented, and their main visitors are hopliine scarab beetles. Several species seem equally attractive to both bees and hopliines, and it is not clear which class of pollinators is the legitimate one, or whether the species have a truly bimodal pollination system that consistently relies on pollination by either of the two insect groups.

More striking are the salver-shaped flowers with an elongate, cylindrical perianth tube in *Romulea hantamensis, R. kamisensis,* and *R. syringodeoflora.* These flowers are pollinated by long-proboscid nemestrinid flies. From what we know about the relationships of *Romulea* species, it is evident that long-proboscid fly pollination evolved independently in each of these species, for all three belong to different sections of the genus.

Readily cultivated, *Romulea* species have a following among bulb enthusiasts. Best grown in containers where they are not overwhelmed by larger, more aggressive plants, they can make a remarkable seasonal display. The large size of most *Romulea* flowers always comes as a surprise, for they are so disproportionate to the small plants.

*Afrocrocus* J. C. Manning & Goldblatt, new genus
Plate 96; Figure 34
Tribe Croceae
TYPE: *Afrocrocus unifolius* (Goldblatt) Goldblatt & J. C. Manning, new combination; basionym: *Syringodea unifolia* Goldblatt (1972)
ETYMOLOGY: named for the resemblance to *Crocus* and its occurrence in Africa

*Geophyta decidua, cormo laterale compresso radicibus infra productis, tunicis plus minusve lignosis, foliis paucis inferioribus unus vel duo cataphyllis, foliis foliosis uno vel duis infra canaliculatis in partem distale teretis, caule subterranea pauciramoso, inflorescentia florum sessile, bracteis membranaceis marginibus infra connatis, floribus hypocrateriformibus violaceis, tubo perianthii cylindrico elongato, tepalis subaequalibus leviter cupulatis, antheris linearibus longitudinaliter dehiscentibus, ovario subterraneo, stylo filiforme ramoris breviter multifidis, capsulis ellipsoideis, seminibus subglobosis rugulosis.*

Deciduous geophytes with laterally compressed corms, lens-shaped, with a wide, fan-shaped basal ridge, axial in origin and rooting from below, the tunics more or less woody, decaying into fine parallel fibrils along the basal ridge. LEAVES few, the lower two or three cataphylls; foliage leaf solitary or two, thick and fleshy, bifacial and lightly channeled in the basal half or for most of its length, terete in the distal part. STEM short, subterranean, few-branched below the ground. INFLORESCENCE composed of sessile flowers terminal on short branches; BRACTS membranous, the margins united below, the inner usually notched apically. FLOWERS radially symmetric, salver-shaped, violet; PERIANTH TUBE cylindric, elongate; TEPALS subequal, lightly cupped. STAMENS symmetrically disposed; FILAMENTS slender, inserted at the mouth of the tube, divergent; ANTHERS ascending, linear, splitting longitudinally. OVARY subterranean, ovoid, sessile; STYLE filiform, the branch tips shortly multifid. CAPSULES ellipsoid; SEEDS globose to weakly angled, rugulose, flattened at the chalazal end, glossy dark brown. BASIC CHROMOSOME NUMBER $x = 11$. Species only *Afrocrocus unifolius*, South Africa, in the southwestern Karoo, on the Roggeveld Escarpment and adjacent mountain ranges, mainly in clay soils in shrubland, flowering in early winter.

Evident only in the early winter, from May to early July, when its violet *Crocus*-like flowers appear in response to the first seasonal rains, *Afrocrocus,* with the single species *A. unifolius,* has had a confused history. It was first described as *Syringodea rosea* by Klatt (1882) but was renamed because the specific epithet was illegitimate. The new and more apt name *S. unifolia* was established in 1971. De Vos's (1974a) revision of *Syringodea* brought into sharp focus the differences between *S. unifolia* and the other seven *Syringodea* species. They are substantial and include the flattened, crescent-shaped corm with tunics composed of unique flattened, plate-like, heavily lignified cells, fringed rather than simple style branches, and especially striking, large, ellipsoid capsules, up to 2 cm long, that split open in the conventional way into three parts as they dry

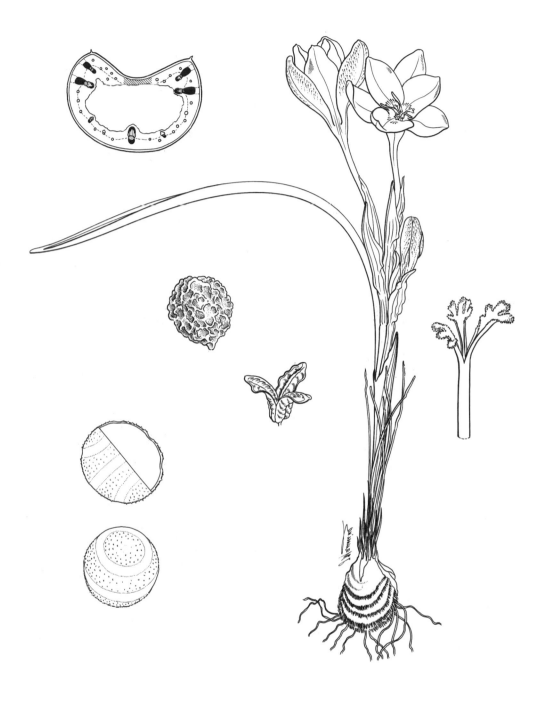

**Figure 34.** *Afrocrocus unifolius* with capsule split open (×1) and seed (×12) at center, detail of stigmas (right, ×12), transection of leaf (upper left, ×20), and pollen (lower left, ×400).

out. The latter feature contrasts with the unusually small (5–10 mm long), specialized, top-shaped capsules of other *Syringodea* species, which split open only when wet into six segments, a unique feature in the Iridaceae. The capsules of *Afrocrocus* also lack the short sterile base of the ovary found in other *Syringodea* species that elongates in fruit, helping to raise the capsule above the ground. In *Afrocrocus* the elongating peduncle alone performs that function, reaching c. 25 mm by the time the capsules are ripe. Even the leaves differ from most *Syringodea* species in being round in cross section in the upper half whereas those of *Syringodea* are typically channeled or grooved and bifacial throughout their length, except in *S. saxatilis* in which the distal part of the leaf is also round but anatomically very different from the leaf of *Afrocrocus*. The leaf of *Afrocrocus* has an adaxial strip of cells with thick walls composed of cellulose, visible as a translucent median band, in the channeled lower section of the blade, whereas those in *Syringodea* do not. It also differs from *Syringodea* in several other features, including the presence of strands or girders of thin-walled parenchyma cells between the main vascular bundles and the epidermis, and in the lack of tannin-containing cells. Basic chromosome number also differs; while *Syringodea* species have $x = 6$, *Afrocrocus* has $x = 11$.

These differences prompted De Vos to place *Syringodea unifolia* in a separate subgenus, *Rhipidiopsis*. We see its features as so unusual that we favor separating the species in its own genus, especially in light of additional differences of a degree that typically characterize separate genera. These include the seeds, which are twice the size of those of *Syringodea* species (2 mm in diameter versus 1 mm) and have a closely wrinkled surface that is glossy and lacks visible cellular details. The seeds are also apparently sticky when fresh as the mature seeds become covered with adhering sand grains when they are shed. Seeds of *Syringodea* are, in contrast,

smoothly rounded in outline, with the individual cells domed. Pollen too, differs, for the pollen grains of *Syringodea* are inaperturate (De Vos 1974), while on close examination we have found the grains of *Afrocrocus* to be trizonasulcate, with a meridional and two polar ring-like apertures.

Like its southern African relative *Syringodea*, *Afrocrocus* closely resembles the Old World temperate genus *Crocus* in general appearance and habit. The acaulescent plants produce their flowers from below the ground on an elongate perianth tube. At the time of flowering, in autumn, the leaves are usually just beginning to emerge, another *Crocus*-like feature. It is clear that the three genera are closely related, but they are readily distinguished by differences in corm and leaf structure, seeds, and pollen grains. The channeled leaves of most *Syringodea* species contrast with those of *Crocus*, which are also bifacial but have an upper surface that is flat rather than channeled, and bisected by a median band of transparent tissue in the midline. In addition, in most species of *Crocus* the lower surface is keeled and ridged. Pollen of *Crocus* is either spiraperturate or inaperturate, suggesting that the trizonasulcate pollen of *Afrocrocus* is a unique and highly specialized condition.

Phylogenetic analysis using DNA sequences indicate that *Afrocrocus*, *Crocus*, and *Syringodea* comprise a clade (Figure 7) that is sister to the African and Eurasian genus *Romulea*, species of which have asymmetric corms with a lateral ridge and woody corm tunics. They also have reduced inflorescences with flowers solitary on the aerial branches, or the plants have stems entirely underground. The narrow, four-grooved leaves of *Romulea* are highly specialized and bear no resemblance to the bifacial or terete leaves of *Afrocrocus*, *Crocus*, or *Syringodea*. The bell-shaped flowers of *Romulea* and deeply divided style branches of the genus also contrast with its allies.

*Syringodea* J. D. Hooker (1873)
Plates 97–98; Figure 35
Tribe Croceae
Conserved name
TYPE: *Syringodea pulchella* J. D. Hooker
ETYMOLOGY: named for the long perianth tube, from the Greek *syrinx,* a pipe
REVISIONARY ACCOUNTS: De Vos (1974a; 1983a: 1–9)

Deciduous geophytes with asymmetric, top-shaped corms with a circular to crescent-shaped basal ridge, rooting from below and axial in origin, the tunics woody to papery. LEAVES few to several, the lower two or three cataphylls; foliage leaves several or solitary, usually entirely bifacial and channeled to flat, without a definite midrib, linear to lanceolate, rarely shortly terete in the distal half. STEM short, subterranean, often branched, sometimes sheathed below by a collar of fibers. INFLORESCENCE composed of sessile flowers terminal on branches; BRACTS membranous, the margins united below, the inner usually notched apically. FLOWERS radially symmetric, salver-shaped, shades of purple to pink, rarely white; PERIANTH TUBE cylindric, elongate; TEPALS equal or subequal, spreading. STAMENS symmetrically disposed; FILAMENTS slender, surrounding the mouth of the tube; ANTHERS erect or ascending. OVARY subterranean, globose, sessile; STYLE filiform, the branches short, undivided or the apices shortly multifid. CAPSULES club-shaped with a narrow sterile tubular base, six-valved and opening when wet; SEEDS globose to weakly angled, smooth, flattened at the chalazal end, lightly wrinkled, matte, the surface cells colliculate or foveolate. BASIC CHROMOSOME NUMBER $x = 6$. Species seven, South Africa, mainly in semiarid parts of the center of the country but extending from northern Namaqualand across the Great Karoo as far north as the Vaal River in Free State and East London in Eastern Cape Province, mainly in clay soils in karroid scrub, but *Syringodea montana* is often found on sandy ground, flowering in autumn.

Poorly known and seldom seen, *Syringodea* species closely resemble the Mediterranean and Eurasian genus *Crocus* in general appearance and habit. Plants are acaulescent and produce their flowers shortly above the ground, raised from the underground ovary on an elongate perianth tube. At the time of flowering, in autumn, the leaves are usually just beginning to emerge, another *Crocus*-like feature. That the two genera are closely related seems certain, but they are readily distinguished by differences in leaf structure and their corms. The leaves of most *Syringodea* species are narrow and channeled, sometimes with a short, laterally compressed, unifacial tip (which resembles the typical leaf blade of most other the Iridaceae). *Syringodea saxatilis* is specialized in having a terete leaf blade and is additionally specialized in having just a single leaf each season. The leaf of *Crocus* is also bifacial, but the upper surface is flat rather than channeled, there is a band of transparent tissue in the midline, and in most species the lower surface is elaborately keeled and ridged.

The corm tunics of *Syringodea* consist of more or less woody, concentric layers, and the corms are asymmetric, with one side somewhat flattened and drawn into a point. In contrast, the corms of *Crocus* species are globose, symmetric, and have leathery, papery, or fibrous tunics. Despite the several detailed differences between the leaves and corms of *Syringodea* and *Crocus,* the two genera do share more than the same general *gestalt.* The leaves are bifacial in both, although those of *Crocus* appear more specialized. Another feature linking the genera is the pollen, which is inaperturate and has small spines in *Syringodea* and many species of *Crocus.* *Syringodea* is exceptional in having the sterile base of the ovary elongating in fruit, thus helping to raise

**Figure 35.** (below) *Syringodea concolor* in habitat (×1), (upper left) *S. longituba* pollen (above, ×400), capsule (center, ×1), and seed (below, ×12), (upper right) *S. pulchella* (×1).

the ripening capsules above the ground prior to release of the seeds.

Elsewhere (Manning and Goldblatt 2001b) we have suggested that *Crocus* and *Syringodea* comprise a clade that is sister to the Eurasian genus *Romulea*, species of which have woody corm tunics, and asymmetric corms with a lateral ridge. They also have reduced inflorescences with flowers solitary on the aerial branches, or the plants have stems entirely underground. The narrow, four-grooved leaves of *Romulea* are highly specialized and bear no resemblance to the bifacial leaves of *Crocus* or *Syringodea*. The flowers of *Romulea* are bell-shaped except in a few derived species, and the style branches are deeply divided, whereas those of *Syringodea* are simple or shortly multifid at the tips. Molecular evidence, using several DNA regions of the chloroplast, available since 2000 confirms that *Crocus* and *Syringodea* are immediately related genera and that they form a clade sister to *Romulea* (Reeves et al. 2001, Goldblatt et al. 2006).

Biologically, species of *Syringodea* are unusual for the Iridaceae—they typically flower in the autumn or early winter following good autumn rain and produce capsules and seeds in the spring. A remarkable feature of the genus is the moisture-responsive (hygrochastic) splitting and opening of the capsules. Unlike other Iridaceae, the capsule valves of these species open in wet weather and close when dry, and these specialized capsules have six valves instead of the usual three. The ecological advantage of this unusual specialization must relate to seed dispersal and germination during wet conditions, presumably so that seeds will be dispersed by water and will germinate and become established in favorable conditions. A more complete explanation awaits further investigation. This type of capsule splitting is not known in other Iridaceae, including the closely allied genus *Crocus*. The unusual, large-flowered species long known as *S. unifolia,* and

exceptional in the genus in its capsules that conform to the normal pattern in the family, opening when dry, is now segregated as the genus *Afrocrocus*. Its peculiar, laterally compressed corms, solitary terete leaf, distinctive pollen, and diploid chromosome number $2n = 22$ also argue for its separation from *Syringodea*.

Pollination biology of *Syringodea* is unknown. The flowers have a long perianth tube, but the thick walls of the tube tightly sheathe the style so that the tube is not hollow. Nectar is evidently not produced, and we assume that *Syringodea* species are pollen flowers, that is, they offer pollen as a reward to female bees and *Apis mellifera* workers for nest provisioning.

**_Crocus_** Linnaeus (1753: 36)
Plates 99–105; Figure 36
Tribe Croceae
TYPE: *Crocus sativus* Linnaeus
ETYMOLOGY: from the Greek *kroko,* saffron, the spice obtained from the styles and stigmas of several of the species
REVISIONARY ACCOUNTS: Maw (1886, somewhat outdated but beautifully illustrated), Mathew (1982)

Deciduous geophytes with globose corms, axial in origin and rooting from below, the tunics leathery, papery, or fibrous. LEAVES few to several, the lower two or three cataphylls; foliage leaves bifacial, the blade linear, without a definite midrib, flat or lightly channeled above and with a broad median band of transparent tissue, with a rounded or rectangular keel beneath, the keel usually ridged and with two prominent wings. STEM short, subterranean, often branched, sometimes sheathed below by a fibrous collar. INFLORESCENCE of solitary flowers terminal on the peduncles; BRACTS membranous, the margins united below, the inner usually notched

**Figure 36.** (top left) *Crocus biflorus* (×0.8), (center right) *C. boryi* (×0.8), (top right, center, and lower left, above) *C. vernus* pollen (×400), detail of stigma (×4), fruit (×0.8), transection of leaf (×8), and seed (×10), and (lower left, below) *C. tommasianus* seed (×10).

apically. FLOWERS radially symmetric, salver- or funnel-shaped, shades of lilac to purple, yellow, or white, evidently without nectar, sometimes sweetly scented; PERIANTH TUBE cylindric, elongate; TEPALS subequal and similarly disposed or occasionally the inner tepals erect and much smaller than the spreading outer tepals. STAMENS symmetrically disposed; FILAMENTS free, slender; ANTHERS linear, erect or diverging, splitting longitudinally. OVARY subterranean, ovoid, sessile; STYLE filiform, dividing into three branches, these either short and undivided, or long and deeply forked or repeatedly divided. CAPSULES usually club- or top-shaped, raised above the ground as they ripen; SEEDS globose or pear-shaped, sometimes lightly angled, flattened or lobed at the chalazal end, sometimes with a prominently ridged or wing-like raphe, the raphe occasionally bearing a white fleshy appendage, matte brown or purple, the surface cells domed, papillate, or tuberculate and seeds then velvety. BASIC CHROMOSOME NUMBER uncertain, possibly $x = 6$, other base numbers 11, 7, 5, 4, and 3. Species c. 85, extending across southern Europe, North Africa, the Middle East, and into the mountains of central Asia as far east as the Tian Shan mountains of Kazakhstan and western China.

One of the best known genera of the Iridaceae, *Crocus* is recognized immediately by its stemless growth habit, with the tubular flowers produced before or just as the leaves emerge from the ground. In fact, its growth habit has given its name to the acaulescent or crocus-type growth form. Plants are stemless at flowering time, and the medium-sized to large flowers are raised above the ground on a long perianth tube. Like other genera of Crocoideae, the flowers of *Crocus* are long lasting and have a fairly firm texture. In spring-blooming species the leaves emerge at the same time the first flowers are produced and reach their full size after the last flowers have faded. Autumn-blooming *Crocus* species may

also have emergent leaves as flowering begins, or the leaves may be well developed before buds begin to open.

The leaves of most *Crocus* species are narrow and bifacial, in stark contrast to nearly all other Crocoideae, and consist of a more or less flat upper surface and an elaborate more or less rectangular ridged keel on the underside. The keel is not developed in the Iberian *C. carpetanus* and *C. nevadensis,* in which the lower surface is rounded and longitudinally grooved. *Crocus* leaves are also distinctive in having a broad, transparent median band of tissue running the entire length of the upper surface. Corms of *Crocus* species are typical of the subfamily in their rounded shape and axial origin, and in the production of roots from the underside. Corm tunics are variable in texture, ranging from hard, leathery or papery layers that split at the base, or parallel or netted fibers. An early classification of *Crocus* was developed based largely on the nature of the corm tunics.

The flowers themselves are often brightly colored, in shades of purple to lilac or yellow to white, and may have contrasting markings at the base of the tepals. The long perianth tube, arising from the underground ovary, an important feature of the genus, seems to function mainly as the means to raise the reproductive parts of the flower above the ground. Unlike the hollow, nectar-filled tubes of most Crocoideae, the perianth tube in some *Crocus* species at least (e.g., *C. alatavicus, C. hyemalis*) has thick walls and the narrow interior space is fully occupied by the style, and the tubes lack nectar. Early pollination studies in *Crocus,* however, record nectar in *C. vernus.* Pollen grains of *Crocus* are unusual for the Crocoideae, being either inaperturate or spiraperturate, though the exine matches the perforate condition of most other members of the subfamily. Another variable feature of *Crocus* flowers is the style, the branches of which range from undivided to forked for some distance or irregularly fringed. The enlarged, prominent style branches of the cultivated *C. sativus* are flattened and unevenly divided toward the tips. The bracts subtending the flowers are membranous and tubular, with their lower margins united, thus the outer bracts enclose the inner one. An important feature within the genus is the presence or absence of a bract-like structure at the base of the flower stalk. The bract condition defines the two sections of the genus: *Crocus*, basal bract present, or *Nudiflorae*, basal bract absent.

The early stages of fruit development take place while the ovary is still below ground, but as the fruit matures into a capsule the flowering stalk elongates, raising the developing fruit several centimeters above the ground. In the allied *Afrocrocus* from southern Africa, the capsules are raised above the ground in the same way, but in the closely related *Syringodea*, which has the same growth habit as *Crocus*, the capsules are raised above the ground by elongation of the lower part of the ovary, a growth pattern unlike that of *Crocus* and one unique in the Iridaceae. Seeds are unusually variable and may be globose or pear-shaped, the latter due to a small lobe at the chalazal end of the seed. The raphe is often prominent and may even be enlarged into a wing-like ridge. Seeds of a few species, including *C. dalmaticus*, have a white, fleshy outgrowth from the raphe, evidently a fat body or elaiosome. Although *Crocus* seeds are often described as having a caruncle, this is not strictly correct, for a true caruncle is an outgrowth from the mouth of the micropyle.

Type genus of subfamily Crocoideae, *Crocus* is one of just three of the 29 genera of the subfamily that occur outside Africa and is the only one that has radiated extensively across the Mediterranean Basin and western Asia. The genus has a pronounced center in southeastern Europe and Turkey, and Turkey alone has more than 30 native species. *Crocus* species show two contrasting flowering patterns. Best known is the early-spring-blooming type, in which the flower emerges soon after the days have begun to lengthen and the ground thaws, sometimes only days after snow melts. The leaves emerge as flowering commences but reach maturity as the capsules ripen. In contrast, a range of species, mostly of the Mediterranean coast, flower in late autumn and early winter, mainly October and November. The leaves usually follow after the flowers have faded, but sometimes they remain within the basal sheaths and emerge only in spring.

The relationships of *Crocus* lie first with the southern African *Afrocrocus* and *Syringodea*, which have the same growth form, and then with the widespread African and Mediterranean *Romulea*. The relationship was first postulated because of the reduction of the flowering axis in all three and the similar asymmetric corm and woody tunics in *Romulea* and *Syringodea*. The relationship has been confirmed by DNA sequence studies (Goldblatt et al. 2006). *Syringodea* and some species of *Crocus* have inaperturate pollen grains, an additional feature linking the two genera. As *Afrocrocus* and *Syringodea* species flower in autumn, it seems likely that autumn-flowering *Crocus* species are closer to the ancestral type than those that bloom in the spring.

Despite its horticultural importance and frequency in the wild, virtually nothing is known of its pollination. One species, examined by the Israeli biologist Amots Dafni, the eastern Mediterranean *Crocus hyemalis*, lacks nectar despite its comparatively long perianth tube. The extended perianth tube functions only to raise the flowers above the ground; they are thus pollen flowers, offering only pollen to visiting female bees. Pollinators captured on *C. hyemalis* include native honeybees, *Apis mellifera*, as well as species of Andrenidae and Halictidae. The sweet scent in *C. hyemalis* is produced by glands on the filaments. Although *C. vernus* is reported to have nectar in the upper part of the tube

(Knuth 1909), our own observations refute this for *C. vernus* and several other species and cultivars. Both *C. vernus* and *C. reticulatus* are visited by various bees and butterflies according to Knuth, but bees are their likely pollinators.

Many species of *Crocus* are cultivated in the northern hemisphere, especially where the winter temperatures fall below freezing for some time. One of the earliest garden plants to bloom, *Crocus* makes remarkable displays of color at the end of winter. Species and cultivars are both prominent in garden, street, and park plantings across Europe and North America, where they flower in mass in late winter. *Crocus sativus* is grown in Spain, Italy, and the Middle East for saffron, a spice used as a food flavoring, occasionally as a dye, and in historic times for medicinal purposes. Only the reddish orange style branches are harvested and dried. The species is a sterile triploid, not known in the wild, and may be clonal polyploid race of the eastern Mediterranean *C. cartwrightianus,* the apparent wild ancestor, or a hybrid with this and a related species (Mathew 1977). The word saffron is of Semitic origin and referred both to the spice and to the *Crocus* plant (see more detail in the section, Economic Importance and Ethnobotany).

*Geissorhiza* Ker Gawler (1804: 223)
Plates 106–114; Figure 37
Tribe Croceae
TYPE: *Geissorhiza obtusata* Ker Gawler = *G. imbricata* (D. Delaroche) Ker Gawler
ETYMOLOGY: from the Greek *geisson,* tile, and *rhizon,* root, for the tiled appearance of the overlapping, segmented corm tunics of subgenus *Geissorhiza*
SYNONYMS: *Sphaerospora* Klatt (1863: 725), illegitimate name, not *Sphaerospora* Sweet ex Loudon (1841), type: *S. exscapa* (Thunberg) Klatt = *Geissorhiza exscapa* (Thunberg) Goldblatt; *Engysiphon*

G. J. Lewis (1941: 19), type: *E. schinzii* (Baker) G. Lewis = *G. schinzii* (Baker) Goldblatt; *Weihea* Ecklon (1827: 22), name without description
REVISIONARY ACCOUNTS: Goldblatt (1985), Goldblatt and Manning (1995b, additional species)

Deciduous perennials with a globose to ovoid, asymmetric or bell-shaped corms, usually with a basal ridge from which the roots emerge, axial in origin, the tunics woody or rarely membranous to fibrous, concentric or imbricate, then notched below. LEAVES few to several, the lower two or three cataphylls; foliage leaves unifacial, usually with a definite midrib, the blades plane to terete or H-shaped in section, sometimes the margins and or midrib raised and winged, occasionally hairy or sticky. FLOWERING STEM aerial, simple or branched, drooping in bud, terete in section, sometimes minutely hairy or scabrid. INFLORESCENCE a spike, flowers usually spirally arranged, rarely solitary on the branches; BRACTS green and soft-textured to membranous, the inner smaller than the outer and forked at the tip. FLOWERS star-like or salver- to funnel-shaped, sometimes the tube elongate, variously colored, often blue to violet, also pink, yellow, cream, purple, red, or bicolored, mostly radially symmetric, weakly zygomorphic in a few species, faintly scented or unscented, usually with nectar from septal nectaries; PERIANTH TUBE short to long, funnel-shaped or cylindric; TEPALS subequal, the inner usually shorter than the outer, cupped or spreading from the base. STAMENS symmetrically disposed or unilateral and arching downward; FILAMENTS filiform, sometimes unequal with one shorter than the other two, usually exserted, sometimes inserted well inside the tube; ANTHERS erect or ascending, rarely included. OVARY globose, sessile; STYLE filiform, eccentric or unilateral and held below the stamens, usually exserted, the branches usually slender and recurved, or broadly

**Figure 37.** (left) *Geissorhiza silenoides* (×1) with flower (×1.2), (center) *G. rupicola* (×1), (lower right) *G. imbricata* capsule (×1) and seed (×12).

expanded above. CAPSULES globose to oblong or cylindric, cartilaginous to bony; SEEDS more or less globose, flattened at the chalazal end, sometimes lightly wrinkled, matte, the surface cells domed or areolate. BASIC CHROMOSOME NUMBER $x = 13$. Species c. 85, restricted to the winter-rainfall zone of South Africa, extending from northern Namaqualand through the western Karoo and southwestern Cape to Grahamstown in the east.

Although named for the distinctive, partially overlapping woody corm tunics that resemble the tiles of a roof, only half the genus, subgenus *Geissorhiza*, has such corm tunics. The other half, subgenus *Weihea*, has concentric corm tunics of a kind found in several other genera, notably *Hesperantha*. The corms of both subgenera are usually asymmetric, having a lateral ridge near the base from which the roots are produced. The asymmetry is not always evident when the tunics are present, but naked corms always show this feature. *Geissorhiza* is otherwise recognized by the long, slender style dividing well above the perianth into short, undivided, recurved branches, and a spike that is nodding in bud. An unusual feature of many species but by no means all of them is the unequal filaments, one of which is shorter than the other two. Most species of both subgenera have relatively small, short-tubed, radially symmetric, star-like flowers. Exceptional in the genus are the large white to pink flowers of section *Engysiphon*, until 1985 regarded as a separate genus. These flowers face to the side and have unilateral stamens, and both the stamens and style arch downward. Except for *G. brevituba*, the species of section *Engysiphon* have flowers with an elongate perianth tube that stand out in this genus of largely short-tubed flowers. The corm development is axial and leaf marginal anatomy is of the ancestral type, with a marginal vein or strand of submarginal sclerenchyma. The basic chromosome number $x = 13$ is unusual in Crocoideae, shared only with *Hesperantha*.

The relationships of *Geissorhiza* have long been thought to be with *Hesperantha* (Lewis 1954a), which has similar woody corm tunics and corms that are often asymmetric. The two genera have the same basic chromosome number, identical corm development, and leaf marginal anatomy. The flowers of *Hesperantha* differ in having the style dividing at the mouth of the perianth tube into three long slender, laxly trailing branches. DNA sequence analysis consistently confirms the close relationship of *Geissorhiza* and *Hesperantha* (Reeves et al. 2001) and like morphological study suggest that the two genera are isolated within Crocoideae. Similar woody corm tunics and asymmetric corm suggest a possible relationship with *Romulea*, but DNA sequences show that this resemblance is convergent. *Geissorhiza* is provisionally included with *Hesperantha* in tribe Croceae of the Crocoideae (Goldblatt et al. 2006).

Radiation in *Geissorhiza* is extensive, and species are adapted to a variety of habitats and pollinators. Notable are a number of species that occur only on cliffs close to or under waterfalls (Goldblatt 1985). The phytogeography corresponds closely to the classic model for members of the Cape flora. Thus there is a marked concentration of species in the southwest, and one or more endemic species are confined to one of six subcenters of the flora. Restricted to the Northwestern Center, *G. cedarmontana* and *G. elsiae* stand out in the genus in having the stamens and style included in the perianth tube. A notable feature of several species is the elaboration of the leaf blade in which the margins and often the midrib as well are raised at right angles to the surface. The resultant marginal wings arch inward, creating an enclosed space sheltered from sun and wind, thus conserving water for the transpiring leaf.

The several long-tubed species of section *Engysiphon*, including *Geissorhiza confusa* and *G. exscapa*, are pollinated by long-proboscid flies, but most other species are pollinated mainly by female bees harvesting pollen or by bee flies and small butterflies searching for nectar. Unexpectedly, the small flowers of *G. inconspicua* are pollinated by empidid flies (Empididae) and halictid bees. A few species have flowers with a dark central marking and are adapted for pollination by hopliine beetles. Pollination of the very striking *G. mathewsii* and *G. radians,* which have violet flowers dark red in the center and dark brown pollen, is uncertain but probably also involves hopliine beetles and perhaps other insects.

*Hesperantha* Ker Gawler (1804: 224)

Plates 115–125; Figure 38

Tribe Croceae

TYPE: *Hesperantha falcata* (Linnaeus fil.) Ker Gawler

ETYMOLOGY: from the Greek *hesperos,* evening, and *anthos,* flower, for the night flowering of many species

SYNONYM: *Schizostylis* Backhouse & Harvey (1864), type: *S. coccinea* Backhouse & Harvey = *Hesperantha coccinea* (Backhouse & Harvey) Goldblatt & J. C. Manning

REVISIONARY ACCOUNTS: Goldblatt (1984b, southern African winter-rainfall zone species; 2003, entire genus), Hilliard and Burtt (1986, species of eastern southern Africa)

Deciduous perennials with globose to ovoid or bell-shaped corms, rarely the rootstock rhizomelike, sometimes with a basal ridge from which the roots emerge, axial in origin, the tunics woody, or rarely firm-papery, concentric or imbricate and then notched below. LEAVES few to several, the lower two or three cataphylls; foliage leaves unifacial, with a definite midrib, two to several, the blades plane to terete, sometimes the margins and/or midrib thickened, sometimes hairy. STEM aerial or subterranean, simple or branched, terete in section.

INFLORESCENCE a spike with the flowers spirally arranged, rarely the flowers solitary; BRACTS green and soft-textured, the inner smaller than the outer and notched apically. FLOWERS star- to salvershaped or nodding, variously colored, mostly white or pink, also yellow or blue to violet or red, usually actinomorphic, rarely weakly zygomorphic, often fragrant and then usually in the evening, with nectar produced from septal nectaries; PERIANTH TUBE cylindric, short or long, sometimes curved near the apex; TEPALS subequal, spreading, sometimes recurved. STAMENS symmetrically disposed or rarely unilateral and declinate; FILAMENTS inserted shortly below the mouth of the tube, sometimes very short, erect or drooping; ANTHERS erect and facing inward or articulated on the filament apices and horizontal, sometimes drooping, occasionally included in the tube; POLLEN monosulcate, operculate, perforate. OVARY globose, sessile; STYLE filiform, dividing at or below the mouth of the tube, the branches filiform, spreading, or erect when included in the tube, stigmatic along their entire length. CAPSULES membranous, globose to oblong or cylindric, sometimes splitting open only in the upper third; SEEDS globose to angular, flattened at the chalazal end, sometimes lightly winged on the angles, smooth or rugulose, the surface cells usually domed. BASIC CHROMOSOME NUMBER $x = 13$. Species c. 82, mainly southern African with a major center in the winter-rainfall zone of southern Africa and a secondary center in the Drakensberg of eastern southern Africa but extending through the tropical African highlands to Ethiopia and Cameroon.

*Hesperantha* is readily recognized by its distinctive style, which is divided from the mouth of the perianth tube into three long, laxly spreading branches stigmatic along their entire length. Species also have corms with woody, or at least unbroken, tunics and the corms are usually asymmetric in having a small lateral ridge near the base from which

**Figure 38.** (left) *Hesperantha coccinea* (×1), (center) *H. brevistyla* capsules (×1) and seed (×12), (right) *H. petitiana* (×1) and flower (×1.25).

the roots arise. The flowers of most species are radially symmetric and have a fairly narrow, cylindrical perianth tube at least as long as the tepals. The eastern southern African *H. grandiflora* has the stamens and style unilateral and arching downward in a half-nodding flower. The predominant flower color among the species of the summer-rainfall part of southern Africa is pink, and flowers are notable for closing tightly at night and showing precise times of opening and closing during the daylight hours. A number of species of the winter-rainfall zone have white flowers that open in the late afternoon and remain open into the night and are then strongly fragrant. In contrast, the flowers of the few white-flowered species of eastern southern Africa are unscented and open for a few hours during the day and close at night. The differences in timing of the opening and closing of the flowers have profound implications for the pollination biology of the genus.

As discussed under *Geissorhiza*, similar woody corm tunics and asymmetric corms and shared basic chromosome number *x* = 13 in *Hesperantha* and *Geissorhiza* indicate a close relationship of the two genera, which has now been confirmed by DNA sequence studies. *Geissorhiza* is readily distinguished by the longer style with short, recurved branches and often a shorter perianth tube. Both genera have axial corm development, ancestral leaf anatomy with a strand of submarginal sclerenchyma, and globose seeds with surface cell outlines prominent. Red- or pink-flowered *H. coccinea*, a semiaquatic plant, long regarded as a separate genus, *Schizostylis*, has all the taxonomically critical features of *Hesperantha* (Goldblatt and Manning 1996), including a basic chromosome number *x* = 13, and is unusual only in its rhizome-like rootstock, anomalous in Crocoideae. The plant often produces cormlets in the upper leaf axils of a shape typical for *Hesperantha*, and it seems clear that the rhizome is a reversal

from a corm, most likely an adaptation associated with its wetland habitat. Comparable reduction of the corm has occurred in a few hygrophilous species of *Geissorhiza* and *Gladiolus.*

One of the more widespread of the African genera of the Iridaceae, *Hesperantha* extends from the southwestern tip of southern Africa northward into arid southern Namibia and eastward through the eastern southern African escarpment into tropical Africa as far north as Ethiopia. Isolated populations also occur in West Africa on Mount Cameroon. *Hesperantha* is equally speciose in the semiarid western Karoo and in the high Drakensberg of Lesotho and KwaZulu-Natal, South Africa. Diversity decreases north of the Drakensberg. Some six species occur in Mpumalanga Province, three in Zimbabwe, and only *H. petitiana* occurs north of Malawi.

Pollination biology of *Hesperantha* is diverse. As predicted as long ago as 1891 by British botanist George Scott Elliot, the small white-flowered species are pollinated primarily by small moths. More critical study shows that the short-tubed, pink-flowed species are pollinated mainly by anthophorine bees and *Apis mellifera* workers, as are white-flowered species of eastern southern Africa. Even the crepuscular, white-flowered species of the winter-rainfall zone are visited by anthophorine bees when they open before sunset but are also visited after dark by settling moths of several different families (Goldblatt et al. 2004c). The several long-tubed species with pink flowers are pollinated by long-proboscid flies of the genus *Prosoeca* (Nemestrinidae). To date, *H. vaginata*, which has bright yellow flowers usually marked with contrasting brown markings, is the only species known to be pollinated exclusively by hopliine beetles. Red-flowered plants of *H. coccinea* are pollinated by large butterflies, including *Papilio* species and *Aeropetes tulbaghia.*

*Hesperantha coccinea*, still better known among horticulturists as *Schizostylis coccinea*, is a popular garden plant not only in southern Africa but in Europe and western North America, and both pink- and red-flowered strains are grown. It is an attractive garden subject, valuable for its late flowering, often continuing to bloom as late in the northern autumn as November and December. It may be grown in conditions simulating the wet habitats it favors in the wild but also thrives in less specialized conditions providing it is watered regularly. There are a number of named cultivars, including pink- and white-flowered strains. Other species of *Hesperantha* are hardly known in cultivation but are ideal subjects for container culture.

*Babiana* Ker Gawler ex Sims (1801)
Plates 126–139; Figure 39
Tribe Croceae
Name conserved against *Beverna* Adanson
TYPE: *Babiana plicata* Ker Gawler = *B. fragrans* (Jacquin) Steudel
ETYMOLOGY: from the Dutch *babianer,* baboon, the native African ape that avidly eats *Babiana* corms
SYNONYMS: *Beverna* Adanson (1763: 20), rejected name, type: not designated; *Acaste* Salisbury (1812: 322), type: *A. venusta* Salisbury = *Babiana rubrocyanea* (Jacquin) Ker Gawler; *Anaclanthe* N. E. Brown (1932: 269), type: *A. plicata* (Linnaeus fil.) N. E. Brown = *B. thunbergii* Ker Gawler; *Antholyza* Linnaeus (1753: 37) in the sense of some authors but not of Linnaeus is sometimes regarded as synonym of *Babiana,* but the designated lectotype is *Gladiolus cunonius* (Linnaeus) Gaertner
REVISIONARY ACCOUNTS: Lewis (1959b: 20, a now much outdated treatment), Goldblatt (1990c, transfer of *Antholyza ringens* and *A. plicata* to *Babiana*), Goldblatt and Manning (2007)

Deciduous geophyte with globose corms, axial in origin and rooting from below, the tunics of tough leathery layers or becoming fibrous. LEAVES several, the lower two or three cataphylls, foliage leaves more or less pleated, with a prominent vein at each fold, usually hairy, often abruptly expanded above the sheath and held obliquely, lanceolate to ovate or linear, sometimes abruptly truncate, rarely more or less terete, margins sometimes undulate or crisped. STEM aerial or subterranean, round in section, often branched, usually hairy or scabrid, usually sheathed below by a thick collar of fibers. INFLORESCENCE a spike, the flowers often facing to one side, or spirally arranged; BRACTS green, usually with dry brown tips, rarely entirely dry, hairy or smooth, the inner usually shorter than the outer, forked apically or divided to the base. FLOWERS usually zygomorphic and bilabiate, sometimes radially symmetric, often shades of blue or purple, or yellow, red, pink, or white, usually with dark or pale markings on the lower tepals, often sweetly fragrant, with nectar from septal nectaries; PERIANTH TUBE short to long, cylindric and straight to curved or funnel-shaped; TEPALS subequal or unequal, then the dorsal enlarged and hooded or curving backward, or erect with margins curved inward enclosing the filaments, the lower tepals sometimes more or less clawed. STAMENS symmetrically disposed and erect or unilateral and arcuate; FILAMENTS free, slender; ANTHERS oblong to linear, or arrow-shaped with the connective broad in the lower half, splitting longitudinally. OVARY globose, sessile, sometimes densely hairy; STYLE slender, the branches filiform, undivided, often somewhat broadened above. CAPSULES globose to oblong, cartilaginous, sometimes hairy; SEEDS pear-shaped, dark brown to blackish, lightly wrinkled, the surface smooth and shiny, with cell outlines obscured by thick cuticle. BASIC CHROMOSOME NUMBER $x = 7$. Species c. 90, centered in the semiarid western half of southern Africa, mainly in Namaqualand and the southwestern Cape of South Africa, but also in southwestern

**Figure 39.** *Babiana toximontana* with (upper left) half-flower and bracts (outer, left, and inner, right) (×1), (center left) *B. melanops* flower (×1), (lower left) *B. ringens* flower (×1), (center right) *B. sinuata* flower (×1), (lower right) *B. noctiflora* flower (×1), (bottom right) *B. villosula* seed (×8) and capsule (×1).

Namibia, and one species extends across southern Africa into Botswana, northern Namibia, southern Zambia, and Zimbabwe.

A widespread southern African genus, *Babiana* has a very characteristic appearance and can nearly always be recognized by the fairly narrow, deeply pleated leaves that are also almost always covered with a silky to velvety pubescence or at least some fine hairs. Even those few species that have seem to have smooth leaves often bear a few hairs along the leaf margins or leaf sheaths. As with most southern African Iridaceae, species are concentrated in the winter-rainfall zone in the southwest of the subcontinent, but *Babiana* is exceptional in having radiated as much in the dry semidesert country surrounding the winter-wet Cape region, and half the species occur in Namaqualand and in adjacent Namibia. Only *B. bainesii* occurs widely in the summer-rainfall region to the north and east of southern Africa, where it extends across northern Namibia and Botswana to Zambia and Zimbabwe. One species, *B. socotrana,* from the island of Socotra in the Indian Ocean, was included by Lewis in her 1959 monograph of *Babiana,* but that species has been shown convincingly to be unrelated and has now been placed in its own genus, *Cyanixia* (Goldblatt et al. 2004a).

The immediate relationships of *Babiana* are obscure, but there is no doubt that it belongs in the Crocoideae for it has the basally rooting corm of the subfamily as well as other characteristic features: flowers with a perianth tube, nectar secreted from septal nectaries, and perforate pollen with a two-banded operculum in the single elliptical aperture. The basic chromosome number in *Babiana,* $x = 7$, offers no guide as to its relationships—the number is shared in the subfamily only with the tropical African *Zygotritonia,* a very different genus perhaps allied to *Lapeirousia* and *Savannosiphon.* Largely because of the green floral bracts and style branches

with expanded tips, *Babiana* has been thought to be most closely allied to *Gladiolus* (Goldblatt 1996). DNA sequences, the only source of reliable information about the relationships of so many genera of Crocoideae, shows *Babiana* to be sister to *Chasmanthe* (Reeves et al. 2001), an alliance that has not before been suggested. This unexpected result is not supported by either morphology or anatomy, but we have no choice but to accept this surprising conclusion. *Babiana* is currently included in section Croceae of the Crocoideae, with which at least its smooth seeds correspond. The seeds are however, unique in Iridaceae in their dark, almost black color and distinctive pear shape.

Like so many other genera of Crocoideae, the flowers of *Babiana* species are extraordinarily variable. The ancestral flower is probably the short-tubed, bilabiate type that is common in the genus and is pollinated by large-bodied, long-tongued bees. Flowers of this kind occur in all both sections of the genus and are usually blue to violet, with white markings on the lower lateral tepals. Several species of section *Teretifolieae* and a few of section *Babiana* have flowers with a slender, elongate perianth tube and are white or dark blue to violet or purple. Section *Babiana* is exceptional in Crocoideae in having the inner floral bracts forked to the base into what are effectively two separate inner bracts. Of relatively recent origin, the section has radiated extensively in the wetter parts of the Cape flora region and does not occur in the surrounding semiarid Namaqualand and western Karoo. A few species of both sections have radially symmetric flowers, evidently adapted for pollination by hopliine beetles. The two species of series *Antholyza* of section *Teretifolieae* have unusually shaped, bright red flowers, and well-exserted stamens.

The range of flower shape, coloration, and perianth tube length reflect major shifts in pollination biology. Species with short-tubed, bilabiate flowers are often scented, and their flowers are adapted for pollination by anthophorid bees (Apidae) and honeybees. Species with radially symmetric flowers, usually associated with a short perianth tube, have two different pollination systems. Those with unscented flowers, often with a contrastingly pigmented center or dark stamens, are adapted for pollination by hopline scarab beetles, but those with scented flowers and pale centers are pollinated by pollen-collecting bees. The species with long-tubed, violet, dark blue, or cream to pink flowers are pollinated by long-proboscid nemestrinid flies in the genera *Prosoeca* (e.g., *Babiana curviscapa, B. framesii, B. sambucina*) and *Moegistorhynchus* (e.g., *B. brachystachys, B. tubulosa*). *Babiana ringens* and *B. thunbergii* of series *Antholyza*, once included in the genus *Antholyza*, have long-tubed, bright red flowers and are pollinated by sunbirds, especially the malachite and dusky sunbird. Moth pollination occurs in the pale yellow, intensely fragrant *B. noctiflora* and is suspected for *B. patersoniae* and *B. virginea*, which also have pale, strongly scented flowers. This diversity of pollination systems in *Babiana* is paralleled in most other genera of African Iridaceae.

*Babiana* corms are edible and form an important part of the diet of baboons, mole rats, and porcupines, and it is not unusual to see plants uprooted with their corms removed. If one looks carefully at the destroyed plants, one can usually see small cormlets scattered about or still lying in the lower leaf axils, and these will ensure survival of the genotype when the parent plants are lost. Often, *Babiana* plants are found in rocky habitats where the corms are afforded protection from predation. *Babiana* corms also provided sustenance for the Khoi and !Kung peoples in past times, and even today in isolated communities in rural Namaqualand the corms of *B. dregei* and other species are eaten by children. The naturalist William Burchell (1824) wrote in detail of the preparation of corms of *B. hypogaea*

for food by the native Griqua people near the modern city of Kimberley. Out of curiosity, we have sampled corms of several species and find that they have a sweet nutty flavor and lack the bitterness that corms of many Iridaceae have.

### *Chasmanthe* N. E. Brown (1932: 273)

Plates 140–141; Figure 40

Tribe Croceae

TYPE: *Chasmanthe aethiopica* (Linnaeus) N. E. Brown

ETYMOLOGY: from the Greek *chasme*, gaping, and *anthos*, flower, alluding to the widely gaping mouth of the flower

REVISIONARY ACCOUNTS: De Vos (1985, 1999: 142–147), Goldblatt et al. (2004b)

Deciduous geophytes with depressed globose corms, axial in origin and rooting from below, the tunics firm-papery, sometimes becoming coarsely fibrous. LEAVES several, the lower two or three cataphylls, foliage leaves unifacial, with a definite midrib composed of more than one pair of veins, mostly basal and forming a two-ranked fan, the blades lanceolate to sword-shaped, plane, cauline leaves few and reduced. STEM aerial, round in section, simple or branched. INFLORESCENCE a two-ranked spike, sometimes one-sided; BRACTS small green, becoming dry at the tips, leathery, the inner as long or shorter than the outer and notched apically. FLOWERS zygomorphic, orange to scarlet, the lower tepals with contrasting markings, unscented, with nectar from septal nectaries; PERIANTH TUBE cylindric below and sometimes spirally twisted, expanded abruptly and tubular and horizontal above; TEPALS unequal, the dorsal largest, extended horizontally and concave, remaining tepals much smaller, usually recurved above. STAMENS unilateral and arcuate; FILAMENTS slender, the lower one slightly longer than the others; ANTHERS parallel, subversatile.

**Figure 40.** *Chasmanthe aethiopica* with corm (lower left), half-flower (upper right), and capsules (upper left) (×1), (center left) *C. floribunda* flower (side view), and seed (×4).

OVARY ovoid, sessile; STYLE well exserted, horizontal, the branches filiform, undivided. CAPSULES globose, leathery, sometimes purple on the inside, warty in *Chasmanthe floribunda;* SEEDS globose, two to four per locule, orange, shiny, and smooth when fresh, the seed coat fleshy in *C. aethiopica,* becoming wrinkled on drying, the ovular vascular trace excluded. BASIC CHROMOSOME NUMBER $x = 10$. Species three, South Africa, mainly in the winter-rainfall zone in the southwest, extending from coastal Namaqualand through the western and southern Cape to the Transkei, usually in coastal bush, or forest margins.

*Chasmanthe* is recognized by the orange to almost scarlet, long-tubed flowers borne above a fan of fairly broad, soft-textured, sword-shaped leaves. The perianth tube is narrow and tubular below and abruptly expanded into a wider tubular upper part, and the tepals are markedly unequal with the enlarged dorsal tepal extended horizontally and concave. The firm filaments are slightly unequal and extend well beyond the mouth of the tube so that the anthers come to lie close to the apex of the dorsal tepal, the median anther extending slightly beyond the adjacent ones. More distinctive than the flowers are the seeds of *Chasmanthe.* Borne in leathery, barrel-shaped capsules, they are bright orange, relatively large, and in *C. aethiopica* the coat is fleshy when first released, later drying and becoming wrinkled. The surface of the epidermal cells of the seed coat are smooth, with the cell wall outlines obscured, and the ovular vascular trace is excluded from the seed during development. Another important but less visible feature of the genus is the leaf anatomy—the leaf marginal epidermal cells are columnar, with thickened walls, and the margins lack a marginal vein or a strand of sclerenchyma. The pollen grains are typical of subfamily Crocoideae, having a perforate exine and the sulcate aperture has a two-banded operculum.

Long considered allied to *Crocosmia* and *Tritonia* (Lewis 1954a, Goldblatt and Manning 2000b), *Chasmanthe* differs from these two genera in its seeds and basic chromosome number $x = 10$, whereas the two former genera have $x = 11$. This hypothetical relationship, however, appears to have been based on little more than shared orange to red flowers and a weak overall similarity. Leaf anatomy of the three genera is similar, and all have seeds with an excluded ovular trace, but those of *Crocosmia* have prominent epidermal cell walls, and the ovular trace is excluded during development in a different manner (Goldblatt et al. 2004b). Moreover, studies using chloroplast DNA sequences give no credence to a relationship with *Crocosmia,* which is quite distantly related to *Chasmanthe. Tritonia* is most closely related to *Ixia* and *Dierama* while *Chasmanthe* is closest to the very different *Babiana.* This alignment is surprising for there is no morphological or anatomical evidence in its favor. The leaf anatomy, seeds, and chromosome number $x = 7$ in *Babiana* all differ from *Chasmanthe.* Additional molecular studies may modify this result, which has only moderate statistical support.

The biology of *Chasmanthe* is closely associated with African sunbirds, *Nectarinia* species. The long-tubed orange to scarlet flowers have exactly the shape and color of many other African species pollinated by sunbirds, and recorded observations confirm that they are pollinated by these birds as they forage for nectar. The flowers produce ample quantities of nectar, which has high proportions of fructose and glucose, sugars preferred by sunbirds, rather than sucrose-dominated nectar in related genera that are pollinated by insects. Birds are also responsible for seed dispersal in the genus. The slightly fleshy, sweet-tasting seeds of *C. aethiopica* are eaten and later eliminated by various fruit-eating species, including red-winged starlings. The dry but bright orange seeds of the other species are apparently deceptive, collectively resembling a berry as they lie in a cluster in the opening capsules, and are most likely also dispersed by birds. Bird dispersal is a more effective means of dispersal than the passive dispersal that occurs in most other Iridaceae, and this probably explains why *Chasmanthe* species, with the exception of *C. bicolor,* are so widely dispersed, especially compared to species of other Crocoideae.

*Chasmanthe* species make admirable garden plants. In areas of suitable climate with mild winters and dry summers, or under glass, all three species respond well to cultivation. In fact, *C. floribunda* was first flowered in cultivation in 1633 in France, and all three species were grown in Europe in the late 17th and early 18th centuries and were described from cultivated specimens. In their native South Africa at Kirstenbosch Botanical Garden in Cape Town *C. floribunda* is grown in masses, providing brilliant splashes of color in spring, August and September. Both wild orange-flowered plants and the yellow-flowered cultivar *C. floribunda* 'Duckittii' are used to advantage. *Chasmanthe aethiopica* and *C. floribunda* are naturalized locally in California and parts of Australia.

*Sparaxis* Ker Gawler (1802b)
Plates 142–147; Figure 41
Tribe Croceae
TYPE: *Sparaxis bulbifera* (Linnaeus) Ker Gawler
ETYMOLOGY: from the Greek *sparasso,* to tear, for the appearance of the floral bracts
SYNONYMS: *Synnotia* Sweet (1826), type: *S. variegata* Sweet = *Sparaxis variegata* (Sweet) Goldblatt; *Streptanthera* Sweet (1827a), type: *S. elegans* Sweet = *Sparaxis elegans* (Sweet) Goldblatt; *Anactorion* Rafinesque (1837: 34), type: *A. bicolor* (Thunberg) Rafinesque = *S. villosa* (Burman fil.) Goldblatt
REVISIONARY ACCOUNTS: Lewis (1954b, *Synnotia* group), Goldblatt (1969: 230, *Sparaxis* group; 1992; 1999: 151–169)

Deciduous geophytes with globose corms, rooting from below and axial in origin, the tunics of fine to coarse fibers sometimes thickened below into vertical claws. LEAVES several, the lower two or three cataphylls; foliage leaves forming a tight, two-ranked fan, sword-shaped to lanceolate, firm and somewhat fleshy, with a definite midrib and usually many fine, closely set secondary veins. STEM aerial, simple or branched either at the base or aboveground, round in section. INFLORESCENCE a spike, the flowers spirally arranged or facing to one side; BRACTS dry, papery, often torn, pale, sometimes with brown streaks, the outer often tricuspidate, the inner bicuspidate, smaller than the outer. FLOWERS zygomorphic and bilabiate or radially symmetric, cream to yellow, orange or red, often with purple shading, or mauve to purple and then often with yellow markings, sometimes sweetly or putrid-scented, usually with nectar from septal nectaries; PERIANTH TUBE short to long, funnel-shaped, the lower cylindrical part short or long, the upper part sometimes bent; TEPALS subequal or unequal with the dorsal sometimes hooded and the lower united with the upper laterals for some distance. STAMENS unilateral, erect or arcuate, or symmetrically disposed; FILAMENTS slender; ANTHERS straight or sometimes sigmoid or coiled. OVARY globose, sessile; STYLE exserted, unilateral or straight and erect, the branches short or long, undivided, filiform or the tips expanded. CAPSULES barrel-shaped to oblong, cartilaginous; SEEDS globose, flattened at the chalazal end, hard, smooth, and shiny, the ovular vascular trace excluded. BASIC CHROMOSOME NUMBER $x = 10$. Species 16, South Africa, restricted to the winter-rainfall zone of the southwest of the country, extending from the Bokkeveld Plateau in the north to the Agulhas Peninsula in the south, mainly on clay soils in renosterveld, less often in coastal sandveld or arid fynbos.

So variable are flowers of *Sparaxis* that the genus is most readily recognized by the dry, papery floral bracts, often somewhat crinkled and flecked with brown, and the distinctive slightly fleshy leaves with a central vein and usually numerous fine, closely set secondary veins. In bright light the leaves also glisten slightly with minute gold flecks. The dry bracts often have long, tapering cusps and readily become torn, a feature that provided the generic name. The relatively small corms resemble those of *Ixia* and *Tritonia*, and like them are axial in origin, forming through the accumulation of reserves at the base of the stem of the current growth cycle. Leaf anatomy of *Sparaxis* is of a specialized type, lacking a subepidermal marginal sclerenchyma strand but with columnar marginal epidermal cells with thick radial walls. The seeds of *Sparaxis* are also specialized in having a hard, smooth surface without surface cell outlines, and the ovular vascular trace is excluded during seed development. Both leaf anatomy and seed morphology point to a relationship with those genera with similar features, including *Dierama*, *Duthieastrum*, *Ixia*, and *Tritonia*. Of these, however, only *Duthieastrum* and *Tritonia* have leaf anatomy that corresponds with that of *Sparaxis*. A close relationship between *Sparaxis* and *Dierama* has also been suggested because the two have similar dry, crinkled floral bracts.

Molecular studies confirm the relationships indicated by morphology and show that *Sparaxis* and *Duthieastrum* may be immediately related, together sister to *Tritonia* and other genera (Figure 4). The monospecific *Duthieastrum* is unusual in lacking an aerial stem and in having a slender perianth tube that raises the flowers above the ground. Additional species of both *Sparaxis* and *Tritonia* need to be included in future molecular studies before we can accept the current evidence of these relationships as convincing.

The taxonomic history of *Sparaxis* has been unusually complex, and as recently as 1969 species now included here were dispersed in three genera. *Sparaxis* was reserved for species with radially symmetric flowers (or at least a symmetric perianth) and straight anthers, *Streptanthera* included species with radially symmetric flowers with coiled anthers, and *Synnotia* was reserved for species with similar bracts but zygomorphic flowers. This taxonomy dates from the early 19th century, prior to which time the species with radially symmetric flowers were included in *Ixia* while those with zygomorphic flowers were assigned to *Gladiolus* (Ker Gawler 1804, Sweet 1826). The coiled anthers were considered to be insufficient grounds for recognizing a genus, particularly as *Sparaxis pillansii* also has slightly twisted anthers, providing a link between *Sparaxis* and *Streptanthera*. In 1992 *Sparaxis* was expanded to include *Synnotia* (Goldblatt 1992). The close relationships of the two genera had never been in doubt, and their separation solely on the basis of a bilabiate perianth was utterly inconsistent with ranges of floral variation in other genera of Iridaceae. Phylogenetic analysis using morphological characters shows that the species with zygomorphic flowers are ancestral and that those with radially symmetric flowers are derived within the genus.

Pollination biology of *Sparaxis* is directly linked to floral morphology (Goldblatt et al. 2000). Thus short-tubed, zygomorphic-flowered species (including *S. galeata* and *S. villosa*) are pollinated by bees, and long-tubed species by long-proboscid flies in the genus *Prosoeca* (Nemestrinidae). The species with radially symmetric flowers are either pollinated by a range of different insects (e.g., *S. bulbifera*), or in those species with dark central markings and a brightly colored background (e.g., *S. elegans*, *S. tricolor*), by hopliine scarab beetles (Scarabaeidae: Hopliinae). These last species produce trace amounts of nectar or none at all, unlike their bee- or fly-pollinated allies, and often have dark pollen. The bright, contrasting

**Figure 41.** (center left) *Sparaxis villosa* flower (three-quarters and front view; ×1), (top left) *S. galeata* flower (three-quarters view and half-flower; ×1), (right) *S. maculosa* (×1) with bracts (lower left: outer, left, and inner, right) (×1.5), (lower right) *S. bulbifera* capsule (left, ×1) and seed (right, ×8).

markings, often shaped like the outline of a beetle, evidently serve to attract potential pollinators.

*Sparaxis* species have long been cultivated in gardens and are surprisingly easy to grow. A range of hybrids between *S. elegans* and *S. tricolor*, and possibly *S. pillansii*, were first flowered in Cape Town in the 1820s, evidently the result of chance hybridization in the garden, and these hybrids, still grown today, make a kaleidoscopic display for a few weeks in spring. A strain of true *S. tricolor* is also grown widely. Equally attractive but less often seen in cultivation are *S. bulbifera* and the yellow-, plum-, or white-flowered subspecies of *S. grandiflora*. There is strong current interest in breeding improved hybrids with larger, longer-lasting flowers, especially for the cut-flower market. The genus has a promising future as a garden subject. Most species not only grow easily but respond well to generous watering and added fertilizer, producing more branches and larger blooms.

*Duthieastrum* M. P. De Vos (1975)
Plate 148; Figure 42
Tribe Croceae
TYPE: *Duthieastrum linifolium* (Phillips) M. P. De Vos
ETYMOLOGY: named for pioneering South African botanist Augusta Vera Duthie (1881–1963), combined with the Latin *aster*, star
SYNONYM: *Duthiella* M. P. De Vos (1974b), illegitimate name, not *Duthiella* Brotherus (1907), type: *D. linifolia* (E. Phillips) M. P. De Vos
REVISIONARY ACCOUNT: De Vos (1999: 139–141)

Deciduous perennials with globose corms, axial in origin and rooting from below, the tunics of fine, reticulate fibers. LEAVES several, the lower two or three cataphylls; foliage leaves unifacial, with a definite midrib, in a tight two-ranked fan, the blades plane. STEM subterranean, branched below the ground. INFLORESCENCE subterranean, simple or branched, flowers one or two per branch; BRACTS membranous, concealed by the leaves, the inner slightly shorter than the outer and notched apically. FLOWERS radially symmetric, salver-shaped, yellow, unscented, with nectar from septal nectaries; PERIANTH TUBE elongate, cylindric; TEPALS subequal, spreading, lanceolate. STAMENS symmetrically disposed, erect; FILAMENTS slender; ANTHERS diverging, linear, splitting longitudinally. OVARY subterranean, ovoid, drawn into a short stalk below; STYLE filiform, the branches undivided, slender and recurved. CAPSULES club-shaped, sterile, and shortly tubular below, cartilaginous; SEEDS globose, flattened at the chalazal end, hard, smooth, and shiny, the surface cell outlines obscured by thick cuticle, the ovular vascular trace excluded. BASIC CHROMOSOME NUMBER $x = 10$. Species only *Duthieastrum linifolium*, restricted to central South Africa.

The *Crocus*-like *Duthieastrum* has an underground stem with a basal tuft of plane, unifacial leaves and long-lived yellow flowers arising from below the ground. While the ovary remains underground during flowering, the sexual parts of the flower are raised above the leaves by the elongate floral tube. As the seeds mature, the underground stem elongates and raises the capsules above ground, where they ripen and split open. The hard, shiny seeds have the ovular vascular trace excluded during development. When the only species of *Duthieastrum* was first discovered it was placed in the genus *Syringodea* on account of their shared acaulescent habit. The cormous rootstock with roots produced from beneath, long-lived flowers with a well-developed perianth tube, and perforate pollen grains with a two-banded operculum, however, place *Duthieastrum* firmly in subfamily Crocoideae. The leaves are sword-shaped and unifacial, unlike the channeled leaves of *Syringodea*. Leaf anatomy is of the derived

**Figure 42.** *Duthieastrum linifolium* with capsules (left, ×1) and seed (right, ×8).

type for the subfamily—the marginal epidermal cells are columnar, with thickened walls, and the blades lack a marginal vein or strand of marginal sclerenchyma. Basic chromosome number in the genus is $x = 10$.

The relationships of *Duthieastrum* evidently lie with the few genera of tribe Croceae that have similar leaf marginal anatomy and hard seeds with a smooth surface and excluded ovular vascular trace. These include *Chasmanthe, Sparaxis,* and *Tritonia.* Although the latter, with its wide range across southern Africa, would seem most likely its closest relative, DNA sequence studies show *Duthieastrum* and *Sparaxis* are sister genera. The genera share the same basic chromosome number, and the molecular results may well be correct. Statistical support for the relationships is, however, relatively weak, leaving the question of phylogenetic relationships among these genera incompletely resolved.

Plants investigated in the field for this volume provided some additional information about this poorly known species. The yellow flowers open in the early afternoon and close shortly after dark each day. The perianth tube, although elongate, has a relatively thick wall, and its interior is completely filled by the long style. The little nectar that is produced is forced by capillary action into the top of the tube, where it is accessible to a range of insects, including small halictid bees, their likely pollinators.

*Tritonia* Ker Gawler (1802c)
Plates 149–156; Figure 43
Tribe Croceae
TYPE: *Tritonia squalida* (Aiton) Ker Gawler
ETYMOLOGY: from the Latin *triton,* a weathervane, for the variable, seemingly random orientation of the stamens in some species
SYNONYMS: *Montbretia* de Candolle (1803), type: *M. securigera* (Aiton) de Candolle = *Tritonia securigera* (Aiton) Ker Gawler; *Bellendenia,* as *Belende-*

*nia,* Rafinesque (1832: 245), illegitimate, superfluous name, type: not designated; *Tritonixia* Klatt (1882: 355), illegitimate superfluous name, type: *T. squalida* (Aiton) Klatt = *Tritonia squalida* (Aiton) Ker Gawler; *Montbretiopsis* L. Bolus (1929b), type: *M. florentiae* (Marloth) L. Bolus = *T. florentiae* (Marloth) Goldblatt
REVISIONARY ACCOUNTS: De Vos (1982, 1983b, 1999: 89–128)

Deciduous perennials with globose to obconic corms, rooting from below and axial in origin, the tunics of fine to coarse fibers. LEAVES several, the lower two or three cataphylls; foliage leaves several, usually with a definite midrib, mostly basal and often forming a two-ranked fan, the blades usually plane and linear to sword-shaped or round to oval in cross section, occasionally the margins undulate to crisped, inrolled, or winged, and thus H-shaped in transverse section, cauline leaves few and reduced. STEM mostly well developed, sometimes very short and virtually subterranean, round in section, simple or branched. INFLORESCENCE a spike, rarely only one flower per branch, flowers mostly facing to one side, rarely spirally arranged; BRACTS fairly small, green and firm, or membranous to dry, the outer usually three-toothed, the inner smaller than the outer and two-toothed or notched apically. FLOWERS usually zygomorphic, rarely radially symmetric, long-lived, bilabiate to salver-shaped, or rotate, mainly orange to yellow, or red, pink, cream, or white, often with darker veins, the lower tepals often bearing a bright yellow median tooth or raised ridge, occasionally sweetly scented, with nectar from septal nectaries; PERIANTH TUBE funnel-shaped or cylindric, short or elongate; TEPALS subequal or unequal with the dorsal largest and the lower tepals forming a lip. STAMENS unilateral and arcuate or symmetrically disposed, then erect or loosely spreading; FILAMENTS slender;

**Figure 43.** (lower left) *Tritonia karrooica* capsule (×1) and seed (×10), (left) *T. securigera* subsp. *watermeyeri* with half-flower at upper left (×1), (upper right) *T. deusta* flower (front view and half-flower) and bracts (inner, left, and outer, right) (×1), (center right) *T. pallida* flower (front and side views; ×1), (lower right) *T. bakeri* flower (front and side views; ×1).

ANTHERS linear, splitting longitudinally. OVARY globose, sessile; STYLE filiform, unilateral and arcuate or central, the branches expanded at the tips and recurved. CAPSULES globose to ellipsoid, cartilaginous; SEEDS globose, flattened at the chalazal end, smooth or rarely lightly wrinkled, shiny, the surface cells obscured by a thick cuticle, the ovular vascular trace excluded. BASIC CHROMOSOME NUMBER $x = 11$. Species c. 30, southern and southern tropical Africa, extending from the southwestern Cape, South Africa, to Mozambique, Malawi, and Tanzania but centered in the southern African winter-rainfall zone, in grassland in areas of summer rainfall, or shrubland and karroid scrub in areas of winter rainfall.

The features of *Tritonia* species are remarkably diverse for a relatively small genus, making its definition difficult. The species are united by membranous to dry, more or less translucent floral bracts, the outer of which is often three-toothed, leaves with specialized marginal anatomy, lacking a sclerenchyma strand, having instead epidermal calls with thickened walls, and more or less smooth, shiny seeds with an excluded ovular trace. Most species have a basic chromosome number $x = 11$ or, exceptionally 10. Although De Vos (1999), in her *Flora of Southern Africa* account of the genus, recognized 26 species in southern Africa and one more in Mozambique, the actual number of species in the genus is probably c. 30. The majority of species have short-tubed, orange to yellow or pink to red, zygomorphic flowers with unilateral, arcuate stamens and the lower tepals, or at least the lowermost, bearing a median, tooth-like ridge of tissue. Species with these features are now referred to *Tritonia* section *Morphixia* and extend from the Little Karoo in South Africa to southern tropical Africa. Better known are the widely cultivated species of section *Tritonia*, like *T. crocata*, which have a radially symmetric perianth and loosely unilateral

stamens, apparently randomly spreading, and lack a raised ridge or tooth on the lower tepals. The three species of the section occur in southern Western Cape, South Africa, an area of winter rainfall. One more species, *T. dubia* (the name reflects uncertainly about its correct genus), has radially symmetric flowers with the filaments arranged around the central style.

Most of the remaining species, assigned to either section *Pectinatae* or section *Montbretia*, have pale pink to cream or white flowers with an elongate perianth, a ridge rather than a tooth on the lower tepals, and are restricted to the southern African winter-rainfall zone, where they are found mostly in montane habitats. The four species of section *Pectinatae*, the most common of which is *Tritonia undulata* (synonym, *T. crispa*), have peculiarly modified leaves, either with tightly crisped and undulate margins or the edges raised into leafy wings held at right angles to the blade. The texture of the flowers is also unusually firm and fleshy compared to other species of the genus. Perhaps most exceptional are two species from the Richtersveld of northern Namaqualand in South Africa, *T. marlothii* and *T. delpierrei*. Sometimes treated as a single species, they have yellow or purple flowers, the latter color otherwise unknown in the genus, an elongate perianth tube, tepals without dark veins, weakly developed ridges on the lower tepals, a basic chromosome number $x = 10$, and perhaps most odd, leaves with a submarginal strand of sclerenchyma and round, thin-walled marginal epidermal cells. Their inclusion in *Tritonia* seems arbitrary, and De Vos's placement of the two in section *Montbretia* is surprising.

It has been suggested, for example, by Lewis (1954a), that the closest relatives of *Tritonia* are *Crocosmia* ($x = 11$) and *Chasmanthe* ($x = 10$), largely on the basis of their shared orange (sometimes reddish) flowers, which are usually zygomorphic.

Subsequent anatomical investigations seemed to endorse this when all three were found to have identical leaf anatomy and seed morphology. *Dierama, Duthieastrum, Ixia,* and *Sparaxis* have similar specialized seeds, hard and round with a smooth shiny surface and with the ovular vascular trace excluded during development, clearly are a natural alliance with *Tritonia. Chasmanthe* has rather different bright orange, smooth, sometimes fleshy seeds, but *Crocosmia* does not have smooth seeds, and the ovular trace is excluded in a somewhat different manner. Studies using plastid DNA sequences show convincingly that *Crocosmia,* despite a chromosome number shared with *Tritonia,* is not closely related to the genus, while *Chasmanthe* is only fairly distantly related within the alliance of species with smooth hard seeds and excluded ovular vasculature. These studies show *Tritonia* to be most closely related to *Ixia,* but the statistical support for the relationship is weak at best. There is, however, fairly strong support for an alliance of *Tritonia, Dierama,* and *Ixia.* We suspect that *Tritonia* is most likely sister to *Dierama* plus *Ixia,* the latter two genera linked by similar leaf anatomy, basic chromosome number, and radially symmetric flowers.

Although not much studied, the diversity of flower types in *Tritonia* is known to signal a corresponding range of pollination systems. *Tritonia marlothii* belongs to a guild of species adapted for pollination by the long-proboscid fly *Prosoeca peringueyi. Tritonia undulata* and its immediate allies appear to be adapted for pollination by the horseflies *Philoliche gulosa* and *P. rostrata,* and other fly species that have elongated mouthparts. Particularly long-tubed races of *T. undulata* are pollinated by *Moegistorhynchus longirostris,* which has the longest mouthparts of any insect except for some Lepidoptera. Species of section *Tritonia,* which have a short-tubed, radially symmetric perianth, are adapted for pollination by hopliine scarab beetles. The ancestral pollination type in the genus appears to be a long-tongued bee system in which anthophorid bees visit flowers to forage for nectar. This system occurs almost throughout the range of the genus but is overshadowed by other pollination systems in the southern African winter-rainfall zone.

It is remarkable that the species of *Tritonia* specialized for long-proboscid fly or hopliine beetle pollination are all restricted to the southern African winter-rainfall zone, whereas outside this area only the ancestral bee pollination occurs. The presence of diverse pollination systems, especially of specialized ones, in this region is a feature repeated in genus after genus of Iridaceae, and the diversity of *Tritonia* in the winter-rainfall zone is obviously linked to the existence of these diverse pollination systems there. Some 18 species occur in the winter-rainfall zone while just nine occur through eastern southern Africa and tropical Africa (three of these shared with the winter-rainfall zone). With so wide a range, *Tritonia* species occur in a wide variety of habitats. These include open grassland, forest margins, and savanna in areas of summer rainfall, but in shrubland vegetation types in the winter-rainfall region, including renosterveld, woodland thicket, semidesert karroid scrub, true stony desert, and fynbos.

**Ixia** Linnaeus (1762: 23)

Plates 157–164; Figure 44

Tribe Croceae

Conserved name

TYPE (conserved): *Ixia polystachya* Linnaeus

ETYMOLOGY: from the Greek *ixias,* the "chameleon plant," the parasite *Loranthus,* possibly because of the sticky seeds, like a chameleon's tongue, but evidently applied arbitrarily by Linnaeus to an African genus of Iridaceae, at the time including what are now *Iris domestica* (*Belamcanda chinensis*) and *Aristea africana;* ironically, neither of them remain in *Ixia*

**Figure 44.** (left) *Ixia superba* with flower (side view), bracts (outer, left, and inner, right), capsules (×0.8), seed (×10), (right) *I.* cf. *paucifolia* with half-flower (right center, ×0.8), (bottom center) *I. acaulis.*

SYNONYMS: *Houttuynia* Houttuyn (1780: 448), rejected name, not *Houttuynia* Thunberg (1784), type: *H. capensis* Houttuyn = *Ixia paniculata* D. Delaroche; *Dichone* Lawson ex Salisbury (1812: 320), name invalid, without description; *Hyalis* Salisbury (1812: 317), name invalid, without description; *Morphixia* Ker Gawler (1827: 105), type: *M. latifolia* (D. Delaroche) Ker Gawler = *I. latifolia* D. Delaroche

REVISIONARY ACCOUNTS: Lewis (1962), De Vos (1999: 3–87)

Deciduous perennials with globose corms, rooting from below and axial in origin, the tunics of fine to moderately coarse, netted fibers. STEM aerial, rarely subterranean, usually slender and wiry, terete, usually branched, the branching often widely spreading. LEAVES several, the lower two or three cataphylls; foliage leaves unifacial, with a definite midrib, the blades usually plane, rarely H-shaped in transverse section with winged margins, sword-shaped, sickle-shaped, or linear, sometimes the margins thickened, occasionally crisped. INFLORESCENCE a spike with the flowers spirally arranged or occasionally in two ranks, often flexuose; BRACTS membranous, occasionally dry, usually translucent, short, the outer usually three-veined and tricuspidate, the inner smaller than the outer and two-veined and bicuspidate. FLOWERS usually actinomorphic, rarely subzygomorphic, variously colored, pink, mauve or yellow, sometimes darker in the center, occasionally fragrant, with nectar from septal nectaries or without nectar; PERIANTH TUBE funnel-shaped or filiform throughout, short or elongate; TEPALS subequal, usually spreading. STAMENS symmetrically disposed; FILAMENTS slender, sometimes included in the tube, free or sometimes partly to entirely united; ANTHERS linear to oblong, splitting longitudinally or sometimes incompletely from the base, occasionally with a bend near the base. OVARY globose, sessile; STYLE filiform, dividing into short to long, undivided, slender branches, either channeled and slightly broadened above or tubular and stigmatic apically. CAPSULES globose, cartilaginous; SEEDS globose or lightly angled, smooth or wrinkled, hard and shiny, the raphal vascular trace excluded. BASIC CHROMOSOME NUMBER $x = 10$. Species c. 67, South Africa, mainly in the winter-rainfall zone in the southwest but extending north into Namaqualand and east to Grahamstown and the central Karoo.

Evidently a relatively specialized genus of subfamily Crocoideae, *Ixia* species have an intriguing combination of apparently primitive and highly derived features. The flowers are typically radially symmetric, and the perianth is always symmetric, a feature usually regarded as primitive. The closest relatives of *Ixia*, however, have zygomorphic flowers, suggesting that the radially symmetry in *Ixia* is derived. Other specialized features are the translucent floral bracts, pollen grains with a single band of exine in the aperture, and hard shiny seeds with the epidermal outlines obscured by thick cuticle and with an excluded ovular trace. The apparently unspecialized nature of the flowers is contradicted by other floral specializations. *Ixia* is one of the few genera of Crocoideae in which the filaments are sometimes united, and it is the only genus in which incomplete anther splitting occurs.

*Ixia* has had a particularly complex taxonomic history. In the Linnaean period all Iridaceae with actinomorphic flowers and a perianth tube were placed in the genus, including such diverse species as *Aristea africana* (subfamily Aristeoideae) and *Iris domestica* (Iridoideae) as well as several that are now understood to belong to at least 10 other genera of Crocoideae. At the end of the 18th century and the beginning of the 19th, the British botanists William Aiton and John Ker Gawler began to remedy the situation. *Aristea* was described by Aiton in 1789, and the genera *Babiana*, *Belamcanda*, *Geissorhiza*,

*Hesperantha, Sparaxis,* and *Tritonia* were described in the period 1802–1805 by Ker Gawler. These activities left *Ixia* circumscribed more or less as it remains today. Species of *Ixia* section *Dichone* were included for many years in *Tritonia* and only transferred to *Ixia* by G. J. Lewis in 1962.

Because of its similar, radially symmetric flowers, dry floral bracts, and often wiry stem, the predominantly eastern African *Dierama* has been considered to be most closely allied to *Ixia* (e.g., Lewis 1962). *Dierama* has, like *Ixia* and several other genera of tribe Croceae, seeds with the ovular trace excluded and hard, shiny, smooth seeds (*Sparaxis* and *Tritonia* are others with this feature), and among these genera only *Dierama* has leaf anatomy like that of *Ixia,* the leaf margins having a subepidermal sclerenchyma trace and undifferentiated marginal epidermis. Other species of Croceae with smooth seeds with an excluded vascular trace lack submarginal sclerenchyma and have specialized marginal epidermis with columnar cells with thickened walls. Studies using chloroplast DNA regions confirm the general relationships of *Ixia* to these genera but so far have not yielded more precise results.

Despite their radial symmetry, the flowers of *Ixia* species vary considerably in color, shape, and the length and nature of the perianth tube. Two subgenera were recognized by Manning and Goldblatt (1999): *Morphixia* and *Ixia.* The former has flowers with a hollow, funnel-shaped or narrowly tapering perianth tube that contains nectar, filaments inserted below the mouth of the tube, and flowers that are often half-nodding or nodding. In contrast, most species of subgenus *Ixia* have upright flowers with a narrow tube, the walls tightly enclosing the style, and filaments inserted at the base of the tepals, thus at the top of the tube, and no nectar is produced. Exceptional are some species of section *Dichone,* which have half-nodding flowers, unusual short anthers splitting incompletely, and tubular style branches stigmatic at the tips. In an earlier classifica-

tion, Lewis (1962) treated section *Dichone* as a subgenus separate from subgenus *Ixia.* While species of section *Dichone* have pink or light purple flowers, those of section *Ixia* range in color from pink to red to dark purple, cream, yellow, or orange, almost always with a dark central mark and sometimes even dark stamens and style.

Restricted to the southern African winter-rainfall zone, species of *Ixia* show a marked concentration in the well-watered southwestern Cape. Representation decreases rapidly to the north and east, semiarid Namaqualand having only three species and the Eastern Cape just one, *I. orientalis.* Unique in the genus in its acaulescent habit, the Namaqualand endemic *I. acaulis* has an entirely underground stem. The ovary is borne a few millimeters below the soil surface, and the flowers are raised above the ground on a fairly long perianth tube. Long floral bracts sheathe the tube and protect its passage through the soil.

The flowers of species of subgenus *Morphixia* produce small to moderate amounts of nectar and are pollinated by insects usually foraging for this carbohydrate source and passively transferring pollen from flower to flower in the process. The short-tubed species are mainly pollinated by anthophorine bees or *Apis mellifera* workers while the few long-tubed species, notably *Ixia paniculata,* are pollinated by long-proboscid flies. *Ixia orientalis,* which has flowers with a very narrow perianth tube, appears to be pollinated by a combination of bees, large butterflies, and even hopliine beetles (Hopliinae). In the specialized section *Ixia,* which has nectarless flowers with narrow, closed perianth tubes and dark central marks, hopliine beetles are the major pollinators. Pollination in section *Dichone* is mixed, with female bees foraging for pollen most important, but the species with incompletely splitting anthers are buzz-pollinated by large anthophorine bees, an adaptation unique in Crocoideae.

**Figure 45.** *Dierama longistylum* (×0.5) with half-flower and style (×1) lower center, (upper left) outer bract (×1), (right) *D. plowesii* (×0.5) with half-flower, style, and outer bract (×1).

*Dierama* K. Koch (1855)
Plates 165–167; Figure 45
Tribe Croceae
TYPE: *Dierama ensifolium* Koch & Bouché = *D. pendulum* (Linnaeus fil.) Baker
ETYMOLOGY: from the Greek *dierama,* a funnel, describing the shape of the flower
REVISIONARY ACCOUNT: Hilliard et al. (1991)

Evergreen geophytes, sometimes growing in clumps, with depressed-globose corms, those of past seasons often not resorbed, axial in origin and rooting from below, the tunics coarsely fibrous, often accumulating in a dense mass. LEAVES several, the lower two or three cataphylls, these often dry and becoming fibrous; foliage leaves often without a definite midrib in mature plants, plane, linear, leathery and fibrotic. STEM aerial, round in section, thin and wiry, usually with several branches, often drooping above, sometimes erect, the subtending bracts dry and thread-like. INFLORESCENCE a drooping or erect spike, the axes wiry; BRACTS dry, usually papery and translucent, occasionally solid, becoming torn above and usually brown-streaked, silvery in a few species, sometimes attenuate, the outer one-veined and acute, the inner smaller than the outer, two-veined, and forked apically. FLOWERS radially symmetric, bell-shaped, usually nodding, often shades of pink to mauve, also red, purple, yellow, or white, with dark markings near the tepal bases, unscented, with nectar from septal nectaries; PERIANTH TUBE funnel-shaped, fairly short; TEPALS subequal, cupped or spreading above, often enclosing the stamens and style. STAMENS symmetrically disposed and central; FILAMENTS slender; ANTHERS linear, splitting longitudinally. OVARY globose, sessile; STYLE surrounded by the stamens, mostly included in the floral cup, the branches short, slender, slightly expanded above and recurved. CAPSULES globose, cartilaginous; SEEDS globose or lightly angled, flattened at the chalazal end, smooth, hard, often shiny, the ovular vascular trace excluded. BASIC CHROMOSOME NUMBER $x = 10$. Species c. 44, centered in eastern southern Africa, with 38 species in southern Africa and 8 in tropical Africa, where they extend from Zimbabwe north through Malawi, Tanzania, and Kenya to Ethiopia, mainly montane but also coastal in South Africa, favoring rocky grassland but also in marshes and along streams.

As described by Hilliard et al. (1990), *Dierama* is a plant of unusual grace and beauty, exceptional in the Iridaceae for its large, nodding, bell-shaped flowers. In fact, the genus is recognized primarily by the drooping spikes borne on wiry flexible branches and the nodding, radially symmetric flowers subtended by large, dry, papery or sometimes solid floral bracts, generally pale with brown streaks and veins. Because of the similarity of their floral bracts, *Dierama* species were for most of the 19th century included in *Sparaxis,* a genus of deciduous plants of semiarid habitats in the southwestern Cape of South Africa. The tough, fibrous, evergreen leaves of *Dierama* are distinctive, as is the frequent absence of a prominent central vein, which is, however, present in seedlings and young plants. Apart from the evergreen habit and characteristic leaves, *Dierama* falls readily in subfamily Crocoideae, having long-lasting flowers with a perianth tube and borne on a spike, corms rooting from the base, pollen with perforate exine and a two-banded operculum, and hard, shiny seeds with the vascular trace to the ovule excluded during development. The leaf anatomy is of the ancestral type for the subfamily, with a prominent strand of sclerenchyma beneath the margins and unmodified epidermal cells. Among the several genera with ovular vasculature excluded from the seeds, the only other genus with similar leaf anatomy is *Ixia.* The latter has often been thought to be closely related to *Dierama* because of their similar, radially symmetric flowers and thin, wiry spike axes. Shared leaf anatomy seems to support this assumption. *Ixia*, however, has pollen grains with a one-banded operculum, and the outer floral bracts have three main veins and are three-dentate at the apex, both important differences between the genera. Data from chloroplast DNA sequences show that *Dierama* is embedded in a cluster of genera with similar specialized hard, smooth seeds and excluded vasculature, including not only *Ixia* but *Sparaxis* and *Tritonia* (Goldblatt et al. 2006). The results are not conclusive beyond this level, for the topology of the phylogenetic tree showing *Dierama* plus *Ixia* sister to *Tritonia* has only weak statistical support.

*Dierama* is primarily a genus of highland grassland, but along the temperate eastern South African seaboard species are also found at low elevations near the coast in similar grassland habitats. The several species that occur in tropical Africa mirror the pattern of favoring highland grassland. *Dierama pauciflorum* and *D. trichorhizum* are unusual in favoring marshy habitats. The flowers are pollinated by a variety of bees that forage both for nectar and pollen. The genus shows only modest floral variation, confined to size and color differences and to the degree of spreading of the tepals. None of these differences suggests a different pollination strategy.

The best known species are *Dierama pendulum* and *D. pulcherrimum*, both from Eastern Cape, South Africa, which have large flowers borne on tall stems. Only gradually, as the interior of Africa was explored botanically, were additional species discovered in northern South Africa and then in Malawi and Tanzania. Some 44 species are now recognized, just eight in tropical Africa. The center of diversity is KwaZulu-Natal in South Africa. *Dierama galpinii*, *D. plowesii*, and *D. tysonii* are exceptional in the genus in having semierect spikes with nearly upright flowers.

Although the first *Dierama* species was collected in the late 18th century, it was not until well into the next century that plants were introduced into cultivation (Hilliard et al. 1990). By the middle of the 19th century, several species were in cultivation in the British Isles, and most likely breeding or simply raising plants from seed produced the first notable variants that were given cultivar names. Today, *Dierama* species and cultivars are widely grown where conditions permit their survival, including the more temperate parts of western Europe, western North America and adjacent Canada, Australia and New Zealand, and of course, their native southern Africa. Almost all the species merit horticultural attention, but few are widely available in the nursery trade, where they are often misidentified as *D. pendulum*, which was for many years the only named species.

## Subfamily **Iridoideae** Eaton (1836)
TYPE: *Iris* Linnaeus

Deciduous or evergreen perennials, rarely annuals, with rhizomes, bulbs or apically rooting corms, roots sometimes tuberous. Leaves unifacial or bifacial and channeled to flat, rarely terete or square in section. INFLORESCENCE units rhipidia enclosed in opposed leafy bracts (spathes). FLOWERS often fugacious, or long-lived, radially symmetric (zygomorphic in *Diplarrena*); tepals free or tubular below, often with nectaries at the base of the outer tepals or on the surface of the inner tepals (septal in *Diplarrena*). STAMENS only two in *Diplarrena*, with filaments free or united below or entirely, alternate with the style branches and/or appressed or joined to the opposed style branch; anthers loculicidal and extrorse or latrorse, or porose, pollen usually monosulcate, or disulcate, occasionally zonasulcate, exine reticulate, rugulate, or verrucate. OVARY inferior; style slender or more often short, divided into three variously developed branches, either thread-like and stigmatic apically, or flattened and sometimes petaloid, then often divided above into paired appendages with a subapical transverse stigma. CAPSULES submembranous to woody; SEEDS globose to angular or discoid, sometimes with fleshy appendages of various types. Genera 30, species c. 890, in five tribes: Diplarreneae Goldblatt (in Rudall and Goldblatt 2001; *Diplarrena*), Irideae M. B. Kittel (1840; *Iris, Dietes, Bobartia, Ferraria, Moraea*), Sisyrinchieae J. S. Presl (1846; *Libertia, Orthrosanthus, Olsynium, Sisyrinchium, Solenomelus, Tapeinia*), Trimezieae P. Ravenna (1981a = Mariceae Hutchinson 1934, illegitimate name); *Trimezia, Pseudotrimezia, Neomarica*), and Tigridieae M. B. Kittel (1840; *Alophia, Calydorea, Cipura, Cobana, Cypella, Eleutherine, Ennealophus, Gelasine, Herbertia, Hesperoxiphion, Larentia, Mastigostyla, Nemastylis, Salpingostylis, Tigridia*).

## Key to Genera of Iridoideae

1  Rootstock a creeping or erect rhizome or indistinct, plants evergreen or deciduous ............ 2

1'  Rootstock a corm, bulb, or tuber, plants always deciduous; leaves bifacial and channeled or unifacial or centric (square, oval, or round in section); plants mostly of Africa and Eurasia, except *Pseudotrimezia* .......................... 15

2  Fertile stamens two; anthers unequal and placed obliquely on the filaments; flowers bilaterally symmetric (zygomorphic)............ ................................. *Diplarrena* (p. 199)

2'  Fertile stamens three; anthers equal, held erect on the filaments and equal; flowers radially symmetric (actinomorphic) ...................... 3

3  Style (to the naked eye) usually dividing into three slender branches, or branches flattened distally, extending between or above the anthers, or style occasionally undivided; tepals not clawed and usually subequal, occasionally those of the outer or inner whorl smaller...... 4

3'  Style usually dividing into three thickened or radially or tangentially compressed more or less petaloid branches remaining opposite appressed to the stamens; tepals subequal or those of the inner whorl smaller or lacking .................. 12

4  Filaments free; pedicels sometimes hairy ...... 5

4'  Filaments united below or entirely; pedicels smooth; plants of Australasia and North and South America ..................................... 7

5  Pedicels hairy below the apices; rhipidia usually several crowded apically and flowering stem consisting of one long internode with a subapical leaf below the rhipidia, or if stem branched then sticky below the nodes; style branches extending between the bases of the anthers; plants of South Africa .......... *Bobartia* (p. 207)

5'  Pedicels smooth; rhipidia not crowded apically on a single long internode and stems not sticky below the nodes; style branches extending between the anthers or above them; plants of South America and East Asia .................... 6

6  Plants repeatedly branched; tepals irregularly speckled red to orange; capsules with cartilaginous walls soon splitting open but seeds remaining attached to axile placentas; seeds globose and glossy black ............ *Iris* (p. 200)

6'  Plants mostly unbranched; tepals not irregularly speckled; capsules walls more or less woody seeds not attached to the placentas; seeds angular, brown ................ *Pseudotrimezia* (p. 229)

7  Stems compressed, often angled or winged; seeds globose or compressed globose, usually with a depression at the chalazal end; seed coat dark brown to blackish ... *Sisyrinchium* (p. 221)

7'  Stems terete; seeds angular or oblong, usually with a chalazal crest; seed coat usually light to dark brown ......................................... 8

8  Evergreen cushion plants to 5 cm high; flowering stems with a single rhipidium bearing one flower............................. *Tapeinia* (p. 226)

8' Not evergreen, low-growing cushion plants, but occasionally acaulescent; flowering stems simple or branched, rhipidia with more than one (to several) flowers ........................... 9

9 Plants with leaves widely spaced, linear to terete, not forming a fan; stems occasionally with one or few slender branches; roots thick and fleshy; stem entirely to partly concealed by long, sheathing leaf bases .... *Olsynium* (p. 219)

9' Plants with a basal fan of two-ranked, sword-shaped to linear leaves; stems usually branched, the lateral branches often fairly short; roots fibrous ............................................. 10

10 Tepals united below in tube; flowers secund; filaments united entirely in a thick column ..................... *Solenomelus* (p. 225)

10' Tepals free to the base; flowers upright; filaments united for up to half their length ....... 11

11 Ovary sessile or nearly so, often lightly hairy; tepals subequal, always blue ..................... ............................... *Orthrosanthus* (p. 216)

11' Ovary usually stalked, never hairy; outer tepals somewhat to much smaller than inner, usually white, blue in one species ...... *Libertia* (p. 215)

12 Style branches thickened, often bearing acute paired terminal appendages; anthers lightly affixed to the abaxial side of the style branches on thread-like filaments not supporting the anther; inner tepals usually folded or bent near base of limb and bearing oil glands on short hairs ................................................. 13

12' Style branches compressed tangentially and petaloid, each bearing flat paired terminal appendages; anthers appressed to the abaxial side of the style branches on sturdy filaments; outer tepals strongly clawed, the base of the limb usually held close to the apex of the style branch and with a prominent nectar guide, inner tepals not abruptly folded back and not glandular ........................................... 14

13 Stem compressed and broadly two-winged; rhipidia crowded apically at the end of a long basal internode and subtended by a subterminal leaf ......................... *Neomarica* (p. 229)

13' Stem terete; rhipidia single at the tip of main axis and of branches, the stem usually branched and bearing leaves below ...... *Trimezia* (p. 226)

14 Tepals usually united below in a tube, rarely free; pedicels smooth; plants deciduous or evergreen ................................... *Iris* (p. 200)

14' Tepals free; pedicels hairy above; plants evergreen ............................... *Dietes* (p. 204)

15 Rootstock a corm, sometimes an erect, rhizome-like organ ............................. 16

15' Rootstock a bulb or tuber ...................... 18

16 Filaments free; plants of South America ........ ............................. *Pseudotrimezia* (p. 229)

16' Filaments partially to fully united, rarely free but contiguous for more of their length; plants of Africa and Eurasia ............................ 17

17 Leaves unifacial, oriented edgewise to the stem; old corms persisting for some years, with tunics membranous and soon decaying; tepals with crisped edges; style branches bearing a fringe of fine hair-like processes, collectively forming a feathery tuft .......... *Ferraria* (p. 209)

17' Leaves bifacial and channeled to flat, oriented with the adaxial surface facing the stem, or terete; old corm usually resorbed annually, with persistent fibrous to woody tunics; tepals with plane or wavy; style branches rarely with marginal processes but other characters not as above ............................. *Moraea* (p. 211)

18 Rootstock a bulb or tuber; leaves slender and often four to many sided; plants of Eurasia and North Africa ......................... *Iris* (p. 200)

18' Rootstock a bulb; leaves unifacial (oriented edgewise to the stem) and pleated or sometimes subterete but at least once folded; plants of South and North America ..................... 19

19 Flowering stem consisting of one long internode and bearing a subterminal leaf subtending one or more short branches or sessile inflorescences...................20

19' Flowering stem not as above, without a subterminal leaf at the base of short branches or sessile inflorescences............................22

20 Stamens opposite style branches and anthers appressed to the thickened style or petaloid style branches; tepals unequal in size and orientation, usually with a distinct limb and claw; at least the outer differentiated into a limb and claw, inner tepals or tepals limbs erect, concealing the anthers and style branches ....................
...................................... *Cipura* (p. 235)

20' Stamens alternate to style branches or style well exceeding the anthers; tepals subequal and spreading, not or obscurely divided into limb and claw..............................................21

21 Style short, dividing into three slender branches extending between the stamens; flowers white......................... *Eleutherine* (p. 240)

21' Style long, dividing above the anther tips into short, flattened branches; flowers violet ........
............ *Tigridia* (p. 253): *Cardiostigma* group

22 Filaments extremely short, less than 1 mm long; anthers porose or splitting near apices; tepals uniformly colored and not clearly differentiated into limb and claw, the surface plane and without glands ...............................23

22' Filaments usually well developed, at least 2 mm long; anthers usually splitting longitudinally; tepals often distinctly clawed and then the inner with secretory hairs on parts of the upper surface ...........................................24

23 Style branches undivided; anthers porose; flowers white.................... *Cobana* (p. 237)

23' Style branches each deeply divided almost to the base; anthers splitting only toward apices; flowers white or yellow........ *Tigridia* (p. 253): *Sessilanthera* group

24 Filaments free or only basally united and style branches variable, simple or divided, and slender to thickened and petaloid...................25

24' Filaments partially to completely united......32

25 Style branches forked for at least half their length into two more or less filiform arms; anthers with a wide, visible connective........26

25' Style not as above; anthers linear or fiddle-shaped with visible connective..................27

26 Tepals subequal or the inner somewhat smaller; anthers fiddle-shaped, attached to the style ........................... *Alophia* (p. 232)

26' Tepals markedly unequal, the inner less than half as long as the outer; anthers linear, collapsing inward after shedding their pollen ............. *Tigridia* (p. 253): *Ainea* group

27 Anthers linear, without visible connective; style dividing either beyond the anther apices below them and then opposite or alternate to style branches ............................................28

27' Anthers fiddle-shaped with visible connective and anther lobes lateral; inner tepal limbs coiled or with a fold at base and spreading distally..............................................31

28 Tepals not obviously clawed; anthers tightly appressed to the style branches or clasping them ...............................................29

28' Inner tepals with conspicuous, long narrow claws ...............................................30

29 Style branches slender, extending between the anthers......................... *Calydorea* (p. 233)

29' Style branches short, expanded and flattened in upper half, held above the anthers ...............
............................... *Salpingostylis* (p. 251)

30 Anthers clasping narrow, more or less linear style branches .................... *Cypella* (p. 238)

30' Anthers appressed to radially compressed, petaloid style branches......... *Larentia* (p. 247)

31 Plants of temperate South America (mainly Brazil, Argentina, Paraguay, and Uruguay)......................... *Cypella* (p. 238)

31' Plants of the Andes of Colombia, Ecuador, and Peru ..................... *Hesperoxiphion* (p. 246)

32 Style branches divided to base into thread-like arms extending either side of an anther or above them; style arms stigmatic terminally and usually more or less horizontal or curving outward ...............................................33

32' Style branches entire, or lobed or divided near apex, never with terminally stigmatic thread-like arms..........................................34

33 Anthers initially erect, collapsing spirally after releasing pollen; arms of the style branches horizontal; filaments partly to nearly completely united..................... *Nemastylis* (p. 250)

33' Anthers diverging or ascending, not collapsing after releasing pollen; arms of the style branches arching outward or suberect; filaments completely united ...... *Tigridia* (p. 253): *Tigridia* group

34 Tepals subequal in length, and shape ............ ..................................... *Gelasine* (p. 242)

34' Tepals usually markedly unequal in shape or length, the inner usually less than half as long as outer, occasionally subequal .................35

35 Inner tepals somewhat shorter to about as long as outer and often differently shaped; tepal claws often forming a well-defined floral cup containing the stamens, or spreading from the base ...............................................36

35' Inner tepals less than half as long as outer....37

36 Style dividing at apex of filament column into well-defined branches appressed to anthers...................... *Ennealophus* (p. 241)

36' Style dividing beyond apex of coherent anthers into minute lobes .............. *Cypella* (p. 238): *Kelissa* group

37 Filament column bottle-shaped; plants always with an aerial stem; tepals free and the inner three spreading and spooned below; anthers exceeding spreading style branches with divergent apices .................... *Herbertia* (p. 243)

37' Filament column cylindric; plants sometimes acaulescent; inner tepals free or basally united in a short tube and the inner more or less erect; anthers usually shorter than apically divided style branches .............. *Mastigostyla* (p. 247)

## *Diplarrena* Labillardière (1800: 157)

Plate 168

Tribe Diplarreneae

TYPE: *Diplarrena moraea* Labillardière

ETYMOLOGY: from the Greek *diploos*, double, and *arren*, male, referring to the presence of only two fertile stamens

REVISIONARY ACCOUNT: Cooke (1986: 26–27)

Medium-sized, more or less evergreen perennials with persistent rhizomes. LEAVES lanceolate to sword-shaped, without a prominent central vein. FLOWERING STEM erect, unbranched, rounded in section, bearing short leaves at the nodes. INFLORESCENCE a few-flowered terminal rhipidium; spathes leathery, green, closely sheathing the flowers buds and membranous floral bracts. FLOWERS zygomorphic, facing to the side, fugacious, borne on long pedicels, white with purple and yellow markings on the lower lateral tepals, honey-scented; TEPALS free, unequal, the outer larger, with the upper two erect and the lower one horizontal, the inner smaller, with the uppermost hooded over the stamens and the lower two longer. STAMENS, only two fertile, the third, lower one reduced to a short sterile cusp; FILAMENTS free, slightly unequal; ANTHERS borne oblique to the filaments, unequal in size. OVARY ovoid, producing nectar from septal nectaries; STYLE slender below, dividing into three unequal, flat stigmatic lobes, upper of these largest and concealing the lower lobes. CAPSULES oblong-cylindric; SEEDS numerous, vertically compressed and discoid, stacked above one another. BASIC CHROMOSOME NUMBER $x = 16$. Species two, southeastern Australia and Tasmania, in open sunny habitats, often among rocks, in heathland and forest gaps.

*Diplarrena* is in many ways a puzzling plant, and its relationships within the Iridaceae have long perplexed botanists. To our minds *Diplarrena* most closely resembles the African *Dietes* in general appearance, even in the shape and color of the flowers. Close examination, however, shows that the flowers are bilaterally symmetric and have unequal and differently marked inner tepals, with only the lower two marked yellow and purple. Most importantly, *Diplarrena* is the only member of Iridaceae that has only two fertile stamens, thereby departing from the family character of three stamens. A third stamen, the lower one, is vestigial and represented by a short slender cusp.

Early phylogenetic studies of the family placed *Diplarrena* in Iridoideae: Sisyrinchieae (Goldblatt 1990). DNA sequence analysis, however, shows that the genus is sister to the large lineage that includes *Iris*, the African *Moraea* and its relatives, and the New World genera, collectively now included in subfamily Iridoideae (Reeves et al. 2001). Interestingly, as befits its odd features, *Diplarrena* is also the only member of the Iridoideae that has septal nectaries, a character of phylogenetic importance in Iridaceae. Septal nectaries occur in families ancestral to the Iridaceae, and within the family in the Crocoideae and the southern African woody genera. Curiously, the less specialized members of the family, including *Aristea*, *Isophysis*, and *Patersonia*, lack nectaries altogether, while other Iridoideae have nectar glands borne on the tepals or walls of the perianth tube. Thus *Diplarrena* seems to have a combination of derived features (bilaterally symmetric flowers and two stamens) and ancestral ones (septal nectaries). It is noteworthy that, like other Australian Iridaceae, the genus falls in an ancestral position in its subfamily.

Although less well known in cultivation than it deserves, *Diplarrena* is amenable to garden con-ditions, and plants we have seen growing at the Royal Botanic Gardens, Kew, make a very attractive display, rather resembling the small-flowered *Iris japonica* from a distance. Reflecting its general resemblance to an *Iris*, species of *Diplarrena* are known as white flag, white iris, or the remarkably apt butterfly flag in Australia, where they are cultivated by wildflower enthusiasts.

The original spelling of the name, *Diplarrena*, is the one used here, although some authorities prefer *Diplarrhena*. The name is quite clearly derived from *diploos* and *arren*, the latter Greek for male. The addition of the *h* seems arbitrary and was done to satisfy some grammatical idiosyncrasy. The original spelling is also used in the *Flora of Australia* (Cooke 1986).

*Iris* Linnaeus (1753: 38)

Plates 169–185; Figure 46

Tribe Irideae

TYPE: *Iris germanica* Linnaeus

ETYMOLOGY: named for *Iris*, goddess of the rainbow, because of the great variety of flower colors in the genus

SYNONYMS: *Hermodactylus* Miller (1754), type: *H. tuberosus* (Linnaeus) Salisbury = *Iris tuberosa* (Linnaeus) Salisbury; *Belamcanda* Adanson (1763: 60, 524), as *Belamkanda*, spelling conserved, type (conserved): *Belamcanda chinensis* (Linnaeus) de Candolle = *I. domestica* (Kaempfer) Goldblatt & Mabberley; *Xiphium* Miller (1768), type: *X. vulgare* Miller = *I. xiphium* Linnaeus; *Pardanthus* Ker Gawler (1804: 246), type: *P. dichotomus* (Pallas) Ker Gawler = *I. dichotoma* Pallas; *Evansia* Salisbury (1812: 312), type not designated; *Juno* Trattinnick (1821: 153), type not designated; *Iridodictyum* Rodionenko (1961: 201), type: *I. reticulatum* (M. Bieberstein) Rodionenko = *Iris reticulata* M. Bieberstein; *Pardanthopsis* (Hance) Lenz (1972), type: *P. dichotomus* (Pallas) Lenz = *I. dichotoma* Pallas; *Siphonostylis* W. Schulze (1965: 330), type: *S. unguicularis*

**Figure 46.** (upper left) *Iris domestica* inflorescence with capsules (center left, ×0.8), (lower left) *I. virginica* flower (×0.8), (center) *I. brevicaulis* (×0.8), (upper right) *I. iberica* seed, with prominent aril around the micropyle (×8), (lower right, above) *I. tuberosa* seed, with diffuse aril (×8), and (below) *I. tenax* capsule (left, ×0.8) and seed (right, ×8).

(Poiret) W. Schulze = *I. unguicularis* Poiret; *Junopsis* W. Schulze (1970: 327), type: *J. decora* (Wallich) W. Schulze = *I. decora* Wallich

REVISIONARY ACCOUNTS: Dykes (1913), Rodionenko (1961), Mathew (1981)

Small to large evergreen or deciduous perennials with rhizomes or bulbs sometimes with swollen roots, the bulbs with papery or netted tunics, or finger-like tubers (*Iris tuberosus*). LEAVES several to single, unifacial, lanceolate to linear, or terete or square in section, or bifacial and channeled, often forming a two-ranked fan. FLOWERING STEM branched, sometimes repeatedly in dichotomous fashion, or simple, sometimes entirely subterranean. INFLORESCENCE a several- to few- or one-flowered rhipidium; spathes green, enclosing membranous floral bracts. FLOWERS not jointed at the top of the ovary, long-lived, mostly yellow or blue to violet, sometimes white, pink or red, purple, green, or blackish, usually with pale yellow or white markings at the base of the outer tepal limbs; TEPALS united with the top of the ovary in a short to long tube, or forming a solid stalk (as when stem underground), usually producing nectar from the inner surface of the tube, unequal or subequal, usually clawed, the outer three larger, claw ascending to erect, limb spreading or reflexed, often with lines of multicellular hairs (a beard) or a serrated ridge of tissue (a crest) in the lower midline, the inner three usually erect, or spreading to reflexed, sometimes much reduced. STAMENS symmetrically arranged; FILAMENTS free, firm, usually flattened and appressed to the style; ANTHERS linear, appressed to the style branch (not in *I. domestica*). OVARY inferior, three- or one-locular (*I. tuberosa*); STYLE slender below, sometimes embedded in the tissue of the floral tube, dividing opposite the filament apices into three flattened, petal-like branches, terminating in flat paired crests, stigma a transverse

lobe on the abaxial surface below the crests, rarely the style branches much reduced. CAPSULES globose to cylindric, sometimes three-lobed, often shortly beaked; SEEDS usually angular, light to dark brown, rarely red, often with a white aril, sometimes discoid or globose, or the coat irregularly corky, covered with glistening glands in a few species. BASIC CHROMOSOME NUMBER $x$ = possibly 12 or 10, but many numbers have been recorded and polyploidy common. Species c. 280, northern hemisphere, especially Middle East to China and Japan but also in Europe and North America.

*Iris,* largest genus of the Iridaceae, is diverse in both vegetative habit and flower form, and several distinctive subgenera and sections are usually recognized, some of which have been treated as separate genera over the period since the mid-1700s. The classification here is the one favored by the expert on the genus, Brian Mathew (1981):

Subgenus *Limniris* (Tausch) Spach: plants with rhizomes; leaves unifacial, plane; stem usually branched, limb of outer tepals without long hairs (beardless) but sometimes crested or finely papillate; seeds without arils, including section *Lophiris* (= section *Evansia*) and section *Limniris,* the latter with several subsections or series. These are the beardless *Iris* species, also called apogon (without a beard) irises.

Subgenus *Iris:* plants with rhizomes; leaves unifacial, plane; stem often unbranched, limb of outer tepals with long hairs (bearded); seeds without arils (section *Iris*) or arillate (sections *Hexapogon, Oncocyclus, Psammiris, Regelia, Pseudoregelia*). This group comprises most of the bearded *Iris* species, or *Pogoniris* (bearded irises).

Subgenus *Xiphium* (Miller) Spach: plants with bulbs with papery to leathery tunics; leaves dorsiventral and bifacial, mostly channeled; flowering stems aerial, unbranched; flowers with erect inner tepals; seeds without arils. Loosely called xiphium irises, these are the Dutch irises, so common in the florist trade.

Subgenus *Hermodactyloides* Spach (= *Iridodictyum* Rodionenko; section *Reticulata* Dykes): plants with bulbs with netted tunics; leaves round or square in section; flowering stem usually subterranean; flowers with a long perianth stalk; seeds arillate. Often called reticulata irises, several species are widely grown in areas with cold climates, where they flower in early spring. DNA data show that the unusual *Iris tuberosa* (better known as *Hermodactylus*) belongs here, but its long stems and remarkable green and black flowers lacking inner tepals stand out as exceptional within the subgenus.

Subgenus *Scorpiris* Spach (= *Juno* Trattinick; subgenus *Juno* (Trattinick) Baker): plants with bulbs and swollen tuberous roots; leaves bifacial and channeled; stems branched or simple, often largely subterranean; flowers with inner tepals usually completely reflexed but sometimes horizontal; seeds sometimes arillate. Strikingly beautiful but difficult to grow, these are the so-called juno irises, which extend from the eastern Mediterranean to central Asia.

Subgenus *Nepalensis* (Dykes) Lawrence (= *Junopsis* Schulz; section *Nepalensis* Dykes): plants with a vestigial rhizome and tuberous persistent roots; leaves unifacial in two ranks, linear to sword-shaped; stems sometimes underground; flowers with inner tepals spreading; seeds arillate.

The taxonomy of *Iris* has undergone several changes, depending on taxonomic philosophy and the growing understanding of relationships among *Iris* and its allies. Authorities favoring narrow generic

circumscriptions have recognized the three groups of species with bulbs as the genera *Iridodictyum*, *Juno*, and *Xiphium*. More recently the British expert Mathew (1981) has included these groups in *Iris* as subgenera: *Hermodactyloides* (= *Iridodictyum*), *Scorpiris* (= *Juno*), and *Xiphium*. *Iris tuberosa* has at times been treated as the genus *Hermodactylus* due largely to its peculiar, finger-like tubers and a one-locular ovary. Its chromosome number $2n = 20$ and leaf blades square in cross section, however, betray its close relationship to the bulbous subgenus *Hermodactyloides*. Another genus long believed to be closely related to *Iris* is the well-known blackberry lily, *Belamcanda*. It has also seemed clear because of their shared chromosome number $2n = 16$ and similar branching pattern that *I. dichotoma* is most closely related to *Belamcanda*—the two can be crossed to produce fertile hybrids, but neither can be crossed with any other *Iris* species. This knowledge was used as evidence in support of the recognition of a separate genus, *Pardanthus*, for *I. dichotoma*.

DNA studies show quite conclusively that all the segregate genera just mentioned are nested in different parts of the *Iris* phylogenetic tree (Tillie et al. 2001, Wilson 2004). Their inclusion in *Iris* is thus fully justified. The phylogeny confirms several traditional species clusters but not subgenus *Limniris*, members of which are scattered across the tree. A new infrageneric classification remains to be developed based on the results of the molecular study.

Spread across the northern hemisphere, *Iris* is most diverse in Asia and has centers in western Asia and the Mediterranean, and in China. The North American species are most closely related to lineages in eastern Asia. *Iris* is the only genus of the tribe Irideae that has radiated extensively north of the equator, where a few species of the largely African *Moraea* also occur. *Moraea monophylla* and *M. sisyrinchium* (= *I. sisyrinchium*) are native to the

Mediterranean and western Asia and were traditionally, and mistakenly, included in *Iris* or else treated as a separate genus, *Gynandriris*. Like most members of the Irideae, *Iris* species have flowers with enlarged, clawed outer tepals marked with nectar guides, and broad, flattened style branches, to the undersurface of which a stamen is appressed. The style branches terminate in a pair of petal-like appendages called crests, at the base of which there is a transverse stigmatic lobe. Each of the three outer tepals and their opposed style branches resemble a single two-lipped, snapdragon-like flower. Thus while an *Iris* flower is by definition radially symmetric, to a visiting insect it comprises three functionally separate floral units, technically called meranthia (partial flowers). Within the Irideae, *Iris* is recognized by its complex flower with free stamens and tepals fused with the top of the ovary into a tube-like structure, the hypanthium, the interior walls of which have nectaries. Vegetatively, *Iris* species are diverse. The rootstock is a fleshy or slender, horizontal or rarely rhizome, a true bulb, or in sections *Nepalensis* and *Scorpiris* a small crown bearing several fleshy roots. Leaves are typically flattened and sword-like, borne in a fan-like arrangement at the end of the rhizome, but may be channeled, round in section, or even, as in most section *Hermodactyloides,* square in section. The vegetative variation together with some floral features forms the basis of most classifications of the genus.

Flowers of most species are pollinated by large bees, especially bumblebees, which climb into the gullet formed by the outer tepal claw and style branch seeking the sweet, sugary nectar exuded from the walls of the floral tube. On entering the gullet, the back of a visiting bee brushes the stigma lobe, depositing any pollen it carries onto the sticky surface. When it exits it not only carries pollen away from the anther but presses the stigma lobe back against the style branch so that deposition of self pollen cannot occur. The North American *Iris fulva,* which has reddish flowers with particularly long outer tepal claws, is adapted for pollination by hummingbirds, hence the elongate gullet, although it is also sometimes visited by bumblebees. Particularly unusual are species of the western and central Asian section *Oncocyclus,* which have large, dark-colored flowers, the outer tepals without nectar guides. Studies of selected species in Israel show that large male bees, including *Anthophora* species, shelter in the gullet overnight. The flowers lack nectar and appear to depend entirely on these male bees for pollen transfer as they inspect various flowers before settling for the night (Sapir et al. 2005). The reward to these bees may not only be a secure site for shelter at night but a source of morning heat (Sapir 2006). The dark-colored flowers absorb heat in the early morning hours and allow the bees to emerge from their shelter earlier than bees sheltering in pale flowers or in holes in the ground.

*Dietes* Salisbury ex Klatt (1866: 583)
Plates 186–187; Figure 47
Tribe Irideae
Conserved name
TYPE: *Dietes compressa* (Linnaeus fil.) Klatt = *D. iridoides* (Linnaeus) Klatt
ETYMOLOGY: from the Greek *di-*, two or dual, and *etes*, affinities, for the mixed features of *Iris* and *Moraea* exhibited by the genus
SYNONYM: *Naron* Medikus (1790: 419), rejected name, type: *N. orientale* Medikus = *Dietes iridoides*
REVISIONARY ACCOUNT: Goldblatt (1981a)

Evergreen perennials with persistent flowering stems and fibrotic creeping rhizomes. LEAVES leathery, sword-shaped to linear, arranged in a two-ranked fan, without a central vein but in some species several veins aggregated in the center. FLOWERING STEM persistent, either paniculately branched or

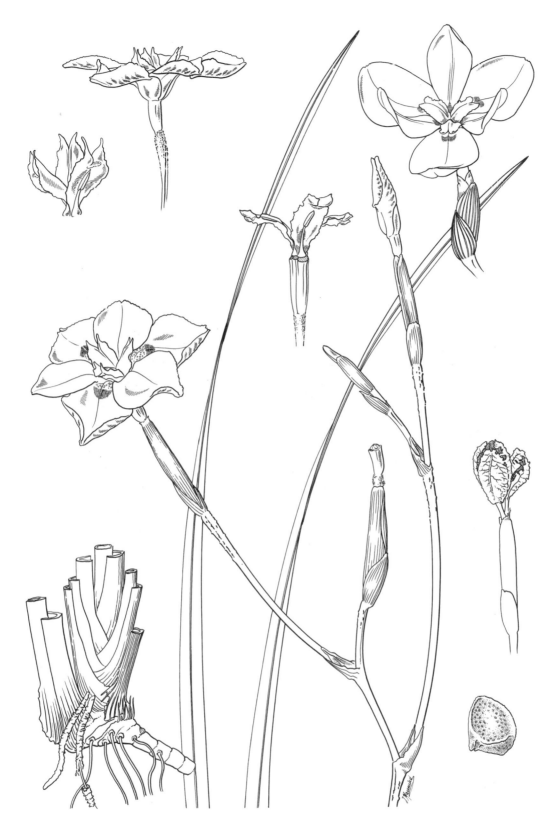

**Figure 47.** *Dietes bicolor* with flower (side view), detail of stamens and style (upper left, ×1.5), rhizome (lower left), capsule (lower right, ×0.8), and seed (bottom right, ×3), (center above the middle) *D. robinsoniana* flower (×0.8) and detail of stamens and style (upper right, ×1.5).

with few branches, but bearing sheathing bract-like leaves at the nodes. INFLORESCENCE a few- to several-flowered rhipidium; spathes leathery, green, tightly sheathing membranous floral bracts. FLOWERS with pedicels hairy above, fugacious (lasting 2–3 days in *Dietes grandiflora*), white to yellow, often with contrasting dark nectar guides on the outer tepals, sometimes with purple style branches; TEPALS free, clawed, the outer often with a line of hairs in the lower midline, larger than the inner. STAMENS symmetrically arranged; FILA-MENTS expanded below, usually free (sometimes basally united in *D. iridoides*); ANTHERS appressed to the opposed style branches. OVARY more or less cylindric, usually exserted from the spathes; STYLE slender below, dividing into broad, petaloid branch-es, each with a transverse abaxial stigma lobe and divided above into paired erect crests. CAPSULE large, woody, partly splitting when ripe or not spit-ting at all and decaying to release the seeds; SEEDS large, angular. BASIC CHROMOSOME NUMBER $x = 10$. Species six, southern and eastern Africa and Lord Howe Island, in evergreen forest, or forest margins, clearings, and bush clumps.

With a fan of sword-shaped leaves borne at the ends of creeping rhizomes, and flowers with broad style branches bearing erect petal-like crests, *Dietes* species closely resemble the northern hemisphere genus *Iris*. Thus it is no surprise that the first spe-cies to be discovered were initially included in that genus. Apart from their evergreen habit, also frequent in *Iris*, *Dietes* flowers differ notably from those of *Iris* mainly in having free tepals that are jointed at the top of the ovary, whereas most *Iris* species have a perianth tube that is continuous with the ovary. The flowers also recall those of the Afri-can genus *Moraea* in their free tepals, but in *Moraea* the stamens are usually partly united, the plants are deciduous, the rootstock is a corm, and the leaves are typically dorsiventral and channeled. Recogniz-ing the combination of features shared with both *Iris* and *Moraea*, the British gardener and botanist Richard A. Salisbury (1812) suggested the name *Dietes*, meaning dual affinities, for the genus, but without providing any description. The name was only formally published with a description by Klatt in 1866. *Dietes* was often ignored by later botanists, and species were simply included in *Moraea*. The resulting confusion has persisted, and even today *Dietes* species are sometimes called *Moraea*.

DNA sequence studies show that *Dietes* is most closely related to the South African *Bobartia*, and the two genera are together sister to *Ferraria* and *Moraea*. As outlined under *Bobartia*, *Dietes* shares with that genus the same basic chromosome num-ber $x = 10$, phloem tissue with fiber cells, and the remarkable hairy pedicels.

The geography of *Dietes* is without precedent in the Iridaceae and is remarkable for all flowering plants. Five species occur in Africa, extending from the southern tip of South Africa to Ethiopia, while the remaining *D. robinsoniana* is restricted to Lord Howe Island in the Tasman Sea between Australia and New Zealand. The morphology of the species, especially the branching pattern, indicate that *D. robinsoniana* is sister to the South African *D. bicolor* (Goldblatt 1981a). DNA sequences (Donato et al. 2000) are not informative about the precise relation-ships of *D. robinsoniana* but confirm its position as relatively unspecialized in the genus. Almost certainly, *D. bicolor* and *D. robinsoniana* are the sister lineage to the remaining four African species. This, together with a postulated minimum age of the genus of c. 35 million years, suggests the remark-able fact that *D. robinsoniana* is a relict species of a genus that dispersed early in its history from an Australasian source to Africa. Pollination of *Dietes* is unknown. The flowers lack nectar and may be pollinated by deceit, by bees visiting flowers vainly searching for nectar.

*Dietes* species are widely cultivated, both in gardens and in street plantings. They are persistent, undemanding of care, drought tolerant, and have a long flowering season. Thus they are cultivated not only in their native Africa but in western North America, New Zealand, southern Europe, and elsewhere. Particularly attractive, *D. grandiflora* has large white flowers with violet style branches that, uniquely in the genus, last 3 days. Another attractive species, *D. bicolor*, has lemon-colored flowers with brown markings that, although lasting only 1 day each, are produced over several months on the multibranched stems, making it very a rewarding garden subject.

*Bobartia* Linnaeus (1747: 17; 1753: 54)
Plates 188–189; Figure 48
Tribe Irideae
TYPE (conserved): *Bobartia indica* Linnaeus
ETYMOLOGY: named for Jakob Bobart (1641–1719), German botanist and first curator of the botanic garden at Oxford, England
REVISIONARY ACCOUNT: Strid (1974)

Evergreen, mostly tufted perennials with creeping or erect rhizomes. LEAVES lanceolate to linear in a two-ranked fan or round in section and then finely grooved longitudinally, often long and trailing. FLOWERING STEMS usually unbranched and bearing several apically crowded, sessile rhipidia, rarely branched and them sometimes with solitary terminal rhipidia, sticky below the nodes in species with branched stems. INFLORESCENCE a few- to several-flowered rhipidium, these often crowded together; spathes closely sheathing the flower buds, green and leathery or more or less dry. FLOWERS borne on pedicels hairy above, fugacious, radially symmetric, usually yellow (blue in *Bobartia lilacina*); TEPALS usually free (united in a short tube in *B. macrospatha*), subequal, spreading, without obvious claws. STAMENS free, symmetrically arranged; FILAMENTS slender, upright; ANTHERS oblong, splitting longitudinally. OVARY excluded or included in the spathes; STYLE slender, dividing into three filiform branches extending between the stamens, stigmatic at the tips. CAPSULES woody, ovoid and truncate, with the central axis separating from the septa; SEEDS angular. BASIC CHROMOSOME NUMBER $x = 10$. Species 15, South Africa, in Western Cape and Eastern Cape Provinces.

Unlike the flowers of other genera of tribe Irideae, those of *Bobartia* are very simple, comprising six subequal spreading tepals, free upright stamens, and a short style that divides into three slender branches stigmatic only at the tips. This contrasts sharply with the *Iris*-like flowers with unequal, clawed tepals of the majority of other species in the tribe. *Bobartia macrospatha* is exceptional in the genus in having the ovary included in the inflorescence spathes, with the perianth exserted from them on a short tube. All but one of the 15 species have yellow flowers, of similar size and shape, but the rare *B. lilacina* has pale violet flowers. That species is also exceptional in having branched stems with a single inflorescence terminal on each branch. Other species have the stem unbranched and bearing several to many individual inflorescences clustered near the stem apex, often at the base of a large terminal leaf. In *B. paniculata* the inflorescences are borne on short branches, a pattern that evidently links *B. lilacina* with the remaining members of the genus. Both species with branched inflorescences, *B. lilacina* and *B. paniculata*, have the stems sticky below the nodes.

*Bobartia* species have tough, fibrous leaves, either plane and isobilateral as is typical of the entire family or round in section with fine longitudinal grooves. The fibrous leaves are apparently unpalatable, and in overgrazed pasture *Bobartia* becomes the dominant plant, the last to be eaten by cattle,

**Figure 48.** *Bobartia indica* with flower (side view) (×1), detail of stamens and style (center, ×4), and stem base (lower left), (lower right) *B. fasciculata* seed (left, ×3) and capsule (right, ×1).

sheep, and goats. Species favor rocky sandstone habitats, which are notoriously nutrient poor, but some are also found on local, nutrient-intermediate, shale outcrops in the mountains of western South Africa. The best known species, *B. indica,* was so named by Linnaeus because the specimens sent to him were thought to have come from the Indies, specifically Ceylon, one of those curious errors that occasionally happen even today.

The relationships of *Bobartia* were misunderstood for many years because the flowers closely resemble those of the New World genus *Sisyrinchium* in their subequal, spreading tepals and three slender style branches alternating with the stamens and stigmatic at the tips. *Bobartia* was accordingly classified with the New World and Australasian genera of Iridaceae tribe Sisyrinchieae. Notably, the basic chromosome number x = 10 corresponds with the African genera of Irideae, and a further two odd features, the hairy pedicels and the presence of fibers in the phloem tissue of the leaves, are unknown in Sisyrinchieae but occur in *Dietes.* DNA sequence data convincingly show that *Bobartia* belongs within tribe Irideae and is most closely related to *Dietes* (Reeves et al. 2001).

*Ferraria* Burman ex Miller (1759, 2: 187, pl. 280)
Plates 190–193; Figure 49
Tribe Irideae
TYPE: *Ferraria crispa* Burman
ETYMOLOGY: named for the 15th century artist Giovanni Ferrari, whose illustrated works were much celebrated by contemporaries; his *Flora seu de florum cultura* (flora of cultivated plants) includes the first illustration of *Ferraria, F. crispa,* drawn from plants grown in Italy
REVISIONARY ACCOUNT: De Vos (1979)

Small to medium-sized seasonal perennials with a flattened corm producing roots from the terminal bud, the corms comprising several internodes, lacking tunics when mature. LEAVES unifacial, sword-shaped to linear, clustered at the base, progressively smaller and bract-like above. FLOWERING STEM usually branched, the branches often short and crowded above. INFLORESCENCE a two- or several flowered rhipidium; SPATHES green, often leafy, enclosing the flower buds. FLOWERS radially symmetric, fugacious or lasting 2 days, often dull-colored, usually cream to buff or brownish, rarely bluish, spotted and blotched dark brown, green, or purple, variously scented, often dull, bitter, or rotting odors; TEPALS free, the inner three somewhat smaller than the outer, clawed, the claws forming a wide or narrow cup, the limbs spreading to lightly reflexed, margins crisped, the tips attenuate and twisted, producing nectar from nectaries near the base of the claws. STAMENS symmetrically arranged; FILAMENTS united below, free and diverging toward the apex; ANTHERS appressed to the style branches, the lobes parallel or diverging from the apex. OVARY included or exserted from the spathes, often with a sterile beak; STYLE short, dividing into short bilobed branches, each densely fringed, stigmatic surface abaxial, below the fringes. CAPSULES globose to ellipsoid, usually pointed or beaked; SEEDS angular or irregularly shaped. BASIC CHROMOSOME NUMBER x = 10. Species c. 14, dry parts of central and southwestern Africa, with a center along the southern African western coast and near interior, with one species extending from interior southern Africa through Namibia to Angola, Congo, Zambia, and Malawi in dry grassland.

The bizarrely mottled flowers of *Ferraria,* with tightly crisped, attenuate tepals, finely fringed style branches, and often unpleasant floral odor, have been a source of fascination ever since plants were first made known to science in 1633 when a woodcut of *F. crispa* was published by Ferrari. The strange

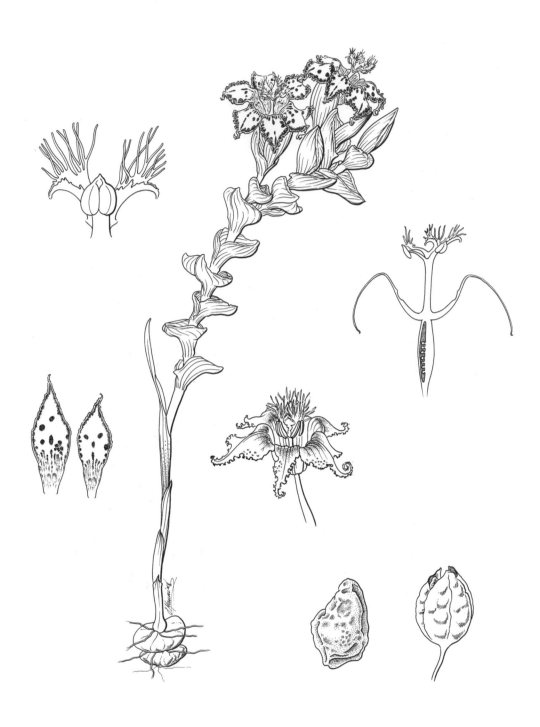

**Figure 49.** *Ferraria ovata* with detached tepals (center left: outer, left, and inner, right) (×1), detail of anther and one stigmatic branch (upper left, ×5), and half-flower (upper right, ×2), (center) *F. divaricata* flower (×1), (lower right) *F. densepunctulata* seed (left, ×6) and capsule (right, ×1).

appearance of the flowers and their curious odors are, as we now know, adapted for pollination by flesh flies, game flies, and houseflies.

*Ferraria* species are recognized not only by the tepal coloring and shape but by several other features. These include the corm, which is more or less discoid, consists of several internodes, and lacks persistent tunics; the long staminal column with the filaments free near the tips; and the short, feathery style branches. The resemblance of the style branches to those of *Iris* and *Moraea* is obscure, although like them the branches are flattened and forked distally, but this is rather obscured by feathery processes of the style branch edges. *Ferraria* is immediately related to *Moraea,* and the molecular clock indicates that the two genera diverged from a common ancestor in the Miocene, c. 25 mya. Like its relatives *Bobartia, Dietes,* and *Iris, Ferraria* also has flattened unifacial and isobilateral leaves while the leaves of *Moraea* are bifacial and dorsiventral, and thus specialized.

The flowers of most *Ferraria* species have broad, spreading tepal claws that form a wide bowl below the spreading style branches. Nectar droplets, exuded from the surface of large nectaries on the lower half of the claws, is consumed by a range of fly species, especially Muscidae and Calliphoridae (game flies), which are attracted to the flowers by their unusual, sometimes rotting odors. As they crawl over the tepals, the upper surface of their bodies brushes against the spreading anthers and becomes covered in a dense coat of the reddish orange pollen. Not all species have such flowers. *Ferraria uncinata* and its allies have fairly narrow tepal claws that are held erect and together form an narrow cup that contains a rather dilute nectar. These species share a prominently beaked ovary and divergent anther lobes with *F. divaricata* and *F. variabilis,* but the flowers of those two species have broad tepal claws, forming a wide cup that contains a pool of watery

nectar. Wasps appear to be the pollinators of this type of flower.

*Ferraria* exhibits a pattern of relatively recent radiation in western southern Africa, which has winter-rainfall and summer-dry climate, but there is one evidently ancestral species, *F. glutinosa,* in southern tropical Africa, where the climate has a hot, wet summer and a dry, cool winter. *Ferraria glutinosa* has an open branching system, and several flowers in each flower cluster, which are both ancestral features, whereas the remaining species always have the branches somewhat crowded together, and only two flowers per inflorescence unit.

## *Moraea* Miller (1759, 2: 159, pl. 238)

Plates 194–210; Figure 50

Tribe Irideae

TYPE (conserved): *Moraea vegeta* Linnaeus

ETYMOLOGY: first named in honor of the English botanist Robert More (1703–1780) and originally spelled *Morea* by Miller but later changed by Linnaeus to *Moraea,* thereby honoring his wife, Elisabeth Moraea; her father, Johan Moraeus, was the town physician in Falun, Sweden

SYNONYMS: *Vieusseuxia* D. Delaroche (1766: 31), type: *V. spiralis* D. Delaroche = *Moraea bellendenii* (Sweet) N. E. Brown; *Galaxia* Thunberg (1782, 2: 50), type: *G. graminea* Linnaeus fil. = *M. fugacissima* (Linnaeus fil.) Druce; *Homeria* Ventenat (1808, 5: no. 2), type: *H. collina* (Thunberg) Salisbury = *M. collina* Thunberg; *Hexaglottis* Ventenat (1808, 6: no. 3), type: *H. longifolia* (Jacquin) Salisbury = *M. longifolia* (Jacquin) Persoon; *Phaianthes* Rafinesque (1837: 30). type: *P. lurida* (Ker Gawler) Rafinesque = *M. lurida* Ker Gawler; *Plantia* Herbert (1844: 89), type: *P. flava* Herbert, probably = *M. virgata* Jacquin; *Hymenostigma* Hochstetter (1844: 24), type: *H. schimperi* Hochstetter = *M. schimperi* (Hochstetter) Pichi-Sermolli; *Gynandriris* Parlatore (1854: 49), type: *G. sisyrinchium* (Linnaeus) Parlatore = *M.*

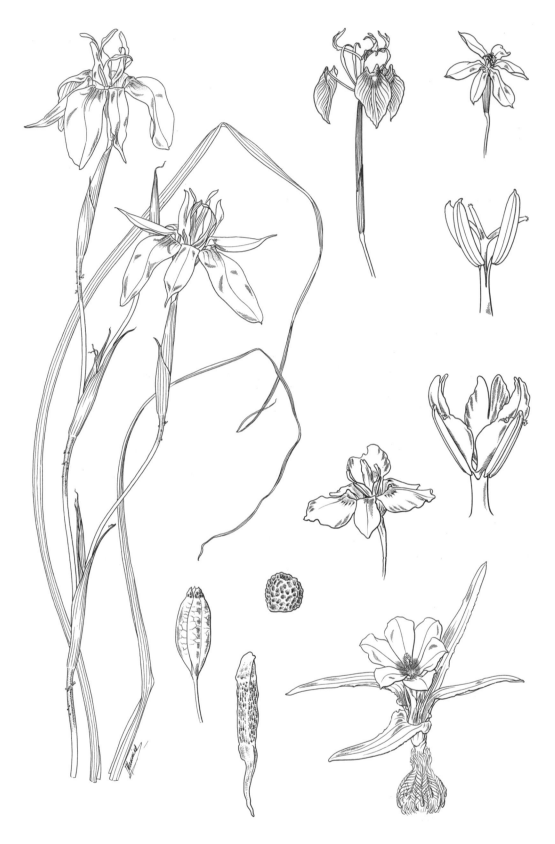

**Figure 50.** (left) *Moraea vespertina* with capsule (×0.8), (top center) *M. regalis* flower (×0.8), (top right) *M. simplex* flower (above, ×0.8) and detail of stamens and style (below, ×5), (center right) *M. cantharophila* flower (left, ×0.8) and detail of stamens and style (right, ×3), (lower right) *M. melanops* (×0.8), (bottom center) seeds of *M. ciliata* (above) and *M. cooperi* (below) (×10).

*sisyrinchium* (Linnaeus) Ker Gawler; *Helixyra* Salisbury ex N. E. Brown (1929: 348), type: *H. flava* Salisbury = *M. longiflora* Ker Gawler; *Barnardiella* Goldblatt (1976: 312), type: *B. spiralis* (N. E. Brown) Goldblatt = *M. herrei* (L. Bolus) Goldblatt; *Roggeveldia* Goldblatt (1979a: 840), type: *R. fistulosa* Goldblatt = *M. fistulosa* (Goldblatt) Goldblatt; *Rheome* Goldblatt (1980a: 92), type: *R. maximiliani* (Schlechter) Goldblatt = *M. maximiliani* (Schlechter) Goldblatt; *Sessilistigma* Goldblatt (1984a: 156), type: *S. radians* Goldblatt = *M. radians* (Goldblatt) Goldblatt

REVISIONARY ACCOUNTS: Goldblatt (1977, 1986; *Galaxia* group, 1979b; *Gynandriris* group, 1980b; *Homeria* group, 1981b; *Hexaglottis* group, 1987)

Large to small seasonal perennials with an apically rooting corm comprising a single internode, with variously fibrous or woody and unbroken tunics. LEAVES few to several, the lowermost without blades, thus cataphylls, blades bifacial and channeled to flat, or margins inrolled, or sometimes terete, without a central vein. FLOWERING STEM several- to few-branched, or simple, sometimes with one long terminal internode and the rhipidia and leaves crowded apically, entirely subterranean in several species, bearing bract-like sheathing leaves at aerial nodes when leaves basal. INFLORESCENCE a one- to several-flowered rhipidium, sometimes several crowded near the stem apex; SPATHES paired, usually firm to leathery, the inner longer, tightly sheathing or the outer curving outward distally, acute or attenuate, rarely with rounded tips, enclosing membranous two-keeled floral bracts. FLOWERS radially symmetric, mostly more or less *Iris*-like, fugacious or lasting up to 3 days, often blue to violet or yellow, also white, pink, red, usually with a yellow mark at the base of the outer tepal limbs, sometimes sweetly or unpleasantly scented, often producing nectar from perigonal nectaries at the tepal bases; TEPALS usually free or united in a solid tube, clawed, subequal to unequal with the outer larger, limbs spreading to reflexed or those of the inner tepals erect, the inner sometimes tricuspidate to hair-like or lacking, claws sometimes short and clasping the base of the filament column. STAMENS symmetrically arranged; FILAMENTS mostly partly to completely united, or free; ANTHERS appressed to the style branches, splitting open longitudinally. OVARY usually pedicellate and exserted, or included or more or less sessile, extending upward as a hollow tube in some species; STYLE slender below, dividing near the apex of the filament column into three branches, these often compressed, petal-like and wider than the anther, terminating in large paired crests (fringed in *Moraea lugubris*), stigma usually transverse and shorter than the width of the style branch, or the style branches reduced and narrow, two-lobed with the stigma terminal and crests lacking, rarely the style branches filiform or divided into paired filiform arms extending between the anther bases and stigmatic at the tips. CAPSULES ovoid to oblong, apex truncate or shortly beaked, leathery to woody or submembranous, usually exserted, or included; SEEDS angular to spindle-shaped, globose or compressed and discoid, the surface cells domed or concave, sometimes smooth. BASIC CHROMOSOME NUMBER $x = 10$ but a wide range of other numbers present. Species c. 198, Africa, the Mediterranean Basin, and the Middle East, most diverse and speciose in western southern Africa and with marked secondary centers in the mountains of eastern southern Africa and the East African highlands, favoring open habitats, including desert scrub, rocky grassland, rock outcrops, and shrubland, often flowering well only after fires.

Resembling *Iris* in many ways, *Moraea* is not immediately related to its northern hemisphere relative but is more closely related to the African genera of tribe Irideae: *Bobartia, Dietes,* and *Ferraria*. *Dietes, Iris,* and *Moraea* stand out in the Iridaceae in having unusual flattened and petaloid style branches with an abaxial transverse stigma lobe and paired terminal crests. *Moraea* and *Ferraria* differ from other members of the Irideae in having a corm, whereas *Dietes* and *Iris* have a rhizome or in the case of *Iris*, sometimes bulbs or tubers. *Moraea* is additionally specialized in having a bifacial leaf (developed independently in some *Iris* species), and its corm differs from that in *Ferraria* in always consisting only of a single swollen internode. The corm in the two genera is distinctive in the family in lacking organized vascular tissue, and perhaps as a consequence, roots are produced from the base of the terminal bud rather than from the corm itself. In other cormous Iridaceae the roots are produced from the base or lower part of the corm. Flowers of *Moraea*, though broadly resembling those of *Iris*, can immediately be distinguished by having filaments partly to completely united and usually lacking a perianth tube. In *Iris* the filaments are free and the tepals usually united in a thick, sometimes solid tube in which the base of the style is embedded. Nectar is secreted from glands on the walls of the tube, whereas in *Moraea* the nectaries are discrete patches of tissue at the base of the tepals, often only the outer tepals.

*Moraea* and *Dietes* are sometimes confused, the result of their being regarded as congeneric by some 19th century botanists. The resemblance is confined to the flowers, which though similar in lacking a perianth tube are readily separated by the free filaments in *Dietes*, species of which are always evergreen and have sword-shaped leaves, and a rhizome. If anything, *Dietes* is more closely related to *Iris* than to *Moraea*.

Species-rich, with c. 198 species, *Moraea* is so diverse in its flowers that several species groups within the genus were at various times segregated as separate genera, all of which have the diagnostic features of *Moraea*, a corm of a single internode, a bifacial (or terete) leaf, and flowers with free tepals and partly united filaments (Goldblatt 1998).

Molecular studies have confirmed that all other species groups with single-internode corms and bifacial leaves are nested within the *Moraea* clade (Goldblatt et al. 2002a), thus endorsing the inclusion in *Moraea* of such apparently distinctive genera as *Galaxia*, *Gynandriris*, and *Homeria* along with several more obscure small ones such as *Barnardiella*, *Hexaglottis*, *Rheome*, and *Roggeveldia*. The specialization that defined most of these genera was the presence of subequal, spreading tepals and narrow, sometimes filiform style branches of various configurations. Species of the *Galaxia* group are additionally stemless, and the flowers have a short, solid perianth tube. In *Hexaglottis* the style branches are divided to the base, thus forming six outspread filiform arms, whereas in *Roggeveldia* the filiform style branches are undivided. *Homeria*, largest of the genera nested in *Moraea*, was defined by having subequal tepals, filaments almost completely united, and style branches narrower than the anthers. The various species included in *Homeria* proved to share an ancestor with different species groups in *Moraea*, and it became impossible to uphold even this apparently distinctive genus.

Species of the *Gynandriris* group were defined primarily by an ovary with a sterile tubular extension and short pedicel, but the flower is otherwise exactly like that of a *Moraea* species. As well as seven in southern Africa, *Gynandriris* has two Mediterranean and Middle Eastern species, one of them the well-known *G. sisyrinchium*, now *M. sisyrinchium*, the Barbary or Spanish nut. That species was for many years treated as *Iris sisyrinchium*, and some current floristic accounts persist in placing the species in *Iris*, ignoring the ample evidence that the species correctly belongs in *Moraea*.

Molecular study has also shown the sister relationship between the two corm-bearing genera of the Irideae: *Moraea* and *Ferraria*. Matching the phylogeny to the molecular clock shows that the two genera diverged in the early Miocene, c. 25 mya (Goldblatt et al. 2002a), a time when the African climate was becoming strongly seasonal and plants with underground storage and reproductive organs were at an adaptive advantage. The center of origin of *Moraea* is southwestern Africa, and it is there that the genus is also most diverse, with both relatively primitive and highly specialized species occurring in the region, which today has a winter-rainfall and summer-dry climate. According to molecular studies, the presence of *Moraea* in eastern southern Africa and tropical Africa is comparatively recent, c. 9–6 mya, and the result of northward range expansion by only three specialized lineages. The large-flowered subgenus *Grandiflora* and section *Polyanthes* of subgenus *Moraea* both extend though tropical Africa to Ethiopia, while one lineage within subgenus *Vieusseuxia* extends into eastern South Africa.

Pollination in *Moraea* is diverse. The ancestral condition appears to be pollination by long-tongued bees foraging for nectar. Several Western Cape species, including the well-known peacock iris, *M. villosa,* are pollinated by monkey beetles (Scarabaeidae: Hopliini), while most species of the *Homeria* group are either pollinated by female bees foraging for pollen or by a combination of these bees and scarab beetles. *Moraea lurida* and *M. ochroleuca* have putrid-scented flowers and are pollinated mainly by game flies, flesh flies, and houseflies in the families Calliphoridae, Scathophagidae, and Muscidae.

Many species are poisonous and contain cardiac glycosides. Stock losses from poisoning, especially of species of the *Homeria* group, locally called tulp (from the Dutch name for tulip, which the flowers resemble), can be considerable in parts of southern Africa. Occasional human deaths occur when corms are eaten by children. Some species are weedy in pastures and orchards in Western Cape Province, notably *Moraea miniata,* and a few are weedy in Australia. A number of other species have edible corms, notably *M. fugax* and *M. lewisiae.* Judging from the frequency of corm tunics in their rock shelters, *Moraea* corms were an important food for hunter-gathering !Kung and Khoi people. The palatability and food value of these species, particularly *M. fugax* (*M. edulis* is a synonym of the species) and *M. lewisiae,* was noted by 17th century European explorers, and *Moraea* corms must have remained an important food source until crops from Europe began to be widely grown in South Africa after 1750.

*Libertia* Sprengel (1824: 127)
Plate 211
Tribe Sisyrinchieae
Conserved name, not *Libertia* Dumortier (1822), rejected name
LECTOTYPE designated by L. B. Moore (1967): *L. ixioides* (Forster fil.) Sprengel
ETYMOLOGY: named after Anne-Marie Libert (1782–1865), Belgian botanist
SYNONYMS: *Tekel* Adanson (1763: 497, 610), rejected name, type not designated; *Renealmia* R. Brown (1810, addendum: 592), illegitimate name, not *Renealmia* Linnaeus (1753), type not designated; *Nematostigma* A. Dietrich (1833: 508), type not designated
REVISIONARY ACCOUNTS: Cooke (1986: 5–8), Blanchon et al. (2002), Goldblatt and Celis (2005)

Small to medium-sized evergreen perennials with creeping rhizomes. LEAVES several, lanceolate to linear, with a prominent central vein. FLOWERING STEM erect, terete, few- to several-branched, branches long or very short and sometimes clustered close to the main axis. INFLORESCENCE a few-flowered rhipidium, usually several per flowering stem; SPATHES short, green or becoming dry, enclosing membranous floral bracts. FLOWERS usually borne on long pedicels, rarely pedicels short or subsessile, radially symmetric, fugacious, white or blue (*Libertia sessiliflora*); TEPALS free, subequal or the outer whorl much smaller. STAMENS symmetrically arranged, erect; FILAMENTS united below in a short tube, slender above; ANTHERS erect. OVARY globose to ovoid; STYLE slender, short, dividing above the filament tube into three slender, apically stigmatic branches extending between the stamens. CAPSULES globose or ovoid, sometimes not splitting open when mature; SEEDS brown and shed immediately or colored yellow or orange and exposed in the open capsule. BASIC CHROMOSOME NUMBER $x = 19$. Species c. 12, Australia, New Guinea, New Zealand, and Andean and temperate South America.

*Libertia* has an unusual disjunct distribution, occurring in Australasia, including eastern Australia, New Guinea, and New Zealand, and on the other side of the Pacific Ocean in temperate and Andean South America. The genus is well represented only in New Zealand and Chile. Of the four South American species, three occur in Chile and the fourth extends through the Andes from Bolivia to Colombia. Flowers of all but one species are white, radially symmetric, and held upright. The genus is distinguished primarily by filaments united in the lower half or third, and the short style has slender branches extended between the filaments, and is distinguished secondarily by the outer tepals, which are slightly to much smaller than the inner. The exception is the Chilean *L. sessiliflora* (= *L. caerulescens*), which has blue flowers, also exceptional in facing to the side instead of being upright. *Libertia sessiliflora* also stands out in having the flowers borne on very short pedicels and in its oblong capsule. All other South American *Libertia* species have globose capsules and the flowers borne on long pedicels, thus held well above the stem. The Australasian species have white flowers and either globose or ovoid to pear-shaped capsules. Cytologically, *Libertia* stands

out in its basic chromosome number, the unusual $x = 19$ (Goldblatt and Takei 1997, Blanchon et al. 2000). Species are diploid or polyploid with some New Zealand species having particularly high levels of polyploidy, thus *L. grandiflora* is hexaploid, $2n = 6x = 114$, and *L. ixioides* dodecaploid, $2n = 12x = 228$. Blue-flowered *L. sessiliflora* is diploid, $2n = 38$. The chromosome number in this unusual *Libertia* species seems to remove any doubt about its generic placement on account of its odd flowers.

*Libertia* is most closely allied to *Orthrosanthus*, a second genus with an Australasian–South American distribution. The latter genus has virtually identical flowers except for a blue perianth, sessile or subsessile flowers, and an oblong ovary that develops into an ellipsoid to almost cylindric capsule. Basic chromosome number in *Orthrosanthus* is uncertain but is possibly $x = 9$, a notable difference from the basic number $x = 19$ in *Libertia*.

New Zealand species of *Libertia* are cultivated in Europe and North America as well as in their land of origin. The fairly large flowers of *L. ixioides* are particularly attractive, and although lasting only a single day each, so many blooms are produced that a flowering period lasts for several weeks. Even in fruit the plants offer an elegant presence in the garden with their bold, upright, sword-shaped leaves. In Australia, *Libertia* species are called grass flags, alluding to their similarity to *Iris*, at least in their foliage.

**Orthrosanthus** Sweet (1829b: pl. 11)
Plate 212; Figure 51
Tribe Sisyrinchieae
TYPE: *Orthrosanthus multiflorus* Sweet
ETYMOLOGY: from the Greek *orthros*, morning, and *anthos*, flower, alluding to the flower buds that open early in the morning and wilt before noon
SYNONYM: *Elvetra* Rafinesque (1837: 30), type: *E. multiflora* (Sweet) Rafinesque = *Orthrosanthus multiflorus* Sweet

**Figure 51.** *Orthrosanthus monadelpus* with fruits, flower (upper right), detached capsule (center left, ×0.8), seed (lower left, ×10), and detail of stamens and style (center right, ×4).

REVISIONARY ACCOUNTS: Cooke (1986: 10–13, for Australian species), Henrich and Goldblatt (1987, for New World species)

Medium-sized to large evergreen rhizomatous perennials, often forming large tufts. LEAVES more or less linear or narrowly sword-shaped, several, in a two-ranked fan, without a prominent central vein. FLOWERING STEM erect, terete, few- to several-branched, the branches often short. INFLORES-CENCE a few-flowered rhipidium, usually several to many per plant in various arrangements; SPATHES relatively short, loosely sheathing the buds and the green to membranous bracts. FLOWERS usually sessile or almost so with the ovary included in the spathes, occasionally the pedicels well developed and elongate in fruit, radially symmetric, fuga-cious, mostly blue (white in *Orthrosanthus occi-pungus*), tepals free, usually subequal, spreading from the base. STAMENS symmetrically arranged, erect; FILAMENTS united below in a short tube, slender above; ANTHERS erect. OVARY oblong to ovoid, included in the spathes, sometimes softly hairy; STYLE short, dividing above the filament column into three slender, apically stigmatic branches extending between the stamens. CAPSULES ellip-soid to cylindric, included (shortly exserted in *O. exsertus*); SEEDS angular to elongate and tapering at the ends. BASIC CHROMOSOME NUMBER prob-ably $x = 9$. Species nine, Australia, and Argentina and Bolivia to Venezuela in South America, and in Central America and southern Mexico, at high elevations, mostly in subpáramo vegetation in South America.

*Orthrosanthus* shares with the closely related genus *Libertia* an unusual disjunct distribution, with species occurring in Australia and in South and Central America, but unlike *Libertia* there are no native species in New Zealand or New Guinea. Flowers of the two genera are largely identical except for their color, and the ovary is usually borne on long pedi-cels in *Libertia,* which typically has white flowers, but is sessile or nearly so in *Orthrosanthus,* which typically has blue flowers. Exceptions occur in both genera, for *L. sessiliflora* has more or less sessile blue flowers, *O. occisapungus* has white flowers, and *O. exsertus* has the ovary borne on well-developed ped-icels exserted from the spathes, as its name suggests. While *Orthrosanthus* has subequal tepals, there is a tendency in *Libertia* for the inner tepals to be larger than the outer, sometimes considerably so, but the tepals are subequal in some species.

Basic chromosome number in *Orthrosanthus* and *Libertia* also differs, offering independent support for their status as separate genera. While *Libertia* has $x = 19$, *Orthrosanthus* probably has $x = 9$. Basic chromosome number in *Orthrosanthus* remains to be confirmed because conflicting counts leave us in some doubt about the correct number. There are differing reports in the Australian *O. polystachyus* of either $2n = 84$ or $2n = 40$ (Goldblatt and Takei 1997), while the South American *O. acorifolius* and *O. chimboracensis* have $2n = 54$ or, alternatively, $2n = 50$ in both *O. chimboracensis* and *O. exsertus.* The difference in the counts seems to concern the identity of four small chromosomes, interpreted either as separate chromosomes or as satellites. The chromosomes are small, making accurate assessment of the number difficult. Nevertheless, it is clear that the base numbers in *Orthrosanthus* and *Libertia* differ. The apparent difference in chromosome base numbers in the Australian and South American species makes us question whether they correctly belong in the same genus.

One species, *Orthrosanthus spicatus,* first referred to *Sisyrinchium,* is very different from other mem-bers of the genus in having a compressed, two-winged stem and pale yellow flowers with the tepals united in a short tube. In other respects is falls within tribe Sisyrinchieae. This plant of southern

Brazil does not belong in *Orthrosanthus,* where a compressed stem and yellow flowers are unknown. The Chilean authority on New World Iridaceae, Pierfelice Ravenna (1968), treated the species as *Phaiophleps brasiliensis,* but the vegetative morphology does not accord with that genus, now a synonym of *Olsynium.* We suspect this species may be an unusual member of *Sisyrinchium* subgenus *Echthronema* in which a compressed stem and yellow flower is universal and only the perianth tube is unusual. Alternatively, it may represent a new genus allied to *Sisyrinchium.*

The South American species are mostly from high elevations, growing in páramo vegetation or immediately below the páramo. In contrast, the Australian species grow in Mediterranean-type shrubland. *Orthrosanthus* is known in Australia as morning flag, recalling its morning blooming habit.

*Olsynium* Rafinesque (1836: 29)
Plates 213–214; Figure 52
Tribe Sisyrinchieae
TYPE: *Olsynium grandiflorum* (Douglas ex Lindley) Rafinesque = *O. douglasii* (A. Dietrich) E. P. Bicknell
ETYMOLOGY: from the Greek *ol,* a little, and *syn-,* joined, referring to the filaments united toward their bases
SYNONYMS: *Phaiophleps* Rafinesque (1837: 29), type: *P. odoratissima* (Cavanilles) Rafinesque = *Olsynium biflorum* (Thunberg) R. C. Foster; *Eriphilema* Herbert (1843a: 85), type: *E. grandiflorum* (Douglas ex Lindley) Herbert = *O. douglasii* (A. Dietrich) Bicknell; *Psithyrisma* Herbert (1843a: 85), type: *P. narcissoides* (Cavanilles) Herbert = *O. biflorum* (Thunberg) R. C. Foster; *Symphyostemon* Miers ex Klatt (1861: 569), type: *S. narcissoides* (Cavanilles) Klatt = *O. biflorum* (Thunberg) R. C. Foster; *Chamelum* Philippi (1864: 250), type: *C. luteum* Philippi = *O. luteum* (Philippi) Goldblatt;

*Ona* P. Ravenna (1972), type: *O. obscura* (Cavanilles) Ravenna = *Olsynium obscurum* (Cavanilles) Goldblatt
REVISIONARY ACCOUNT: Goldblatt et al. (1990)

Small to medium-sized seasonal or evergreen perennials with thickened roots and a short rhizome, or the rootstock indistinct. LEAVES in a basal tuft, the upper partly sheathing the stem, linear or terete, hollow, or cross-shaped in transverse section. FLOWERING STEM aerial and simple or branched or subterranean. INFLORESCENCE a few- to several-flowered rhipidium; spathes green, soft-textured, tightly enclosing the buds and floral bracts. FLOWERS usually borne on long pedicels, rarely shortly pedicellate and borne at ground level, pink, red, orange, white, or yellow, sometimes with dark stripes, often facing to the side or more or less nodding, fugacious or lasting 2 days; TEPALS united below in a short or well-developed tube, subequal, often cupped below and including stamens and style. STAMENS symmetrically arranged; FILAMENTS united in the lower half or entirely, the column usually inflated above the base; ANTHERS parallel or diverging above. OVARY globose; STYLE slender, dividing into three short to long branches reaching or exceeding the anthers. CAPSULES more or less globose, sometimes apically truncate, often borne on elongate pedicels held well above the spathes; SEEDS more or less angular and prismatic. BASIC CHROMOSOME NUMBER $x = 9$. Species c. 12, Andean and temperate South America, the Falkland Islands, and western North America.

Described as early as 1837 by the eccentric botanist Constantine Rafinesque, *Olsynium* at first included only the native western North American plant until then known as *Sisyrinchium grandiflorum* (*S. douglasii* is an earlier name for this plant). Then in 1843, William Herbert described *Eriphilema,* including only *S. grandiflorum,* and *Psithyrisma* for three more

**Figure 52.** *Olsynium douglasii* (×1) with staminal column and style (right, ×5), capsules (center left, ×1), and seed (lower left, ×12).

species now included in *Olsynium. Eriphilema* was submerged in *Sisyrinchium* as subgenus *Eriphilema* by Bentham and Hooker (1883) and remained so treated until the 1990s when Goldblatt et al. (1990) showed that *O. grandiflorum* and several South American species then placed in the genera *Chamelum, Ona,* and *Phaiophleps* shared several features that set them apart. These included the short, hollow leaves rounded in cross section, globose capsules borne on unusually elongated pedicels, and perhaps most significantly, tepals united at least basally and sometimes for a considerable distance. The flowers also often face to the side or are almost completely nodding, but flowers of the dwarf or acaulescent species are, of course, held upright.

Like other members of the *Sisyrinchium* group of genera, the filaments are united, and the filament column is also distinctively swollen below. Although the filament column is also sometimes swollen below in *Sisyrinchium,* it is always lightly to densely hairy in that genus but smooth in *Olsynium.* The significance of the swollen filament column was not understood when Goldblatt et al. (1990) recognized *Olsynium* and united *Chamelum, Ona,* and *Phaiophleps* with it. Studies of the pollination biology of *O. douglasii* in North America and *O. junceum* in South America show that the bulbous part of the column is highly vascularized and exudes sugary nectar through the epidermis into the base of the perianth tube (Rudall et al. 2003). The secretion of nectar from the filaments in *Olsynium* is unique in Iridaceae and is evidently the only genus of the *Sisyrinchium* group that normally secretes true nectar. The other genera appear to be pollen flowers, thus offering only pollen as a reward to visiting insects, or they offer oils or, rarely, sugar nectar produced from the glandular hairs on the filament column in some *Sisyrinchium* species. Our pollination studies conducted on *O. douglasii* show that it is pollinated by a range of bees, including female bumblebees

(*Bombus* species) and *Osmia* (Megachilidae), foraging for nectar as well as pollen. The southern South American *Olsynium philippi* seems exceptional in the genus in not producing nectar and thus provides only pollen for foraging female bees (Cocucci and Vogel 2001).

*Olsynium* has an unusual distribution with a center in temperate South America but with species extending through the southern Andes to Peru; one species, *O. douglasii,* is in western North America, and *O. filifolium* on the Falkland Islands. The genus includes species with aerial stems and two that are acaulescent, the latter segregated in the past in the genus *Chamelum,* which has flowers with a particularly elongate tube that raises the flower above the ground. Known as widow grass in North America, in reference to its rather somber-colored, nodding flowers, *O. douglasii* is occasionally cultivated in is native range and in the British Isles. It makes an interesting rock garden subject, but the flowering season is short and plants each produce only a few blooms. Unlike other genera of the *Sisyrinchium* group, flowers of *Olsynium,* or at least *O. douglasii,* last more than a single day, though they do deliquesce on fading like those of the other genera of the tribe.

## *Sisyrinchium* Linnaeus (1753: 954)

Plates 215–219; Figure 53

Tribe Sisyrinchieae

TYPE: *Sisyrinchium bermudianum* Linnaeus

ETYMOLOGY: the Greek name for *Moraea sisyrinchium,* so called because its corm tunics recall a shaggy coat (Greek, *sisyra*) or, alternatively but unlikely, derived from the Latin *sus,* pig, and Greek *rhynchos,* snout, alluding to swine digging the roots of some bulbous plant for food, spoken of by Pliny and Theophrastus (W. J. Hooker 1830); the reason for applying the name to a genus of New World Iridaceae was apparently arbitrary

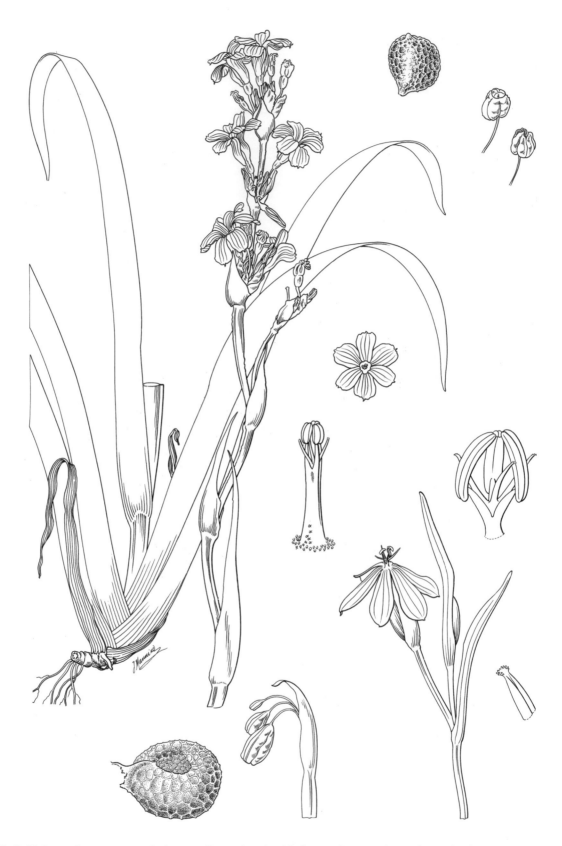

**Figure 53.** (left) *Sisyrinchium striatum* (subgenus *Sisyrinchium*) with flower (center above, front view) and capsules (above right) (×0.8), seed (top center, ×12), and detail of staminal column (center below, ×3), (lower right) *S. convolutum* (subgenus *Echthronema*) inflorescence (×1), detail of staminal column (×3), and detail of stigmatic branch (×6), (lower left) *S. tinctorium* seed (left, ×10) and capsules (right, ×1).

SYNONYMS: *Bermudiana* Miller (1754), invalid superfluous name for *Sisyrinchium*, type not designated; *Souza* Vellozo (1825: 258, and 7: pl. 1), type: *S. marchio* Vellozo = *Sisyrinchium vaginatum* Sprengel; *Pogadelphia* Rafinesque (1837: 29), type: *P. graminifolia* (Lindley) Rafinesque = *S. graminifolium* Lindley (lectotype designated by Goldblatt et al. 1990: 507); *Paneguia* Rafinesque (1837: 34), type: *P. striata* (Smith) Rafinesque = *S. striatum* Smith; *Echthronema* Herbert (1843a: 85), type: *E. tenuifolium* (Kunth) Herbert = *S. tenuifolium* Kunth; *Glumosia* Herbert (1843a: 85), type: *G. palmifolium* (Linnaeus) Herbert = *S. palmifolium* Linnaeus; *Hydastylus* Bicknell (1900: 373), type: *H. californicus* (Ker-Gawler) Salisbury ex Bicknell = *S. californicum* (Ker-Gawler) Aiton
REVISIONARY ACCOUNTS: R. Rodríguez (1986, Chilean species), Goldblatt and Henrich (1994, Central American species), Cholewa and Henderson (2002)

Small to medium-sized seasonal perennials or rarely annuals with rhizomes or the rootstock indistinct, roots often thick and fleshy or tuberous, or fibrous in annual species. LEAVES lanceolate to linear or sometimes terete, without a distinct central vein. FLOWERING STEM variously branched or simple, compressed and angled to winged, sometimes comprising a single extended terminal internode. FLOWERS borne on slender pedicels, radially symmetric, fugacious, mostly either shades of pale or dark blue or violet, often with a yellow center, or entirely yellow; TEPALS free, subequal, spreading from the base or cupped below and then often including the stamens and style. STAMENS symmetrically arranged; FILAMENTS united in the lower half and diverging above or entirely united, the filament column sometimes inflated and often glandular-pubescent; ANTHERS diverging or coherent. OVARY globose, included or exserted; STYLE short to long, dividing into three short to long branches, these usually

extending between the stamens. CAPSULES globose to cylindric, sometimes truncate; SEEDS globose, often with a deep depression at the chalazal end. BASIC CHROMOSOME NUMBER $x = 9$, other numbers $n = 8, 17$, with many polyploid species. Species c. 140, throughout South, Central, and North America, including one species in Greenland. Populations of a *Sisyrinchium* species in western Ireland, often referred to *S. bermudianum*, are considered by some as native there, unlikely as this seems.

Often a conspicuous member of the flora of grasslands, prairies, and páramo, *Sisyrinchium* is the largest genus of the Iridaceae in the New World and one that remains poorly understood. The genus was revised for *Flora of North America* by Cholewa and Henderson (2002), where 37 species are recognized. There are also modern floristic accounts of the genus for Central America (Goldblatt and Henrich 1994), Chile (R. Rodríguez 1986), and all of temperate South America, where some 92 species occur (G. Roitman, pers. comm.). Knowledge of *Sisyrinchium* in Mexico, a major center for the genus, as well as for much of South America, however, remains incomplete. For this reason we are unable to assess accurately the number of species in the genus but conservatively estimate c. 140.

*Sisyrinchium* is the central genus of Sisyrinchieae, a tribe that includes five other genera: *Libertia*, *Olsynium*, *Orthrosanthus*, *Solenomelus*, and *Tapeinia*. Members of the tribe have either a rhizomatous rootstock or a fibrous root system, sometimes with thickened tuberous roots, and they are recognized by the partially or entirely united filaments and filiform, undivided style branches stigmatic at the tips. *Olsynium* was included in *Sisyrinchium* as subgenus *Eriphilema* by most modern authors until a study by Goldblatt et al. (1990) showed that treatment as a separate genus was preferable. The earliest name for subgenus *Eriphilema* at generic rank is *Olsynium*. With the exclusion of this last genus, *Sisyrinchium* is distinguished by a compressed stem and globose seeds, often with the chalazal end flattened or sunken, both derived features. *Olsynium* shares with many *Sisyrinchium* species an unusual anatomical feature—the fiber caps of the vascular traces are situated on the interior side of the phloem (Rudall et al. 1986), whereas in most plants, not only the Iridaceae, the fiber caps are on the outside. *Olsynium* species, however, have angular seeds and rounded stems, ancestral features for the tribe and family.

Species of *Sisyrinchium* fall into two major groups: subgenus *Sisyrinchium*, the blue-eyed grasses, and a heterogeneous group of mostly yellow-flowered species, often treated as subgenus *Echthronema*. Subgenus *Sisyrinchium* is well represented in North America, where flowers range in color from shades of pale to dark blue or violet with a cream or yellow center, and the flowers themselves are cup- or bell-shaped. Yellow-flowered species are well represented in Central and South America, and two or three species extend into western North America. The well-known garden plant *S. striatum*, native to Chile, has the floral morphology of subgenus *Sisyrinchium* but pale yellow flowers. The filaments in subgenus *Sisyrinchium* are united for most of their length, if not entirely, and the anthers are usually parallel and coherent. The filament column is usually sparsely to densely hairy, and in some South American species the hairs are crowded toward the base of the column with the tips gold-colored. They are glandular and secrete oil as a reward for pollinating insects, always female bees (Cocucci and Vogel 2001). At least one species secretes sugary nectar from the filament hairs (Roitman and Medan 1995).

In contrast, flowers of most yellow-flowered species have tepals spreading from the base instead of being cupped, the filaments are united only in the lower half, and the anthers diverge from one another. These flowers lack hairs of any kind, produce no oil reward for pollinators, and presumably rely on pollen-collecting bees for pollination. Species with this type of flower are sometimes called yellow-eyed grasses. The subgenus is best developed in Central and northern South America. Differences between the flowers of the two subgenera of *Sisyrinchium* are not clear-cut, and a more complex infrageneric classification seems called for. Ancestral basic chromosome number in the genus is $x = 9$, but both blue- and yellow-flowered species also have the derived number $n = 8$. In subgenus *Sisyrinchium* there is an extended polyploid series culminating in the hexaploid $n = 48$ in several North American species. *Sisyrinchium* is the only genus of Iridaceae that has annual species. The handful of annuals include the Central American *S. micranthum* and a few species in temperate South America. It seems likely that the two or three annual species that occur in the southern United States are fairly recent introductions from South America and not native.

Studies using DNA sequences confirm that *Sisyrinchium* is sister to the temperate and largely South American genus *Olsynium*, and the pair are in turn sister to the Andean genus *Solenomelus* (L. Karst, pers. comm.). This tree topology is identical to the earlier study of Goldblatt et al. (1990).

*Sisyrinchium striatum* (Plate 53) is an elegant plant for the perennial border and is widely grown in areas of relatively mild winters, but it will survive temperatures as low as −8°C (18°F). A few other species are sometimes seen in gardens, and despite their small flowers they can make effective displays. At the Rancho Santa Ana Botanic Garden in Claremont in southern California, banks densely planted with the native *S. bellum* can be one of the highlights of a visit in late spring. The pale blue flowers produced in great numbers from the branched stems offer a striking contrast to the deep orange of the California poppy (*Eschscholzia californica*) and suggest that the value of *Sisyrinchium* as a garden subject should be reconsidered. Yellow-flowered *S.*

*californicum* and its allies, the yellow-eyed grasses, also make interesting plants in rock gardens and low perennial borders. *Sisyrinchium macrocephalum* has particularly large flowers, and it, too, can make a striking garden display.

## *Solenomelus* Miers (1841: 122; 1842)
Plate 220
Tribe Sisyrinchieae
TYPE: *Solenomelus chilensis* Miers = *S. pedunculatus* (Gillies ex W. J. Hooker) Hochreutiner
ETYMOLOGY: from the Greek *solen,* tube, and *melos,* member, for the union of the filaments and anthers in a tube containing the style
SYNONYM: *Cruckshanksia* Miers (1826, 2: 529), name invalid, without description, not *Cruckshanksia* W. J. Hooker (1831), type: *C. graminea* Miers = *Solenomelus pedunculatus* (Gillies ex W. J. Hooker) Hochreutiner

Medium-sized seasonal perennials with short rhizomes. LEAVES sword-shaped to linear, in a basal tuft, without a central vein. FLOWERING STEM erect, simple or few-branched, round in section. INFLORESCENCE a few-flowered rhipidium; SPATHES leathery, green, somewhat inflated. FLOWERS subsessile, facing to the side, fugacious, yellow or blue, weakly bell-shaped, tubular below; PERIANTH TUBE slender, curving outward, partly included in the spathes; TEPALS subequal, cupped below, spreading above; PERIANTH TUBE short, narrow, curving outward. STAMENS symmetrically arranged; FILAMENTS united in a smooth or densely hairy column; ANTHERS parallel and contiguous. OVARY ovoid, included in the spathes; STYLE slender, obscurely three-lobed above. CAPSULES ellipsoid, borne on short pedicels and included in the spathes; SEEDS ovoid, with foveolate sculpturing. BASIC CHROMOSOME NUMBER $x = 9$. Species two, Andes of Chile and Argentina.

Comprising just two species, *Solenomelus* is restricted to the southern Andes of South America. The more common *S. pedunculatus,* the type of the genus, has yellow flowers, a branched stem, and fairly softly textured leaves, whereas *S. segethii* has violet flowers, an unbranched stem, and narrow, fibrotic leaves. The genus first appears in the literature under the name *Cruckshanksia* but without description in the British mining engineer John Miers's account of his experiences in Chile in the 1820s (Miers 1826). By the time Miers published a formal description in 1841, the name *Cruckshanksia* was unavailable because of the existence of two other genera called *Cruckshanksia,* one in the family Geraniaceae and one in Rubiaceae. Miers replaced his *Cruckshanksia* with the more euphonious *Solenomelus.* The genus is recognized by the nearly sessile flowers with the ovary included in the inflorescence spathes and the tepals united in a tube, which raises the rest of the flower beyond the spathes. Equally important, the filaments are completely united in a tube and the anthers are coherent, somewhat different from the condition in the related genera *Olsynium* and *Sisyrinchium,* in both of which the filaments may be free distally but are fully united in some *Sisyrinchium* species. Unusual, large, ovoid seeds also link the two species of *Solenomelus.* The ovoid seeds have shallow depressions arranged in longitudinal rows across their surface in marked contrast to the nearly smooth, more or less globose seeds of *Sisyrinchium* species with one end flattened or somewhat concave. Basic chromosome number in *Solenomelus* is $x = 9$, the same base as in *Olsynium* and *Sisyrinchium.*

The relationships of *Solenomelus* are evidently with *Sisyrinchium,* and studies using chloroplast DNA sequences place the genus as sister to the lineage consisting of *Sisyrinchium* and *Olsynium* (L. Karst, pers. comm.). Both species of *Solenomelus* are occasionally cultivated as alpines or rock garden subjects. *Solenomelus pedunculatus* makes a very attractive sight planted in drifts among boulders.

*Tapeinia* Commerson ex Jussieu (1789: 59)
Tribe Sisyrinchieae
TYPE: *Ixia magellanica* Lamarck = *Tapeinia pumila* (Forster fil.) Baillon
ETYMOLOGY: from the Greek *tapeinos,* low, referring to the short stature of the cushion-forming plants
REVISIONARY ACCOUNTS: D. M. Moore (1971; 1983: 340)

Small, evergreen, cushion-like, rhizomatous perennials. LEAVES crowded along the stems in two ranks, more or less linear, without a prominent central vein. FLOWERING STEMS several per plant, mostly unbranched. INFLORESCENCE a solitary flower enclosed by a pair of leafy spathes smaller than the leaves. FLOWERS radially symmetric, fugacious, more or less sessile, white, greenish on the reverse; TEPALS united basally in a very short tube, subequal, ascending below, more or less spreading above. STAMENS symmetrically arranged; FILAMENTS erect, united in the lower fourth; ANTHERS linear. OVARY ovoid; STYLE dividing opposite the middle of the anthers into three slender, ascending branches extending above the anther tips. CAPSULES globose, more or less woody; SEEDS obovoid, restricted to the lower part of the locules, ovoid, with foveolate sculpturing. BASIC CHROMOSOME NUMBER unknown. Species only *Tapeinia pumila,* southern Argentina and southern Chile, mainly Tierra del Fuego.

*Tapeinia,* a monospecific genus (a second species, *T. obscura,* has been transferred to *Olsynium*), has an unusual growth form for the Iridaceae. Plants have a slender creeping rhizome and low, cushion-like habit, thus producing numerous short branchlets densely covered with short leaves. The flowers are blue and cup-like with only the tips of the ascending tepals curved outward. As in other genera of Sisyrinchieae, the filaments are united in the lower half, but the style branches are ascending, reaching above the anther tips, unlike other members of the tribe, in which the style branches extend outward between the upper half of the filaments. A phylogenetic study of the genera of Sisyrinchieae suggests that *Tapeinia* is most closely related to *Orthrosanthus,* a result based only on the shared subsessile ovary found in both genera. The seeds are distinctive, being restricted to the lower half of the capsule and with a foveolate sculpturing, features not present in *Orthrosanthus* (Goldblatt et al. 1990).

Although we now see *Tapeinia* as an undoubted member of the Sisyrinchieae, its affinities were by no means clear when the plant was first discovered. The perennial stems and evergreen habit suggested a relationship with the southern African *Witsenia* to early 19th century botanists, and the single species was first referred to this genus. *Witsenia* is one of three woody southern African genera of Iridaceae, all of which have true secondary growth, unlike the stems of *Tapeinia,* and also have the tepals united in a well-developed perianth tube. The three woody genera are now placed in a separate subfamily, Nivenioideae. *Tapeinia* seems to be most closely related to *Libertia* and *Orthrosanthus* rather than to *Sisyrinchium* and its immediate allies. An unpublished molecular study confirms this relationship (G. Reeves, pers. comm.).

*Trimezia* Salisbury ex Herbert (1844: 88)
Plate 221; Figure 54
Tribe Trimezieae
TYPE: *Trimezia meridensis* Herbert = *T. martinicensis* (Jacquin) Herbert
ETYMOLOGY: from the Greek *tri,* three, and *meze,* greater, referring to the three outer tepals that are much larger than the inner

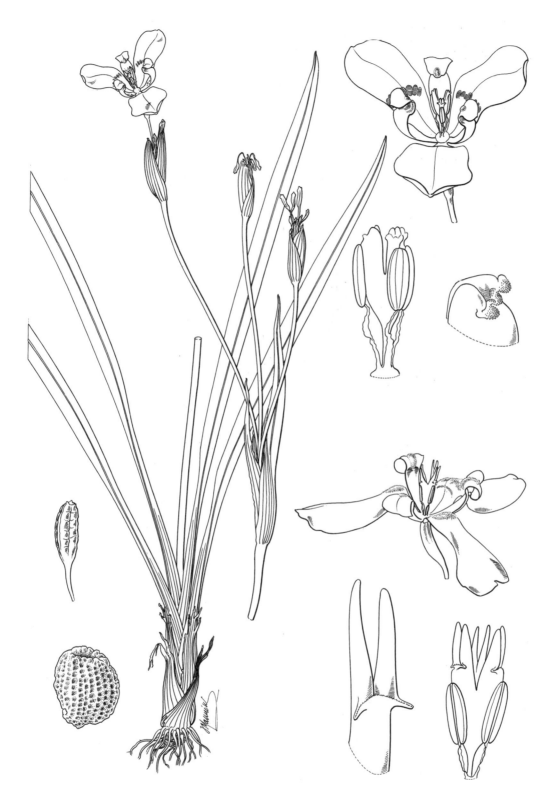

**Figure 54.** (left) *Trimezia martinicensis* with capsule (lower left, ×1), seed (below, ×12), flower (upper right, ×1.5), detail of stamens and style (center, ×6), and detail of single style branch (center right, ×18), (lower right) *T. steyermarkii* flower (×1.5) with details of single style branch (left, ×18) and stamens and style (right, ×6).

SYNONYM: *Anomalostylus* R. C. Foster (1947: 110), type: *A. crateriformis* R. C. Foster = *Trimezia spathata* (Klatt) Baker

REVISIONARY ACCOUNT: Ravenna (1982)

Small to large evergreen or seasonal perennials with an erect rhizome or corm with brownish, sometimes fleshy or sometimes glutinous leaf bases. LEAVES lanceolate to linear, straight or sickle-shaped, with the blades plane or terete and then either hollow or with narrow vertical grooves. FLOWERING STEM erect, simple or branched, sometimes compressed. INFLORESCENCE a several-flowered rhipidium; SPATHES leathery, tightly enclosing the flower buds and membranous bracts. FLOWERS radially symmetric, fugacious, yellow or violet to purple, bearing contrasting markings on the tepal claws; TEPALS free, prominently clawed, the outer larger, the inner with oil glands in the lower half, partly concealed by a fold at the base of the limb. STAMENS symmetrically arranged; FILAMENTS free, thickened below, slender and weak; ANTHERS appressed to the style branches, with a broad connective and laterally placed locules. OVARY usually exserted, STYLE thickened above, dividing opposite the anther bases into three branches, often each terminating in paired acute crests and with an abaxial transverse stigma, or bilobed to truncate and apically stigmatic. CAPSULES globose to cylindric, truncate; SEEDS angular. BASIC CHROMOSOME NUMBER $x = 16$ or 14, with a dysploid series $n = 13$, 12, and 10. Species c. 20, South and Central America and the West Indies.

In the sense used here, *Trimezia* is a genus of evergreen or seasonal perennials that have a distinctive rootstock, identified either an erect rhizome or as a corm, comprising several internodes of stem tissue enclosed by dry, tough, sometimes glutinous cataphylls (Chueiri-Chiaretto and Menezes 1980). Terminology fails us here for the *Trimezia* rootstock seems very much intermediate between a rhizome, which is usually prostrate, frequently branched, and lacks sheathing cataphylls, and a corm, which is erect, unbranched, sheathing cataphylls, and is typically, but not always, replaced annually. The "corms" in *Trimezia* differ substantially from those in all genera of subfamily Crocoideae and most closely resemble the erect rhizomes of some species of *Bobartia* (Iridoideae: Irideae). The flowers of *Trimezia* are very like those of *Neomarica* and some bulbous genera of the tribe Tigridieae, for example, *Cypella*. Thus they have broadly clawed tepals, the outer larger and with plane, spreading limbs, and the inner with a fold at the base of the limb, usually partly concealing a zone of stalked oil glands. In addition, the stamens are free and have slender, weak filaments and anthers appressed to the thickened style branches. The latter bear transverse stigmatic lobes, usually with acute erect crests above them, very much as in *Cypella* and *Neomarica*.

The name *Trimezia*, often attributed to Richard A. Salisbury, was proposed by him with the spelling *Trimeza* in 1812 for the common Caribbean *T. martinicensis* but without any description. The genus was validated by William Herbert in 1844, who spelled the name *Trimezia*. Although the genus is widespread, extending from Paraguay in the south to Mexico and the West Indies in the north, most of the c. 20 species occur in Brazil and the adjacent Guiana Highlands of Venezuela and Guyana. Only *T. martinicensis* extends into the West Indies, while *T. steyermarkii* is native to Central America and southern Mexico. Both these species are widely cultivated, and it is difficult to tell where *T. martinicensis* is native. Plants are self-fertile and reproduce rapidly in cultivation. The species is polyploid, with populations having $n = 20$ and 40. Closely related *T. sincorana* has $n = 30$. Other species of *Trimezia* have $n = 14$ (*T. spathata* and a few more) or 13 (*T. fosteriana*), while

*T. steyermarkii* is tetraploid, *n* = 26. The diversity in chromosome number is surprising in a relatively small genus, and when more species are counted the pattern should throw light on its evolution. On available evidence, ancestral number is probably *x* = 14, but a decreasing dysploid series has resulted in species with base numbers *x* = 13, 12, and 10.

The immediate relationships of *Trimezia* lie with *Neomarica*, the latter distinguished by its creeping rhizome and broadly winged, leafy flowering stem. *Neomarica* has been included in *Trimezia* by Ravenna (1977b), an action that has not been widely followed. Both *T. martinicensis* and *T. steyermarkii* are widely cultivated in the tropics and subtropics, and are rewarding garden plants. The latter species is often seen in street and garden plantings, their flowering season lasting several months.

*Pseudotrimezia* R. C. Foster (1945: 8–9)
Tribe Trimezieae
TYPE: *Pseudotrimezia barretoi* R. C. Foster
ETYMOLOGY: from the Greek *pseudo,* false, and the genus *Trimezia,* some species of which it resembles in vegetative features
REVISIONARY ACCOUNT: Chukr and Giulietti (2003)

Small seasonal perennials with a thick erect rhizome (or corm) surrounded by leathery to dry, more or less fibrous tunics. LEAVES few, often with only one large basal leaf, either plane and then without a central vein or terete and then sometimes hollow, erect or sickle-shaped. FLOWERING STEM erect, unbranched, round in section, leafless or bearing one or two sheathing leaves. INFLORESCENCE a few-flowered rhipidium; SPATHES leathery, tightly enclosing the flower buds and membranous floral bracts. FLOWERS radially symmetric, fugacious, yellow, sometimes with contrasting marks at the tepal bases; TEPALS free, subequal, spreading from

the base or cupped below. STAMENS symmetrically arranged; FILAMENTS free or basally united, slender; ANTHERS erect, coherent or diverging, opposed to the style or style branches. OVARY obovoid, STYLE slender, dividing toward the upper part of the anthers into three short to long and slender branches. CAPSULES globose; SEEDS angular, wrinkled. BASIC CHROMOSOME NUMBER *x* = 16. Species c. 12, restricted to central Brazil in the state of Minas Gerais, in sandy, nutrient-poor soils.

This small genus, entirely restricted to the rocky sandstone mountains of Minas Gerais in Brazil, has been poorly understood. Studies by the Brazilian botanists Nadia Chukr and Anna Maria Giulietti have remedied that situation, and we now know that there are some 12 species of *Pseudotrimezia.* Most are narrow endemics, limited to single mountain ranges. The species show interesting adaptations to dry or nutrient-poor habitats, such as leathery leaves with the blades round in cross section and either rigid or hollow. Plants have a corm-like rootstock, more often interpreted as an erect rhizome.

The flowers are fairly simple in organization and have free, subequal, spreading yellow tepals, usually free filaments, and anthers appressed to the style or the style branches. The latter are simple, slender, and apically stigmatic, unlike the elaborate style branches of the closely related genera *Neomarica* and *Trimezia.* It is probably to *Trimezia* that the genus is most closely related. With chromosome number determined for only one species of *Pseudotrimezia,* base number for the genus is evidently *x* = 16, a number also recorded in *Trimezia.*

*Neomarica* Sprague (1928: 280)
Plates 222–224; Figure 55
Tribe Trimezieae
TYPE: *Neomarica northiana* (Schneevogt) Sprague
ETYMOLOGY: from the Greek *neo,* new, and *marica,* the nymph, fabled mother of the Latins, the

**Figure 55.** *Neomarica caerulea* (×0.8); note the broad, two-winged flowering stem and inflorescences crowded at the stem apex.

name replacing *Marica,* which although used for the genus has as its type *Cipura paludosa*
REVISIONARY ACCOUNT: Chukr and Giulietti (2001)

Medium-sized to large evergreen perennials with a creeping to suberect rhizome or a corm. LEAVES sword-shaped to lanceolate, the blades plane, leathery, forming a two-ranked basal fan. FLOWERING STEM suberect to inclined, compressed and broadly winged, comprising one long aerial internode, terminating in a leaf and one to several stalked or sessile rhipidia. INFLORESCENCE a several-flowered rhipidium; spathes leathery, tightly enclosing the flower buds and membranous bracts. FLOWERS radially symmetric, fugacious, cream, yellow, or blue, the claws patterned with contrasting bands of dark and pale color; TEPALS free, with broad claws, the outer larger, spreading to reflexed distally, the inner bearing oil glands in the lower half, partly concealed by a fold at the apex of the claws. STAMENS symmetrically arranged; FILAMENTS free, slender, and weak, thickened below; ANTHERS affixed to the style branches, splitting longitudinally. OVARY included in the spathes or exserted; STYLE thickened above, dividing toward the anther tips into three branches, each terminating in paired acute crests and with an abaxial transverse stigma lobe at the base of the crests, the center of the stigmatic lobe sometimes bearing one or a pair of short erect appendages. CAPSULES obovoid to cylindric, truncate; SEEDS angular and brownish, or globose, fleshy, and reddish, then retained in the capsule. BASIC CHROMOSOME NUMBER probably $x = 9$. Species c. 12, South and Central America and Mexico.

Primarily a genus of evergreen forest and forest margins, *Neomarica* is readily recognized by the flattened, broadly winged flowering stem that resembles a leaf, with the branches typically clustered close to the stem apex and subtended by a short subapical leaf. The complex flowers broadly resemble those of an *Iris,* having large outer tepals with drooping limbs, smaller inner tepals, and fairly prominent, colored style branches to which the anthers are appressed. The resemblance is superficial, however, and does not indicate a close relationship. Like several other genera of South American Iridaceae, the flowers of *Neomarica* have inner tepals with a prominent fold at the base of the limb that partly conceals a zone of stalked oil glands. Also like those genera, the filaments are free, weak, and thread-like, and the anthers are appressed to the opposed style branches. These are thickened and terminate in a pair of acute crests that extend above the transverse stigma lobe, which bears a secondary erect appendage or pair of appendages. Diploid numbers $2n = 18$ and 16 have been recorded in the genus, together with the polyploid species *N. caerulea* and *N. rupestris,* $2n = 32$. The pattern suggests an ancestral chromosome number $x = 9$ for *Neomarica* (Goldblatt and Takei 1997).

*Neomarica* has been treated as a subgenus of *Trimezia,* perhaps because the flowers of the two genera are virtually identical (Ravenna 1977b) although they consistently differ vegetatively. We prefer to maintain *Neomarica* until more convincing evidence of their interrelationships is available. There seems no doubt, however, that these two genera are immediately related. The genus name *Marica,* often applied to species of *Neomarica* in the past, has as its type *M. paludosa,* which is also the type of *Cipura.* This makes *Marica* an illegitimate nomenclatural synonym of *Cipura. Marica* was applied subsequently to species of *Neomarica,* but the name remains illegitimate in its revised sense. Sprague corrected the unsatisfactory nomenclatural situation by proposing the new name *Neomarica* for the genus.

Flowers of most species are predominantly white to cream with yellow to brown or even violet markings, but *Neomarica caerulea* has handsome blue-violet tepals. Several species are cultivated in gardens in the tropics or in greenhouses in areas of cold winters, including the walking-stick plant, *N. northiana*, the stems of which incline toward the ground and root at the tips after flowering. The genus is centered in Brazil, where species are found largely in the Atlantic coastal forests. The white-flowered *N. variegata* of Central America and southern Mexico is unusual not only in its isolated geographic distribution but in fruit morphology. The seeds have a bright red, fleshy coat and are retained on the opened capsule, thus resembling a berry. They are presumably dispersed by fruit-eating birds.

*Alophia* Herbert (1840: below pl. 3,779)
Figure 56
Tribe Tigridieae
TYPE: *Alophia drummondii* (Graham) Herbert, as *drummondiana*

ETYMOLOGY: from the Greek *a-*, without, and *lophos*, a crest
SYNONYM: *Eustylis* Engelmann & Gray (1847: 236), type: *E. purpurea* = *Alophia drummondii* (Graham) Herbert
REVISIONARY ACCOUNT: Goldblatt and Howard (1992)

Small to medium-sized seasonal perennials with bulbs with dark brown papery tunics. LEAVES few, sword-shaped to linear, the blades pleated. FLOWERING STEM simple or few-branched. INFLORESCENCE a few- to several-flowered rhipidium; SPATHES leafy in texture, acute, tightly enclosing membranous floral bracts. FLOWERS radially symmetric, fugacious, shades of blue to violet or purple, with contrasting dark and white markings in the center; TEPALS free, unequal, spreading from the base, with broad claws, the outer larger, the inner

**Figure 56.** *Alophia veracruzana* flower (×1), staminal column (top right), separate style (bottom right, both ×3), and detail of stigmatic branch tips (center right, ×6).

with oil glands scattered on the lower half, sometimes partly covered by a fold. STAMENS symmetrically arranged; FILAMENTS free or partly to entirely united; ANTHERS with a broad, fiddle-shaped connective. OVARY ovoid, exserted from the spathes; STYLE slender below, thickened above and dividing opposite or above the anthers into short branches, each deeply divided into filiform arms arching outward above the anthers. CAPSULES obovoid-truncate; SEEDS angular. BASIC CHROMOSOME NUMBER $x = 14$. Species approximately five, South and Central America to Texas and Louisiana.

One of several New World genera of the tribe Tigridieae, *Alophia* closely resembles *Tigridia* in vegetative features and even in some floral characters. A major difference is that the filaments are usually free, and the anthers are fiddle-shaped, with a broad connective so that the pollen chambers are placed laterally at the edges of the anther. When free, as they usually are, the filaments are weak and thread-like, and the anthers are attached to the style by sticky mucilage. The style is sturdy, and the three branches are divided at or above the level of the anthers into paired filiform arms that arch outward. In *Tigridia*, with a few exceptions, the filaments are entirely united, the anthers are linear, and the style branches are deeply divided, often to the base, with their paired arms extending to either side of the anthers. Another important difference between the genera is that the pollen grains of *Tigridia* are bisulcate while those of *Alophia* are monosulcate and quite typical of other genera of subfamily Iridoideae.

The name *Alophia* has had a confused history and was for many years applied to species now included in *Herbertia*. The error has its roots in the identity of the type species, *A. drummondii* (or the illegitimate variant spelling, *A. drummondiana*). No type specimen is known, but there is little doubt that the description applies to the southern U.S. species with deeply divided and thread-like style arms

and not to *Herbertia* (Goldblatt 1975). When the name was used for species of the latter genus, those species now regarded as *Alophia* were treated as the genus *Eustylis*, now a synonym of *Alophia*.

The immediate relationships of *Alophia* are uncertain, but molecular study (Figure 8) shows the genus is ancestral the entire Central American clade of the Tigridieae plus several South American genera, including *Hesperoxiphion*, *Gelasine* plus *Eleutherine*, and *Ennealophus* and the South American *Tigridia* group. *Alophia* is one of few bulbous genera of Iridaceae that are native in North America, where the fairly common *A. drummondii* extends across southern Louisiana and Texas, west into Mexico. Plants currently called *A. drummondii* from Guyana in South America have slightly smaller, dark purple flowers with the filaments united basally and shorter style branches; we suspect they represent a separate species. Other species occur in Mexico, Central America, and Brazil. In North America, *A. drummondii* is sometimes called the propeller flower.

*Calydorea* Herbert (1843a: 85)
Figure 57
Tribe Tigridieae
TYPE: *Calydorea speciosa* (J. D. Hooker) Herbert = *C. xiphioides* (Poeppig) Espinosa
ETYMOLOGY: from the Greek *caly*, sheathed or covered, and *dorea*, a spear, most likely referring to the spear-shaped buds enclosed within the spathes until anthesis
SYNONYMS: *Catila* Ravenna (1983a: 197–198), type: *C. amabilis* Ravenna = *Calydorea amabilis* (Ravenna) Goldblatt; *Itysa* Ravenna (1986: 582), type: *I. gardneri* (Baker) Ravenna = *C. gardneri* Baker; ?*Lethia* Ravenna (1986: 585), not fully understood, type: *L. umbellata* (Klatt) Ravenna = ?*Calydorea*; *Tamia* Ravenna (2001: 15), type: *T. pallidens* (Grisebach) Ravenna = *C. pallidens* Grisebach
REVISIONARY ACCOUNT: Goldblatt and Henrich (1991)

**Figure 57.** (left) *Calydorea* sp., fruiting plant (×0.8) and seed (×12), (upper left) *C. xiphoides* flower (×1.5) with details of stigma (above, ×30) and stamens and style (top, ×3), (upper right) *C. pallens* flower (×1.5) with details of stigma (above left, ×12) and stamens and style (above right, ×4), (lower right) *C. amabilis* flower (×1.5) with details of stigma (above right, ×24) and stamens and style (below right, ×6).

Small seasonal perennials with bulbs with dark brown papery tunics, rarely leafless when in bloom. LEAVES few, sword-shaped to linear, with pleated blades. FLOWERING STEM simple or few-branched, smooth, round in section. INFLORESCENCE a few-flowered rhipidium; spathes green, leafy to leathery in texture, tightly sheathing, enclosing membranous bracts. FLOWERS radially symmetric, borne on long, slender pedicels, shades of pale to deep blue to violet, with contrasting dark and white markings; TEPALS free, subequal or the outer markedly larger than the inner, spreading from the base, usually obviously clawed, often with stalked oil glands on the inner tepals. STAMENS symmetrically arranged; FILAMENTS free, ascending; ANTHERS suberect or diverging, often closely associated with the style branches. OVARY oblong, usually exserted; STYLE short or exceeding the anthers, dividing into three short to long, slender branches appressed to the anthers or extending between or above the stamens, stigmatic at the tips. CAPSULES obovoid to cylindric, truncate; SEEDS angular. BASIC CHROMOSOME NUMBER $x = 7$. Species c. 16, South America.

Vegetatively typical of tribe Tigridieae with its pleated leaves and bulbous rootstock, *Calydorea* species have a deceptively simple flower recognized by the free stamens, short style, and filiform style branches that either lie opposite to or extend between the stamens. The type species, *C. xiphioides* (= *C. speciosa*), from central Chile, has relatively large flowers with bright blue-purple tepals with yellow at the base, and its tepals are smooth, without folds or zones of oil glands. Species added to *Calydorea* over the years have expanded its circumscription. The Argentinean *C. pallens* has pale bluish tepals darkly speckled in the lower half, and although the stamens and style branches are very similar to those of *C. xiphioides*, the style branches lie opposite the stamens. In *C. amabilis* the anthers lie appressed to the style branches, and the outer tepals have a fold in the distal half.

Maintaining a narrow generic concept, Ravenna (1983a) treated *Calydorea amabilis* as the monotypic genus *Catila* and referred *Calydorea pallens* to a second monotypic genus, *Tamia*, which we include here in *Calydorea*. Plants from Venezuela placed by *Ravenna* in *Lethia* and *Itysa* share a similar floral form and critical features of *Calydorea*, with the small exception that the style is elongate so that the style branches are remote from the anthers. *Lethia* is now included in *Calydorea*, where *Itysa* may also belong (Goldblatt and Henrich 1991).

The puzzling genus *Cardiostigma*, which has four species in Mexico, was included by Goldblatt and Henrich (1991) in *Calydorea*, as was *Salpingostylis*, a monospecific genus of Florida. Three species of *Cardiostigma* and *Salpingostylis* have spreading, subequal tepals and an elongate style with broadly lobed style branches that are completely undivided, and the anthers split open via apical pores. Evidently this decision was incorrect, for A. Rodríguez (1999) has shown that the single species of *Cardiostigma* that he studied is nested in *Tigridia*. The relationships of species of *Cardiostigma* have long been puzzling, and botanists have referred species to, among other genera, *Calydorea*, *Gelasine*, and *Sphenostigma*, the type species of which is a *Gelasine*. The *Cardiostigma* group must now be included in *Tigridia*, but it is not yet clear whether the Florida member of the alliance, *Salpingostylis coelestina*, correctly belongs with the Mexican species, and until this is known we treat *Salpingostylis* as a separate genus.

*Cipura* Aublet (1775: 38, pl. 13)
Tribe Tigridieae
TYPE: *Cipura paludosa* Aublet
ETYMOLOGY: unknown
SYNONYM: *Marica* Schreber (1789: 37), illegitimate name, superfluous for *Cipura* Aublet, type: *M. paludosa* (Aublet) Schreber = *C. paludosa* Aublet
REVISIONARY ACCOUNTS: Goldblatt and Henrich (1987), Ravenna (1988), Celis et al. (2003)

Small to medium-sized seasonal perennials with bulbs usually with brown to blackish papery tunics, sometimes held together with glutinous resin. LEAVES few, sword-shaped to linear, with pleated blades. FLOWERING STEM simple or few branched, smooth, round in section, bearing a prominent subapical leaf. INFLORESCENCE a few- to several-flowered rhipidium, these solitary or several, clustered at the stem apex; SPATHES green, leafy to leathery in texture, tightly sheathing, enclosing membranous floral bracts. FLOWERS fugacious, radially symmetric, borne on short or long, slender pedicels, shades of white, yellow, or pale to deep blue to violet, sometimes with contrasting dark and pale markings; TEPALS free, subequal or unequal, with the outer larger, ascending or spreading, clawed, the inner ascending or erect and then partly concealing the stamens and style, sometimes lacking claws and sometimes bearing oil glands below, these then enclosed by folds. STAMENS symmetrically arranged; FILAMENTS free and slender or sometimes united below; ANTHERS loosely attached to the style branches or parallel and contiguous around the style. OVARY oblong, exserted or subsessile and included in the spathes; STYLE thickened distally and three-lobed, either with sessile stigmatic lobes apically or prominently three-branched, the branches compressed, stigmatic lobes abaxial, at base of paired crests. CAPSULES stalked or subsessile, obovoid to subcylindric, truncate; SEEDS angular. BASIC CHROMOSOME NUMBER $x = 7$. Species approximately nine, tropical South America to Mexico and the West Indies.

*Cipura,* first genus of the New World tribe Tigridieae to be described, is recognized first by its specialized vegetative morphology and second by some unusual features of its flowers. The flowering stem consists of one long internode that bears a subterminal leaf subtending several crowded short branches, each bearing a terminal inflorescence of one or more flowers within tightly sheathing spathes. The leaves

themselves are pleated and differ not at all from those of other genera of Tigridieae. The flowers, which range in color from blue to violet, yellow, or white, have the inner tepals more or less erect, sometimes lacking claws and then partly to entirely concealing the stamens and style. Most significantly, the stamens are free (or united basally) and have thread-like, weak filaments, and the style is thickened distally and either lacks discrete style branches, so that the stigmas are terminal on the style, or branches are developed and bear paired terminal crests above the stigma.

The best-known and most widespread species is *Cipura paludosa,* described from French Guiana by the French naturalist Jean Baptiste Christophore Fusée Aublet in 1775. This widespread species occurs almost throughout tropical South America and into Central America and the West Indies. It is a relatively small plant, often less than 15 cm high, distinctive in having the inner tepals erect, without claws, and overlapping to form an urn-shaped flask that conceals the stamens and thick style. It is readily confused with the Central American *C. campanulata,* which generally has linear leaves and half-nodding flowers, also with the inner tepals lacking claws but forming a wider cup. Other species include the Brazilian *C. xanthomelas,* which has yellow flowers with brown markings, and *C. formosa,* with large violet flowers. The two well-known species *C. campanulata* and *C. paludosa* are typical for the genus in their clawless inner tepals and reduced style branches, but these features are mostly likely specialized. *Cipura rupicola,* a Venezuelan species, has narrowly clawed inner tepals and quite prominent style branches that recall other genera of Tigridieae, notably *Cypella. Cipura* is unusually variable in pollen morphology, with different species having mono-, di-, or trisulcate pollen. The latter pollen aperture types are derived and occur in the most specialized species.

The immediate relationships of *Cipura* have been uncertain, but DNA sequence studies (A. Rodríguez

1999, A. Rodríguez and Sytsma 2006) and continuing investigations (Figure 8) show that the genus is sister to a clade of species often included in *Cypella* but also treated as a separate genus, *Larentia*. The molecular evidence has led us to examine *Larentia* more closely, with the result that we see some similarities with *Cipura,* especially in the structure of the style branches and crests, first noted by Ravenna (1977a), an authority on South American Tigridieae. The anthers lightly adhere to the style branches in both genera, and the structure of style branches of *Larentia* recall especially that in *Cipura rupicola.* Further study will allow us to determine whether *Cipura* and *Larentia* can be maintained as separate from one another and from their sister lineage, *Cypella,* but it is clear that *Larentia* cannot be retained in *Cypella* unless that genus is expanded to several more genera, including *Cipura.*

*Cipura paludosa* is one of a few Neotropical species used for its medicinal properties and, like another medicinal species of the family, *Eleutherine bulbosa,* occurs almost throughout tropical South America. It is uncertain whether its wide range is the result of human activity, but this seems likely, for no other species of New World Iridaceae has such a wide range. A decoction of the boiled bulbs is used to relieve diarrhea. Finely pulverized dried bulbs in syrup are used for heart ailments. Other documented uses of *C. paludosa* include relief of inflammation, pain, digestive ailments, and more specifically, bronchitis.

## *Cobana* Ravenna (1974)
Tribe Tigridieae
TYPE: *Cobana guatemalensis* (Standley) Ravenna
ETYMOLOGY: unknown

Medium-sized seasonal perennial with bulbs with dark papery tunics. LEAVES few, pleated, lanceolate. FLOWERING STEM erect, round in cross section, simple or branched. INFLORESCENCE a few- to several-flowered rhipidium; spathes green, enclosing membranous floral bracts. FLOWERS white, upright; TEPALS free, spreading from the base, unequal, the inner three smaller, without oil glands or nectaries. STAMENS symmetrically arranged; FILAMENTS short, free; ANTHERS linear, suberect, opening by apical slits, pollen bisulcate. OVARY globose, on long pedicels; STYLE slender, dividing at the base of the anthers, style branches filiform, undivided, extending between the anthers, stigmatic at the tips. CAPSULES obovoid- to cylindric-truncate; SEEDS angular. BASIC CHROMOSOME NUMBER $x = 14$. Species only *Cobana guatemalensis,* Guatemala and Honduras.

In its general appearance *Cobana* conforms closely to *Tigridia,* and the basic chromosome number $x = 14$ and bisulcate pollen grains provide convincing evidence that the two genera are closely allied. The flowers of *Cobana* are, however, very different from those of any *Tigridia,* having unequal, spreading tepals and short filaments and style, the latter dividing at the base of the anthers into threadlike branches. Unlike *Tigridia,* the style branches are undivided. The anthers are also unusual as they split open at the tips instead of longitudinally as in nearly all other Iridoideae. Porose anthers usually signal buzz or vibratile pollination, and we suggest this pollination system for the single species of this genus. The short stamens and style are also consistent with this pollination system.

Sequence studies using both nuclear and plastid DNA regions show *Cobana* is sister to the large Mexican *Tigridia* clade, most members of which have divided style branches and nectaries or oil glands on the inner tepals. Members of the *Sessilanthera* group of *Tigridia* have flowers similar to those of *Cobana* in their spreading tepals, very short filaments, and porose anthers, but they have typical deeply divided style branches of the *Tigridia* type. The *Cardiostigma* group of *Tigridia* also has spreading, glandless tepals, very like those of *Cobana,* but the styles are long and slender, and divide well above the anthers. Recognition of a monotypic genus immediately related to a large, florally diverse genus such as *Tigridia* is not satisfactory taxonomically, particularly when the floral differences appear to represent nothing more than a specialized pollination strategy. Available evidence, however, leaves the genus outside the main Mexican *Tigridia* clade, and we provisionally continue to recognize *Cobana*.

### *Cypella* Herbert (1826)
Plates 225–228; Figure 58
Tribe Tigridieae
TYPE: *Cypella herbertii* (Lindley) Herbert
ETYMOLOGY: probably from the Greek *kyphella*, the hollow of the ear, used to describe the cup-shaped structure of some lichens, thus most likely alluding to the ear-like folding of the inner tepals in *Cypella* species
SYNONYMS: *Phalocallis* Herbert (1839), type: *P. plumbea* (Lindley) Herbert = *Cypella coelestis* (Lehmann) Diels; *Polia* Tenore (1845: 92), illegitimate name, not *Polia* Louriero (1790), type: *P. bonariensis* Tenore = *C. herbertii* (Lindley) Herbert; *Kelissa* Ravenna (1981c), new synonym, type: *K. brasiliensis* (Baker) Ravenna = *C. brasiliensis* (Baker)

Roitman & A. Castillo; *Onira* Ravenna (1983a: 204), new synonym, type: *O. unguiculata* (Baker) Ravenna = *C. unguiculata* (Baker) Roitman & A. Castillo
REVISIONARY ACCOUNT: Baker (1892: 63–72)

Small to large seasonal perennials with bulbs usually with brown to blackish, papery or glutinous tunics. LEAVES few, sword-shaped to linear, blades pleated. FLOWERING STEM simple or few-branched, smooth, round in cross section. INFLORESCENCE a few-flowered rhipidium; SPATHES green, leafy to leathery in texture, tightly sheathing, enclosing membranous floral bracts. FLOWERS radially symmetric, borne on slender pedicels, fugacious, mostly shades of yellow or pale to deep blue to violet, with contrasting dark and pale markings on the tepal claws; TEPALS free, subequal or the outer markedly larger, spreading from the base, often with broad claws forming a central bowl, usually with stalked oil glands on the inner tepals, often concealed by a fold at the base of the limb. STAMENS symmetrically arranged; FILAMENTS usually free or united below, slender and weak or thickened below and sturdy, entirely united in *Cypella brasiliensis*; ANTHERS attached at least apically to the opposed style branches, often with a wide connective and locules

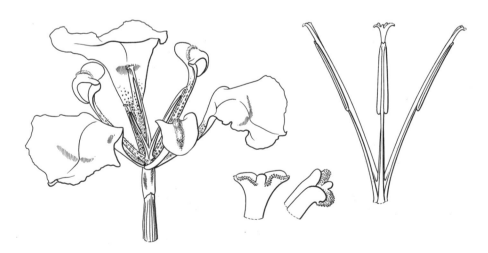

**Figure 58.** *Cypella unguiculata* flower (×1), stamens and style (lower right, ×3), and details of stigmas (×6).

placed laterally, or linear. OVARY oblong, usually exserted; STYLE slender below, with branches usually well developed, often compressed, usually divided above into prominent acute crests and with a transverse stigmatic surface on the abaxial surface at the base of the crests, the stigma also sometimes with short, acute appendages in the center, rarely style dividing at the anther tips into three vestigial branches. CAPSULES obovoid to cylindric, truncate; SEEDS angular. BASIC CHROMOSOME NUMBER $x = 7$. Species c. 30, mainly temperate South America.

*Cypella*, a genus of bulbous plants with pleated leaves, is widespread across temperate and tropical America. *Cypella* species are occasionally cultivated in gardens, the most frequently encountered species being *C. herbertii*, which has been grown in Great Britain since the 1820s. In its narrow sense, *Cypella* is restricted to temperate South America and includes medium-sized plants with yellow flowers with broadly clawed tepals with conspicuous dark transverse banding. Both Baker (1892) and Foster (1945) included *Larentia* and *Phalocallis* in *Cypella*, Foster also placing *Hesperoxiphion* in the genus. Ravenna (1964, 1977a) likewise initially included *Hesperoxiphion*, *Larentia*, and *Phalocallis* in *Cypella* but later reversed himself (Ravenna 1981d) and recognized all four genera, which have slightly different floral features but always inner tepals with a prominent fold at the base of the limb and mostly free, weak filaments. *Cypella* and *Phalocallis* share thickened style branches with paired crests, a transverse stigma lobe, often with secondary appendages in the center, and anthers with a wide connective so that anther lobes are more or less laterally placed. Basic chromosome number in *Cypella* is $x = 7$, but *C. coelestis*, the type of *Phalocallis*, has $x = 5$. The relationships of the *Phalocallis* group of *Cypella*, long included in this genus, remain to be determined using molecular methods. *Phalocallis* remains provisionally retained in *Cypella*.

The monotypic genera *Kelissa* and *Onira*, described by Ravenna 1981 and 1983, respectively, are also poorly differentiated from *Cypella*, and indeed, the Argentinean botanist Gérman Roitman (in prep.) has included both in *Cypella*. His argument is based on the close similarity of the plants and their flowers to several species of *Cypella*, for example *C. aquatilis* and *C. laxa* of section *Nais*. Flowers of *Onira* have unusually narrow style branches, small style crests, and linear anthers that clasp the anthers. *Kelissa* has an even more reduced style with vestigial branches, united filaments, and linear anthers. Both have tepals with strongly clawed tepals, the claws cream, speckled with red to brown and blue to mauve tepal limbs. The flowers fairly closely resemble those of *C. plumbea*, *C. oreophila*, and even more so, *C. hauthalii*. Roitman sees a clear series of reductions of the style and its branches in the two genera and progressive fusion of the filaments, which although usually free in *Cypella* are partially fused in some *Cypella* species. We agree that the differences in the stamens and style branches that defined *Kelissa* and *Onira* are trivial and follow Roitman's taxonomy.

Despite the similarity in style and stamen structure between the typical *Cypella* flower (section *Cypella*) and the genus *Hesperoxiphion*, however, studies using plastid DNA sequences (Reeves et al. 2001 and more recent work) indicate that the latter does not fall close to true *Cypella* but is sister to *Gelasine* plus *Eleutherine*. That convinces us to regard *Hesperoxiphion* as separate from *Cypella*. *Cypella roseii* and *C. mexicanum*, however, which have floral features that define *Larentia*, appear unrelated to *Cypella* and on the basis of molecular data appear most closely allied to *Cipura* (A. Rodríguez 1999, Goldblatt et al. 2007). This new information makes it impossible to include *Larentia* in *Cypella*, and it is here regarded as a separate genus, allied to *Cipura*.

*Eleutherine* Herbert (1843b)
Figure 59
Tribe Tigridieae
TYPE: *Eleutherine plicata* Herbert = *E. bulbosa* (Miller) Urban
ETYMOLOGY: uncertain, possibly for the free stamens, from the Greek *eleuthera*, meaning free
SYNONYMS: *Galatea* Salisbury, (1812: 310), name invalid, without description; *Keitia* Regel (1877: 639), type: *K. natalensis* Regel = *Eleutherine bulbosa* (Miller) Urban
REVISIONARY ACCOUNT: Goldblatt and Snow (1991)

Small seasonal perennials with bulbs with dark reddish, somewhat fleshy tunics. LEAVES few, sword-shaped to linear, with pleated blades. FLOWERING STEM with a long basal internode with a prominent subterminal leaf subtending one to many short branches, often short, smooth, round in section. INFLORESCENCE a few- to several-flowered rhipidium; SPATHES green, leafy to leathery in texture, tightly enclosing the buds and membranous bracts. FLOWERS radially symmetric, borne on short pedicels, fugacious, white, sometimes scented; TEPALS free, subequal, spreading from the base, lacking claws, without nectaries or oil glands. STAMENS symmetrically arranged; FILAMENTS free; ANTHERS diverging. OVARY oblong, usually exserted; STYLE short, dividing into three filiform branches extending between the filaments, the style branches stigmatic at the tips. CAPSULES obovoid to oblong, truncate; SEEDS angular. BASIC CHROMOSOME NUMBER $x = 6$. Species two, Mexico, West Indies, Central America, and tropical South America.

Among the bulbous, pleat-leaved Iridaceae, *Eleutherine* is readily recognized by its small, radially symmetric white flowers with subequal spreading tepals, free stamens, and simple, filiform style branches that extend outward between the filaments. The genus also stands out among genera of Tigridieae in its derived basic chromosome number $x = 6$, where $x = 7$ is ancestral and the most common base number. *Eleutherine latifolia*, recognized by its long capsules and short stem, has an interesting disjunct distribution, occurring in Central America–Mexico and northern Argentina. The second species, *E. bulbosa*, is widespread in the Neotropics but over most of its range is sterile and is largely if not entirely associated with human cultivation for medicinal uses. The most consistently fertile collections of *E. bulbosa* that produce capsules and seeds are from the Andean foothills of eastern Peru, but occasional fertile collections are recorded from eastern Brazil and the West Indies. The reasons for the sterility are chromosomal heterozygosity for an inversion and tandem duplication in one of the two longer chromosomes. Pairing during meiosis of these mismatched long chromosomes results in the disruption of cell division and abortion of the ovules.

*Eleutherine bulbosa* is an important part of the American Indian pharmacopeia, hence its frequent

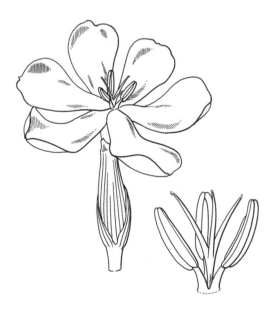

**Figure 59.** *Eleutherine bulbosa* flower (×1) with detail of stamens and style (right, ×3).

cultivation. It is one of the few Neotropical Iridaceae with known medicinal uses. Its uses include as a vermifuge, a diuretic, a treatment for bloody diarrhea and open wounds, and as a contraceptive and hallucinogen. The species has been introduced into the Philippines, Indochina, and southern Africa, where plants escaped from cultivation and assumed to be native were described in 1877 as the genus *Keitia*. The active medicinal principles of *E. bulbosa* are not known.

The relationships of *Eleutherine* are uncertain. Its deceptively simple flowers are unlike those of any other genera of Tigridieae, but the relatively short rhipidial spathes with the tips of the floral bracts protruding are known in some species of *Ennealophus*. A relationship with this genus, however, seems improbable. DNA sequence analysis (Reeves et al. 2001 and more recent studies) shows that *Eleutherine* is most closely related to *Gelasine*, but species of that small genus always have united filaments and a violet to purple perianth.

*Ennealophus* N. E. Brown (1909: 361)
Figure 60
Tribe Tigridieae
TYPE: *Ennealophus amazonicus* N. E. Brown = *E. foliosus* (Kunth) Ravenna
ETYMOLOGY: from the Greek *ennea*, nine, and *lophus*, a crest, for the three-lobed tips of each of the three style branches of the type species
SYNONYMS: *Eurynotia* R. C. Foster (1945: 6–7), type: *E. penlandii* R. C. Foster = *Ennealophus foliosus* (Kunth) Ravenna; *Tucma* Ravenna (1973: 43), new synonym, type: *T. simplex* Ravenna = *E. simplex* (Ravenna) Roitman & A. Castillo
REVISIONARY ACCOUNTS: Ravenna (1977a, 1983b)

Medium-sized seasonal perennials with bulbs usually with brown to blackish, papery tunics. LEAVES lanceolate to linear, pleated. FLOWERING STEM usually branched, smooth, round in section. INFLORESCENCE a several-flowered rhipidium; spathes soft-textured, sometimes only partially enclosing the flower buds and membranous floral bracts. FLOWERS radially symmetric, borne on slender pedicels, blue to violet, with white markings on the outer tepals; TEPALS free, subequal or unequal, then the outer three larger, broadly clawed, and more or less widely cupped below, the inner three usually bearing stalked oil glands in the lower half, these usually partly enclosed by folds of the tepal surface. STAMENS symmetrically arranged; FILAMENTS partly to fully united; ANTHERS appressed to the opposed style branches, splitting longitudinally, the

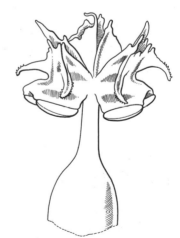

**Figure 60.** *Ennealophus fimbriatus* flower (×2) with detail of staminal column (below, ×8).

lobes lateral on a broad connective. OVARY globose, usually exserted; STYLE divided into broad, petal-like branches with transverse stigmatic surfaces or nearly linear and divided above and stigmatic at the tips. CAPSULES obovoid to cylindric, truncate, sometimes borne on elongate, recurving pedicels; SEEDS angular. BASIC CHROMOSOME NUMBER $x = 7$. Species five, South America, from Ecuador to Northern Argentina.

As with most of the South American bulbous Iridaceae, the genus *Ennealophus* is difficult to define. Important features are the united filaments that form a smooth, bottle-shaped column widest in the lower half, and diverging anthers closely appressed to the style branches. The anthers have slightly expanded connectives, wider toward the base, so that the anther lobes are laterally placed, and the style branches are usually fairly broad but narrow in one species. The flowers are always blue to violet and, like other Tigridieae, fugacious, each lasting part of one day. Basic chromosome number $x = 7$, the ancestral condition in the tribe, but the karyotype for the two species counted is distinctive in having the single large chromosome pair metacentric, a feature that provides independent evidence of the monophyly of the genus.

The species fall into two subgenera. Subgenus *Ennealophus* has flower buds enclosed until anthesis within relatively large, sheathing spathes, while in subgenus *Actine* the flower buds are borne on long, arching pedicels that are exserted from the short, slightly diverging spathes. The monospecific genus *Tucma*, which we here reduce to synonymy, belongs in the latter subgenus and differs from other members of *Ennealophus* in having the spreading tepals subequal, with obscure claws not forming a cup, and nearly linear style branches forked only near the tips. The vegetative resemblance to subgenus *Actine* provides the main justification for the reduction of *Tucma*, which has the short inflorescence spathes and long, arching pedicels characteristic of the subgenus.

*Ennealophus* is largely Andean and extends from Ecuador in the north to Jujuy Province in northern Argentina in the south. The most common species, *E. foliosus* (= *E. amazonicus*), is the only member of the genus in Ecuador and Peru. This species plus *E. euryandrus* and *E. fimbriatus* have the stamens and style branches enclosed by the inner tepal claws, which form a well-developed triangular cup and bear stalked oil glands. The few observations available indicate that the flowers are pollinated by oil-collecting bees, including *Chalepogenus* (Apidae; Vogel 1974, C. Rasmussen, pers. comm. 2000).

The immediate relationships of *Ennealophus* are not evident from morphology. DNA sequence studies of Tigridieae (Figure 8) similarly show no immediate relatives of *Ennealophus*, which is isolated among a large lineage including *Tigridia* and close allies and South American *Tigridia* plus the *Mastigostyla* group, an unexpected result. *Ennealophus* shares united filaments with both groups and is diploid, unlike the tetraploid *Tigridia* complex of Central America and Mexico.

## *Gelasine* Herbert (1840)

Plate 229; Figure 61

Tribe Tigridieae

TYPE: *Gelasine azurea* Herbert = *G. elongata* (R. Graham) Ravenna

ETYMOLOGY: from the From the Greek *gelasinus*, a dimple, alluding to the dark blue spot near the base of the tepals in the type species

SYNONYM: *Sphenostigma* Baker, (1877: 124), type: *S. sellowianum* (Klatt) Baker = *Gelasine coerulea* (Vellozo) Ravenna

REVISIONARY ACCOUNT: Ravenna (1984)

Medium-sized to large seasonal perennials with bulbs, usually with brown to blackish, papery or glutinous tunics. LEAVES few, sword-shaped to linear, with pleated blades. FLOWERING STEM simple or few-branched, smooth, round in cross section. INFLORESCENCE a few-flowered rhipidium; SPATHES green, leafy in texture, tightly sheathing, enclosing membranous floral bracts. FLOWERS radially symmetric, borne on long, slender pedicels, fugacious, blue to violet, often with white or darker purple markings; TEPALS free, subequal or the outer markedly larger, spreading from the base, sometimes with broad claws forming a central bowl, usually with stalked oil glands on the inner tepals, usually concealed by folds. STAMENS symmetrically arranged; FILAMENTS united in a column; ANTHERS erect, appressed to the style branches or extending between them when simple. OVARY oblong, usually exserted; STYLE slender, reaching or exceeding the anthers, with branches slender or flattened and usually divided above into prominent acute crests and with a transverse stigmatic surface on the abaxial surface at the base of the crests. CAPSULES obovoid to cylindric, truncate; SEEDS angular. BASIC CHROMOSOME NUMBER $x = 7$. Species approximately six, South America, northern Argentina, Brazil, Uruguay.

*Gelasine* is poorly understood, and its generic circumscription remains weak. The type species, *G. elongata*, widely known in cultivation by its later synonym, *G. azurea*, has subequal tepals of a striking deep blue with white markings, and undivided, fairly slender style branches, somewhat flattened and expanded at the tips. Other species have more complex flowers with unequal tepals, the inner smaller than the outer. The most conspicuous features of *Gelasine* are the united filaments and, with the exception of *G. elongata*, style branches with broad stigmatic lobes and short crest-like appendages. All the species are fairly robust plants, often exceeding 50 cm in height.

Basic chromosome number in *Gelasine* is assumed to be $x = 7$, based on the count of $2n = 14$ (Ravenna 1984) for *G. uruguaiensis*, which matches the base number for most genera of tribe Tigrideae. *Gelasine elongata*, however, has $2n = 12$ (i.e., $n = 6$); thus both its morphology and the derived chromosome number mark the species as derived. In addition, the chromosomes of *G. elongata* form a ring at meiosis, indicating that it is a complex heterozygote (Kenton and Rudall 1987). The reduced chromosome number of *G. elongata* recalls the base number in *Eleutherine*, also $x = 6$, and suggests a possible relationship between *Gelasine* and *Eleutherine*, in which the style branches are undivided as they are in *G. elongata* but more slender than in that species. Molecular studies by Reeves et al. (2001) also show an immediate relationship between the two genera. Molecular analysis (Figure 8) shows *Gelasine* sister to *Eleutherine* and the pair sister to the Andean *Hesperoxiphion*.

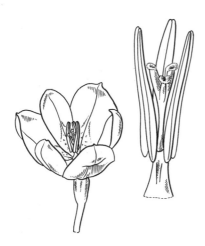

**Figure 61.** *Gelasine elongata* flower (×1) with detail of staminal column (right, ×3).

*Herbertia* Sweet (1827b)
Plate 230; Figure 62
Tribe Tigridieae
TYPE: *Herbertia pulchella* Sweet
ETYMOLOGY: named in honor of the British expert of bulbous plants, William Herbert (1778–1847)
SYNONYMS: *Trifurcia* Herbert (1840: below pl. 3,779), type: *T. caerulea* Herbert = *Herbertia lahue* (Molina) Goldblatt; *Sympa* P. Ravenna (1981b), type: *S. riograndensis* Ravenna = *H.* cf. *lahue* (Molina) Goldblatt

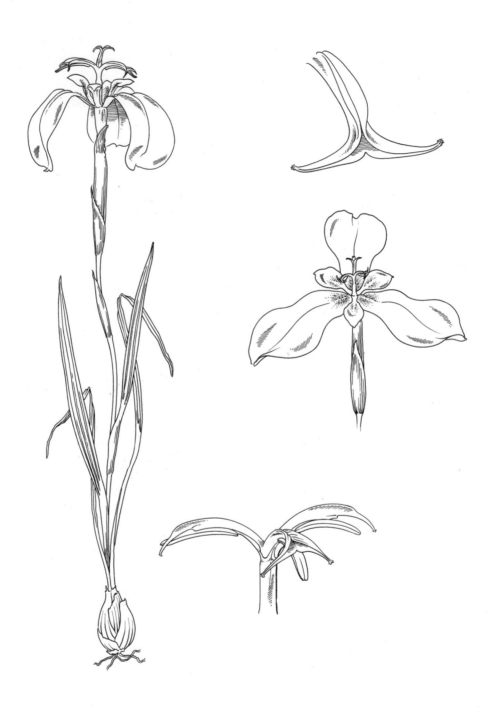

**Figure 62.** (left) *Herbertia pulchella* (×1) with stamens and style (below, ×3), (upper right) *H. lahue* flower (×1.5) with detail of style branch (above, ×10).

Small seasonal perennials with bulbs with dark brown, papery tunics. LEAVES few, sword-shaped to linear, with pleated blades. FLOWERING STEM simple or few-branched, smooth, round in section. INFLORESCENCE a few-flowered rhipidium; spathes green leafy to leathery in texture, tightly sheathing, enclosing membranous bracts. FLOWERS radially symmetric, borne on slender pedicels, pale to deep blue or violet, with contrasting dark and white markings; TEPALS free, unequal, spreading from the base, the outer three larger and obviously clawed, the inner much smaller and bearing oil glands in the lower part. STAMENS symmetrically arranged; FILAMENTS united or free in upper part, the column often bottle-shaped; ANTHERS diverging, each appressed to an opposed style branch. OVARY oblong, usually exserted; STYLE dividing into flattened, spreading branches, each forked apically and stigmatic at the tips. CAPSULES obovoid to cylindric, truncate; SEEDS angular. BASIC CHROMOSOME NUMBER $x = 7$. Species approximately seven, temperate South America, including southern Brazil, Uruguay, Argentina, central Chile, with one subspecies in the southern United States and Mexico.

A bulbous rootstock, pleated leaves, and free tepals place the genus *Herbertia* in tribe Tigridieae, in which it is distinguished by a relatively short stature, blue to violet flowers with outer tepals somewhat to much exceeding the inner, and stamens with united filaments. The stamens lie opposite the style branches, to which the anthers are closely appressed. The inner tepals, either clawed or lacking a well-defined claw, bear a zone of stalked glandular, oil-secreting hairs on the upper surface while the outer tepals are more or less smooth, or have a few scattered hairs. Known by the name *Alophia* for many years, *Herbertia* is actually not even closely related to *Alophia*, which is also a member of Tigridieae but has divided, filiform style branches and is probably more closely related to *Tigridia*. The confusion was due to a misinterpretation of the identity of the type of *Alophia*, a question discussed in more detail under that genus. The name *Trifurcia* was used for *Herbertia* when that name was regarded as a homonym for *Herberta*, a genus of moss. The two names are now regarded as separate, valid names and not homonyms.

DNA sequence studies (Reeves et al. 2001) show that the relationships of *Herbertia* lie with the widespread South American genus *Cypella* (including *Onira*), and together these genera form a clade with *Calydorea* and *Cipura*. The American *Nemastylis* and *Calydorea* are immediately allied to this clade of largely diploid species. Basic chromosome number for this entire assemblage is $x = 7$, but a few species are polyploid, with $n = 14$ or 28. *Herbertia* has an interesting distribution with a center in southern Brazil, Uruguay, and northern Argentina, but *H. lahue* subsp. *lahue* is endemic to central Chile, and subspecies *caerulea* occurs in the southern United States. The latter differs hardly at all from subspecies *amoena* of southeastern South America and is probably a fairly recent arrival in North America, possibly a post-Columbian introduction.

As mentioned, plastid DNA sequences show that *Herbertia* is sister genus to *Cypella*. The two genera are often identical in vegetative habit, but unlike *Herbertia*, *Cypella* usually has free stamens, always well-developed tepal claws and limbs, the inner three tepals somewhat to considerably smaller than the outer, and inner tepals with a zone of stalked oil glands in the middle part at the base of a fold at the base of the limb. There is a trend in *Cypella* for the reduction of the inner tepals, and in a few species for partial or in one species complete fusion of the filaments. Free filaments are unknown in *Herbertia* as usually circumscribed, but a survey of *Herbertia* species shows that while *H. lahue* has the filaments fully united, they are free in the upper half in *H.*

*pulchella,* which also has clawed inner tepals. Further molecular study may well show *Herbertia* to be nested in *Cypella.*

### *Hesperoxiphion* Baker (1877: 76)
Tribe Tigridieae
TYPE: *Cypella peruviana* Baker = *Hesperoxiphion peruviana* (Baker) Baker
ETYMOLOGY: from the Greek *hesperos,* western, and *xiphos,* sword, referring to the leaves and the source of the plants, western South America

Medium-sized to large seasonal perennials with bulbs usually with brown to blackish, papery or glutinous tunics. LEAVES few, lanceolate, with pleated blades. FLOWERING STEM usually branched, smooth, round in cross section. INFLORESCENCE a few-flowered rhipidium; SPATHES green, leafy in texture, tightly sheathing, enclosing membranous floral bracts. FLOWERS radially symmetric, borne on long, slender pedicels, fugacious, yellow, white, or blue, with contrasting white and yellow to brown bands in the tepal claws; TEPALS free, prominently clawed, the outer larger, spreading from the base, the inner with stalked oil glands in the upper half of the inner tepals partly concealed by a fold. STAMENS symmetrically arranged; FILAMENTS free, slender and weak; ANTHERS attached at least apically to the opposed style branches, with a wide connective and locules placed laterally. OVARY ovoid, usually exserted; STYLE slender below, style branches well developed, compressed, divided above into petaloid crests, with a transverse stigmatic surface on the abaxial surface at the base of the crests, also with short, acute appendages in the center. CAPSULES obovoid, truncate; SEEDS angular. BASIC CHROMOSOME NUMBER $x = 7$. Species approximately four, Andes of South America, from Peru to Colombia.

A fairly typical member of the Tigridieae, *Hesperoxiphion* consists of fairly robust plants with broad, pleated leaves and large, yellow, white, or blue, fugacious flowers. No obvious features distinguish the genus for it has large outer tepals with broad claws and inner tepals with a band of prominent distal band of secretory hairs partly concealed by an S-shaped fold. The stamens and style branches are virtually identical to those of *Cypella* and *Neomarica*—the free stamens have weak filaments, and the anthers, which have a broad connective, are loosely attached to thickened style branches. The style branches each have a pair of prominent petaloid crests, and the transverse stigma has secondary crests in the center. This elaborate structure says little about the relationships of the genus as it is the ancestral state for the Tigridieae. Foster (1945) included *Hesperoxiphion* in *Cypella,* and Ravenna (1977a) followed this taxonomy. Ravenna (1981d) later changed his mind and recognized *Hesperoxiphion* as a separate genus. Basic chromosome number in *Hesperoxiphion* is $x = 7$, the same number as in *Cypella,* but their chromosome complements are significantly different. *Hesperoxiphion* has two large acrocentric chromosomes with large satellites and 12 short chromosomes. All *Cypella* species as well as the allied genera *Calydorea, Cipura,* and *Herbertia* have a diploid karyotype of two large chromosome pairs, two acrocentric and two metacentric, and five small chromosome pairs.

Studies using DNA sequences likewise run counter to the belief that *Hesperoxiphion* should be included within *Cypella,* for it falls outside the *Cypella* clade and close to genera of the *Tigridia* group, including *Alophia* and *Gelasine* (Reeves et al. 2001). While we think additional study of the relationships of the genera of Tigridieae is needed, we cannot support the inclusion of *Hesperoxiphion* in *Cypella,* and we retain it as a separate genus, somewhat poorly defined but according to available information (Figure 8) most closely allied to the *Gelasine–Ennealophus* clade.

*Larentia* Klatt

Klatt (1882). Type: *L linearis* (Kunth) Klatt.
ETYMOLOGY: unknown
SYNONYM: *Zygella* S. Moore (1896), type: *Z. graminea* S. Moore = *Larentia linearis* (Kunth) Klatt

Small to medium-sized seasonal perennials with bulbs with brown, papery tunics. LEAVES few, sword-shaped to linear, with pleated blades. FLOWERING STEM simple or few-branched, smooth, round in section. INFLORESCENCE a few- to several-flowered rhipidium; SPATHES green, leafy in texture, tightly sheathing, enclosing membranous floral bracts. FLOWERS fugacious, radially symmetric, borne on short or long, slender pedicels, shades yellow or pale to deep blue to violet, sometimes with contrasting dark and pale markings; TEPALS free, prominently clawed, subequal, with the outer larger, ascending, the inner ascending or suberect, with a pouched fold at the top of the claw. STAMENS symmetrically arranged; FILAMENTS free and slender; ANTHERS linear, loosely appressed to the style branches. OVARY oblong, exserted from the spathes; STYLE thickened distally and three-branched, the branches compressed, stigmatic lobes abaxial, at base of paired crests. CAPSULES stalked, obovoid to cylindric, truncate; SEEDS angular. BASIC CHROMOSOME NUMBER $x = 7$. Species approximately four, northern South America to Mexico and central Brazil.

Poorly understood, *Larentia*, was described by Klatt in 1882 to accommodate the Venezuelan species *Moraea linearis*, obviously misplaced in that genus. Not particularly distinctive in leaf or flower, *Larentia* was transferred to *Cypella* by Baker in 1892, where it seems unusual in occurring north of the equator whereas other species of *Cypella* are found in temperate South America. It also differs from all other *Cypella* species in its violet to purple flower color, linear anthers without a visible connective, and small details of the style branches. Although *Larentia* has free stamens, as does *Cypella,* the anthers are weakly appressed to the style branches, contrasting with the closely adhering anthers of *Cypella*. Ravenna (1977a) noted the structural differences in the stamens and style branches of *Larentia* and *Cypella* and revived the genus. More recent studies using DNA sequences show that the two Mexican species of *Cypella* allied to *L. linearis* are immediately related to *Cipura* rather than to *Cypella*. The only acceptable taxonomic solution to the situation is to continue to recognize *Larentia* as a separate genus or, alternatively, unite both it and *Cipura* with *Cypella*. We await more information about relationships in this alliance before taking that seemingly radical step. Thus we provisionally endorse recognition of *Larentia*.

The genus currently includes just two species, *Larentia linearis* and *L. rosei,* but at least *Cypella mexicana* belongs here, and possibly one more species of *Cypella*. These await formal transfer to *Larentia*.

*Mastigostyla* I. M. Johnston (1925: 85)

Tribe Tigridieae

TYPE: *Mastigostyla cyrtophylla* I. M. Johnston
ETYMOLOGY: from the Greek *mastigos,* a flagellum or whip, and *stylos,* a style, for the distinctive style that characterized species of the genus then known
SYNONYM: *Cardenanthus* R. C. Foster (1945: 3), new synonym, type: *C. boliviensis* R. C. Foster (1945: 4) = *Mastigostyla boliviensis* (R. C. Foster) Goldblatt, new combination
REVISIONARY ACCOUNT: Foster (1962: 292–298, for the *Mastigostyla* group; 298–303, for the *Cardenanthus* group)

Small to medium-sized seasonal perennials with bulbs with brown to blackish, papery tunics, acaulescent in a few species. LEAVES few, sword-shaped to linear, blades pleated. INFLORESCENCE a few-flowered rhipidium; SPATHES green, leafy to leathery in texture, tightly sheathing, enclosing the buds and membranous floral bracts. FLOWERING STEM aerial and simple or branched, or subterranean, smooth, round in cross section. FLOWERS radially symmetric, on slender pedicels or subsessile, fugacious, usually blue to purple; TEPALS free or basally united, unequal, the outer larger, with ascending to suberect claws, inner often erect and without folds or pockets, sometimes bearing stalked oil glands near the base. STAMENS symmetrically arranged; FILAMENTS united in a column; ANTHERS each loosely appressed to an opposed style branch. OVARY oblong, included in the spathes or exserted; STYLE slender below, the branches flattened, usually deeply divided, sometimes to below the level of the stigmas, often terminating as slender, whip-like crests, stigmas terminal or lateral at or above the bases of the crests on their outer edges. CAPSULES oblong; SEEDS angular. BASIC CHROMOSOME NUMBER $x = 14$. Species c. 20, Andean South America from Bolivia and Peru to Ecuador in the north, Argentina in the south.

The first species of this moderate-sized genus to be discovered were referred to *Cypella,* and vegetatively the two genera are virtually identical. As pointed out by Johnston, who described *Mastigostyla,* and later by Foster (1945), however, the flowers of *Mastigostyla* in the narrow sense differ in some important ways. While the flowers of *Cypella* have broad spreading tepal claws forming a shallow cup, the tepals of *Mastigostyla* have narrow suberect claws. The inner tepals are also much smaller than the outer and lack the band of glandular hairs and pouch-like fold at the top of the claw typical of *Cypella* species. Equally important, the filaments are united in a fairly slender column, and the flattened style branches are deeply divided into narrow erect crests. The latter are narrow enough to be described

as whip-like in the type species, *M. cyrtophylla,* and have the stigmas placed on the outer edges of the crests. That the style branches are forked below the level of the stigmas seems particularly important, for in other Tigridieae with petaloid style branches the style forks at or shortly above the stigma lobe. Foster also noted that the tepals are united for a short distance above the base, but we place little reliance on his interpretation of this feature, which on examination seems to differ hardly at all from other Tigridieae.

We include in *Mastigostyla* here for the first time a second Andean genus, the poorly understood *Cardenanthus* (Foster 1945). The flowers of the genera match those of *Mastigostyla* fairly closely in their erect outer tepals claws, smaller inner tepals, and anthers opposed to flattened style branches. The main distinguishing feature of *Cardenanthus* is the reduced stem, largely or entirely underground. That character alone is a poor reason for recognition of a genus, for acaulescence is developed repeatedly in genera of the Iridaceae. Flowers of some species of *Cardenanthus* are reported to have the tepals united in a short tube (as have those of *Mastigostyla*). Some species of the *Cardenanthus* group have the ovary included in the spathes, with the style branches truncated, shorter than the anthers, and vestigial crests.

Other features of *Mastigostyla* are monosulcate pollen grains and an apparent basic chromosome number $x = 14$ (there is a chromosome count for only one species of the genus), marking the genus, at least on the basis of the one count, as paleopolyploid. The relationships of *Mastigostyla* are uncertain, but DNA sequence studies show it plus *Cardenanthus* as constituting a separate lineage together with two South American species of *Tigridia.* This seems reasonable, for South American *Tigridia* species also have united filaments and whip-like style branches. They differ, however, in having stigmas

**Figure 63.** *Nemastylis geminiflora* (×0.7) with details of flower (×1.3), capsule (upper right, ×0.7), and seed (lower right, ×10).

terminal on the style crests, and spreading rather than erect tepals. Further study is needed before these species can be transferred to *Mastigostyla*. Additional collections of the species of this alliance will be helpful in assessing their relationships, and in particular, photographs of flowers are needed to better understand their structure.

*Nemastylis* Nuttall (1835: 157)
Plate 231; Figure 63
Tribe Tigridieae
TYPE: *Nemastylis geminiflora* Nuttall
ETYMOLOGY: from the Greek *nema*, thread, and *stylos*, a pillar or rod, alluding to the straight but very slender style branches
SYNONYM: *Chlamydostylus* Baker (1876: 188), type: *C. tenuis* (Herbert) Baker = *Nemastylis tenuis* (Herbert) Bentham
REVISIONARY ACCOUNTS: Foster (1945: 26–44), Goldblatt (1975: 375–380; 2002)

Small to medium-sized seasonal perennials with bulbs with brownish papery tunics. LEAVES several to single, sword-shaped to linear, the blades pleated. FLOWERING STEM simple to several-branched, round in section. INFLORESCENCE a few- to several-flowered rhipidium; SPATHES green, leafy in texture, tightly enclosing the membranous floral bracts. FLOWERS radially symmetric, fugacious, blue to purple, often white in the center; TEPALS free, spreading from the base, without obvious claws, subequal or the inner slightly smaller than the outer. STAMENS symmetrically arranged; FILAMENTS free or united partly to entirely; ANTHERS much longer than the filaments, initially erect, collapsing and coiling inward after shedding their pollen. OVARY exserted; STYLE deeply divided almost to the base into paired filiform arms extended horizontally between the anther bases, apically stigmatic. CAPSULES obovoid-truncate; SEEDS angular or the

ends flattened into wings. BASIC CHROMOSOME NUMBER $x = 7$. Species four, southern United States and Mexico to Guatemala.

Species of *Nemastylis* are readily recognized by their flower, unusual among the bulbous Tigridieae in having subequal tepals without apparent claws, long anthers that collapse spirally after shedding their pollen, and above all the style branches, which are each divided to the base into a pair of long, thread-like arms, the character for which the genus is named. The straight style branches extend horizontally between the bases of the anthers and are stigmatic at their tips. The best-known species, *N. geminiflora* of the southern and central United States, has the largest flowers and is worth cultivating despite the short life span of individual flowers. The widespread *N. tenuis* extends from New Mexico to Guatemala and is so variable in appearance that four subspecies are recognized (Foster 1945, Goldblatt 1975).

The flowers apparently lack nectaries and offer pollen alone as a reward to potential pollinators, which in *Nemastylis floridana* have been established to be female bees, the most important of which are two species of the family Halictidae (Mackiernan and Norman 1979).

The immediate relationships of *Nemastylis* are uncertain. The yellow-flowered *N. convoluta* is certainly misplaced in the genus—it has unequal tepals, and the anthers do not collapse after anthesis. DNA sequence studies (A. Rodríguez 1999, A. Rodríguez and Sytsma 2006) show that this species is nested within *Tigridia* and matches that genus especially in its bisulcate pollen. Molecular study also shows that two typical, blue-flowered species of *Nemastylis* are not related to *Tigridia* but are most closely related to *Calydorea*, and the genus is part of a clade that includes *Cipura* and *Cypella*. Sampling in these genera is too incomplete for this result to be regarded as conclusive, but it is nevertheless a useful guide.

**Figure 64.** *Salpingostylis coelestina* with capsule (center right) (×1) and style (lower right, ×3).

*Salpingostylis* Small (1931: 161)

Figure 64

Tribe Tigridieae

TYPE: *Salpingostylis coelestina* (Bartram) Small

ETYMOLOGY: from the Greek *salpiggon*, small trumpet, and *stylos*, a column, referring to the shape of the style, the short branches of which are directed forward in a trumpet shape

REVISIONARY ACCOUNT: Goldblatt (1975)

Small seasonal perennials with bulbs with dark brown, papery tunics. LEAVES few, with obscurely pleated blades. FLOWERING STEM simple, or rarely one-branched, smooth, round in cross section. INFLORESCENCE a few-flowered rhipidium; spathes green, leafy in texture, tightly sheathing, enclosing membranous bracts. FLOWERS radially symmetric, facing sideways, borne on pedicels just reaching the top of the spathes, blue-violet; TEPALS free, subequal, spreading from the base, not obviously clawed, without stalked oil glands. STAMENS symmetrically arranged; FILAMENTS free; ANTHERS slightly diverging. OVARY oblong, usually exserted; STYLE slender, exceeding the anthers, arching toward the ground, dividing above the anthers into three short, flattened, ascending branches, the tips stigmatic and spreading. CAPSULES narrowly obovoid, truncate; SEEDS angular. BASIC CHROMOSOME NUMBER $x = 28$. Species only *Salpingostylis coelestina*, piney woods in Florida.

Although typical of tribe Tigridieae in its vegetative features, including pleated leaves and bulbous rootstock, *Salpingostylis* has a seemingly unspecialized flower with subequal, spreading tepals not obviously divided into a claw and limb, and without nectar glands on the surface. The stamens are free, and the slender style divides beyond the top of the anthers into three simple branches flattened and spreading at the tips. The only species, *S. coelestina*,

is a fairly rare species restricted to central Florida. It has relatively large flowers with bright blue-violet tepals. First discovered by the botanist-explorer William Bartram in 1765–1766, this plant remained something of a mystery until its rediscovery in 1931.

The genus and its type and sole species have a checkered taxonomic history. *Salpingostylis coelestina* was first assigned to the southern African genus *Ixia*, then to *Trichonema*, a synonym of *Romulea*. A more realistic treatment was its transfer to the North American *Nemastylis* by Thomas Nuttall in 1833, who noted its obvious similarity in leaf and bulb to that genus. John Kunkel Small, an expert on the flora of the southeastern United States, who rediscovered the species in 1931, then placed it in a new genus, *Salpingostylis*, noting that the flowers are was unlike those of *Nemastylis*, the latter having upright rather than nodding flowers and a short style, the three branches of which are divided almost to the base into a pair of thread-like arms that extend outward below the anthers.

Further generic transfers included removal to *Marica*, then *Beatonia* (now a synonym of *Tigridia*), and after that to *Sphenostigma*, a South American genus, the type of which is a species of *Gelasine*. Its last transfer was to a second South American genus, *Calydorea*, by Goldblatt and Henrich (1991), who were impressed by the similar, undivided style branches of both that genus and *Salpingostylis*. Goldblatt and Henrich associated *S. coelestina* (as *Calydorea*) with a group of Mexican species that had been treated as the genus *Cardiostigma* before their transfer to *Calydorea*. DNA sequence studies now show that the type of *Cardiostigma* is nested within *Tigridia* (A. Rodríguez and Sytsma 2006), and accordingly we treat *Cardiostigma* as a synonym of *Tigridia*. It remains to be seen whether *Salpingostylis* is also nested in *Tigridia*, but no material for DNA extraction has come to hand. Recognition here of *Salpingostylis* is thus provisional, and we suspect that when molecular study has been undertaken the genus will be found to belong to *Tigridia*. We note that *Salpingostylis* does not have the distinctive subapical leaf of typical *Cardiostigma* species, but their long style with short, somewhat flattened style branches is similar.

Small's rediscovery of *Salpingostylis coelestina* also yielded some interesting information about its biology. The delicate flowers are extraordinarily fleeting. They open soon after sunrise and last just 3 hours, the tepals rapidly collapsing at about 9:00 a.m. So short a flowering period is rare but known in a few other Iridaceae, notably the late-afternoon-flowering *Moraea vespertina* and the *M. crispa* group of species.

*Tigridia* Jussieu (1789: 57)
Plates 232–233; Figure 65
Tribe Tigridieae
TYPE: *Tigridia pavonia* (Linnaeus fil.) de Candolle in Redouté (1802)
ETYMOLOGY: tiger-like, in reference to the spotted and streaked flower of *Tigridia pavonia*, the type species
SYNONYMS: *Hydrotaenia* Lindley (1838), type: *H. meleagris* Lindley = *Tigridia meleagris* (Lindley) Nicholson; *Beatonia* Herbert (1840: below pl. 3,779), type: *B. purpurea* Herbert = *T. violacea* Schiede ex Schlechtendal; *Rigidella* Lindley (1840), type: *R. flammea* Lindley = *T. flammea* (Lindley) Ravenna; *Cardiostigma* Baker (1877: 102), new synonym, type: *C. longispathum* Baker (1877: 189) = *T. longispathum* (Baker) Goldblatt, new combination; *Fosteria* Molseed (1968), new synonym, type: *F. oaxacana* Molseed (1968: 234) = *T. oaxacana* (Molseed) Goldblatt, new combination; *Sessilanthera* Molseed & Cruden (1969), new synonym, type: *S. latifolia* Molseed & Cruden (1969: 192) = *T. latifolia* (Molseed & Cruden) Goldblatt, new combination;

*Colima* (Ravenna) A. Rodríguez & Ortíz-Catedral (2003: 53), new synonym, *Nemastylis* section *Colima* Ravenna (1968: 282), type: *C. convoluta* (Ravenna) A. Rodríguez & Ortíz-Catedral = *T. convoluta* (Ravenna) Goldblatt, new combination; *Ainea* Ravenna (1979), new synonym, type: *A. conzattii* (R. C. Foster) Ravenna (= *Sphenostigma conzattii* R. C. Foster 1947: 106) = *T. conzattii* (R. C. Foster) Goldblatt, new combination
REVISIONARY ACCOUNTS: Molseed (1970, the *Tigridia* group), Cruden (1971, the *Rigidella* group; 1975: 108, the *Sessilanthera* group)

Small to medium-sized seasonal perennials with bulbs with dark, papery tunics. LEAVES few, pleated, lanceolate to linear. FLOWERING STEM erect or drooping, round in cross section, often branched or simple, sometimes consisting of a single internode with a subterminal leaflet. INFLORESCENCE a few- to several-flowered rhipidium; spathes green, leafy, acute or subacute, enclosing membranous floral bracts. FLOWERS radially symmetric, variously colored, often yellow, purple, brownish, or red, usually with contrasting dark or pale markings, often in striking patterns, upright, facing sideways, or nodding; TEPALS free, subequal or unequal with the inner three somewhat to much smaller, usually clawed, claws often broad, often forming a wide cup, sometimes a narrow cylinder, limbs spreading to reflexed, the claws bearing stalked oil glands or nectaries, often partly concealed by a fold formed by the tepal arching forward below the base of the limb, in a few species the tepals spreading from the base and without claws and lacking oil glands. STAMENS symmetrically arranged; FILAMENTS mostly united in a well-developed column, sometimes short and free, rarely vestigial; ANTHERS linear, diverging, mostly splitting longitudinally, or by apical slits, sterile below in one species, laterally placed with broad connective and collapsing and coiling

**Figure 65.** *Tigridia pavonia* with flowers, capsule (lower left) (×0.9), and details of stamens and style branches (lower right, ×3.5) and seed (bottom center, ×9).

inward (*Tigridia conzattii*); pollen bisulcate. OVARY globose, on long pedicels, usually exserted; STYLE slender below, often dividing at the base of the anthers, the branches usually each divided more or less to the base into two slender diverging or rarely suberect arms, usually extending outward on either side of the opposed anther, often with a distinct mucro in the sinus between the two arms, rarely the style branches undivided, central or eccentric, stigmas terminal on the style arms or papillate and evidently stigmatic along their entire length (*T. oaxacana*). CAPSULES obovoid- to cylindric-truncate; SEEDS angular. BASIC CHROMOSOME NUMBER $x = 14$. Species c. 55, Mexico and adjacent countries of Central America; *Tigridia* species of Peru, Bolivia and Ecuador fall outside the genus.

*Tigridia* is most well known outside its center of diversity in Mexico and Central America by the widely cultivated *T. pavonia*, sometimes called the tiger flower or Aztec lily. This species is not the best example of the genus but nevertheless has the classic features that usually associated with *Tigridia:* filaments united in a smooth column, diverging anthers, and a style with three deeply divided arms. The circumscription of *Tigridia* has changed considerably over the years, and Elwood Molseed, in his 1970 account of the genus in Mexico and Guatemala, recognized 23 species in two subgenera. These are subgenera *Tigridia* and *Hydrotaenia*, the two distinguished primarily by differences in the nectar glands of the flowers. In subgenus *Tigridia* the glands are restricted to the inner tepals and are hidden in folds of the tepal surface, and they consist of club-shaped cells that secrete oils. In contrast, the nectar glands of subgenus *Hydrotaenia* are exposed, glistening areas on the lower half of the inner tepals, also composed of short secretory cells.

Our treatment here of *Tigridia* departs from the traditional one in including for the first time several genera until now regarded as separate and not always even closely allied to *Tigridia*. Our expanded circumscription of the genus is based on information derived from sequences of nuclear and plastid genes, and the results show conclusively that these several genera are nested within *Tigridia* (A. Rodríguez 1999, A. Rodríguez and Sytsma 2006). The conclusion is that their distinctive flowers are adapted for pollination systems different from those of other *Tigridia* species. Perhaps the best known of these genera is *Rigidella*, described in 1840, and when revised by Robert Cruden in 1971 it was expanded to include four species. All have bright scarlet to red flowers and secrete quantities of sugary nectar offered to hummingbirds, their pollinators. Surprisingly, molecular study shows that *Rigidella* is not even monophyletic—species with the *Rigidella* flower type evolved independently from different ancestors in *Tigridia*. We believe that species until now included in *Rigidella* are best included in *Tigridia* and must be viewed as species of that genus adapted for hummingbird pollination.

The molecular studies just cited and subsequent analyses (Figure 8) show that the plant called *Nemastylis convoluta*, also treated as the monospecific genus *Colima*, as well as species assigned to the genus *Sessilanthera* are nested in *Tigridia*. *Colima* and *Sessilanthera* are distinguished by their subsessile anthers, opening by apical slits, and spreading tepals without nectaries. *Sessilanthera*, with three species of central to southern Mexico and Guatemala, has style branches exactly like those of typical *Tigridia* species, having a mucro between the divergent pairs of style arms of each style branch, whereas *Colima* has style branches dividing below the level of the anthers. As with *Rigidella*, the genera *Colima* and *Sessilanthera* must now be included in *Tigridia*. The absence of nectaries and, of course, of nectar in flowers of the *Sessilanthera* group strongly suggests that they have evolved a different pollination system from that in other *Tigridia* species.

Molecular study also shows that the mono-specific *Fosteria* and mono- or dispecific *Ainea*, both *Tigridia*-like in leaf and fruit feature, are nested in *Tigridia*. *Fosteria* differs in having nodding style arms stigmatic along their entire length, and *Ainea* has free stamens and unusual, laterally placed anthers on a broad connective. After shedding their pollen, the anthers collapse and coil inward, a feature also known in *Nemastylis*. These taxonomic changes expand the circumscription of *Tigridia* and enlarge it to some 55 species. With hindsight, we can now see that the narrowly circumscribed *Tigridia* encompassed a range of species adapted for pollination by insects, mainly bees and wasps, foraging for a nectar reward. There is no reason to exclude species pollinated by hummingbirds that belong to the same lineage despite the rather different floral specializations.

Significantly, *Tigridia* and the genera we now include in the genus all share a basic chromosome number $x = 14$ (thus are ancestrally tetraploid) and a distinctive karyotype. They also have bisulcate pollen grains (A. Rodríguez and Ortíz-Catedral 2002). Apart from the main *Tigridia* group, only *Cobana*, with a single species, *C. guatemalensis*, of the highlands of Guatemala and Honduras, has these two features. This plant has white flowers that most closely resemble those of the *Sessilanthera* group of *Tigridia*, but they differ in the subsessile anthers splitting only near the tips and the style branches, which are undivided and lie between the anthers. DNA sequences place *Cobana* outside the main *Tigridia* lineage, but we suspect that when more species are included in such analyses, *Cobana* will be found to be nested in *Tigridia*. Provisionally, we have accepted the genus, which is easy to recognize because of its undivided, thread-like style branches and subsessile anthers.

Flowers of *Cobana*, the *Sessilanthera* group, and *Tigridia* (*Colima*) *convoluta* exhibit another specialized pollination system for the *Tigridia* lineage, one that offers just pollen as a reward for pollinators, presumably female bees. Anthers opening by apical slits are a feature of buzz pollination in which a bee vibrates its wings at a high frequency, thereby driving pollen out of the anther and onto its body, where it is collected for nest provisioning. In its expanded circumscription, *Tigridia* is now seen as one more example, and a particularly striking one, of a genus of Iridaceae that has undergone explosive adaptive radiation, leading to profound floral diversification.

# GLOSSARY

abaxial. Of the side or face of an organ facing away from the axis; usually the lower face

acaulescent. Stemless

achlorophyllous. Lacking chlorophyll

acrocentric. Of a chromosome that has a sub-terminal centromere

actinomorphic. Radially symmetric

adaxial. Of the side or face of an organ facing toward the axis; usually the upper face

androecium. Male part of a flower, consisting of one or more stamens

anther. Pollen-bearing organ, top of part of a stamen (male part of the flower), borne at the top of a stalk, the filament

anthesis. Time of opening of the flower

antipodals. Cells in the embryo sac opposite the micropyle

appressed. Lying flat against

arcuate. Arched upward like a bow, often of stamens

areolate. Of pollen exine in which the perforations in the surface are crushed and angular

aril (adjective, arillate). Fleshy appendage on a seed, more specifically a structure derived from the funicle, usually fleshy or waxy

astelic. Of an organ lacking a stele (ring of vascular tissue)

autogamy (adjective, autogamous). Production of seed from self-pollination

awn. Bristle-like appendage

axil (adjective, axillary). Angle formed between a leaf or bract and the stem bearing it

axile. Of placentation in which the ovules are borne along the axis in the center of a compound ovary

basifixed. Attached at or by the base

bifacial. Of leaves, either flat or channeled, that have two anatomically distinct faces, typically flattened at 90° to the stem axis

bilabiate. Two-lipped, of a flower

bract. Leaf-like structure lacking an axillary bud at its base and often subtending a flower or inflorescence, usually differing from foliage leaves in form or size

bulb. Specialized storage structure in which the storage function has been transferred from the stem to the leaves; the stem is reduced to a small disk of tissue bearing apical and axillary buds, all closely wrapped by enlarged, persistent leaves or leaf bases (tunics) that constitute the main storage tissues

bulbiferous. Bearing a small or secondary bulb, also called a bulblet

c. Circa, approximately

calyx. Sepals or outer, usually green, sterile whorl of a flower

capsule. Dry fruit formed from two or more united carpels (i.e., with two or more locules) and splitting at maturity to release the seeds

carpel. Unit of the gynoecium (female portion of the flower), often fused into a compound structure, as in the Iridaceae where the gynoecium consists of three united carpels

cataphyll. Scale-like leaf, usually associated with a vegetatively propagating organ such as a corm or perennating bud

caudex. Woody underground part of a stem

cauline. Borne along the stem or trunk

centric. Of leaves oval to rounded in cross section and more or less radially symmetric internally

centrifixed. Of an anther appearing basifixed but the filament attached to the center of the anther through a sheath or collar

cf. Confer (i.e., compare), similar to

chalazal. Signifying the end of an ovule or seed, often opposite the micropyle, the point of entry of the vascular tissue into the ovule

chromosome. Organelle within the nucleus of a cell that carries genetic material, always constant in number within an individual, population, and usually a species

clade. Lineage of organisms with a common ancestor

claw. Differentiated basal portion, usually of a tepal, often narrower than the distal portion of the tepal, the limb

clone (adjective, clonal). Single genotype maintained in plants through vegetative reproduction

coleoptile. Sheath-like outgrowth of the cotyledon (embryonic leaf) protecting the growing tip of the seedling

colliculate. Of cells with domed outer walls

complex heterozygosity. Anomalous chromosomal arrangement in which the normal rules of meiosis are not followed and the chromosomes segregate in linked sets, preserving particular genotypes

corm (adjective, cormous). Underground organ, essentially a shortened rhizome with relatively few nodes and usually renewed annually, comprising a fairly dry, starchy nugget of stem tissue topped by a small, fleshy apical bud

cormlet. Small or secondary corm, also called a cormel

corymb (adjective, corymbose). An inflorescence in which the branches form a flat-topped structure

corolla. Petals or inner sterile whorl of a flower

cortex. Tissue of the stem or root located between the epidermis and the vascular tissue

corymb (adjective, corymbose). Inflorescence in which the pedicels of the lower flowers are longer than those of the upper flowers, bringing all flowers to about the same level and resulting in a more or less flat-topped inflorescence

cuspidate. Tapering into a sharp, rigid point

cyme. Inflorescence in which each flower, in turn, is formed at the tip of the growing axis, and further flowers are formed on branches arising below it, the terminal flower being the first to bloom

declinate. Arched downward and forward

decurrent. Extending downward below the point of insertion

dehiscent. Breaking open at maturity to release the contents

depressed. Flattened as if pressed down from the top or end

dichotomous. Forked in equal pairs

diploid. Chromosome number of somatic cells of a plant, consisting of two matching chromosome sets

disjunct. A geographic distribution with a significant gap in the range

distylous. See heterostyly

diurnal. During the day, for example, of flowers that open in the daylight and close at night

dorsiventral. Of leaves that are flattened and provided with definite upper and lower surfaces

dysploidy (adjective, dysploid). Incremental increase or decrease in chromosome number

eccentric. Of a style that is off-center

elaiophore. Oil-secreting gland

elaiosome. White, fleshy seed appendage, typically containing fatty or waxy material (literally, fat-body)

embryo sac. Cell within the ovule that contains the egg nucleus, and in which the embryo is formed after fertilization

endodermis (adjective, endodermal). Tissue, usually a single layer thick at the inner edge of the cortex, enclosing the vascular tissue

endosperm. Storage tissue within a seed, often composed of cells filled with starch, oil, and protein

endothecium (adjective, endothecial). Tissue of an anther, specifically the cell layer responsible for the opening of the locules, and distinguished by characteristic cell wall thickening patterns

epidermis. Outermost tissue of plant organs, usually a single cell layer thick

exine. Outer layer of the wall of a pollen grain

exodermis. Outermost layer of internal tissue of the root, located immediately below the epidermis and corresponding to the hypodermis of the stem

exostome. Seed coat layers around the micropyle

exserted. Protruding

extrorse. Of anthers opening away from the center of the flower

fibrotic. Tough and full of fibers

-fid. Divided, at the tip

filament. Stalk of a stamen

filiform. Thread-like

flexuose. Bent from side to side in a zigzag form

foveolate. With small depressions

fugacious. Fleeting, lasting only a few hours

funicle. Stalk of an ovule

fused. Joined together, united

fynbos. Heathy shrubland vegetation characteristic of sandy soils in the winter-rainfall zone of South Africa, dominated by small to large evergreen shrubs with tough, often small and needle-like leaves

genotype. Distinct genetic strain

geophyte (adjective, geophytic). Plant whose storage organs and perennating buds are underground

globose. Spherical, globe-shaped

gynoecium. Female part of a flower, consisting of an ovary, style, and stigma

haploid. Half the chromosome number of somatic (diploid) cells of an organism

helobial. Type of endosperm development in which the first and only cell division is very unequal, producing one large and one tiny cell

heterostyly (adjective, heterostylous). Condition is some plant species in which some individuals have different style and stamen lengths than others; for example, there may be two (distylous) sets of style–stamen forms in certain Iridaceae

heterozygosity (adjective, heterozygous). Condition in which an organism has different expressions of a gene or genes

hexaploid. Of an organism with six times the haploid number compared with related species

hysteranthy (adjective, hysteranthous). Of leaves that appear after the flowers

inaperturate. Of pollen without germination pores

inferior. Of an ovary that is below the level of attachment of the other floral parts

inflorescence. Group or arrangement in which flowers are borne on the plant

integument. Outer layer of an ovule, of which there are two, an inner and an outer, or less often one

internode. Portion of stem between two adjacent leaf attachments (nodes)

involute. Rolled inward

isobilateral. Of leaves with identical surfaces and oriented in the same plane as the stem

Karoo. Semiarid central plateau of South Africa

karroid. Describing the dwarf, shrubby, drought-adapted vegetation characteristic of the Karoo

karyotype. Appearance of the chromosome complement manifested during cell division

lanceolate. Broadest in the lower half and tapering toward the tip, about four times as long as broad

latrorse. Of anthers opening laterally (i.e., toward adjacent anthers)

lectotype. Deliberately chosen type of a taxon when a selection has to be made because it was not designated when the taxon was first described and named

lignification (adjective, lignified). Process by which structures become woody

limb. Blade-like portion of a tepal

locule (adjective, locular). Enclosed compartment within an organ, usually the ovary

loculicidal. Of the splitting of a fruit along lines coinciding with the center of the locules

meiosis. Type of cell division that yields four daughter cells, each with half the chromosome number of the parental cells

meristem. Tissue concerned primarily with the formation of new cells through division

mesophyll. Internal tissue of the leaf, not including the vascular tissue and associated cells

metacentric. Of a chromosome that has the centromere more or less in the middle, thus with equal arms

metaxylem. Xylem cells produced later during the first year of development, composed of large cells

micropyle (adjective, micropylar). Opening of the ovule though which the sperm nuclei enter the embryo sac

monochasial. Branching from one side only

monocot. Colloquial abbreviation for monocotyledon, a class of flowering plants whose embryo has only one cotyledon; this group includes palms, lilies, orchids, grasses, and Iridaceae

monophyly (adjective, monophyletic). A lineage with a single common ancestor

mucro. A small but prominent extension of the apex of an organ

multifid. Cleft into many parts

mya. Million years ago

nectar. Sugary fluid produced by flowers

nectary. Multicellular gland secreting nectar

node. Joint of a stem or site at which a leaf is inserted

nucellus (adjective, nucellate). Tissue within the ovule surrounding the embryo sac

ob-. Prefix denoting reversed or inverted

oblong. Longer than broad with the sides parallel most of their length

operculum (adjective, operculate). Lid or cover, often of pollen grains, loosely applied to the bands of exine in the aperture of many Crocoideae

ovate. Oval in shape and attached at the broader end

ovoid. Egg-shaped in three dimensions and attached at the broader end

ovule. Organ inside the ovary that houses the embryo sac and becomes the seed following fertilization and development

panicle (adjective, paniculate). Branched or compound inflorescence of stalked flowers

papilla (adjective, papillate). Small, elongate cellular projection on the surface of an organ

parenchyma (adjective, parenchymatous). Unspecialized cell with equal vertical and horizontal diameters and thin walls, or tissue composed of such cells

parietal. Of placentation in which the ovules are borne on the walls of an ovary

pedicel (adjective, pedicellate). Stalk of an individual flower

perennating. Self-renewing, of perennial plants

perianth. Calyx and corolla of a flower, used particularly when the two are similar in appearance

pericycle (adjective, pericyclic). That part of the ground tissue of the vascular bundle located between the phloem and the endodermis, or outermost layer of the vascular cylinder, and regularly present in roots but rarely in stems

periderm. Protective tissue of secondary origin that replaces the epidermis of stems and roots, commonly evident in woody plants as cork tissue

perigonal. Of the perianth, from *perigone,* a synonym of perianth

petaloid. Petal-like in texture and color

phloem. Vascular tissue responsible for conduction of sap, consisting of thin-walled, elongate cells

phylogeny (adjective, phylogenetic). Evolutionary relationship between groups of organisms

phytomelan (adjective, phytomelanous). Brittle, black pigment found in the outer layer of the seed coat

pilose. Softly hairy

placenta. Region within an ovary to which the ovules are attached

placentation. Arrangement of placentas, hence ovules, within an ovary

plane. Of a leaf blade that is flat, that is, without ridges, grooves, raised veins, undulations, etc.

plastid. Organelle of a cell, for example, a chloroplast or mitochondrion

polyploidy. Increase in an entire set or sets of chromosomes

porose. Of anthers splitting open through discrete, rounded pores

protandry (adjective, protandrous). Maturing and shedding of pollen from anthers before the stigmas become receptive

raceme (adjective, racemose). Indeterminate inflorescence in which the main axis produces a series of flowers on lateral stalks, the oldest at the base and the youngest at the top

radical. Of leaves clustered at the base of the stem

raphe (adjective, raphal). Portion of the funicle joined to the integument of the ovule

recurved. Curved or curled downward or backward

reflexed. Bent abruptly downward or backward

renosterveld. Low heathy shrubland dominated by the small-leaved evergreen shrub *Elytropappus rhinocerotis* (Asteraceae), characteristic of clay soils in the winter-rainfall zone of southern Africa

reticulate. Of seeds of pollen with a surface that resembles a network

rhipidium (adjective, rhipidial; plural, rhipidia). Laterally compressed compound cyme with the lateral branches developed alternately on one side, then the other, and all pedicels or flowers arising from a single point

rhizodermis. Outermost layer of the root, analogous to the epidermis of the stem

rhizome (adjective, rhizomatous). More or less horizontal stem that is fleshy, filled with stored food (often starch), and produces roots from the underside and leaves at the apex

rootstock. Organ from which the roots are produced, often a corm or bulb

rugulate. Irregularly wrinkled

rugulose. Minutely and irregularly wrinkled

salver-shaped. With a long, narrow tube abruptly expanded into a flat or spreading limb

sandveld. Terrain of deep coarse sand

saprophyte. Plant that is unable to photosynthesize carbohydrate, and absorbs food from decaying vegetation

scabrid (scabrate when applied to pollen sculpturing). Rough to the touch

scalariform. Arranged regularly in a ladder-like sequence

scale. Of a bulb covering that is narrower than a tunic and not completely sheathing

sclerenchyma (adjective, sclerenchymatous). Type of cell or tissue in which parenchyma-like cells have heavily thickened walls of woody tissue

secund. With all the parts grouped on one side or turned to one side

seed. Reproductive unit of a flowering plant developed from the ovule after fertilization

self-compatible. Of plants with flowers in which the pollen can fertilize the same plant

self-incompatible. Of plants with flowers in which the pollen cannot fertilize the same plant

selfing. Placing pollen on stigmas of the same plant

semi-. Prefix denoting half

sepal. Member of the outer whorl of nonfertile floral parts, often green

septum (adjective, septal). Partition, specifically in flowers between the locules of the ovary, or of a nectary located within the septum

serrate. Toothed, with teeth pointing forward

sessile. Not stalked

sp. A species but not further identified

spathe. Large bract enclosing the inflorescence

spathulate. Spoon-shaped

spike (adjective, spicate). Unbranched indeterminate inflorescence in which the flowers are sessile (without stalks on the axis)

spiraperturate. Of pollen with a single helical aperture

stamen (adjective, staminal). One to many in number, units of the male portion of the flower, usually consisting of an anther, containing pollen, and a stalk or filament the anther; in the *Iris* family there are nearly always three stamens per flower

stele. Central ring of vascular tissue

stomata (adjective, stomatal). Pores in leaf and stem tissue, consisting of two guard cells, able to expand or contract, opening or closing the pore

style (adjective, stylar). Organ connecting the ovary to the bearing the pollen-receptive stigma; may be divided distally into lobes or branches

styloid. Column-shaped, multisided crystal of calcium oxalate

sub-. Prefix denoting approximately, more or less

subsp. Abbreviation for subspecies

sulculus (adjective, sulculate). An aperture of a pollen grain that resembles a sulcus, but its location with respect to the poles of the grain is unknown

sulcus (adjective, sulcate). Elongate germination groove of a pollen grain located at the pole, with the number of grooves often indicated, as in monosulcate, etc.

superior. Of an ovary borne above the level of attachment of the other floral parts

synergids. Two cells associated with the egg cell at the entrance to the embryo sac, which play a vital role in fertilization

systematics. Study of plant classification, relationships, and identification

tapetum. Specialized inner surface layer of cells of the locules of the anther, responsible for secretion of the exine layer of the pollen grain

taxa (singular, taxon). A taxonomic group at any rank, thus species, subspecies, etc.

taxonomy. Study of naming and classification

tectate. Of pollen with a layer of exine borne above the layer of small columns

tectum. Roof (or outer layer) of the pollen exine

tegmen. Inner layer of the seed coat, derived from the inner integument

tepal. Member of the nonfertile whorls of floral parts when both whorls, inner and outer, are similar rather than consisting of a green, leafy outer whorl of sepals (the calyx) and an inner whorl of colored petals (the corolla)

terete. Rounded in cross section

terminal. Borne at the tip

testa. Seed coat, derived from the integuments of the ovule

tetrad. Product of reduction division of a cell in which four haploid cells are produced from a single diploid mother cell, also of pollen in which four grains produced during division remain attached as mature pollen and are shed together

tetraploid. Of an organism with four times the haploid number compared with related species

transpiration. Process by which plants absorb carbon dioxide and eliminate oxygen through stomatal pores, coincidentally losing water by evaporation

tri-. Prefix denoting three

tuber. Swollen storage stem but typically not covered by tunics and having initiation buds scattered over the surface, often developing from the tips of rhizomes and not as discrete as corms nor as upright

tubercle. Small wart-like outgrowth

tuberculate. Covered with tubercles

tunic. Dry corm covering wrapping entirely around the organ, often of fibrous material

type. The single species upon which a genus or infrageneric taxon is based, or the single genus upon which a family or infrafamilial taxon is based, or the single specimen upon which a species is based, usually cited as such when a plant is first described (see also lectotype) umbel (adjective, umbellate). Inflorescence in which all the individual flower stalks arise at the same point in a cluster from the top of the peduncle and are of about equal length

undulate. Wavy, often applied to leaves or leaf margins

unifacial. Of leaves with both surfaces anatomically identical, typically flattened parallel to the stem axis

veld. Vegetation other than forest in southern Africa

verrucate. Covered with wart-like outgrowths (verrucae)

versatile. Of an anther attached near its center to the filament and moving freely

vessel. Water-conducting cell, usually of wide diameter, in which parts of the end walls are dissolved to allow unimpeded water flow (also see xylem)

xylem. Vascular tissue responsible for water conduction, consisting of open-ended vessels and narrow-diameter tracheids, elongate cells with walls thickened in various patterns with lignin (wood) deposited in the thickened parts

zonasulcate. Of pollen encircled with a ring-like germination pore passing through the poles

zonasulculate. Resembling zonasulcate pollen but the orientation of the aperture with respect to the poles is unknown

zygomorphic. Bilaterally symmetric

# LITERATURE CITED

Adamson, R. S. 1926. On the phylogeny of some shrubby Iridaceae. Transactions of the Royal Society of South Africa 13: 373–378.

Adanson, M. 1763. Familles des plantes, vol. 2. Vincent, Paris.

Aiton, W. 1789. Hortus Kewensis, vol. 1. George Nicol, London.

Anderson, B., W. W. Cole, and S. C. H. Barrett. 2005. Specialized bird perch aids cross-pollination. Nature 435: 41–42.

Arber, A. R. 1921. The leaf structure of the Iridaceae, considered in relation to the phyllode theory. Annals of Botany 35: 301–336.

Aublet, F. 1775. Histoire des plantes de la Guiane Française, vol. 1. Didot, Paris.

Backhouse, J., and W. Harvey. 1864. *Schizostylis coccinea.* Curtis's Botanical Magazine 90: pl. 5,422.

Baillon, H. 1894. Une Iridacée sans matière verte. Bulletin Mensuel de la Société Linnéene, Paris, 2(146): 1,149–1,150.

Baker, J. G. 1876. On *Chlamydostylus,* a new genus of Iridaceae from tropical America, and its allies. Journal of Botany 14: 184–188.

Baker, J. G. 1877 [as 1878]. Systema iridearum. Journal of the Linnean Society, Botany 16: 61–180.

Baker, J. G. 1892. Handbook of the Irideae. George Bell and Co., London.

Baker, J. G. 1896. Irideae, pp. 6–171 *in* W. T. Thiselton-Dyer (editor), Flora capensis, vol. 6. Reeve & Co., London.

Barthlott, W., and D. Frolich. 1983. Mikromorphologie und Orientierungsmuster epicuticularer Wachs-Kristalloide: Ein neues systematisches Merkmal bei Monokotylen. Plant Systematics and Evolution 142: 171–185.

Baumann, H. 1993. The Greek plant world in myth, art and literature (translated by W. T. Stearn and E. R. Stearn). Timber Press, Portland, Oregon.

Baytop, T., B. Mathew, and C. Brighton. 1975. Four new taxa in Turkish *Crocus* (Iridaceae). Kew Bulletin 30: 241–246.

Beerling, D. J., and F. I. Woodward. 2001. Vegetation and the terrestrial carbon cycle: Modeling the first 400 million years. Cambridge University Press, Cambridge.

Behnke, H.-D. 1981. Siebelement-Plastiden, Phloem-Protein und Evolution der Blütenpflanzen: II. Monocotyledonen. Berichte der Deutschen Botanischen Gesellschaft 94: 647–662.

Bentham, G., and J. D. Hooker. 1883. Iridaceae, pp. 681–710 *in* Genera plantarum, vol. 3. A. Black, London.

Bernhardt P. 2000. Convergent evolution and adaptive radiation of beetle-pollinated angiosperms. Plant Systematics and Evolution 222: 293–320.

Bicknell, E. P. 1900. Studies in *Sisyrinchium* VIII. *Sisyrinchium californicum* and related species of the neglected genus *Hydastylus*. Bulletin of the Torrey Botanical Club 27: 373–387.

Blanchon, D., B. G. Murray, and J. E. Braggins. 2000. Chromosome numbers in the genus *Libertia* (Iridaceae). New Zealand Journal of Botany 38: 245–250.

Blanchon, D., B. G. Murray, and J. E. Braggins. 2002. A taxonomic revision of *Libertia* in New Zealand. New Zealand Journal of Botany 40: 437–456.

Bolus, H. M. L. 1915. Novitates Africanae. Annals of the Bolus Herbarium 1: 20–21.

Bolus, H. M. L. 1929a. Plants—New and noteworthy. South African Gardening and Country Life 19: 123.

Bolus, H. M. L. 1929b. Plants—New and noteworthy. South African Gardening and Country Life 19: 215.

Boyd, L. 1932. Monocotylous seedlings. Transactions and Proceedings of the Botanical Society of Edinburgh 31: 5–224.

Brown, N. E. 1909. Decades Kewenses. Decas LIV. Kew Bulletin of Miscellaneous Information 1909: 357–362.

Brown, N. E. 1929. Contributions to a knowledge of the Transvaal Iridaceae. Transactions of the Royal Society of South Africa 17: 341–352.

Brown, N. E. 1932. Contributions to a knowledge of the Transvaal Iridaceae. 2. Transactions of the Royal Society of South Africa 20: 261–280.

Brown, N. E. 1935. *Freesia* Klatt and its history. Journal of South African Botany 1: 1–31.

Brown, R. 1810. Prodromus florae Novae Hollandiae. London.

Bullock, A. A. 1930. A new genus of Iridaceae from East Africa. Kew Bulletin of Miscellaneous Information 1930(10): 465–466.

Burchell, W. J. 1824. Travels in the interior of southern Africa, vol. 2. Longman, Hurst, Rees, Orme, Brown and Green, London.

Burman, N. L. 1768. Prodromus plantae Capensis. Cornelius Haak, Leiden.

Burnett, G. T. 1835. Outlines of botany, including a general history of the vegetable kingdom, in which plants are arranged according to the system of natural affinities. H. Renshaw, London.

Burtt, B. L. 1970. The evolution and taxonomic significance of a subterranean ovary in certain monocotyledons. Israel Journal of Botany 19: 77–90.

Candolle, A. P. de. 1803. Note sur deux genres nouveaux de la famille des Iridées. Bulletin des Sciences, par la Société Philomatique de Paris 3: 151.

Carter, S. 1962. *Radinosiphon leptostachya.* Flowering plants of Africa 35: pl. 1,384.

Celis, M., P. Goldblatt, and J. Betancur. 2003. A new species of *Cipura* Aubl. (Iridaceae) from Colombia and Venezuela. Novon 13: 419–422.

Chase, M. W., D. E. Soltis, P. S. Soltis, P. J. Rudall, M. F. Fay, W. J. Hahn, S. Sullivan, J. Joseph, M. Molvray, P. J. Kores, T. J. Givnish, K. J. Sytsma, and J. C. Pires. 2000. Higher-level systematics of the monocotyledons: An assessment of current knowledge and a new classification, pp. 3–16 *in* K. L. Wilson and D. A. Morrison (editors), Proceedings of monocots II: The second international symposium on the comparative biology of the monocotyledons, Sydney, Australia. CSIRO Press, Sydney.

Chase, M. W., M. F. Fay, D. S. Devey, O. Maurin, N. Ronstad, J. T. Davies, Y. Pillon, G. Peterson, O. Seberg, M. N. Tamura, C. B. Asmussen, K. Hilu, T. Borsch, J. I. Davis, D. W. Stevenson, J. C. Pires, T. J. Givnish, K. J. Sytsma, M. A. McPherson, and S. W. Graham. 2006. Multi-gene analysis of monocot relationships: A summary, pp. 63–75 *in* J. T. Columbus, E. A. Friar, J. M. Porter, L. M. Prince, and M. G. Simpson (editors). Monocots: Comparative biology and evolution, 1. Rancho Santa Ana Botanic Garden, Claremont, California.

Cheadle, V. I. 1963. Vessels in Iridaceae. Phytomorphology 13: 245–248.

Chevalier, A. 1937. Deux nouvelles Iridées de l'Afrique tropicale. Bulletin du Muséum National d'Histoire Naturelle, Paris, 2 sér., 9: 401–404.

Chichiriccò, G. 1996. Intra- and interspecific reproductive barriers in *Crocus* (Iridaceae). Plant Systematics and Evolution 201: 83–92.

Cholewa, A. F., and D. M. Henderson. 2002. *Sisyrinchium,* pp. 351–371 *in* Flora of North America, vol. 26. Oxford University Press, New York.

Chueiri-Chiaretto, I. A., and N. L. de Menezes. 1980. Considerações sobre as características morfológicas e filogenéticas do cormo de *Trimezia* (Iridaceae). Boletin Botânica, Universidade São Paulo 8: 1–6.

Chukr, N. S., and A. M. Giulietti. 2001. New combinations in the genus *Neomarica* (Iridaceae) and its segregation from *Trimezia* on the basis of morphological features. Novon 11: 376–380.

Chukr, N. S., and A. M. Giulietti. 2003. Revisão de *Pseudotrimezia* Foster (Iridaceae). Sitiéntibus, ser. Ciências Biológicas 3: 44–80.

Clarke, A. E., J. A. Considine, R. Ward, and R. B. Knox. 1977. Mechanism of pollination in *Gladiolus:* Roles of the stigma and pollen-tube guide. Annals of Botany 41: 15–20.

Cocucci, A. A., and S. Vogel. 2001. Oil-producing flowers of *Sisyrinchium* species (Iridaceae) and their pollinators in southern South America. Flora 196: 26–46.

Cooke, D. 1986. Flora of Australia 46: 1–66. Australian Government Publishing Service, Canberra.

Cox, C. B., and P. D. Moore. 2000. Biogeography: An ecological and evolutionary approach. Blackwell Science, Oxford.

Cruden, R. W. 1972. Systematics of *Rigidella* (Iridaceae). Brittonia 23: 217–225.

Cruden, R. W. 1975. New Tigridieae (Iridaceae) from Mexico. Brittonia 27: 103–109.

Dahlgren, R., H. T. Clifford, and P. Yeo. 1985. The families of the monocotyledons. Springer-Verlag, Berlin.

Dalziel, J. M. 1937. The useful plants of West Tropical Africa. Crown Agents for the Colonies. London.

Daumann, E. 1970. Das Blütennektarium der Monocotyledonen unter besonderer Berucksichtigung seiner systematischen und phylogenetischen Bedeutung. Feddes Repertorium 80: 463–590.

Davies, T. J., T. G. Barraclough, V. Savolainen, and M. W. Chase. 1974. The environmental causes of plant of biodiversity gradients. Philosophical Transactions of the Royal Society, London, B, 359: 1,645–1,656.

Delaroche, D. 1766. Decriptiones plantarum aliquot novarum. Verbeek, Leiden.

De Vos, M. P. 1972. The genus *Romulea* in South Africa. Journal of South African Botany, supplementary volume 9.

De Vos, M. P. 1974a. Die Suid-Afrikaanse genus *Syringodea.* Journal of South African Botany 40: 201–254.

De Vos, M. P. 1974b. *Duthiella,* 'n Nuwe genus van die Iridaceae. Journal of South African Botany 40: 301–309.

De Vos, M. P. 1975. 'n Nuwe naam vir *Duthiella.* Journal of South African Botany 41: 91.

De Vos, M. P. 1977. Knol ontwikkeling by sommige genera van die Iridaceae en die systematiese posisie. Tydskrif vir Natuurwetenskap 17: 9–19.

De Vos, M. P. 1979. The African genus *Ferraria.* Journal of South African Botany 45: 295–375.

De Vos, M. P. 1982. The African genus *Tritonia* Ker-Gawler 1. Journal of South African Botany 48: 105–163.

De Vos, M. P. 1983a. *Syringodea, Romulea.* Flora of Southern Africa 7(2), fascicle 2: 1–76.

De Vos, M. P. 1983b. The African genus *Tritonia* Ker-Gawler 2. Journal of South African Botany 49: 347–422.

De Vos, M. P. 1984. The African genus *Crocosmia* Planchon. Journal of South African Botany 50: 463–502.

De Vos, M. P. 1985. Revision of the South African genus *Chasmanthe* (Iridaceae). South African Journal of Botany 51: 253–261.

De Vos, M. P. 1999. *Ixia, Tritonia, Crocosmia, Duthieastrum, Chasmanthe.* Flora of Southern Africa 7(2), fascicle 1: 1–147.

Diels, F. 1930. Iridaceae, pp. 469–505 *in* A. Engler and K. Prantl, Die natürlichen Pflanzenfamilien, ed. 2, vol. 15a. W. Engelmann, Leipzig.

Dietrich, A. 1833. Species plantarum, vol. 2. G. C. Nauck, Berlin.

Donato, R., C. Leach, and J. G. Conran. 2000. Relationships of *Dietes* (Iridaceae) inferred from ITS2 sequences, pp. 407–413 *in* K. L. Wilson & D. A. Morrison (editors), Monocots: Systematics and evolution. CSIRO, Melbourne.

Dumortier, B. C. 1822. Commentationes botanicae. Tournay.

Dykes, W. R. 1913. The genus *Iris.* Dover, New York (reprint).

Eaton, A. 1836. A botanical dictionary, ed. 4. Howe and Spaulding, New Haven.

Ecklon, C. F. 1827. Topographisches Verzeichniss der Pflanzensammlung. Reiseverein, Esslingen.

Engelmann, G., and A. Gray. 1847. Plantae Lindheimerae. Boston Journal of Natural History 5: 210–264.

Ferrence, S. C., and G. Bendersky. 2004. Therapy with saffron and the goddess at Thera. Perspectives in Biology and Medicine 47: 199–226.

Foster, R. C. 1939. Studies in the Iridaceae, 1. Contributions from the Gray Herbarium of Harvard University 127: 33–48.

Foster, R. C. 1945. Studies in the Iridaceae, III. Contributions from the Gray Herbarium of Harvard University 155: 3–54.

Foster, R. C. 1947. Studies in the Iridaceae, IV. Contributions from the Gray Herbarium of Harvard University 165: 106–111.

Foster, R. C. 1962. Studies in the Iridaceae, VII. Rhodora 64: 291–312.

Frakes, L. A., J. E. Francis, and J. I. Syktus. 1992. Climate modes of the Phanerozoic. Cambridge University Press, Cambridge.

Furness, C. A., and P. J. Rudall. 1999. Inaperturate pollen in monocotyledons. International Journal of Plant Science 160: 395–414.

Gibson, L. J., M. F. Ashby, and K. E. Easterling. 1988. Structure and mechanics of the *Iris* leaf. Journal of Material Science 23: 3,041–3,048.

Goldblatt, P. 1969. The genus *Sparaxis.* Journal of South African Botany 35: 219–252.

Goldblatt, P. 1971a. Cytological and morphological studies in the southern African Iridaceae. Journal of South African Botany 37: 317–460.

Goldblatt, P. 1971b. *Syringodea unifolia.* Flowering Plants of Africa 41: pl. 1638.

Goldblatt, P. 1972. A revision of the genera *Lapeirousia* Pourret and *Anomatheca* Ker in the winter-rainfall region of South Africa. Contributions from the Bolus Herbarium 4: 1–111.

Goldblatt, P. 1975. Revision of the bulbous Iridaceae of North America. Brittonia 27: 373–385.

Goldblatt, P. 1976. *Barnardiella:* A new genus of the Iridaceae and its relationship to *Gynandriris* and *Moraea.* Annals of the Missouri Botanical Garden 63: 309–313.

Goldblatt, P. 1977. Systematics of *Moraea* (Iridaceae) in tropical Africa. Annals of the Missouri Botanical Garden 64: 243–295.

Goldblatt, P. 1979a. *Roggeveldia,* a new genus of southern African Iridaceae—Irideae. Annals of the Missouri Botanical Garden 66: 839–844.

Goldblatt, P. 1979b. The South African genus *Galaxia* (Iridaceae). Journal of South African Botany 45: 385–423.

Goldblatt, P. 1980a. Redefinition of *Homeria* and *Moraea* (Iridaceae) in the light of biosystematic data, with *Rheome* gen. nov. Botaniska Notiser 133: 85–95.

Goldblatt, P. 1980b. Systematics of *Gynandriris* (Iridaceae), a Mediterranean–southern African disjunct. Botaniska Notiser 133: 239–260.

Goldblatt, P. 1981a. Systematics, phylogeny and evolution of *Dietes* (Iridaceae). Annals of the Missouri Botanical Garden 68: 132–153.

Goldblatt, P. 1981b. Systematics and biology of *Homeria* (Iridaceae). Annals of the Missouri Botanical Garden 68: 413–503.

Goldblatt, P. 1982a. Corm morphology in *Hesperantha* (Iridaceae, Ixioideae) and a proposed infrageneric taxonomy. Annals of the Missouri Botanical Garden 69: 370–378.

Goldblatt, P. 1982b. Systematics of *Freesia* Klatt (Iridaceae). Journal of South African Botany 48: 39–91.

Goldblatt, P. 1982c. Chromosome cytology in relation to suprageneric systematics of Neotropical Iridaceae. Systematic Botany 7: 186–198.

Goldblatt, P. 1984a. *Sessilistigma,* a new monotypic genus of Iridaceae—Iridoideae from the southwestern Cape. Journal of South African Botany 50: 149–157.

Goldblatt, P. 1984b. A revision of *Hesperantha* (Iridaceae) in the winter-rainfall area of southern Africa. Journal of South African Botany 50: 15–141.

Goldblatt, P. 1985. Revision of the southern African genus *Geissorhiza* (Iridaceae: Ixioideae). Annals of the Missouri Botanical Garden 72: 277–447.

Goldblatt, P. 1986. The moraeas of southern Africa. Annals of Kirstenbosch Botanical Garden 14.

Goldblatt, P. 1987. Systematics of the southern African genus *Hexaglottis* (Iridaceae—Iridoideae). Annals of the Missouri Botanical Garden 74: 542–569.

Goldblatt, P. 1989a. The genus *Watsonia.* Annals of Kirstenbosch Botanic Gardens 19.

Goldblatt, P. 1989b. Revision of the tropical African genus *Zygotritonia* (Iridaceae). Bulletin du Museum d'Histoire Naturelle, 4 sér., sect. B, Adansonia 11: 199–212.

Goldblatt, P. 1990a. Phylogeny and classification of Iridaceae. Annals of the Missouri Botanical Garden 77: 607–627.

Goldblatt, P. 1990b. Systematics of *Lapeirousia* (Iridaceae—Ixioideae) in tropical Africa. Annals of the Missouri Botanical Garden 77: 430–484.

Goldblatt, P. 1990c. Status of the southern African *Anapalina* and *Antholyza* (Iridaceae), genera based solely on characters for bird pollination, and a new species of *Tritoniopsis.* South African Journal of Botany 56: 577–582.

Goldblatt, P. 1991. Iridaceae—Famille 45 (2me éd.), *in* Flore de Madagascar et des Comores, pp. 1–45. Muséum National d'Histoire Naturelle, Paris.

Goldblatt, P. 1992. Phylogenetic analysis of the South African genus *Sparaxis* including *Synnotia* (Iridaceae: Ixioideae), with two new species and a review of the genus. Annals of the Missouri Botanical Garden 79: 143–159.

Goldblatt, P. 1993a. The woody Iridaceae: *Nivenia, Klattia* & *Witsenia:* Systematics, biology & evolution. Timber Press, Portland, Oregon.

Goldblatt, P. 1993b. Iridaceae. Flora Zambesiaca 12(4): 1–106.

Goldblatt, P. 1996a. *Gladiolus* in tropical Africa. Timber Press, Portland, Oregon.

Goldblatt, P. 1996b. Iridaceae, *in* R. M. Polhill (editor), Flora of tropical East Africa. A. A. Balkema, Rotterdam.

Goldblatt, P. 1998. Reduction of *Barnardiella, Galaxia, Gynandriris, Hexaglottis, Homeria* and *Roggeveldia* in *Moraea* (Iridaceae: Irideae). Novon 8: 371–377.

Goldblatt, P. 1999. *Devia, Sparaxis.* Flora of southern Africa 7(2), fascicle 1: 148–169.

Goldblatt, P. 2002. *Nemastylis,* pp. 398–400 *in* Flora of North America, vol. 26. Oxford University Press, New York.

Goldblatt, P. 2003. A synoptic review of the African genus *Hesperantha* (Iridaceae: Crocoideae). Annals of the Missouri Botanical Garden 90(3): 390–443.

Goldblatt, P., and P. Bernhardt. 1990. Pollination biology of *Nivenia* (Iridaceae) and the presence of heterostylous self-compatibility. Israel Journal of Botany 39: 93–111.

Goldblatt, P., and M. Celis. 2005. Notes on *Libertia* Spreng. (Iridaceae: Sisyrinchieae) in South America. Sida 21: 2,105–2,112.

Goldblatt, P., and M. P. De Vos. 1989. The reduction of *Oenostachys, Homoglossum* and *Anomalesia,* putative sunbird pollinated genera, in *Gladiolus* L. (Iridaceae—Ixioideae). Bulletin du Muséum National de l'Histoire Naturelle, 4 sér., sect. B, Adansonia 11: 417–428.

Goldblatt, P., and J. E. Henrich. 1987. Notes on *Cipura* (Iridaceae) in South and Central America, and a new species from Venezuela. Annals of the Missouri Botanical Garden 74: 333–340.

Goldblatt, P., and J. E. Henrich. 1991. *Calydorea* Herbert (Iridoideae—Tigridieae): Notes on this New World genus and reduction to synonymy of *Catila, Cardiostigma, Itysa,* and *Salpingostylis.* Annals of the Missouri Botanical Garden 78: 504–511.

Goldblatt, P., and J. E. Henrich. 1994. Iridaceae, *in* G. Davidse et al. (editors), Flora Mesoamericana 6: 71–80. Ciudad Universitaria, Universidad Nacional Autónoma de México.

Goldblatt, P., and T. Howard. 1992. Notes on *Alophia* (Iridaceae) and a new species, *A. veracruzana,* from Vera Cruz, Mexico. Annals of the Missouri Botanical Garden 79: 901–905.

Goldblatt, P., and A. Le Thomas. 1992. Pollen apertures, exine sculpturing and phylogeny in Iridaceae subfamily Iridoideae. Review of Palaeobotany and Palynology 75: 301–315.

Goldblatt, P., and A. Le Thomas. 1997. Palynology, phylogenetic reconstruction and the classification of the Afro-Madagascan genus *Aristea* Aiton (Iridaceae). Annals of the Missouri Botanical Garden 84: 263–284.

Goldblatt, P., and J. C. Manning. 1990. *Devia xeromorpha,* a new genus and species of Iridaceae—Ixioideae from the Cape Province, S. Africa. Annals of the Missouri Botanical Garden 77: 359–364.

Goldblatt, P., and J. C. Manning. 1992. Systematics of the southern African *Lapeirousia corymbosa* (Iridaceae—Ixioideae) complex (sect. *Fastigiata*) and a new species of sect. *Paniculata.* South African Journal of Botany 58: 326–336.

Goldblatt, P., and J. C. Manning. 1995a. Phylogeny of the African genera *Anomatheca* and *Freesia* (Iridaceae—Ixioideae), and a new genus *Xenoscapa.* Systematic Botany 20: 161–178.

Goldblatt, P., and J. C. Manning. 1995b. New species of the southern African genus *Geissorhiza* (Iridaceae: Ixioideae). Novon 5: 156–161.

Goldblatt, P., and J. C. Manning. 1996. Reduction of *Schizostylis* (Iridaceae: Ixioideae) in *Hesperantha.* Novon 6: 262–264.

Goldblatt, P., and J. C. Manning. 1997a. New species of *Aristea* (Iridaceae) from South Africa and notes on the taxonomy and pollination biology of section *Pseudaristea.* Novon 7: 137–144.

Goldblatt, P., and J. C. Manning. 1997b. New species of *Aristea* section *Racemosae* (Iridaceae) from the Cape Flora, South Africa. Novon 7: 357–365.

Goldblatt, P., and J. C. Manning. 1997c. *Nivenia parviflora,* a new species of shrubby Iridaceae from the Klein Swartberg, South Africa. Bothalia 27: 101 103.

Goldblatt, P., and J. C. Manning. 1998. *Gladiolus* in southern Africa. Fernwood Press, Cape Town.

Goldblatt, P., and J. C. Manning. 2000a. Cape plants. Strelitzia 7.

Goldblatt, P., and J. C. Manning. 2000b. Iridaceae, pp. 623–638 *in* O. A. Leistner (editor), Seed plants of southern Africa: Families and genera. Strelitzia 10.

Goldblatt, P., and J. C. Manning. 2000c. The long-proboscid fly pollination system in southern Africa. Annals of the Missouri Botanical Garden 87: 146–170.

Goldblatt, P., and J. C. Manning. 2002. Evidence for moth and butterfly pollination in *Gladiolus* (Iridaceae: Crocoideae). Annals of the Missouri Botanical Garden 89: 110–124.

Goldblatt, P., and J. C. Manning. 2006. Radiation of pollination systems in the Iridaceae of sub-Saharan Africa. Annals Botany 97: 317–344.

Goldblatt, P., and J. C. Manning. 2007. A revision of the southern African genus *Babiana* (Iridaceae: Crocoideae). Strelitzia 18.

Goldblatt, P., and W. Marais. 1979. *Savannosiphon* gen. nov., a segregate of *Lapeirousia* (Iridaceae: Ixioideae). Annals of the Missouri Botanical Garden 66: 845–850.

Goldblatt, P., and N. Snow. 1991. Systematics and chromosome cytology of *Eleutherine* Herbert (Iridaceae). Annals of the Missouri Botanical Garden 78: 942–949.

Goldblatt, P., and M. Takei. 1993. Chromosome cytology of the African genus *Lapeirousia* (Iridaceae—Ixioideae). Annals of the Missouri Botanical Garden 80: 961–973.

Goldblatt, P., and M. Takei. 1997. Chromosome cytology of Iridaceae, base numbers, patterns of variation and modes of karyotype change. Annals of the Missouri Botanical Garden 84: 285–304.

Goldblatt, P., J. E. Henrich, and P. Rudall. 1984. Occurrence of crystals in Iridaceae and allied families and their phylogenetic significance. Annals of the Missouri Botanical Garden 71: 1,013–1,020.

Goldblatt, P., P. J. Rudall, V. I. Cheadle, L. J. Dorr, and C. A. Williams. 1987. Affinities of the Madagascan endemic *Geosiris,* Iridaceae or Geosiridaceae. Bulletin du Museum National de Histoire Naturelle, 4 sér., sect. B, Adansonia 9: 239–248.

Goldblatt, P., P. J. Rudall, and J. E. Henrich. 1990. The genera of the *Sisyrinchium* alliance (Iridaceae—Iridoideae): Phylogeny and relationships. Systematic Botany 15: 497–510.

Goldblatt, P., A. Bari, and J. C. Manning. 1991. Sulcus variability in the pollen grains of Iridaceae subfamily Ixioideae. Annals of the Missouri Botanical Garden 78: 950–961.

Goldblatt, P., M. Takei, and Z. A. Razzaq. 1993. Chromosome cytology in tropical African *Gladiolus* (Iridaceae). Annals of the Missouri Botanical Garden 80: 461–470.

Goldblatt, P., J. C. Manning, and P. Bernhardt. 1995. Pollination biology of *Lapeirousia* subgenus *Lapeirousia* (Iridaceae) in southern Africa: Floral divergence and adaptation for long-tongued fly pollination. Annals of the Missouri Botanical Garden 82: 517–534.

Goldblatt, P., P. Bernhardt, and J. C. Manning. 1998. Pollination of petaloid geophytes by monkey beetles (Scarabaeidae: Rutelinae: Hopliini) in southern Africa. Annals of the Missouri Botanical Garden 85: 215–230.

Goldblatt, P., J. C. Manning, and P. Bernhardt. 1999. Evidence of bird pollination in the Iridaceae of southern Africa. Adansonia, 3 sér., 21: 25–40.

Goldblatt, P., J. C. Manning, and P. Bernhardt. 2000. Adaptive radiation of pollination mechanisms in *Sparaxis* (Iridaceae: Ixioideae). Adansonia, 3 sér., 22: 57–70.

Goldblatt, P., J. C. Manning, and P. Bernhardt. 2001. Radiation of pollination systems in *Gladiolus* (Iridaceae: Crocoideae) in southern Africa. Annals of the Missouri Botanical Garden 88: 713–734.

Goldblatt, P., V. Savolainen, O. Porteous, I. Sostaric, M. Powell, G. Reeves, J. C. Manning, T. G. Barraclough, and M. W. Chase. 2002a. Radiation in the Cape flora and the phylogeny of peacock irises *Moraea* (Iridaceae) based on four plastid DNA regions. Molecular Phylogeny and Evolution 25: 341–360.

Goldblatt, P., P. Bernhardt, and J. C. Manning. 2002b. Floral biology of *Romulea* (Iridaceae: Crocoideae): A progression from a generalist to a specialist pollination system. Adansonia 3 sér., 24: 243–262.

Goldblatt, P., J. C. Manning, J. Davies, V. Savolainen, and S. Rezai. 2004a. *Cyanixia,* a new genus for the Socotran endemic, *Babiana socotrana* (Iridaceae subfamily Crocoideae). Edinburgh Journal of Botany 60: 517–532.

Goldblatt, P., J. C. Manning, G. Dunlop, and A. Batten. 2004b. *Crocosmia* and *Chasmanthe.* Timber Press, Portland, Oregon.

Goldblatt, P., I. Nänni, P. Bernhardt, and J. C. Manning. 2004c. Floral biology of *Hesperantha* (Iridaceae: Crocoideae): Shifts in flower color and timing of floral opening and closing radically change the pollination system. Annals of the Missouri Botanical Garden 91: 186–206.

Goldblatt, P., P. Bernhardt, and J. C. Manning. 2005a. Pollination mechanisms in the African genus *Moraea* (Iridaceae: Iridoideae): Floral divergence and adaptation for pollen vector variability. Adansonia 27: 21–46.

Goldblatt, P., P. Bernhardt, and J. C. Manning. 2005b. Observations on the floral biology of *Melasphaerula* (Iridaceae: Crocoideae): Is this monotypic genus pollinated by March flies (Diptera: Bibionidae)? Annals of the Missouri Botanical Garden 92: 268–274.

Goldblatt, P., J. Davies, V. Savolainen, J. C. Manning, and M. van der Bank. 2006. Phylogeny of Iridaceae subfamily Crocoideae based on combined multigene plastid DNA analysis, pp. 399–411 *in* J. T. Columbus, E. A. Friar, J. M. Porter, L. M. Prince, and M. G. Simpson (editors), Monocots: Comparative biology and evolution, vol. 1. Rancho Santa Ana Botanic Garden, Claremont, California.

Grilli Caiola, M., and F. Brandizzi. 1997. Pollen-pistil interactions in *Hermodactylus tuberosus* Mill. (Iridaceae). Plant Biosystems 131(3): 197–205.

Haeckel, I. 1930. Über Iridaceen. Flora 215: 1–82.

Henrich, J. E., and P. Goldblatt. 1987. A review of the New World species of *Orthrosanthus* Sweet (Iridaceae). Annals of the Missouri Botanical Garden 74: 577–582.

Herbert, W. 1826. *Cypella herbertii.* Curtis's Botanical Magazine 53: below pl. 2,637.

Herbert, W. 1839. *Phalocallis plumbea.* Lead-coloured phalocallis. Curtis's Botanical Magazine 65: pl. 3710.

Herbert, W. 1840. *Gelasine azurea.* Azure gelasine. Curtis's Botanical Magazine 66: pl. 3,779.

Herbert, W. 1841. *Rigidella immaculata.* Edwards's Botanical Register 27: pl. 68.

Herbert, W. 1843a. De sisyrinchiis spuriis tentamina. Edwards's Botanical Register 29: 84–85.

Herbert, W. 1843b. *Eleutherine anomala.* Anomalous eleutherine. Edwards's Botanical Register 29: pl. 57.

Herbert, W. 1844. Miscellaneous matter. Edwards's Botanical Register 30: 88–89.

Heslop-Harrison, Y. 1977. The pollen-stigma interaction: Pollen tube penetration in *Crocus.* Annals of Botany 41: 913–922.

Heslop-Harrison, Y., and K. R. Shivanna. 1977. The receptive surface of the angiosperm stigma. Annals of Botany 41: 1,233–1,258.

Hilliard, O. M., and B. L. Burtt. 1986. *Hesperantha* (Iridaceae) in Natal and nearby. Notes from the Royal Botanic Garden, Edinburgh 43: 407–438.

Hilliard, O. M., B. L. Burtt, and A. Batten. 1991. *Dierama:* The hairbells of Africa. Acorn Press, Johannesburg.

Hochstetter, C. F. 1844. Nova genera plantarum Africae. Flora 27: 17–32.

Hooker, J. D. 1873. *Syringodea pulchella.* Curtis's Botanical Magazine 99: pl. 6,072.

Hooker, J. D. 1881. *Babiana socotrana.* Curtis's Botanical Magazine, ser. 3, 37: pl. 6,585.

Hooker, W. J. 1830. *Sisyrinchium pedunculatum.* Long-stalked sisyrinchium. Curtis's Botanical Magazine, new ser., 4: pl. 2,965.

Hooker, W. J. 1852. *Hewardia tasmanica,* Hook. Icones Plantarum 9: pl. 858.

Horn, W. 1962. Breeding research on South African plants: III. Intra- and interspecific compatibility in *Ixia* L., *Sparaxis* Ker., *Watsonia* Mill. and *Zantedeschia* Spreng. Journal of South African Botany 28: 269–277.

Houttuyn, M. 1780. Natuurlijke historie 2, 12. F. Houttuyn, Amsterdam.

Huber, H. 1969. Die Samenmerkmale und Verwandtschaftsverhaltnisse der Liliiflorae. Mitteilungen der Botanische Staatssammlung München 8: 219–538.

Hutchinson, J. 1934. The families of flowering plants, vol. 2, monocotyledons. Macmillan, London.

Irvine, F. R. 1930. Plants of the Gold Coast. Oxford University Press, London.

Johnston, I. M. 1925. Some undescribed American spermatophytes. Contributions from the Gray Herbarium of Harvard University 81: 85–98.

Jussieu, A. L. de. 1789. Genera plantarum. Herissant, Paris.

Kenton, A., and C. A. Heywood. 1984. Cytological studies in South American Iridaceae. Plant Systematics and Evolution 146: 87–104.

Kenton, A., and P. Rudall. 1987. An unusual case of complex heterozygosity in *Gelasine azurea* (Iridaceae), and its implications for reproductive biology. Evolutionary Trends in Plants 1: 95–103.

Kenton, A., P. J. Rudall, and A. R. Johnson. 1987. Genome size variation in *Sisyrinchium* L. (Iridaceae) and its relationship to phenotype and habitat. Botanical Gazette 147: 342–354.

Kenton, A., J. B. Dickie, D. H. Langton, and M. D. Bennett. 1990. Nuclear DNA amount and karyotype symmetry in *Cypella* and *Hesperoxiphion* (Tigridieae; Iridaceae). Evolutionary Trends in Plants 4: 59–69.

Ker Gawler, J. 1802a. *Trichonema cruciatum.* Curtis's Botanical Magazine 16: pl. 575.

Ker Gawler, J. 1802b. *Ixia bicolor.* Curtis's Botanical Magazine 15: pl. 548.

Ker Gawler, J. 1802c. *Tritonia squalida.* Curtis's Botanical Magazine 16: pl. 581.

Ker Gawler, J. 1803. *Melasphaerula graminea.* Curtis's Botanical Magazine 17: pl. 615.

Ker Gawler, J. 1804. Ensatorum ordo. Annals of Botany (König & Sims) 1: 219–247.

Ker Gawler, J. 1807. *Patersonia sericea.* Curtis's Botanical Magazine 26: pl. 1,041.

Ker Gawler, J. 1827. Iridearum generum. De Mat, Brussels.

Kittel, M. B. 1840. Achilles Richard's Grundriss der Botanik und der Pflanzenphysiologie. Nürnburg.

Klatt, F. W. 1861. Specimen e familia Iridearum. Linnaea 31: 533–570.

Klatt, F. W. 1863. Revisio Iridearum. Linnaea 32: 689–784.

Klatt, F. W. 1866. Revisio Iridearum (conclusio). Linnaea 34: 537–689.

Klatt, F. W. 1882. Ergänzungen und Berichtigungen zu Baker's Systema Iridacearum. Abhandlungen der Naturforschenden Gesellschaft zu Halle 15: 44–404.

Knuth, P. 1909. Handbook of flower pollination, vol. 3 (translated by J. R. Ainsworth Davis). Clarendon Press, Oxford.

Koch, K. H. E. 1855. Index seminum Hortus Berolinensis 1854, Appendix 10.

Kuntze, O. 1898. Revisio generum plantarum, vol. 3, part 3. A. Felix, Leipzig.

Labillardière, J.-J. H. de. 1800. Relation du voyage à la recherche de La Pérouse, vol. 1. H. J. Jansen, Paris.

Labillardière, J.-J. H. de. 1805. Novae Hollandiae plantae, vol. 1. Huzard, Paris.

Larsen, P. O., F. T. Sorensen, E. Wieczorkowska, and P. Goldblatt. 1981. *Meta*-carboxy-substituted aromatic amino acids and à-glutamyl peptides: Chemical characters for classification in the Iridaceae. Biochemical Systematics and Ecology 9: 313–323.

Lee, J. 1994. Fatty oil production by *Alophia drummondii* (Iridaceae) and modified oil collecting behavior of *Centris* (Centridini—Apidae). Master's thesis, University of Texas, Austin.

Lenz, L. W. 1959. Hybridization and speciation in the Pacific coast irises. Aliso 4: 237–309.

Lenz, L. W. 1971. The status of *Pardanthopsis* (Iridaceae). Aliso 7: 401–403.

Lewis, G. J. 1941. Iridaceae. New genera and species and miscellaneous notes. Journal of South African Botany 7: 19–59.

Lewis, G. J. 1954a. Some aspects of the morphology, phylogeny and taxonomy of the South African Iridaceae. Annals of the South African Museum 40: 15–113.

Lewis, G. J. 1954b. A revision of the genus *Synnotia.* Annals of the South African Museum 40: 137–151.

Lewis, G. J. 1959a. South African Iridaceae. A revision of *Hexaglottis.* Journal of South African Botany 25: 215–230.

Lewis, G. J. 1959b. The genus *Babiana.* Journal of South African Botany, supplementary vol. 3.

Lewis, G. J. 1959c. South African Iridaceae. The genus *Tritoniopsis.* Journal of South African Botany 25: 319–355.

Lewis, G. J. 1960. South African Iridaceae. The genus *Anapalina.* Journal of South African Botany 26: 51–72.

Lewis, G. J. 1962. South African Iridaceae. The genus *Ixia.* Journal of South African Botany 28: 45–195.

Lewis, G. J., A. A. Obermeyer, and T. T. Barnard. 1972. *Gladiolus* in South Africa. Journal of South African Botany, supplementary vol. 8.

Lindley, J. 1838. Miscellaneous matter. Edwards's Botanical Register 24: 69.

Lindley, J. 1840. *Rigidella flammea*. Edwards's Botanical Register 26: pl. 16.

Linnaeus, C. 1747. Flora Zeylanica. Van der Vecht, Leiden.

Linnaeus, C. 1753. Species plantarum. Laurentius Salvius, Stockholm.

Linnaeus, C. 1762. Genera plantarum. Laurentius Salvius, Stockholm.

Loudon, J. W. 1841. Ladies' flower garden of ornamental bulbous plants. William Smith, London.

Mackiernan, J. M., and E. M. Norman. 1979. Reproductive biology of *Nemastylis floridana* Small (Iridaceae). Florida Scientist 42: 229–236.

Manning, J. C., and P. Goldblatt. 1990. Endothecium in Iridaceae and its systematic implications. American Journal of Botany 77: 527–532.

Manning, J. C., and Goldblatt, P. 1991. Seed coat structure in the shrubby Cape Iridaceae, *Nivenia*, *Klattia* and *Witsenia*. Botanical Journal of the Linnean Society 107: 387–404.

Manning, J. C., and P. Goldblatt. 1999. New species of *Sparaxis* and *Ixia* (Iridaceae: Ixioideae) from Western Cape, South Africa, and taxonomic notes on *Ixia* and *Gladiolus*. Bothalia 29: 59–63.

Manning, J. C., and P. Goldblatt. 2001a. Three new species of *Tritoniopsis* (Iridaceae: Crocoideae) from the Cape region of South Africa. Bothalia 31: 175–181.

Manning, J. C., and P. Goldblatt. 2001b. A synoptic review of *Romulea* (Iridaceae: Crocoideae) in sub-Saharan Africa, the Arabian Peninsula and Socotra, including new species, biological notes, and a new infrageneric classification. Adansonia, sér. 3, 23: 59–108.

Manning, J. C., and P. Goldblatt. 2002. The pollination of *Tritoniopsis parviflora* (Iridaceae) by oil-collecting *Rediviva gigas* (Hymenoptera: Melittidae): The first record of oil-secretion in African Iridaceae. South African Journal of Botany 68: 171–176.

Manning, J. C., and P. Goldblatt. 2004. A new species of *Thereianthus* (Iridaceae: Crocoideae) from Western Cape, South Africa,

nomenclatural notes and a key to the genus. Bothalia 34: 103–106.

Manning, J. C., and P. Goldblatt. 2005. Radiation of pollination systems in the Cape genus *Tritoniopsis* (Iridaceae: Crocoideae) and the development of bimodal pollination strategies. International Journal of Plant Sciences 166: 459–474.

Manning, J. C., and P. Goldblatt. 2007. *Nivenia argentea* misunderstood, and the new species *Nivenia inaequalis* (Iridaceae: Nivenioideae). Bothalia 37.

Maratti, G. F. 1772. Plantarum Romuleae, et Saturniae, etc. A. Casaletti, Rome.

Mathew, B. 1977. *Crocus sativus* and its allies (Iridaceae). Plant Systematics and Evolution 128: 89–103.

Mathew, B. 1981. The *Iris*. Batsford, London.

Mathew, B. 1982. The *Crocus*. Batsford, London.

Mathew, B. 1989. A taxonomic revision of *Iris* subgenus *Hermodactyloides* (Iridaceae), pp. 81–109 *in* K. Tan (editor), Plant taxonomy, phytogeography and related subjects. Edinburgh University Press, Edinburgh.

Mathew, B., and C. Brighton. 1977. *Crocus tournefortii* and its allies (Iridaceae). Kew Bulletin 31: 775–786.

Maw, G. 1886. A monograph of the genus *Crocus*. Dulau, London.

Medikus, F. K. [1790]. Über den gynandrischen Situs der Staubfäden und Pistille einiger Pflanzen. Historiae et Commentationes Academiae Electoralis Scientiarum et Elegantiarum Theodosa-Palatinae 6.

Miami Museum of Science. 1997. Miami Museum of Science—Ecolinks—World Vegetation Map, *http://bird.miamisci.org/ecolinks/mapbiosphere. html.*

Miers, J. 1826. Travels in Chile and La Plata. Baldwin, Cradock and Joy, London.

Miers, J. 1841. On a new genus of plants from Chile. Proceedings of the Linnean Society 1: 122–123.

Miers, J. 1842. On a new genus of plants from Chile. Transactions of the Linnean Society, London. 19: 95–97, pl. 8.

Mildbraed, J. 1923. Iridaceae Africanae. Botanische Jahrbücher für Systematik, Pflanzengeschichte und Pflanzengeographie 58: 230–233.

Miller, P. 1754. The gardener's dictionary, abridged ed. 4 [unpaged], vol. 1. P. Miller, London.

Miller, P. 1759. Figures of plants in the Gardener's dictionary. P. Miller, London.

Miller, P. 1768. The gardener's dictionary, ed. 8. P. Miller, London.

Molseed, E. 1968. *Fosteria*, a new genus of Mexican Iridaceae. Brittonia 20: 232–234.

Molseed, E. 1970. The genus *Tigridia* (Iridaceae) of Mexico and Central America. University of California Publications in Botany 54: 1–128.

Molseed, E., and R. W. Cruden. 1969. *Sessilanthera*, a new genus of American Iridaceae. Brittonia 21: 191–193.

Moore, D. M. 1971. *Tapeinia* Comm. ex Juss. (Iridaceae) and the rediscovery of *Galaxia obscura* Cav. Botaniska Notiser 124: 82–86.

Moore, D. M. 1983. Flora of Tierra del Fuego. Anthony Nelson, England.

Moore, L. B. 1967. The New Zealand species of *Libertia* (Iridaceae). New Zealand Journal of Botany 5: 255–275.

Moore, S. Le M. 1896. The phanerogamic botany of the Matto Grosso Expedition, 1892–32. Transactions of the Linnean Society, London, Botany 4: 265–516.

Moore, T. 1853. On venation as a generic character in ferns: With observations on *Hewardia*, J. Smith, and *Cionidium*, Moore. Proceedings of the Linnean Society 2: 210–213.

Nuttall, T. 1835. Collections towards a flora of the Arkansas territory. Transactions of the American Philosophical Society, new ser., 5: 139–203.

Obermeyer, A. A. 1962. *Pillansia templemannii.* Flowering Plants of Africa 35: pl. 1,381.

Parlatore, F. 1854. Nuovi generi et nuovi specie di piante monocotyledoni. Le Monnier, Florence.

Pax, F. 1888. Iridaceae, pp. 137–157 *in* A. Engler and K. Prantl, Die natürlichen Pflanzenfamilien, vol. 2(5). W. Engelmann, Leipzig.

Perrier de la Bâthie, H. 1946. Iridacées, pp. 1–21 *in* H. Humbert (editor), Flore de Madagascar

et des Comores 45. Imprimerie Officielle, Tananarive.

Persoon, H. 1805. Synopsis plantarum, vol. 1. C. H. Cramer, Paris.

Peters, W. C. H. 1864. Naturwissenschaftliche Reise nach Mossambique, Band 6, Botanik, 2 Abteilung. Georg Reimer, Berlin.

Philippi, R. A. 1864. Plantarum novarum Chilensium centuria, inclusis Mendocinis et Patagonicis. Linnaea 33: 1–308.

Planchon, G. 1851. *Crocosmia aurea.* Flore des Serres et des Jardins de l'Europe 7: 161.

Poiret, J. L. M. 1826. *Peyrousia*, in F. G. Lebrault (editor), Dictionnaire des sciences naturelles 39: 363–366. Le Normant, Paris.

Pourret, P. A. 1788. Description de deux nouveaux genres de la famille de Liliacées designées sous le nom *Lomenia* et de *Lapeirousia*. Histoire et Mémoires de l'Académie Royale des Sciences, Toulouse 3: 74–82, pl. 5.

Presl, J. S. 1846. Wšeobecný Rostlinopsis, vol. 2. Kronberg, Prague.

Rafinesque, C. S. 1832. Retrospective criticism. The Gardener's Magazine 8: 244–248.

Rafinesque, C. S. 1836. *Olsynium, in* New Flora of North America 4. Published by author, Philadelphia.

Rafinesque, C. S. 1837 [as 1836]. Flora Telluriana 4. Published by author, Philadelphia.

Ravenna, P. 1964. Notas sobre Iridaceae. Revista, Instituto Municipal de Botánica, Jardin Botánico 'Carlos Thays' 2(1962): 51–60.

Ravenna, P. 1968. Notas sobre Iridaceae III. Bonplandia 2(16): 273–291.

Ravenna, P. 1972. *Ona*, genero nuevo de Iridaceae nativo de Iridaceae de las provinicas de Magellanes (Chile) y Tierra del Fuego (Argentina). Anales del Museo de Historia Natural de Valparaiso 5: 97–101.

Ravenna, P. 1973. *Tucma*, genero nuevo de Iridaceae de la precordillera de los Andes del norte de Argentina. Anales del Museo de Historia Natural de Valparaiso 6: 41–47.

Ravenna, P. 1974. *Cobana*, a new genus of Central American Iridaceae. Botaniska Notiser 127: 104–108.

Ravenna, P. 1977a. Notas sobre Iridaceae V. Noticiario Mensual del Museo Nacional de Historia Natural (Santiago) 21(249): 7–9.

Ravenna, P. 1977b. Neotropical species threatened and endangered by human activity in the Iridaceae, Amaryllidaceae and allied bulbous families, pp. 257–263 in G. T. Prance and T. S. Elias (editors), Extinction is forever. New York Botanical Garden, New York.

Ravenna, P. 1979. *Ainea*, a new genus of Iridaceae from Mexico. Botaniska Notiser 132: 467–469.

Ravenna, P. 1981a. The tribe Trimezieae of the Iridaceae. Wrightia 7: 12.

Ravenna, P. 1981b. *Sympa*, a new genus of Iridaceae from Rio Grande do Sul, Brazil. Wrightia 7: 10–11.

Ravenna, P. 1981c. *Kelissa*, a new genus of Iridaceae from south Brazil. Bulletin du Museum National d'Histoire Naturelle, 4 sér., sect. B, Adansonia 3: 105–110.

Ravenna, P. 1981d. A submerged new species of *Cypella* (Iridaceae), and a new section for the genus (s. str.). Nordic Journal of Botany 1: 489–492.

Ravenna, P. 1982. New species and miscellaneous notes in the genus *Trimezia* (Iridaceae)—1. Wrightia 7: 90–95.

Ravenna, P. 1983a. *Catila* and *Onira*, two new genera of South American Iridaceae. Nordic Journal of Botany 3: 197–205.

Ravenna, P. 1983b. A new species and a new subgenus in *Ennealophus* (Iridaceae). Wrightia 7: 232–234.

Ravenna, P. 1984. The delimitation of *Gelasine* (Iridaceae) and *G. uruguiaensis* sp. nov. from Uruguay. Nordic Journal of Botany 4: 347–350.

Ravenna, P. 1986. *Itysa* and *Lethia*, two new genera of Neotropical Iridaceae. Nordic Journal of Botany 6: 581–588.

Ravenna, P. 1988. Revisional studies in the genus *Cipura* (Iridaceae). Onira 1(5): 35–44.

Ravenna, P. 2001. The Iridaceae of the Cuyo region, Argentina. Onira, Botanical Leaflets 6: 1–18.

Redouté, P. 1802. Les Liliacées, vol. 1: 5, fig. 6. Paris.

Reeves, G., M. W. Chase, P. Goldblatt, P. J. Rudall, M. F. Fay, A. V. Cox, B. Lejeune, and T. Souza-Chies. 2001. A phylogenetic analysis of Iridaceae based on four plastid sequence regions: *trn*L intron, *trn*L–F spacer, *rps*4 and *rbc*L. American Journal of Botany 88: 2,074–2,087.

Regel, E. 1877. Plantarum diversarum in horto botanico imperiale Petropolitano cultarum descriptiones. Acta Horti Petropolitanum 5: 638–641.

Ridley, H. N. 1930. The dispersal of plants throughout the world. Reeve & Co., Ashford, Kent.

Rodionenko, G. I. 1961. Rod *Iris* = *Iris* L. Izd-vo Akademiia Nauk, Moskva. (Translation published by the British Iris Society, London, in 1987: The genus *Iris* L.: Questions of morphology, biology, evolution and systematics.)

Rodriguez, A. 1999. Molecular and morphological systematics of the "tiger flower" group (tribe Tigridieae: Iridaceae), biogeography and evidence for the adaptive radiation of the subtribe Tigridiinae. Doctoral thesis, University of Wisconsin, Madison.

Rodriguez, A., and L. Ortíz-Catedral. 2002. Cytology and pollen morphology of *Ainea conzatti* and *Cardiostigma hintonii* (Tigridieae: Iridaceae) and their phylogenetic consequences. Abstract, American Society of Plant Taxonomists 2002 Conference.

Rodriguez, A., and L. Ortíz-Catedral. 2003. *Colima* (Tigridieae: Iridaceae), a new genus from western Mexico and a new species: *Colima tuitensis* from Jalisco. Acta Botánica Mexicana 65: 51–60.

Rodriguez, A., and K. Sytsma. 2006. Phylogeny of the tiger-flower group (Tigirideae: Iridaceae): molecular and morphological evidence, pp. 412–424 in J. T. Columbus, E. A. Friar, J. M. Porter, L. M. Prince, and M. G. Simpson (editors), Monocots: Comparative biology and evolution, vol. 1. Claremont, California: Rancho Santa Ana Botanic Garden.

Rodríguez, R. 1986. Die chilenischen Arten der Gattung *Sisyrinchium* L. (Iridaceae). Mitteilungen der Staatssammlungen München 22: 97–201.

Roemer, J. J., and J. A. Schultes. 1817. Systema vegetabilium, vol. 1. J. G. Cotta, Stuttgart.

Roitman, G., and D. Medan. 1995. Biología reproductiva de Iridáceas de los pastizales húmedos de la Depresión del Río Salado, prov. de Buenos Aires, pp. 114 *in* XVII Reunión Argentina de Ecología.

Rudall, P. 1983. Leaf anatomy and relationships of *Dietes* (Iridaceae). Nordic Journal of Botany 3: 471–478.

Rudall, P. 1984. Taxonomic and evolutionary implications of rhizome structure and secondary thickening in Iridaceae. Botanical Gazette 145: 524–534.

Rudall, P. 1991. Leaf anatomy in Tigridieae (Iridaceae). Plant Systematics and Evolution 175: 1–10.

Rudall, P. 1995. Anatomy of the monocotyledons: Iridaceae. Clarendon Press, Oxford.

Rudall, P., and Goldblatt, P. 1991. Leaf anatomy and phylogeny of Ixioideae (Iridaceae). Botanical Journal of the Linnean Society 106: 329–345.

Rudall, P., and Goldblatt, P. 2001. Floral anatomy and systematic position of *Diplarrhena* (Iridaceae): A new tribe Diplarrheneae, pp. 59–66 *in* M. A. Colasante and P. J. Rudall (editors), Irises and Iridaceae: Biodiversity and systematics. Annali di Botanica (Roma), nuov. ser. 1.

Rudall, P., A. Y. Kenton, and T. J. Lawrence. 1986. An anatomical and chromosomal investigation of *Sisyrinchium* and allied genera. Botanical Gazette 147: 466–477.

Rudall, P. J., J. C. Manning, and P. Goldblatt. 2003. Evolution of floral nectaries in Iridaceae. Annals of the Missouri Botanical Garden 90: 613–631.

Rübsamen-Weustenfeld, T., V. Mukielka, and U. Hamann. 1994. Zur Embryologie, Morphologie und systematischen Stellung von *Geosiris aphylla* Baillon (Monocotyledoneae, Geosiridaceae / Iridaceae). Botanische Jahrbücher für Systematik, Pflanzengeschichte und Pflanzengeographie 115: 475–545.

Salisbury, R. A. 1812. On the cultivation of rare plants, etc. Transactions of the Horticultural Society (London) 1: 261–366.

Salisbury, R. A. 1866. The genera of plants. Van Voort, London.

Sapir, Y., A. Schmida, and G. Ne'eman. 2005. Pollination of *Oncocyclus* irises (*Iris*: Iridaceae) by night sheltering male bees. Plant Biology 7: 417–424.

Sapir, Y., A. Schmida, and G. Ne'eman. 2006. Morning floral heat as a reward to the pollinators of the *Oncocyclus* irises. Oecologia 147: 53–59.

Saward, S. A. 1992. A global view of Cretaceous vegetation patterns. Geological Society of America Special Paper 267: 17–35.

Schreber, J. C. D. 1789. Genera plantarum. Varrentrapp & Wenner, Frankfurt.

Schultes, R. E., and R. F. Raffauf. 1990. The healing forest: Medicinal and toxic plants of the northwest Amazonia. Dioscorides Press, Portland, Oregon.

Schulze, W. 1965. *Siphonostylis*, eine neue Gattung der Iridaceae. Österreichische Botanische Zeitschrift 112: 330–343.

Schulze, W. 1970. *Junopsis*, eine neue Gattung der Iridaceae. Österreichische Botanische Zeitschrift 117: 327–332.

Schulze, W. 1971. Beiträge zur Pollenmorphologie der Gattungen um *Iris* L. Feddes Repertorium 81: 507–517.

Scott, D. H., and G. Brebner. 1893. On the secondary tissues of certain monocotyledons. Annals of Botany 7: 21–62.

Simpson, B. B., and J. L. Neff. 1981. Floral rewards: Alternatives to pollen and nectar. Annals of the Missouri Botanical Garden 68: 310–322.

Sims, J. 1801. Curtis's Botanical Magazine 15: pl. 539.

Small, J. E. 1931. Bartram's *Ixia coelestina* rediscovered. Journal of the New York Botanical Garden 32: 155–161.

Souza-Chies, T. T., G. Bittar, S. Nadot, L. Carter, E. Besin, and B. Lejeune. 1997. Phylogenetic analysis of Iridaceae with parsimony and distance methods using the plastid gene *rps4*. Plant Systematics and Evolution 204: 109–123.

Species Group of the British Society. 1997. A guide to species irises: Their identification and cultivation. Cambridge University Press, Cambridge.

Sprague, T. A. 1928. *Marica* and *Neomarica*. Kew Bulletin of Miscellaneous Information 1928: 278–281.

Sprengel, K. P, J. 1817. Anleitung zur Kenntniss der Gewächse, ed. 2, vol. 2. Kümmel, Halle.

Sprengel, K. P. J. 1824. Systema vegetabilium, vol. 1. Dieterich, Göttingen.

Stapf, O. 1927. *Zygotritonia crocea*. Hooker's Icones Plantarum, ser. 5, 2: pl. 3,120.

Stebbins, G. L. 1970. Adaptive radiation of reproductive characteristics in angiosperms. 1. Pollination mechanisms. Annual Review of Ecology and Systematics 1: 307–326.

Steiner, K. E. 1998. Beetle pollination of peacock moraeas in South Africa. Plant Systematics and Evolution 209: 47–65.

Steudel, E. G. 1821. Nomenclator botanicus, vol. 1. J. G. Cotta, Stuttgart.

Steyn, E. 1973. 'n Embriologiese ondersoek van *Romulea rosea* Eckl. var. *reflexa* Beg. Journal of South African Botany 39: 113–121.

Stock, W. D., F. van der Heyde, and O. M. Lewis. 1992. Plant structure and function, pp. 226–240 *in* R. M. Cowling (editor), The ecology of fynbos. Oxford University Press, Oxford.

Stones, M., and W. Curtis. 1969. The endemic flora of Tasmania, vol. 2. Ariel, London.

Strid, A. K. 1974. A taxonomic revision of *Bobartia* L. (Iridaceae). Opera Botanica 37.

Suárez-Cervera, M., A. Le Thomas, J. Márquez, J. A. Seaone-Camba, and P. Goldblatt. 2000. The channelled intine of *Aristea major*: Ultrastructural changes during development, activation and germination, pp. 57–71 *in* M. M. Harley, C. M. Morton, and S. Blackmore (editors), Pollen and spores: Morphology and biology. Royal Botanic Gardens, Kew.

Sweet, R. 1826. *Synnotia variegata*. British Flower Garden 2: pl. 150.

Sweet, R. 1827a. *Streptanthera elegans*. British Flower Garden 3: pl. 209.

Sweet, R. 1827b. *Herbertia pulchella*. British Flower Garden 3: pl. 222.

Sweet, R. 1829a. *Spatalanthus speciosus*. British Flower Garden 3: pl. 300.

Sweet, R. 1829b. Flora Australasiaca. James Ridgway, London.

Sweet, R. 1830. Hortus Britannicus, ed. 2. James Ridgway, London.

Takhtajan, A. 1980. Outline of the classification of flowering plants (Magnoliophyta). Botanical Review 46: 225–359.

Tenore, M. 1845. Catalogo delle piante che si coltivano nel R. Orto Botanico di Napoli. 5. Puzziello, Naples.

Thorne, R. F. 2007. An updated classification of the class Magnoliopsida ("Angiospermae"). Botanical Review 73: 67–102.

Thunberg, C. P. 1782. Nova genera plantarum. Edman, Uppsala.

Tillich, H.-J. 2003. Seedling morphology in Iridaceae: Indications for relationships within the family and to related families. Flora 198: 220–242.

Tillie, N., M. W. Chase, and T. Hall. 2001. Molecular studies in the genus *Iris* L.: A preliminary study. Annali di Botanica (Roma), nuov. ser., 1: 105–122.

Trattinnick, L. [1821]. Auswahl Gartenpflanzen. [Archiv der Gewächskunde.] Wien.

Trew, C. J. 1754. Plantae selectae, vol. 4. C. J. Trew, Nuremberg.

Upchurch, G. R., B. L. Otto-Bliesner, and C. Scotese. 1998. Vegetation-atmosphere interactions and their role in global warming during the latest Cretaceous. Philosophical Transactions of the Royal Society B341: 317–326.

Van Wyk, B.-E., F. van Heerden, and B. van Oudtshoorn. 2002. Poisonous plants of southern Africa. Briza, Pretoria.

Vellozo, J. M. 1825. Flora Fluminensis. Rio de Janeiro.

Ventenat, E. P. 1808. Decas generum novorum aut parum cognitarum. E. Dufart, Paris.

Vickers, W. T., and T. Plowman. 1984. Useful plants of the Siona and Secoya Indians of Ecuador. Fieldiana, Botany, new ser., 15.

Vincent, L. P. D. 1985. A partial revision of the genus *Aristea* (Iridaceae) in South Africa, Swaziland, Lesotho, Transkei and Ciskei. South African Journal of Botany 51: 209–252.

Vines, S. H. 1895. A students' text-book of botany. Swan Sonnenscheinm, London.

Vlok, J. 2005. Why do some flowers close at night? Veld & Flora 2005: 76–79.

Vogel, S. 1974. Ölblumen und Ölsammelnde Bienen. Tropische and Subtropische Pflanzenwelt 7: 1–267.

Watt, J. M., and M. G. Breyer-Brandwijk. 1962. Medicinal and poisonous plants of southern and eastern Africa, ed. 2. Livingstone, Edinburgh.

Weimarck, H. 1939. Types of inflorescences in *Aristea* and some allied genera. Botaniska Notiser 1939: 616–626.

Weimarck, H. 1940a. Monograph of the genus *Aristea*. Lunds Universitets Årsskrift, new ser. 2, 36(1): 1–140.

Weimarck, H. 1940b. A revision of the genus *Nivenia* Vent. Svensk Botanisk Tidskrift 34: 355–372.

Williams, C., J. B. Harborne, and P. Goldblatt. 1986. Correlations between phenolic patterns and tribal classification in the family Iridaceae. Phytochemistry 25: 2,135–2,154.

Wilson, C. A. 1998. A cladistic analysis of *Iris* series *Californicae* based on morphological data. Systematic Botany 23: 73–88.

Wilson, C. A. 2004. Phylogeny of *Iris* based on chloroplast *mat*K gene and *trn*K intron sequence data. Molecular Phylogeny and Evolution 33: 402–412.

Wolf, J. A. 1985. Distribution of major vegetation types during the Tertiary, pp. 357–375 *in* E. T. Sundquist and W. S. Broecker (editors), The global carbon cycle and atmospheric $CO_2$: Natural variations Archean to present. American Geophysical Union Research Monographs 32.

Wunderlich, R. 1959. Zur Frage der Phylogenie der Endospermtypen bei den Angiospermen. Österreichische Botanische Zeitschrift 106: 203–293.

# INDEX

Names of genera in parentheses are the current names for the listed synonyms.